William Plumer

of

NEW HAMPSHIRE

1759-1850

The Institute of Early American History and Culture is sponsored jointly by the College of William and Mary and Colonial Williamsburg, Incorporated. Publication of this book has been assisted by a grant from the Lilly Endowment, Inc.

WILLIAM PLUMER

In his autobiography, Plumer wrote that "this portrait was taken, at the city of Washington, in January, 1804, by Charles St. Memin, & was at that time a correct likeness." Reproduced from Elias Dexter, *The St.-Memin Collection of Portraits* (New York, 1862).

William Plumer

of

NEW HAMPSHIRE

1759-1850

by LYNN W. TURNER

PUBLISHED FOR THE
Institute of Early American History and Culture
at Williamsburg, Virginia
by The University of North Carolina Press · Chapel Hill

Manufactured in the United States of America

Van Rees Press • New York

Dedication

To Vera, who knows William Plumer as intimately as her husband, and has tolerated, yea, even encouraged this strange domestic triangle.

Preface

THE time and energy spent on this book are justified, in my opinion, by the conviction that William Plumer is a figure in American history deserving more than the fleeting recognition he has hitherto received. I stumbled upon him while searching for a suitable dissertation topic, but hundreds of serious students of American history have never encountered him. Yet it seems to me that he embodies so much of the essential character of his times that his biography serves as a significant commentary on forty years of American history.

During the years in which I have worked on this book I have incurred so many obligations to so many generous professors, librarians, editors, and administrators that I cannot possibly name them all. I hope that some of them will read this book, and remember the part they played in making it possible. One name, however, I must mention. I began this study as a doctoral dissertation under Professor Frederick L. Merk at Harvard—for me, a most fortunate circumstance. His patient assistance, his constant encouragement, and the communication of his own deep insights into American history, are responsible for much of whatever merit this book may possess.

Contents

Preface   vii

CHAPTER I   Newburyport and Epping   1

CHAPTER II   Politics and Law   13

CHAPTER III   Constitution Maker   36

CHAPTER IV   Lawyer and Federalist   54

CHAPTER V   The Decline of Federalism   74

CHAPTER VI   United States Senator   92

CHAPTER VII   Constitutional Issues   109

CHAPTER VIII   The Secession Plot   133

CHAPTER IX   Farewell to Washington   151

CHAPTER X   The Apostate   177

CHAPTER XI   War Governor   202

CHAPTER XII   A Waiting Period   224

CHAPTER XIII   Dartmouth College and the Courts   240

CHAPTER XIV   Trials and Errors   258

CHAPTER XV   The Era of Good Feelings   282

CHAPTER XVI   Elder Statesman   305

CHAPTER XVII   The Last Years   334

Appendix   345

Note on the Sources   349

Index   357

William Plumer
of
NEW HAMPSHIRE
1759-1850

CHAPTER I

Newburyport and Epping

"The little knowledge I have gain'd
Was all from simple nature drain'd;
Hence my life's maxims took their rise,
And hence my first hatred unto vice." [1]

O N June 25, 1780, a dark, slender, New England farmer boy named
William Plumer reached his majority. Although he had better
than average intelligence, there was nothing very remarkable about the
young man; his formal education was slight, he had little property and
no important connections.

Yet, the Plumer family tree was rooted deeply in New England soil.
Young William could trace his paternal ancestry through five generations to a progenitor who participated in the Puritan migration of the
1630's. Francis Plumer had come from either England or Wales in 1633
and settled as one of the original proprietors at Newbury, Massachusetts,
in 1635. From this fountainhead, the Plumer clan had flowed copiously
until, by 1780, the descendants of Francis were scattered widely throughout northern New England and as far westward as the Ohio country.
For the most part, the Plumers had been respectable, substantial yeomen
and artisans, supporting the church and civil authority by their taxes,
taking their turns at the onerous duties of town office, drilling in trainbands, and fighting when their leaders decided that fighting was necessary. Here and there a Plumer had risen above the level of mere good
citizenship and had entered a profession, become a master-mariner,
gained wealth in trade, or represented his town in the colonial legislature.

William's father, Samuel Plumer, was the third child in a family of
twelve. Three such prolific generations had so far subdivided the lands
of the clan that Samuel could not be provided with a farm when he

1. Plumer used this quotation as the heading for his autobiography, a manuscript
folio volume of 419 pages, purchased by the Library of Congress in 1923 (hereafter
cited as Plumer, Autobiography).

I

married. Accordingly he was bred to a trade in Newburyport and set up a cordwainer's shop in which he prospered. But his love of the soil was strong, and as soon as he had accumulated enough money he purchased a good farm in Epping, New Hampshire, and moved there with his family in the autumn of 1768. The records do not reveal why Samuel Plumer chose to settle in Epping rather than join other members of the family who were migrating to the frontiers of New England and New York. Whatever the reason, the ex-cordwainer quickly became a hardworking, thrifty Yankee farmer. He regarded debt with abhorrence, interfered as little as possible with his neighbors, shunned lawsuits, made cautious donations to the poor, avoided politics, and "preserved thro life the character of a man of unblemished integrity—honest, fair & honorable in all his dealing & transactions." A powerful man, six feet in height, with the physique of an athlete, he was a keen participant in the village weight-lifting and wrestling contests, in which he subdued no less an opponent than Henry Dearborn, although the future Secretary of War was thirty years his junior.[2]

Unlike his father, William was a frail boy inheriting his slender constitution from his mother, nee Mary Dole, who was also descended from one of Newbury's first families. In spite of her small stature, poor health, and constant toil, she bore six children and lived to be sixty-nine years of age. William, who was not much given to sentimentalism, described his mother with prosaic tenderness: "She was a woman of good understanding, but not much improved by education, or reading, except religious books. Her piety was pure, practical, & unaffected.... No person had a better disposition—& during the many years I lived with her I never saw her angry—no, not for a moment."[3]

William, the eldest son of this exemplary couple, was born on June 25, 1759, in his father's house in Newburyport. His schooling began when he was four, but ended when he was seventeen, and consisted entirely of reading, writing, spelling, and arithmetic "so far as thro the *square root*." Plumer spent five years in the South Writing School of Newburyport, a town noted throughout New England for the way in which its schools were "honorably supported."[4] With the sympathetic help of his instructor Stephen Sewall, young Plumer made rapid progress in his

2. Sidney Perley, "Plumer Genealogy," Essex Institute, *Historical Collections,* 50 (1914), 17, 337; 51 (1915), 83; Plumer, Autobiography, 5-6; William Plumer, Jr., *Life of William Plumer* (Boston, 1856), 4-5.

3. Plumer, Autobiography, 6.

4. *Ibid.,* 9; Joshua Coffin, *A Sketch of the History of Newbury* (Boston, 1845), 229.

elementary studies and stood at the head of his class in the still inchoate science of orthography.

William did so well that Sewall urged Samuel Plumer to prepare his boy for college. The father, however, believed that the time and money which William would expend at preparatory school and college could be better used elsewhere, and William was not eager to leave home for the strange environment of a boarding school. In later life he realized that he would have profited by college training, although he retained a naive mixture of admiration and contempt for "book-learning" that is a frequent characteristic of self-made men. "I lost the advantages that others enjoyed at colleges," he wrote, "but I escaped the evil examples that too often prevail at those seats of science." [5] Indeed, William somehow acquired a genuine thirst for knowledge and love of learning which often escape the college graduate.

At the age of nine, William Plumer moved from the busy life of a bustling seaport to rural New Hampshire. Although Epping lay in the oldest settled part of the colony, only twenty miles west of Portsmouth, the capital and metropolis, it was an isolated spot of no particular importance. Epping, in 1768, was a good place to carry on agriculture and the worship of Calvin's Jehovah, but the town had little else to recommend it. It did not have a post office, a newspaper, a physician, a lawyer, or a library, and the school system was woefully inadequate. During his seven years in Epping schools, William probably spent less time in the classroom than he had during his four years in Newbury-port, for it was difficult to find a school in Epping that remained open as long as four months in each year. Plumer later described with stark realism the educational facilities in Epping:

Previous to 1775 the town was divided into four or five school districts, in each of which a building was erected for a school house. The houses were . . . small & dark, warm in summer, but cold in winter; & often . . . out of repair. . . . Almost every year, & sometimes oftener, we had new schoolmasters, each of whom varied from his predecessor in the mode of instruction. The selectmen of the town, who employed them, were themselves in general illiterate, & like the people who elected them, thot the principal object was to procure such men as would accept the *lowest wages*. They usually gave from five to eight dollars the month & boarded them; & deemed it extravagant to give more wages than what they gave to those who labored in the fields.[6]

5. Plumer, Autobiography, 10.
6. *Ibid.*, 9.

The selectmen of Epping hired a teacher in 1775 who happened to be proficient in mathematics; from him Plumer learned enough to understand the mysteries of public finance in later years. But the schools had nothing further to offer him, and his formal education ended in the winter of that year.

William Plumer lacked the inspiration of fine teachers, but his education progressed more rapidly after he left school than before. Exclusion from the schoolroom seemed to stimulate his desire for knowledge, and he quickly developed a voracious appetite for books. The Bible, the *Morals of Epictetus,* and a few books on divinity comprised the household library; Samuel Plumer did not even subscribe to the *New Hampshire Gazette,* the only newspaper then published in the province.[7] But the Congregationalist minister, the Reverend Josiah Stearns, owned many books, and young Plumer quickly exhausted the resources of his library, which contained more Calvinism than general information.[8] The scarcity of reading matter caused him to master thoroughly all that he encountered, and he acquired solid if not extensive information. His habits of reading and study not only continued, but grew throughout life. Plumer's writings betray many faults in composition, grammar, and spelling, but he succeeded in developing a literary style that was vigorous, clear, and usually devoid of ornate verbosity.

In the midst of dramatic events that shook the world and tumbled empires, the Plumer family lived peacefully on their farm near the center of Epping. Samuel Plumer, like most of his neighbors, practiced a self-sufficient kind of agriculture, selling occasional surpluses. His farm produced most of the necessities of life, and he clothed his family with household manufactures, including expertly made shoes. William's father differed considerably from his neighbors, however, in his inclination to stay at home and mind his own business. The only time he entered a court room was as a juryman, and he had none of the litigious spirit which was to make his son's later career profitable in New England. When the quarrel with England progressed from protest to revolution, he remained a loyalist, "but," said the son, "he took no measures to oppose our government—indeed, no man was more punctual in the payment of the *war taxes.* The spirit & temper of the times, imposed

7. See Frank Miller, *History of the New Hampshire Gazette* (Boston, 1872).

8. J. H. Stearns, "Congregational Church in Epping," in D. H. Hurd, ed., *Rockingham and Strafford Counties* (Philadelphia, 1882), 215. The contributor of this sketch was the grandson of Plumer's contemporary.

silence on political subjects, upon those who questioned the policy of the revolution; & he prudently acquiesced." His prudence even extended to signing the Association Test in 1776, by which he pledged to the utmost of his power, at the risk of life and fortune, to oppose with arms the hostile proceedings of the British fleets and armies against the united American colonies.[9]

In 1775, William Plumer was sixteen, no younger than many of the New Hampshire lads who joined Stark and Reed at the siege of Boston, but he betrayed no inclination for the army. Nor does he mention ever having served in the militia, in which, according to law, he should have been enrolled in 1775. Perhaps his father's loyalism and his own frail health prevented military service. The state legislature passed a conscription act in 1776, but it obviously did not affect him.[10] Rather than resort to the unpopular necessity of drafting native citizens, Epping hired soldiers from other places to fill her quota. In one way or another Plumer evaded military duty throughout the war. If any explanation was needed, Plumer did not, at that time or any later date, offer one.

In later life he insisted, however, that he became a Whig during the armed conflict. He claimed that, deliberately resisting his father's influence, he investigated the issues of the revolution for himself and came to "a thorough conviction of the justice . . . of the measure, & a firm belief that we should eventually establish our independence." From then until the end of the war, he insisted that he "was anxiously attentive to the occurrences of the times, read the journals of the day with avidity, & diligently sought information from every source to which [he] could gain access." [11] This change in attitude, however, did not result in any active assistance to the patriot cause. Since Plumer remained passive, and since his father's patriotism was noticeably lukewarm, it was inevitable that later political opponents would attempt to besmirch him with the Tory label. While this may have been good politics, it was poor history. It seems clear enough that the Plumers were neither Tories nor zealous revolutionaries, nor was there any necessity that they should have been either. So far as the record shows, they may be included with

9. Plumer, Autobiography, 4-5; Nathaniel Bouton *et al.*, eds., *Documents and Records Relating to the Province [Towns and State] of New Hampshire* [1623-1800], 39 vols. (Concord, 1867-1943), VIII, 204-96 (hereafter cited as *N. H. State Papers*). Only 773 men in New Hampshire had the fortitude to refuse assent to this pledge. Samuel Plumer's name is recorded among the signers in Epping on p. 230.

10. *Ibid.*, 393n.

11. Plumer, Autobiography, 14.

that third of the population which, according to John Adams, lived passively through the winning of independence without participating on either side.

The most exciting event of the year 1779 for the villagers of Epping was not the conquest of Georgia by the British nor the collapse of the Franco-American offensive against Newport, nor even the defection of western New Hampshire from the state government. Far more stirring than these occurrences was a local revival of religion among the various sects of "New Lights." "Religious meetings were frequent," said Plumer in recalling these days; "people were deeply & zealously engaged, enthusiasm & superstition pervaded the assemblies, & spread from mind to mind like a contagious disease, or the fire in a forest impelled by a strong wind." [12] At one of these meetings young Plumer was converted to the Baptist faith. A few months later he made his debut in public life as a Baptist preacher. By so doing, he became, unconsciously, as much a revolutionary as if he had joined the Continental army.

New Hampshire was a Congregationalist as well as a royal province in 1775, and Baptists were as much rebels against the one establishment as Whigs were against the other. In the topsy-turvy world of the Revolution, however, the Congregationalists were Whigs whereas the Baptists tended to lean upon royal protection. This may have been the principal reason for the Plumers' loyalist proclivities, since the family had long been at odds with the orthodox clergy. William's ancestor, Francis Plumer, had incurred the wrath of the General Court of Massachusetts for objecting to its policy of religious intolerance in 1653.[13] Samuel Plumer had been a convert to the New Lights while still living in Newburyport. When the family moved to Epping, however, they found that the new light had not yet penetrated so far north. There the pious elder Plumer had no choice but to attend the regular Congregational meetinghouse and listen to the rigidly orthodox sermons of the Reverend Josiah Stearns. Consequently, he was delighted to transfer his allegiance to the Baptists when a class was organized in Epping by Dr. Samuel Shepard, a remarkable New Hampshire physician who had also become a highly successful evangelist.[14] This minister to both body and soul was the apostle of the revival that drew William Plumer into its net in 1779.

The story of Plumer's conversion provides an excellent case history

12. *Ibid.*, 10.
13. Perley, "Plumer Genealogy," Essex Institute, *Hist. Collections,* 50 (1914), 23-25.
14. William Plumer, "Samuel Shepard," in Biographies, V, 73, New Hampshire Historical Society.

of a phenomenon that has loomed large in American life from the days of Jonathan Edwards and George Whitefield. He first entered the house, where an excited crowd of worshipers had gathered, in a spirit of skepticism, which was increased by the noise and confusion. But "before I was aware I was deeply affected, & alarmed with the apprehension of everlasting misery; & what rendered it peculiarly distressing, I thot I deserved it." For several days, the stricken youth was depressed by a heavy sense of guilt, finding it difficult even to eat or sleep. Then, "on a sudden, I was strongly impressed with the idea that God had forgiven my sins, which releived my distress & filled my mind with transports of joy." [15] Thereafter, the young farmer spent all of his leisure time in prayer, Bible reading, and exhortation, and became a pillar of the local Baptist society.

Dr. Shepard found an able and enthusiastic co-worker in this twenty-one-year-old farmer lad. In the late spring of 1780, William set out on a six-week missionary tour of the north and west. He was an earnest, eloquent, and forceful preacher. In Holderness, he made a vivid impression upon young Arthur Livermore, who was later to become a political associate.[16] In Canaan, he was heckled as a Tory, and the incident formed the basis of a campaign slander thirty-six years later. He preached sometimes twice a day and traveled through every county of the state except Cheshire.[17] Much of his effort was expended on the northern and western frontier of New Hampshire, for it was in the more newly settled areas and in the poorer towns that the Baptists reaped their greatest harvests.[18] The success of his first experiment suggested that a notable career in the Baptist itineracy lay ahead of him, but Plumer's religious metamorphosis was yet to be completed—he was to finish in a state at once more solitary and less constricted than that of the Baptist ministry.

Throughout the summer of 1780, Plumer continued to fast one day in every month, to pray and study the Scriptures four hours in every day, and to participate in frequent religious meetings. But suddenly, in

15. Plumer, Autobiography, 10.
16. Plumer, Jr., *Life of Plumer*, 35.
17. Plumer, Autobiography, 11. After he returned to Epping, Plumer occasionally entered upon similar preaching missions in Rockingham County.
18. Isaac Backus, *History of New England Baptists*, 2d ed. (Newton, Mass., 1871), II, 308-9. During the war, Baptist enthusiasm spread until there were some 24 distinct congregations in the state, extending as far northward as Rumney and Holderness. It is possible that Plumer paved the way for some of these organizations by his pioneering tour.

September, doubts began to disturb his faith. He struggled with them alone; he sought advice from his ministerial friends; he read books that had been written for the benefit of just such waverers—but all to no avail. Within a few weeks, his faith changed to skepticism and his zeal to disillusionment. "No man, unless he has been in my situation, can realize the anxiety I suffered. I knew there [were] some men who professed & preached religion for money, & others who preached doctrines they did not believe, but that was not my case," he afterward recalled.[19] Reason struggled painfully with faith until finally the young man decided that his religious creed was inconsistent with the existence of a rational and benevolent deity. Thus, within a period of eighteen months, he had become a convert first to antipedobaptist theology and then to deism.

For some time Plumer was almost as enthusiastic in propagating the latter as the former faith, but he soon learned that New England was an exceptionally barren field for such labors. His Baptist brethren grew alarmed at his sudden change of tone and brought him to informal trial, whereupon he withdrew from their brotherhood. After a few more quarrels he confessed to a friend that arguments over religion only "alienated my friends & embittered my enemies against me. In disputes, its easier to silence men's arguments than to convince their judgements. . . . The effect of a conquest in such a war is to arm the passions of the conquered against the victor." [20]

This extraordinary series of spiritual struggles, which occupied the twenty-second year of Plumer's life, left an indelible mark upon his later career. His deism was not another temporary fancy of impressionable youth, but remained the basis of his philosophy until he died. It is difficult to discover the influences that caused him to adopt a set of religious ideas that in this one respect distinguished him from the mass of his New England contemporaries. Plumer insisted that his doubts arose entirely from his own mind, but were confirmed by later reading. It is possible that Plumer picked up some of his ideas from America's French allies, who, according to the complaints of ministers in 1780, had introduced a "flood of deism and infidelity" which threatened "to deluge the land." [21] Yet the remoteness of Epping must have been a considerable

19. Plumer, Autobiography, 12.
20. *Ibid.*, 13; Plumer to Jesse Johnson, Dec. 23, 1784, William Plumer Letters, I (1784-1804), Plumer Papers, Lib. Cong. (hereafter cited as Letter Book, I).
21. Backus, *New England Baptists*, II, 542. See also Lucius Thayer, *Religious Condition of New Hampshire at the Beginning of the Nineteenth Century* (Rochester, N. H., 1901), 27.

barricade against this flood. It is much more likely that Plumer worked out his religious beliefs with the help of the writings of the older and more familiar English rationalists. His final tenets were cast in their mold.

The earliest of Plumer's surviving letters were written in 1781-82 as he worked out his personal creed. One letter was taken up with a discourse on the proofs of immortality; Plumer quoted Addison, Sherlock, Akenside, and Cato to buttress his belief that immortality could rationally be expected. In another Plumer outlined his religious philosophy. He believed, he said, in one God, "infinite & eternal—the unoriginated & uncreated source of truth, faithfulness, goodness, love, mercy, spotless purity, justice, impartiality, power, & in fine, the center and unimpaired original of all possible excellence & perfection." [22] Plumer insisted that finite creatures could not even understand God, much less add to His happiness. Man was not created, therefore, as the Calvinists said, to worship God, but to be happy. Human happiness consisted merely in achieving perfect harmony with the benevolent purposes of Providence. It followed therefore that "the laws of nature and reason owe their origin to the Deity—& are at all times & in all places obligatory on all orders & degrees of men."

Plumer's God was not the impersonal and indifferent First Cause of many deists. His world was a rational one, but the rule of reason behind it was social, not scientific. Plumer believed that "all men are bound to practise the moral & social virtues." Civil government was necessary but rulers were required to govern with justice and the people to obey honest rulers. To practice virtue and shun vice was simply good sense. "The man whose passions & appetites are duly regulated, quietly submits to the laws of nature, sees their propriety & adores their author; but he whose passions are unsubdued, finds the order of nature opposed to his measures & renders his schemes abortive." Plumer believed in the "essential & eternal difference" between good and evil, in repentance and pardon, and in the moral duty of man to obey God's laws. Yet none of this was couched in the terms of Christian theology; there was no eschatology, no human depravity, no necessity for salvation, and no eternal damnation. His was a religion of practice, not profession—of deeds, not words. It all seemed so simple to Plumer that no intelligent person could fail to understand it, yet he conceded that prejudice and bad education still turned the great majority of mankind away from the "refulgent

22. Plumer to John Hale, Feb. 22, 1781, Mar. 25, 1782, Letter Book, I, Lib. Cong.

rays" of truth. But "the volume of nature is open & legible . . . & man's duty plain." [23]

Plumer never wandered far from the general principles of this credo, either in belief or practice. As long as he lived, he manifested a clinical interest in religion. When the Shakers first established their peculiar communistic villages in New England, Plumer was intrigued by the experiment and made them several visits, which he described at great length in some fascinating letters.[24] He was never averse to attending religious meetings when the speakers dilated upon the social and moral virtues, but he disliked Calvinistic theology. His life and religious experience spanned the century between rationalism and transcendentalism —between the Pietists and the Unitarians.

When he abandoned organized religion in 1780, Plumer took a fateful step, for the New Englander's entire life usually centered around the meetinghouse. The Congregationalist clergy were powerful leaders of public opinion and dangerous men to cross, and the leaders of the sects, as Plumer acknowledged, exceeded even the "standing order" in their fanaticism. It might be thought that a man who had once been a preacher, particularly a Baptist preacher, and then had deliberately turned his back on all religion, could never hope for a successful career in New Hampshire. Yet Plumer's difference from his brethren, although it was used against him in politics, did not prevent his ultimate attainment of the highest office in the state. One reason was that he had political shrewdness and an accommodating temper, the other that he built his career, in part at least, upon a platform of championing religious freedom.

Plumer's first published writing was a newspaper article in 1782 in which he attacked the religious intolerance written into the proposed state constitution. Only a year had elapsed since he had withdrawn from the Baptist communion. In February, a few weeks before the constitution was to be voted upon in town meetings, Plumer sent an article to the *New Hampshire Gazette,* attacking that part of the bill of rights which dealt with religion. Plumer took exception to the partiality of Article VI, which guaranteed the protection of the laws equally to every denomination of Christians. "Why then have not those who profess a religion different from that of Christianity, an equal right to be protected by those laws, to whose support they contribute, & under whose government they reside," he asked his fellow citizens. "I appeal to your wisdom, candor, & impartiality, whether. . . it would not be more safe

23. Plumer to Hale, Mar. 25, 1782, *ibid.*
24. Plumer to Lydia Coombs, June 17, 1782, Feb. 19, 23, 1783, *ibid.*

& honorable expressly to declare that the protection of the law shall extend to each individual, to all sects & denominations whatsoever; provided their conduct is moral." [25]

Plumer devoted most of the article to an attack upon the Protestant test for officeholding, first introduced into the state by this constitution. The provision reflected fears current in New England that the French alliance was likely to bring popery to America. But Plumer perhaps opposed it for a different reason—because its rigid application would exclude himself, for instance, from office. He argued that it was an unnecessary restriction of doubtful validity; that it "would in fact exclude only the honest & honorable, for dishonest men cannot be excluded by test-laws." [26] In urging a more liberal spirit in the basis of government, he made an eloquent plea for the rights of minorities: "That system which provides for an equal administration of justice & equality, & preserves the natural rights & priviledges of the people in the greatest latitude, is the best suited to the humour & disposition of freemen. . . . If [the majority] deny that liberty, which they enjoy themselves, to others because their ecclesiastical sentiments is different from their's, then their determination is partial & unequal. The ideas of power & equality are in their nature distinct, & ought not to be confounded." [27]

But young Plumer's was a lonely voice in 1782. The people rejected many other features of the constitution but retained its religious restrictions. Some estimate of public feeling on this question may be made from the fact that Plumer had to pay the editor of the *Gazette* three dollars in order to persuade the cautious man even to print his article. [28]

Plumer's sentiments brought him into open and persistent conflict with the religious establishment in New Hampshire, where taxpayers had been required from earliest times to support in every town the legally chosen minister, who was, with very few exceptions, a Congregationalist. The Revolutionary state constitution contained a toleration clause which permitted a person of such prominence as Plumer later became to escape religious taxation by stating in town meeting that he was not of the same sect as the established minister. [29] In spite of the

25. William Plumer, Essays, I (1782-1838), 3-5, Plumer Papers, Lib. Cong.
26. Plumer, Autobiography, 15.
27. Plumer, Essays, I, 5, Lib. Cong. See also *New Hampshire Gazette* (Portsmouth), Feb. 18, 1782.
28. Plumer, Autobiography, 15.
29. *Ibid.*, 55. Plumer copied into his Register the formal letter to the Congregational Society of Epping, dated Jan. 1, 1793, in which he and a fellow townsman declared their separation and determination not to pay religious taxes. William Plumer, Register, I (1805-7), 60, Plumer Papers, Lib. Cong.

toleration clause, however, many of the sectarians fared badly at the hands of overly zealous magistrates and judges.[30] The Baptists, and other nonconformists after them, were inclined to resist the union of church and state in its entirety, and refused to pay taxes that they considered to be in violation of their consciences as well as their rights. Plumer was in complete agreement with this position. His active sympathy soon produced a strange spectacle in New Hampshire public life— a deist allied with religious zealots whom he often despised personally, against the ruling class of orthodox clergymen, lawyers, and squires with whom he naturally associated.

30. For specific examples of such persecution, culled from local histories and court records, see Charles Kinney, *Church and State: The Struggle for Separation in New Hampshire, 1630-1900* (New York, 1955), 86-97.

CHAPTER II

Politics and Law

"There's a report the General Court,
To regulate the sawyer,
Of late in fact have pass'd an act,
But quite forgot the lawyer." [1]

THE collapse of William Plumer's brief career in the Baptist ministry left him perplexed, restless, and dissatisfied. He had finished his schooling, exhausted the intellectual resources of his community, and returned to the endless round of farm labor. Although William's father was determined to make him a farmer, the young man found agricultural labor distasteful, partly because of his slender constitution, but chiefly because it did not challenge his mind. There was nothing stimulating about an agricultural career in New England in the eighteenth century. Men farmed as their fathers and grandfathers had farmed, with the same primitive equipment and in the same unimaginative routine. The rocky soil of New England tested the muscle and endurance of the Yankee husbandman, but not his vision. By 1781, young Plumer realized that the time was fast approaching when he should have to make a permanent choice of career, or remain bound to the soil forever.

For three years the young man wavered among law, medicine, and commerce. With his shrewd business sense and habits of industry, Plumer might have had a successful commercial career, but grubbing for money did not appeal to him and he did not consider it very seriously. Medicine lured the young farmer much more strongly. It was a profession that supported a surprisingly large number of practitioners in those days and paid them with prestige as well as cash. But medical science was still in its infancy, and physicians, in Plumer's opinion, had made less progress than either lawyers or the clergy. He was vain enough to believe that his high ethical standards would put him at a

1. *N. H. Gazette* (Portsmouth), Aug. 26, 1785.

disadvantage with the quacks who infested the country. After having read a considerable amount of medical literature, Plumer reluctantly concluded that the profession was in a chaotic condition, and he abandoned the field with a curious prejudice against physicians that he retained throughout life.[2]

By the time he was twenty-six Plumer had made up his mind to become a lawyer. His earlier hesitation had been due in part to the disturbed condition of the country, and particularly of the judiciary. During the Revolution, when the courts had often been suspended, the majority of New Hampshire's lawyers had either been avowed loyalists or conspicuously neutral. When the courts reopened in the latter period of the war, the lawyers alienated the people by their alliance with creditors; debtors were harassed not only by creditors and lawyers but also by the deflationary policy of the state government. Plumer's relatives, being simple people, had their full share of this popular anti-lawyer feeling. In an effort to draw William away from the law, Samuel Plumer purchased a sixty-acre tract on the Dearborn homestead in the center of Epping and made an outright gift of it to his son.[3] But even this $2,500 bribe was not sufficient to overcome William's yearning for an expanded stage of activity, and he finally obtained his parents' consent to begin his legal education.

Perhaps Plumer's decision had been influenced by his entry into politics as a selectman and justice of the peace. In 1783 the voters of Epping chose the twenty-four-year-old farmer as one of the town's elders. The Baptists were undoubtedly annoyed with him for having so recently forsaken their ranks, and the dominant Congregationalists must have been no less irritated by his deism, yet he was continued in office for three successive years. He launched a consistently unorthodox political career by making an affirmation before the magistrate rather than taking the prescribed oath. "I considered it irreverent & degrading to the character of the Supreme being to invoke his name as a witness to our petty transactions," he explained.[4] The duties of his office, which were prescribed by state law, were not such as to tax unduly either Plumer's capacities or his fellow citizens' pocketbooks. He performed them easily

2. In New Hampshire, physicians outnumbered clergymen or lawyers. Nathaniel Bouton printed an interesting table of the comparative numbers in the professions as an appendix to his discourse on the history of education in 1833. "History of Education in New Hampshire," New Hampshire Historical Society, *Collections*, 4 (1834), 37-38.

3. Plumer, Autobiography, 17; Plumer to William Coleman, Aug. 27, 1784, Letter Book, I, Lib. Cong.

4. Plumer, Autobiography, 16.

and to the satisfaction of the townspeople; testimonial of their regard was a petition to the president and council of state, begging that William Plumer "of this town Whome We humbly Conseive is Quallifyed for the Office" should be appointed a justice of the peace.[5]

When the new justice of the peace decided to study law, he had little choice but to follow the eighteenth-century practice of attaching himself to a practicing attorney for a few months as a combination student, apprentice, clerk, and boarder. The quality of legal education under these conditions depended almost entirely upon the industry, intelligence, and initiative of the apprentice.[6] This was certainly true in Plumer's case, for he was not particularly fortunate in his instructors. He applied first to Theophilus Bradbury of Newburyport, one of New England's most distinguished lawyers, and then to John Pickering of Portsmouth, probably the busiest attorney in New Hampshire, but neither of these men was able at the time to accept another student.[7] He next tried Joshua Atherton, who lived in the New Hampshire village of Amherst, and was accepted. A "man of a haughty imperious disposition," Atherton had held office under the royal governor of the colony and had continued after 1775 as a staunch loyalist, for which offense he had been mobbed and jailed.[8] However, he had finally taken the oath of loyalty to the new government in 1779, and thereafter rapidly regained his professional standing. His practice soon returned to its former extent, and he was sent by Amherst as a delegate to the convention which framed the state constitution in 1783.

It was a year after Atherton's return from this work that young William Plumer, thin and spare, wearing a snuff-colored coat, and still looking a good deal like a Baptist preacher, appeared at his door to begin the study of law. Atherton set him to work reading *Coke upon Littleton,* but four weeks later abruptly told him that he must study Latin grammar before he could appreciate English law. This Spartan regimen was too much for Plumer, who, concluding that he had chosen the wrong vocation after all, returned to Epping. The only thing he had

5. *N. H. State Papers,* XI, 625-27.

6. The first law school in New England was not founded until 1784, the very year that Plumer began his training, and none was attached to any college in New England until 1817. See Edwin Dexter, *History of Education in the United States* (N. Y., 1904), 316-18.

7. Plumer, Autobiography, 16. Bradbury would have taken him but advised against it since Massachusetts law differed from that of New Hampshire.

8. Plumer, "Joshua Atherton," Biographies, IV, 484, N. H. Hist. Soc.; Charles Bell, *The Bench and Bar of New Hampshire* (Boston, 1894), 150.

gained from this false start was the friendship of William Coleman, a fellow student in Atherton's office, who was to become the editor of the *New-York Evening Post* and the "field marshal of federalism." [9]

From this disappointment, Plumer plunged once more into politics. In March 1785, only a few days after he had taken possession of his farm and installed a tenant, young Plumer was chosen by his fellow townsmen to be their representative in the state legislature. By this time, the first flush of postwar prosperity had faded into the drab shades of depression. The state of public affairs in New Hampshire was "gloomy & menacing," Plumer wrote; "they approached an alarming crisis, threatening the destruction of order & civil government." [10] The chief problem was economic. Like all her sister states, New Hampshire in 1782 was flooded with paper money that had depreciated to one seventy-fifth of its face value. Professional men with fixed incomes saw their purchasing power dwindle to the vanishing point, and creditors, as Plumer noted, "instead of seeking avoided their debtors, & used every effort to prevent payment." The situation had produced an inevitable deflationary reaction. First, the money printing had been stopped; then the hard money advocates in the legislature had partially repudiated the old currency and attempted to restore specie payment for debts. For a few months the deflationary policy was supported by a continuing artificial war prosperity. Plumer noted that: "In this interval British merchants, & our own merchants, imported an immense quantity of goods into this country, a great portion of which were articles of luxury & superfluity. These importations in a few months drained the money from the country, & it became scarce & valuable." [11] By November 1783, the agricultural towns were complaining of the complete absence of gold and silver. In the absence of legal currency, no amount of hard work or good intentions would pay debts or taxes. A group of malcontents put the whole matter succinctly when they said, "the war with all its Calamitys did not seem near so distressing as the present times." [12]

9. Plumer, Jr., *Life of Plumer,* 56; Plumer, Autobiography, 17.

10. Plumer, Autobiography, 19, 21. Plumer's defeated opponent threatened to contest his right to the seat on the ground of failure to fulfill the religious qualification, but eventually thought better of it.

11. *N. H. State Papers,* VIII, 907, 913; Plumer, Autobiography, 22; Richard Upton, *Revolutionary New Hampshire* (Hanover, 1936), 141-43. For the effect of inflation upon a minister's standard of living, see Jane Marcou, *Life of Jeremy Belknap, D. D.* (N. Y., 1847), 33 ff.

12. *N. H. State Papers,* XII, 765.

As a farmer, Plumer might have been expected to join the rising clamor for debt cancellation and inflation. One of his campaign promises, on the contrary, was an assurance that he would vote against any further extensions of time on the payment of past-due taxes by delinquent towns.[13] This attitude was obviously dictated by sectional interests, since most of the tax-debtor towns were on the northern and western frontier, while Epping had faithfully met its obligations and was tired of carrying a disproportionate burden.[14]

Tax delinquency greatly augmented the appalling problem of the public debt, which imposed a per capita obligation of eighteen dollars upon every resident of New Hampshire.[15] This obligation could be met only by grinding taxation that fell with peculiar severity upon the poor.[16] After 1782, however, New Hampshire fell further and further behind in meeting her obligations to the national treasury, and the conservatives in general, including Plumer, regarded this financial infidelity with shame and apprehension. As if all this were not enough, the title to every acre in the richest and oldest two-thirds of the state's territory was suddenly jeopardized by the revival of an ancient dispute.

In 1783 the so-called Allen claim to this area was acquired by a group of speculators who promptly declared all other titles invalid. Since every land title in a score of New Hampshire towns derived from the so-called Masonian Proprietors, who had purchased the original proprietary claim in 1746, public indignation was extreme. Plumer, who later became an attorney for one of the Masonian Proprietors,[17] may not have been an unprejudiced observer, but he noted that the land dispute aroused deep anxiety. "Many people," he declared, "believed it was the intention of

13. The obligation of the delinquent towns to the state treasury had mounted to a sum of £399,877. Upton, *Revolutionary N. H.*, 137. Plumer's election promises are preserved in Plumer, Repository, IV (1741-1805), 279-81, Plumer Papers, New Hampshire State Library.

14. For the problems of the delinquent towns, see the petition of Dorchester, Grafton County, in *N. H. State Papers*, XI, 502-3. Dozens of such petitions are scattered among the *Town Papers* volumes in this series. See especially XII, 406-9, XIII, 121-23.

15. Allan Nevins, *American States During and After the Revolution, 1775-1789* (N. Y., 1927), 477.

16. *N. H. Gazette* (Portsmouth), June 3, 1785. New Hampshire followed Massachusetts' lead in levying heavy specie taxes and trying to discharge its debts. Virginia, on the other hand, discharged its state debt by repudiating its paper currency and paying its soldiers with land grants. Virginia's policy, of course, was easy on debtors; New Hampshire's added to their burdens. See Merrill Jensen, *The New Nation* (N. Y., 1950), 304-8.

17. George Jaffrey to Plumer, June 5, 1794, *N. H. State Papers*, XXIX, 363-71.

[the Allenites] to establish lordships, & reduce people to vassallage." [18]

Such was the explosive state of public opinion in 1785 when William Plumer rode to Portsmouth to take his seat in the legislature. "Numerous applications were made to the legislature," he wrote, "requesting relief against the scarsity of money, & the claims of the Allenites." The legislature voted overwhelmingly against a paper currency issue, but, feeling that some gesture of conciliation should be made, passed by a large majority an act to exempt debtors from arrest if they tendered real or personal property in satisfaction of executions. Representative Plumer was one of seventeen members "who strenuously opposed its passage," and he supported the senate in several efforts to modify or repeal the bill. It may seem inconsistent that a man who always considered imprisonment for debt barbaric should have been unwilling to sanction the small measure of relief that this law seemed to afford. But Plumer's judgment that the act was a defective palliative rather than true relief seemed to be borne out by experience. "People were afraid to loan their money, lest when they called for it they should receive a tender of old houses, uncultivated lands, or property of little value," he wrote.[19]

The legislature of 1785 made another ill-digested effort to stop the clamor against the lower courts by passing an act for the expeditious recovery of small debts, which allowed justices of the peace to try civil suits involving ten pounds or less. Plumer claimed that the bill was passed "at a time when there was scarse a quorum of the House present —& the number of justices who were members was more than ten to one who was not in Commission." [20] The Epping representative courageously, or theatrically, entered his single dissent against this act on the journals. He reasoned that the act was unconstitutional, and within a few months he had the satisfaction of seeing it so pronounced by the courts, after it had led to some ridiculous miscarriages of justice. The other enactments of this addled parliament were in the same character. When its final session had stumbled to adjournment, Jeremy Belknap, the state historian, wrote to a friend, "Our G.C. quarrelled among themselves, and broke up. . . . Fine times!" [21]

18. Plumer, Autobiography, 22. For a thorough discussion of the tangled land title question in New Hampshire, see Otis Hammond, *The Mason Title and Its Relations to New Hampshire and Massachusetts* (Worcester, 1916).

19. *N. H. State Papers,* XX, 434-35, 445, 518; Plumer, Autobiography, 22-23.

20. Plumer to William Coleman, May 31, 1786, Letter Book, I, Lib. Cong.

21. *N. H. State Papers,* XX, 450; Plumer, Autobiography, 382; Massachusetts Historical Society, *Collections,* 5th Ser., 2 (1877), 422-23, 433.

In his first session, Plumer had taken little part in debate. In the second session, which met at Concord in November, he had been much more articulate and his name began to appear frequently in the proceedings. By the end of this session, he had decided to forsake his farm in Epping and resume his legal studies. When the third session of this assembly met at Portsmouth in February 1786, Plumer was no longer only a farmer, but a law student and a companion of great men. "I was treated with much attention by many of the members & respectable families in Portsmouth," he recalled.[22] Plumer had certainly demonstrated that he was about as far from being a radical extremist at it was possible to be. Whether Epping approved of its representative's conservatism would be hard to say, for he did not subject it to the test of re-election. Instead he devoted himself to the completion of his legal studies and, consequently, lacked any opportunity to influence by his vote the course of action during the year 1786.

Plumer acquired his knowledge of the law in the office of his second preceptor, John Prentice, a Londonderry lawyer and a fellow legislator. Prentice was an undisciplined character, with a professional status even more obscure than Plumer's first tutor, but he was a good neighbor and companion and he had a pleasant home. The bargain between the instructor and his pupil provided that Plumer would pay five hundred dollars and "perform the usual business of the office" in return for two years of board, lodging, and instruction.[23] The board and lodging were excellent, but the instruction was negligible.

Prentice knew very little law, was not fond of reading, and had a library that Plumer thought extremely meager. His legal practice was largely that of a conveyancer, and he seldom appeared at the bar in important cases. Plumer was particularly irked at his instructor's complete ignorance of special pleading, which led to his own serious deficiency in that art.[24] Left largely to his own devices, Plumer began to wade laboriously through Blackstone. He presently found his task lighter, then intensely interesting. Long before his two years were finished, he had devoured his host's small library and transcribed virtually the whole of it into notebooks. By dint of hard work, long hours of study, and persistent effort, he mastered all that Prentice had to offer and much besides. Plumer was not sufficiently interested in the study of law to become a profound legal scholar. His legal education was adequate for

22. Plumer, Autobiography, 21.
23. *Ibid.,* 19-20.
24. Plumer, "John Prentice," Biographies, IV, 445, N. H. Hist. Soc.

his time and purpose. It is probable, however, that he gained more of it in Prentice's office than he did in Prentice's library.

Plumer's pursuit of legal learning was disrupted by a courtship, a term in the state legislature, and the exciting events of 1786 that culminated in the Exeter riot. Nevertheless, in spite of all distractions, he finished his two years with Prentice, intending to apply for admission to the bar at the February term in 1788. Three months earlier, he happened to be present at a session of the Court of Common Pleas in Exeter, when the court unexpectedly directed him to take the necessary affirmation and admitted him to practice. This action was taken upon the recommendation of the bar, without Plumer's knowledge and without examination.[25] It was an unusual procedure, contrasting strangely with the experience of Jeremiah Smith, a Harvard graduate from Peterborough, who knew a great deal more law than did Plumer. In the spring of the previous year, young Smith had been refused even an examination by the bar in Hillsborough County and had only been admitted by the court against the malevolent opposition of the lawyers, including Atherton. " 'Tis devlishly provoking to be denied admittance into *bad company*," he had written to Plumer.[26]

Although Plumer was not a member of the legislature that met in June 1786, he attended its sessions, drafting bills and petitions, and supporting them before committees. Such lobbying was a regular part of the lawyer's practice in Plumer's day, and the experience was more valuable to him than weeks of study in Prentice's office. In the taverns of Concord he encountered several men who had been elected from nearby towns to a paper money convention, which was expected to browbeat the legislature into acquiescence.[27] Noting that the delegates seemed uncertain as to the proper revolutionary procedure, Plumer and several young lawyer friends conceived the idea of turning the convention into a farce. They assumed the character of delegates from their respective towns and suggested to the genuine members that they proceed immediately to organize without waiting for further reinforcements. When two delegates from a Hillsborough County convention, who would have been the leaders of the lobby under more conventional circumstances, arrived in Concord, they found matters already out of hand, and were even unwilling, by exposing the hoax, to share the ridicule which would be heaped upon their fellows. They had brought

25. Plumer, Autobiography, 31.
26. Jeremiah Smith to Plumer, Oct. 31, 1787, Letter Book, I, Lib. Cong.
27. Plumer, Autobiography, 24.

to Concord a memorial from the Hillsborough County convention for submission to the legislature, but decided to leave town without presenting their ultimatum.

In the meantime, the Concord wits, artfully opposing each other in debate, had joined with the innocent delegates in adopting a set of extravagant resolutions, including one that the state should "emit *three million* of dollars in paper money," and another that there should be "but two lawyers in each county." At this point, Plumer thought that the comedy had proceeded to its proper climax and demurred at presenting such resolutions to the legislature. But his companions were enjoying themselves too much to stop so soon, and they assured the delegates that brother Plumer had made his declaration merely to test their courage and perseverance. Accordingly, the next day all the members marched solemnly to the assembly room and presented their memorial to the legislators, who had been apprised beforehand of the deception and were greatly amused. The whole procedure excited so much contempt for the so-called state convention that the delegates slunk home and the legislature was spared any further pressure for paper money during that session.[28]

It soon appeared, however, that the paper money mania was no laughing matter. The resolutions adopted in the spurious convention were not one whit more extravagant than those being voted in town meetings on every hand. The example of Rhode Island, where paper had depreciated 500 per cent during the summer, filled New Hampshire conservatives with dread. Calling upon his memory of Scripture, Plumer wrote with grim humor to a friend: "It seems the zealous advocates of paper currency intend to convince an infidel age of the truth of a part, at least, of the Scriptures, by demonstrating *that riches take to themselves wings & flee away*—That notes, bonds & other obligations are *vanity & vexation*—That it is best to revive the Apostolic age, & *have all things in common*—that the indolent, extravagant & wicked may divide the blessings of life with the industrious, the prudent & the virtuous." [29]

The New Hampshire farmers were enraged because the legislature had ignored their petitions in June, and they were inflamed by the bold action of their neighbors across the southern border. They were also, in young Plumer's opinion, secretly encouraged by "others of more

28. *Ibid.,* 25, 26; Plumer to Samuel Plumer, July 22, 1786, Colonial Society of Massachusetts, *Publications,* 11 (1910), 385.
29. Plumer to John Hale, Aug. 13, 1786, Letter Book, I, Lib. Cong.

consequence . . . by men who are bankrupts in fame and fortune, by men who are disaffected with the government because they are unable to obtain offices of honor and profit." [30] In July, Plumer had an excellent opportunity to take the pulse of their desperation when a self-styled Rockingham County convention met in Londonderry, where he was studying law. The chairman of this convention was an honest, gullible farmer from Hampstead, Joseph French, who later aspired to be the Daniel Shays of New Hampshire. Still convinced that ridicule was the only weapon likely to discourage such people, Plumer and his friends attempted to repeat their Concord comedy when the Rockingham Convention met again in August in nearby Chester. The law student sent a copy of the fabulous resolutions drawn up by his mock convention to the Exeter *Freeman's Oracle,* accompanied by a letter of explanation in which he revealed the full virulence of his conservative instincts. He believed that his account, if printed, would serve as a fitting introduction to:

. . . the proceedings of the *real* Convention—in which the consummate Statesmen appeared, formed not by the specious rules of Art but by simple *uninstructed* nature—whose externals (adorned with leather doublets and shoe strings) corresponded with their internal faculties . . . the Members of our Convention without ever turning a page of history, perusing a sheet of Law, or even reading the title page of human Nature, are equal to the more than Herculean task, of giving Laws to the State. Their knowledge is Intuitive. Who would wish for the *dim taper of science* to direct their wandering steps, that is blessed with the full collection of the efulgent rays of Intuition? [31]

But ridicule, this time, only served to inflame the passions of the outraged masses. The Chester convention voted to raise a force of armed men to enforce their claims if the legislature persisted in its neglect. "I hope these visionary schemes will not end in acts of rebellion against the constituted authorities—tho' much I fear it," wrote Plumer in genuine alarm.[32]

The legislature that met at Exeter in September 1786 was under heavier popular pressure than any since the early days of the Revolutionary War. It received an enormous number of petitions from county conventions, towns, and groups of clamorous citizens. "Paper money

30. Plumer to Hale, Sept. 18, 1786, Col. Soc. of Mass., *Publications,* 11 (1910), 387.
31. Plumer to Randlet and Lampson, Printers, Aug. 25, 1786, Plumer, Repository, IV, 269-70, N. H. State Lib.
32. Col. Soc. of Mass., *Publications,* 11 (1910), 386.

was what they requested," observed Plumer, "nothing else would satisfy them, tho every well informed man knew, if it was made, it would depreciate, & prove a fertile source of fraud & iniquity." [33] Plumer, who had again deserted his books in favor of the more exciting educational opportunities at Exeter, was inclined to take a very lofty attitude toward legislators who bent before this gale. There were enough of them, however, to send to the towns, for a referendum vote, a complicated scheme for issuing interest-bearing state notes that would not be legal tender. In the meantime, three years after the Treaty of Paris had been signed, a bill for removing the legal impediments in New Hampshire to the collection of debts by British subjects was finally passed.[34] A report was immediately spread that the lawmakers had promised the Tories to return their confiscated property. This spark touched off armed insurrection in New Hampshire.[35]

Upon receipt of this inflammatory falsehood, earnest Joseph French hastened to Londonderry and called another meeting of the Rockingham Convention delegates; this time they were armed with staves, pitchforks, and a few Revolutionary muskets. On the afternoon of the twentieth, while the assembly was debating a new ferry over the Connecticut, Plumer saw this motley army of two hundred men and boys march into Exeter with colors flying, drums beating, and arms clubbed.[36] Ignoring a vigorous warning against their treasonable course by Major General Sullivan, the president of the state,[37] the rioters surrounded the meetinghouse, placed sentinels with fixed bayonets at all doors and windows and declared "that unless the Genl Court would grant their Petition [they] would Starve them till they would comply & much more." [38]

The subsequent events are nowhere so graphically described as in the unpublished autobiography of Plumer. He was himself outside the meetinghouse, in an excellent position to see what occurred and even to participate in events. At sunset, when the mob prevented Sullivan and

33. Plumer, Autobiography, 23.
34. *N. H. State Papers*, XI, 127-30; XX, 699. Orin Libby reported the vote on this bill incorrectly in his *The Geographical Distribution of the Vote of the Thirteen States on the Federal Constitution, 1787-1788* (Madison, 1894), 54.
35. Plumer, Autobiography, 27; Col. Soc. of Mass., *Publications,* 11 (1910), 390, 395.
36. The mob first mistakenly marched to the townhouse where the Superior Court was sitting. Chief Justice Livermore ignored the rioters and sternly forbade anyone inside the courtroom to look out the windows. Bell, *Bench and Bar,* 37.
37. *New Hampshire Mercury*, Sept. 24, 1786, quoted in N. H. Hist. Soc., *Collections,* 3 (1832), 122; Plumer to John Hale, Sept. 20, 1786, Letter Book, I, Lib. Cong.
38. *N. H. State Papers,* XVIII, 744, 745.

the senators from leaving the building, twenty men, of whom Plumer was one, formed a company and marched upon the rioters. Since they were joined by many of the spectators, the prospect of a serious clash and the "effusion of blood" appeared imminent.[39] Sullivan effected a temporary truce by which French agreed to withdraw his men and camp outside the town on the assurance that the legislature would do no more business that night but would consider their grievances on the next morning. Plumer, who had been highly critical of the slightest evidence of concession to the mob, found no fault with the legislature when it reconvened as soon as the insurgents were out of town and authorized Sullivan to call out the militia. The young man who had felt no compulsion to fight during the Revolution, now procured arms and joined as a volunteer in the Exeter militia company commanded by Nicholas Gilman, a New Hampshire delegate to Congress. In the early morning, Plumer and five other citizen-soldiers were detached to arrest a Revolutionary veteran from Londonderry "who was lurking as a spy." Six other deputies from French who came to seek their comrade's release were also thrown into jail.

By eight o'clock, a well-armed militia force including cavalry units, had assembled in Exeter, and marched out to meet French's ragged force, which had begun moving toward town. Fortunately, no battle ensued. A cavalry charge put the insurgents to flight and most of their leaders were captured. "We returned to the town, in good order," wrote Plumer exultantly, "not a man on either side received any considerable injury. . . . We took thirty nine prisoners, who after marching thro our columns with their heads uncovered & hats under their arms, the music playing *the rogues march,* were lodged in the gaol." [40]

No one was more pleased with the collapse of the rebellion than William Plumer, who returned in October to Londonderry, the chief center of revolt. "President Sullivan has acquired credit by his prudence

---

39. Plumer, Autobiography, 28-29.
40. *Ibid.,* 29-30. Contemporary accounts of the riot may be found in Col. Soc. of Mass., *Publications,* 11 (1910), 390-96; Marcou, *Life of Jeremy Belknap,* 124-25; Charles Warren Brewster, *Rambles About Portsmouth* (Portsmouth, 1869), II, 139-42; N. H. Hist. Soc., *Collections,* 3 (1832), 122; *Historical Magazine,* 15 (1869), 37-38. The legislative journals are printed in *N. H. State Papers,* XX, 671-713, and a few documents connected with the affair may be found in *ibid.,* XVIII. The Exeter Riot has also been treated in at least two unpublished master's theses: Abraham Sondak, The Paper Money Struggle in New Hampshire, 1786-1788 (Columbia University, 1936); and Sturgis Wilson, The Riot at Exeter, New Hampshire, September 20 and 21, 1786 (no place, 1928 [typescript in N. H. Hist. Soc.]). Neither of these authors made use of the Plumer Papers.

caution & firmness," he declared.[41] In November, when Sullivan visited Londonderry on a grand military tour of the state, Plumer was chosen by the town to write the welcoming address to the president, and the young law student gave Sullivan a liberal dose of the flattery he loved. "The Spirit & wisdom with which your *Excellency* so happily extinguished the flame of sedition at the very crisis when it became most alarming, merits the thanks of every friend to order & to mankind," he declaimed.[42] Thus early in his career did William Plumer align himself with those conservatives who reacted in alarm against the excesses of populism.

The civil commotions of the fall and winter convinced Plumer and many others in all parts of the Confederation that strong measures were necessary for a restoration of stability and prosperity. "I fear to look forward, anarchy, confusion & sometimes bloodshed rise full to my view. . . . Is it not . . . all over with this Republican country?" queried William Coleman, Plumer's former fellow student at Amherst, who had just spent a month's service against the Shaysites in Massachusetts.[43] "There is an absolute necessity of establishing a more efficient system of government," wrote Plumer in response to this pessimism.[44] Most of New Hampshire's leaders, including John Langdon and Nicholas Gilman, the two delegates whom the state sent belatedly to the Philadelphia convention, were in complete sympathy with these views. When the new Federal Constitution, which these men helped to construct, was finally revealed to the public and the magnificent extent of its renovating power became apparent, the New Hampshire conservatives were overjoyed. "Men of talents, information, & attachment to their country, seem to have turned their whole attention to the Constitution reported by the late Federal Convention," wrote Plumer in December 1787. " 'Tis an object of much importance to this nation." Here was a transformation worked in the national government such as the "men of talents" had not yet achieved in the state. "Our liberties, our rights & property are now the sport of ignorant unprincipled State legislators," Plumer went on to say, but he believed that the adoption of the new system would end their tyranny. The young lawyer was indeed disappointed that the medicine was not even stronger. He wished more authority granted to the President and fewer restrictions placed

41. Plumer to John Hale, Sept. 21, 1786, Letter Book, I, Lib. Cong.
42. Plumer, Repository, IV, 283, N. H. State Lib.
43. William Coleman to Plumer, Mar. 28, 1787, Letter Book, I, Lib. Cong.
44. Plumer to William Coleman, May 31, 1786, *ibid*.

upon the powers of Congress, but he recognized that a formidable opposition existed, which would render any greater centralization altogether hopeless.[45]

Plumer was one of the first to feel the effects of this opposition. When the state legislature ordered the towns to elect delegates to a convention which would meet at Exeter in February to consider the new Constitution,[46] Plumer, who had only just returned to Epping to open up his law office, offered himself as a candidate. He buttonholed "most of the freeholders of Epping" and obtained the unanimous support of the Federalists, but all in vain. It developed that Epping, although it had not been one of the paper money towns, was suspicious of the new Constitution, and elected Plumer's Antifederalist rival, Nathaniel Ladd, who subsequently did not even bother to attend the convention.[47]

It soon became apparent that the overly confident Federal leaders could have used Plumer's vote in the convention. At the first session, in February, the Antifederal delegates were obviously in the majority, and their opponents were fortunate to secure an adjournment without an adverse vote. New Hampshire finally ratified in June by a close, sectional vote which clearly foreshadowed the future lines of political battles within the state. But for the moment, New Hampshire's men of "wealth and talents" had secured control and brought their state into firm union with the rest of the nation.

This was a result with which William Plumer was thoroughly in sympathy, but he gave it little immediate attention. At the moment he was more concerned with his new law practice and his new wife. Plumer's courtship occupies a minimum of space in his autobiography, for he was little given to romantic memories. Nevertheless, he had carried on with certain friends a lively correspondence dealing with girls, parties, good dinners, and amusements, as well as with law, religion, and politics. The letters that he considered worthy of preservation include those from the number of young ladies whom a busy and somewhat diffident young man might be expected to know, and at least one of them suggests the existence of an early love affair which was ended by the death of the girl.[48] A poem addressed to this young lady reveals

45. Plumer to Daniel Tilton, Dec. 16, 1787, *ibid.*
46. *N. H. State Papers,* XXI, 149, 160.
47. Plumer, Autobiography, 34. Plumer later insisted, somewhat erroneously, that this was one of only three offices he had ever sought for himself, and that in every such case he had been defeated.
48. Sophia Murray to Plumer, Dec. 8, 1785, Letter Book, I, Lib. Cong.

Plumer's character, demonstrating at once the prosaic quality of his mind and the genuine sincerity of his emotion:

> Attend, fair maid, to what I shall impart,
> Let the precepts of truth sink in thy heart;
> So shall the virtues of thy mind, adorn
> With lustre, the elegance of thy form—
> And as the Rose, tho past its bloom, is sweet,
> Thy beauty, even in age, shall be compleat.
> In spring of youth & morning of thy days,
> When men with joy & rapture on thee gaze—
> And Nature tells thee what their looks impart,
> 'Gainst their seducing words guard well thy heart.
> Thou wast not made Man's loose desires to gratify,
> And with his passions only to comply—
> Kind Heaven did thee, fairest creature, form,
> Man's soul with love & tenderness to warm—
> The roughness of his sen's to humanize,
> And all his cares & joys to realize—
> Such is the lovely maid that wins his soul,
> And shall reign in my breast without controul.[49]

If any broken heart resulted from this short reign, it was soon mended, for in the spring of 1787, Plumer met his future wife, Sally Fowler. The daughter of a respectable landowner in Newmarket, New Hampshire, she was on a visit to Londonderry at the time of the encounter. In July, Plumer wrote in high spirits to his friend, Moses Neal, that he had taken up a new sport since Neal's departure:

You well know that I frequently expressed strong doubts of the lawfulness of depriving either beasts or *fowls* of their existence.... Notwithstanding my former sentiments & aversion, *fowling* now constitutes a principal source of my delight.... Some are pleased to say that this *fowling game* will eventually tend more to the reproduction of life than to its destruction. Should that be the case I shall enjoy the double pleasure of playing with a *fair Fowler* & not destroying that *tenderness* which I have long cherished in favor of the world of life.... But whether the *game* will end with the season or terminate but with life, is equally uncertain.[50]

---

49. Plumer to Sophia Murray, Nov. 7, 1785, *ibid.* It should come as no surprise, after reading this sample, that Plumer concluded: "nature had not formed me for a poet." Plumer, Autobiography, 14.

50. Plumer to Moses Neal, July 6, 1787, Letter Book, I, Lib. Cong.

The game did indeed terminate but with life, for William Plumer and his wife lived together for the remarkable span of sixty-three years. Mrs. Plumer did not appear to have any strong influence over her husband, and she certainly shared little, if at all, in his manifold public interests. Nevertheless, their life together was happy and placid. She bore him six children, managed his household during his numerous absences, and provided for him an indispensable domestic surcease from the distractions of his public life. Plumer unquestionably loved and appreciated her, but it was not within his nature to perpetuate his sentiments in epic or sonnet. Almost the last mention which he makes of his wife in his autobiography occurs shortly after they were married— a classic of succinctness: "On the 13th day of February [1788] I was married to Miss Fowler; on the first day of April moved her to my house; & have since enjoyed as much happiness in the marriage state as I had any right to expect." [51]

Plumer's entry into marriage and the law almost coincided. Admitted to the bar three months before his wedding, Plumer found himself a member of a select and distinguished company. In 1787, New Hampshire had only twenty-nine lawyers, one for every 4,600 inhabitants.[52] Seven months after Plumer's admission to the bar, a majority of the attorneys met at Concord and organized the New Hampshire Bar Association. Plumer could not be present, but he was represented by proxy [53] and became a charter member. The group included a goodly portion of the genius and ability of New Hampshire; besides Prentice and Atherton, there were John Pickering of Portsmouth, whom Plumer greatly admired and would have preferred as his instructor; Major General John Sullivan of Durham, who had become a national figure during the War of Independence; Benjamin West of Charlestown, a man of painful modesty but commanding eloquence; and Samuel Livermore, the chief justice, a frontier aristocrat, and constitution maker.[54]

These men were the patriarchs of the New Hampshire bar, rounding out their last years of service in 1788. It was principally with their sons

51. Plumer, Autobiography, 34.
52. N. H. Hist. Soc., *Collections,* 4 (1834), 38.
53. Plumer kept a record of the minutes of the state meeting and of the Rockingham County meeting in 1788. See William Plumer, Repository, IV, 271-76, N. H. State Lib.
54. Plumer, "John Pickering," "Benjamin West," "John Sullivan," "Samuel Livermore," *N. H. State Papers,* XXII, 839-40, 861; XXI, 818. Thirty-four of Plumer's biographical sketches of men prominent in the state government just after the Revolution were published as appendices to vols. XXI and XXII of the *N. H. State Papers.*

and a group of younger contemporaries that Plumer was to ride the circuits over muddy trails and unbridged rivers, dine and sleep in wayside taverns, and fight the endless legal battles of the turn of the century. Prominent among this generation were two sons of Samuel Livermore, Edward St. Loe and Arthur, who, according to Plumer, inherited full portions of those "strong intellectual powers ... decision of character," and "arbitrary" conduct that had characterized their father.[55] Clifton Claggett, however, was a humorless man who suffered severely in comparison with his gifted father, Wyseman Claggett, the aggressive attorney-general of New Hampshire in colonial times. The Atherton name was carried on by Charles Humphrey Atherton, a son of Joshua, who was a more eminent lawyer than his father had been. Joshua Atherton's son-in-law, William Gordon, was also a contemporary of Plumer at the bar and a good friend. Another famous son of a noted father was George Sullivan, an able orator who settled at Exeter and adorned the Rockingham County bar throughout this period. Jonathan Steele, who studied with General Sullivan and married his preceptor's daughter, was admitted to the bar at the same time as Plumer. He showed early promise, acquired an extensive practice, and was appointed to the Superior Court bench, but his gloomy disposition and irritable temper prevented him from attaining pre-eminence in either law or politics.[56] Plumer seemed to get along amiably with most of his colleagues at the bar except for John Samuel Sherburne, a Portsmouth lawyer whose guile and hypocrisy were especially distasteful. Jeremiah Smith perverted Scripture in order to say of him, "I hate him with a pure heart, fervently." [57]

Plumer's deep friendships were as few as his ineradicable hatreds. A promising friend was John Hale, a young Portsmouth attorney with whom he maintained his earliest correspondence, but who died in 1796. More important was his friendship with Jeremiah Smith, the brilliant young Scotch-Irish scholar who had welcomed him to the bar with generous wit: "I hate a monopolizing spirit; and though the profession seems somewhat crowded at present, the harvest small, and the laborers very many, yet I cannot help thinking that there is room for as many good characters as may be disposed to enter into the profession." [58] This friendship grew within the next few years, and after Smith was

55. Plumer, "Samuel Livermore," *ibid.,* XXI, 818.
56. Plumer, "Jonathan Steele," Biographies, V, 327, N. H. Hist. Soc.
57. Plumer, Jr., *Life of Plumer,* 114*n.*
58. Jeremiah Smith to Plumer, Oct. 31, 1787, Letter Book, I, Lib. Cong.

elected to Congress, the two men corresponded untiringly. In 1797, Plumer had an opportunity to repay Smith's generosity with interest, when he helped his friend settle in Exeter, where Smith would necessarily take away some of his business. Until 1805, the serious, persistent lawyer in Epping and the witty, industrious lawyer in Exeter were good friends, but in that year they quarreled. After that, their rivalry was part of the history of the state.

It was with such men as these, rather than among the frontier evangelists, the country squires, the merchant princes of Portsmouth, or the ill-trained physicians of New Hampshire, that William Plumer had cast his lot. In the winter of 1787, he opened in his house the first law office in Epping, and was soon engaged in as much business as he could handle. Despite his late start, he had qualities that commanded success— industry, persistence, shrewdness, and integrity. "I was always ready & prepared for my clients," he boasted; "their causes were not delayed by my inattention. I managed their business as if it had been my own . . . my fees were moderate & reasonable. By this course of conduct I gained the confidence & esteem of the people, & acquired property & reputation." [59]

Plumer's greatest activity at the bar fell between his admission to practice before the Superior Court in 1789 and his election to the United States Senate in 1802. During these busy years he attended nearly every session of the courts held in Rockingham and Strafford counties. The Rockingham bar, at this time, contained a particularly distinguished galaxy of legal talent. Accustomed to outstanding performances by the lawyers already mentioned, the courts in southeastern New Hampshire were later dazzled by the appearance of two meteoric newcomers: Jeremiah Mason and Daniel Webster. Mason, a physical and intellectual giant with a persistent Yankee nasal twang, came to Portsmouth in 1797 and soon earned the reputation of being the greatest lawyer who had ever practiced in New Hampshire.[60] This he retained until 1807 when Daniel Webster opened an office in Portsmouth. As if this native talent were not enough to bewilder the simple New Hampshire judges and juries, such brilliant Massachusetts lawyers as Theophilus Parsons, Samuel Dexter, and Theophilus Bradbury regularly practiced in the Rockingham County courts.[61]

59. Plumer, Autobiography, 35-36.
60. George Hillard, *Memoir and Correspondence of Jeremiah Mason* (Cambridge, 1873), 38.
61. Plumer, Jr., *Life of Plumer,* chap. 6.

How well William Plumer fared in such distinguished company is difficult to determine. The records of the courts in his time were not printed, and evidence of what went on in them consists largely of later reminiscences and exaggerated impressions. In the course of preparing his father's biography, William Plumer, Jr., solicited a large number of testimonials from people ranging in importance from the clerk of the Superior Court to Daniel Webster—testimonials that unanimously praised Plumer's industry, shrewdness, skill, courtesy, and effectiveness. In classical simile, William, Jr., described the "strife of Titans" in the Rockingham County courts: "If... my father, from age or character, was the Nestor or Ulysses of this assembly; Smith, the Menelaus, with a touch of the Thersites humor; and Mason, the Ajax or Agamemnon, towering head and shoulders above the rest; the youthful vigor of Webster, in this first exhibition of his unrivalled power, 'the flash and outbreak of a fiery mind,' stamped itself boldly on all beholders, as the Achilles, *impiger, iracundus, inexorabilis, acer,* of the scene." [62]

Since young Plumer was himself a witness to some of these memorable contests, his miniature Iliad may be accepted as an approximate picture of this concentration of powerful minds within a limited sphere of action. The elder Plumer had less pretension to learning or genius than many of his colleagues. Unlike Webster he could never have dazzled the Supreme Court of the United States with learned eloquence, but he was able to win cases from Webster before a New Hampshire jury. He did not have time for such profound legal research as distinguished the two Jeremiahs of the New Hampshire bar, Smith and Mason, but he could clarify the fundamental issues of a case in simple language, a device which was more effective with a New Hampshire judge and jury than innumerable citations or the most biting sarcasm. He was also shrewd enough to take advantage of a court's prejudice. On one occasion, he carried a point with a patriotic judge against no less an opponent than Theophilus Parsons backed by Coke and Blackstone, simply by quoting a Mosaic law that contradicted the English authorities. [63]

As he became a familiar figure in New Hampshire's courtrooms, Plumer made a strong impression upon his younger contemporaries. His tall, spare figure, black hair, and piercing dark eyes were accentuated rather than subdued by the simplicity of his dress and manners. A casual observer, watching him chewing raisins in apparent absent-mindedness

62. *Ibid.,* 179.
63. *Ibid.,* 206.

while counsel for the other side had the floor, might even have thought him torpid; but when he rose to his feet he was "keen, and ready, always prepared." [64] In addressing the court he was respectful, "gentlemanly in his demeanor to the senior members of the bar, and more than others affable and courteous to those . . . who were his Juniors." [65] He was not a courtroom actor; his jury speeches were "fluent, plain and always intelligible . . . unshowy, but full of good sense, and to the point." It is unlikely that he ever lost a case through inattention to detail; "there was a minute correctness in his mode of doing business." The clerk of the Superior Court, who heard him argue hundreds of cases, declared that he was "shrewd, sagacious, forbearing, and calculating, of an high order of intellect." He made many friends among his fellow itinerants as they followed the judicial circuits, for he was a good conversationalist who had a fund of experience upon which to draw; he was also a good listener when a still better speaker was in their midst. Perhaps the greatest compliment to him was that "he understood human nature." [66]

Bench and bar presented a curious anomaly in Plumer's day, for whereas the lawyers were clearly distinguished, the judges were, at best, mediocre. Judicial salaries were ridiculously low, judicial duties were onerous, and legislative interference with judicial decisions was a constant irritant. Under these circumstances, well-trained lawyers could seldom be persuaded to accept judicial appointments, and the state executives tended to avoid disappointing refusals by filling the bench with ill-trained and sometimes illiterate farmers, shopkeepers, and politicans. This resulted in needless delays, conflicting decisions, and legal uncertainty. "What a Superior Court we have to judge of special pleading to decide nice & abstruse questions of law," Plumer once exclaimed in disgust. "Who of them can resort to first principles? . . . These are your $800 judges." [67]

These conditions cried for reform, and a number of the younger lawyers, led by Plumer and Smith, dedicated themselves to the task.

64. Nicholas Emery to William Plumer, Jr., Jan. 12, 1854, Plumer Papers, N. H. State Lib.
65. Moody Kent to William Plumer, Jr., Mar. 4, 1853, Plumer Papers, N. H. State Lib. The quotations in this paragraph are all from this letter and the one in the preceding citation.
66. William Plumer, Jr.'s biography of his father contains in chap. 6, pp. 191-238, many delightful anecdotes of Plumer's experience as a lawyer and his courtroom battles with Smith, Mason, Webster, Sullivan, and other eminent men. Most of the accounts rest upon the author's memory or were related to him by the participants. They are worth reading.
67. Plumer to William Gordon, Apr. 2, 1798, Letter Book, I, Lib. Cong.

In the courts themselves, they worked constantly for the clarification, improvement, and standardization of legal practice. Plumer's greatest victory in this campaign occurred in 1791, when, in the case of *McClary* v. *Gilman*, he argued that an act by which the legislature had restored the plaintiff to her law, that is, permitted her a second suit in the same court, was unconstitutional.[68] Plumer's contention was that the law either reversed the court's judgment or demanded a new trial without reversing the court's judgment, either of which was a palpable violation of the Bill of Rights.[69] The Superior Court accepted his argument, declared the law unconstitutional, and dismissed the plaintiff's plea.[70] Such opportunities, however, were rare before 1802, at which time Plumer had ceased to practice regularly in the courts, and he did not, like Smith, carry on the work of reform from the bench. It was in his political, rather than his professional capacity, that he was to perform his most effective labors for the improvement of the judiciary. In the revision of the state constitution, in the passage of new laws, and in the executive appointment of judges, he kept the perfect dispensation of justice before him as a constant ideal.

During his active years at the bar, Plumer figured prominently in legal battles over the issue of the ecclesiastical tax. He invariably refused to take the cases of town officers seeking to compel dissenters to pay their taxes, but he readily defended those who claimed exemptions. Most of these cases in Rockingham and Strafford, he asserted, were confided to him. He acted in this matter on principle, not prejudice. Plumer had no religious sympathies with the sectarians, but he warmly approved the principle of religious freedom for which they were contending. "It was my opinion," he wrote, "that no man ought to be *compelled* to contribute any thing to the support of religion, but every man left to the perfect freedom of his own will to join or not join any society, & to contribute or not to its support, as he pleased."[71] Plumer, indeed, re-

68. In this suit Plumer was counsel for the defendant, for whom the Superior Court rendered judgment based on a report of referees to whom both parties had agreed to submit their case. Nevertheless, Elizabeth McClary, the plaintiff, appealed to the legislature, which ordered the case re-entered on the Superior Court's docket. See *N. H. State Papers,* XXII, 22, 59, 67, 104, 113, 156, 168.

69. Plumer, Jr., *Life of Plumer,* 170. See also Walter Dodd, "The Constitutional History of New Hampshire, 1775-1792," New Hampshire Bar Association, *Proceedings,* 2 (1906), 399-400.

70. Plumer, Repository, IV, 303-6, N. H. State Lib. About this same time, Jeremiah Mason argued a similar *cause célèbre* in Cheshire County and carried it against two legislative orders to the courts. See Hillard, *Mason,* 26-27.

71. Plumer, Autobiography, 74.

garded the multiplicity of sects as a strong guarantee of freedom and security.

His labor in behalf of religious freedom was hardly remunerative, since the zealots whom he defended were usually the poorer members of each community, often able to repay him only with gratitude. This sentiment might indeed have been useful to Plumer if his intention had been to turn it into votes, but at the time he was most active in the courts he had much to lose and little to gain by his policy. He was then a leading Federalist; his political friends were the men who upheld the religious establishment and expected it, in turn, to prop up their government. Some of them were judges who considered it their sacred duty to interpose the bench between their church and such legal assaults as Plumer seemed to be making upon it. Judge Paine Wingate of the Superior Court was particularly insistent upon making "every man tributary to the dominant sect of congregational priests," and he highly disapproved of Plumer's efforts to block his purpose. On one occasion, Plumer was counsel for a Universalist who claimed damages for property taken by distraint to support a rigidly Calvinist minister. Judge Wingate asked the lawyer if he expected to prove that Calvinists and Universalists were different sects. Plumer replied that "it did not require either argument or testimony to *shew* there was an essential difference between the chastisements of this short life & eternal flagellation in the next, & between the doctrine of the eternal salvation of *all men*, & the everlasting misery of nearly the whole human family." [72] Nevertheless, the judge directed the jury to find costs for the defendant. Plumer may have lost his case by the very bluntness with which he outlined the salient features of the judge's theology.[73]

In spite of such experiences with judicial bias, however, Plumer always had an instinctive respect for a strong and independent judiciary. In 1786, as a young and rather extreme conservative, he wrote: "If our elective government is long supported, it will owe its existence to the

72. *Ibid.*, 79.

73. A few years later (in 1803), Judge Wingate dissented from the opinion of the court, pronounced by Chief Justice Jeremiah Smith, Judge Arthur Livermore concurring, which declared that Presbyterians constituted a sect different from Congregationalists and were not subject to church taxes. See *Muzzy* v. *Wilkins*, Jeremiah Smith, *New Hampshire Reports* (Boston, 1879), 1-37. This decision reversed the precedents established by Wingate and others in such cases as the ones Plumer defended and in *Henderson, et al.* v. *Erskine* (1802), in which a Universalist was declared not to differ from a Congregationalist. It is an interesting fact that the first case ever reported in the New Hampshire courts, *Muzzy* v. *Wilkins*, mentioned above, involved this issue of religious taxation.

Judiciary. That is the only body of men who will have an effective check upon a numerous Assembly." [74] In 1825, as an old and moderate Republican, he still maintained that the judiciary was the ultimate repository of the people's liberties, and that they had less to fear from it than from any other branch of the government.[75]

74. Plumer to William Coleman, May 31, 1786, Letter Book, I, Lib. Cong.
75. "Cincinnatus," No. 126, in William Plumer, Essays, III (1823-29), 136-41, Plumer Papers, N. H. State Lib.

CHAPTER III

Constitution Maker

"I commenced public life with a resolution that I would attach myself to no party or faction, but perform my duty regardless of its consequences as it related to my popularity." [1]

In the years of readjustment and political realignments following the adoption of the Federal Constitution, William Plumer rose to the first rank of politicians in New Hampshire. Although he had been defeated for a seat in the ratifying convention in February 1788, he was promptly elected in March to the state legislature by his fellow townsmen, who thus proved that they did not associate Federalism with any permanent principles. In his second term as a lawmaker, Plumer played a leading role, serving on so many important committees that he was forced to plead the rules of the House to avoid being completely enmeshed in committee duty. "I had the satisfaction of knowing that I possessed the confidence of the legislature," he recalled, "& had considerable influence upon its deliberations." [2] He spoke frequently and learned to develop a succinct, closely reasoned, and impersonal style, which served him well in political debate.

Representative Plumer won his political spurs by the active role he assumed in the arrangements for New Hampshire's first national elections. Although the immediate necessity of choosing two United States senators and three representatives as well as five presidential electors presented almost irresistible temptations to logrolling and intrigue, Plumer's actions were guided by his instinct for national strength and conservatism. At the same time, however, he gave evidence of a talent for parliamentary maneuver that commanded the respect of older colleagues.

1. Plumer, Autobiography, 53.
2. Ibid., 34.

Plumer joined in the virtually unanimous election of John Langdon, the Revolutionary patriot and ardent supporter of the Constitution, as the senior senator. He was determined, however, to prevent the second senatorial seat from going to Dr. Nathaniel Peabody of Atkinson, also a Revolutionary hero, but a notorious speculator who was strongly suspected of playing an underhanded role in the paper money agitation and uprising of 1786. Fearing that many who sympathized with the easy money party might vote for Peabody under cover of the secret ballot which the House had decided to employ, Plumer devised an ingenious parliamentary trick.[3] He first persuaded the House that their choice of senator should be made by a regular resolution, which could be sent to the Senate for concurrence. Then he sprang his surprise by calling for the yeas and nays in the voting, as any single member had a right to do in the case of a regular resolution. Having thus circumvented the secret ballot, Plumer made a forthright speech against Peabody and promised to hold individual members accountable to the people for their votes if they supported him. The resolution for Peabody's election received only forty votes in the House and was decisively rejected by the Senate.[4] It is said that the Atkinson physician, understandably angry, threatened Plumer with bodily chastisement, but was promptly met with a promise of still further financial exposures.[5]

True to his conservative principles, Plumer opposed the popular election of the state's five presidential electors, but the measure passed.[6] It provided, however, that when popular majorities were not obtained, the electors should be chosen by the legislature. In the absence of party machinery, this contingency proved to be inevitable. At its December session, therefore, the legislature had the opportunity of choosing five electors from among the ten highest candidates, but the two houses immediately began quarreling as to whether the choice should be by joint or concurrent resolution. Since by the former method, the vote of the twelve senators would be swallowed up in the much more numerous House, and their constitutional role as a conservative counterweight destroyed, Plumer took the side of the Senate against his own colleagues.

The electors had to be chosen before midnight of January 7, 1789. As the winter shadows lengthened in the old Exeter meetinghouse on

3. *Ibid.*, 35.
4. *N. H. State Papers*, XXI, 357, 359, 425.
5. Plumer, Jr., *Life of Plumer*, 103.
6. *N. H. State Papers*, XXI, 355, 876.

that day, frantic efforts were made to wear down the opposition. Watching the political temperature carefully, Plumer detected signs that the House was cooling, and he kept the Senate posted in order to bolster its determination. Just before midnight, the House gave in and concurred in the Senate's choice of electors. General Sullivan, who had favored joint action, then requested that the speaker appoint Plumer to carry the glad tidings to the Senate, *"as [he] knew the way to [their] chamber."* [7] Plumer and his colleagues recognized this sardonic remark for what it was—a tribute of grudging respect from a veteran politician to a victorious neophyte. Their disagreement had nothing to do with candidates or politics; it was simply a struggle for the future control of electoral machinery, in which Plumer had helped gain a victory for conservatism.

Plumer may have been unusually successful with his fellow legislators, but he neglected to curry favor with the voters at home. One of the measures he opposed in the winter session was a more stringent blue law against Sunday travel. [8] Other skeptics were politic enough in this matter to yield "to the rabble," but Plumer led the fight against it on the floor and lost his seat in the House as a consequence. [9] In 1790, however, he returned to the political wars with his third election to the state legislature and served briefly as clerk of the House until the former clerk had recovered from a temporary illness. Re-elected in 1791, Plumer was chosen speaker of the House when Nathaniel Peabody resigned. This was a considerable honor to come to a man of thirty-one who was serving only his fourth year in the legislature, but the former Baptist preacher righteously concluded that it was not undeserved. "The duties of speaker required my constant attention," he admitted, "but by introducing a greater degree of order & method than had been previously practised, I performed its duties with greater ease & more dispatch than I expected. My promptness & uprightness was rewarded by the approbation of the house." By the end of the year 1792, Plumer could state with smug satisfaction that he had "already enjoyed office & influence beyond my expectations." [10]

The confusion of principles and factions within the state during these years did not make it easy for Plumer to discover his place in local poli-

7. Plumer, Autobiography, 36-37.
8. *N. H. State Papers,* XXI, 488-92.
9. Plumer, Autobiography, 37.
10. *Ibid.,* 38, 49, 53.

tics. Although he had vigorously advocated the adoption of the Constitution and was to become an almost fanatical Federalist, he was rather more Jeffersonian than otherwise in 1790 and 1791.[11] He wrote to New Hampshire congressmen approving Madison's proposal to discriminate between original holders and speculators in the funding of the national debt, and in June he opposed Hamilton's assumption scheme, begging his congressman to vote "agt the adoption of a system so partial & injurious to some of the States, particularly to this." [12] Plumer's indignation at New Hampshire's treatment in Philadelphia did not, however, dissolve his nationalism. He thought that Virginia had gone too far in attacking the constitutionality of the Assumption Act, and he helped secure the defeat of a resolution in the New Hampshire House stating that the law was "an infringement on the rights of the legislature of this state." In 1791, however, when he was speaker of the House, a second such memorial was introduced. Since it "was in decent & respectful language," Plumer made no objection to it, "& it passed with apparent unanimity." [13]

The young lawyer of Epping had not risen high enough to profit by the first distribution of federal offices, which were divided largely between the supporters of John Langdon and John Sullivan. Unfortunately for his modest efforts at plum-gathering,[14] Plumer was not inclined to cultivate influential friends. On the contrary, he seemed to seek opportunities for antagonizing such powerful politicians as Senator Langdon and his intriguing brother-in-law John Samuel Sherburne. In 1790, he moved for Sherburne's expulsion from the state House of Representatives on the ground that he held office under the United States government as a war pensioner. This was rather an excessively strict construction of the state constitution's clause against pluralism, and Plumer's motion was decisively beaten. Sherburne was subsequently

11. So were New Hampshire's first congressmen. See Orin Libby, "Political Factions in Washington's Administrations," University of North Dakota, *Quarterly Journal,* 3 (1913), 298, 304. According to the criteria selected by Libby, the four New Hampshire representatives in the lower house voted with the administration 93 times and against it 43 times between 1789 and 1793.

12. Plumer to Abiel Foster, June 28, 1790, Letter Book, I, Lib. Cong.

13. *N. H. State Papers,* XXII, 146, 227; Plumer, Autobiography, 41, 46, 49; Charles Wingate, *Life of Paine Wingate* (Medford, Mass., 1930), II, 543-44. Wingate was the author of this memorial.

14. Plumer to Jeremiah Smith, Mar. 22, 1794, Letter Book, I, Lib. Cong. Plumer hinted to Smith that he would not be averse to accepting appointment to the federal district court if a vacancy should occur.

adroit enough to obtain a resolution from the House that its members were not precluded from holding federal offices.[15]

In 1791 when the laws of the state were being revised, an ex-Congregational minister proposed to substitute for the old law against blasphemy, a more stringent one providing the penalty of boring through the tongue with a hot iron. To his amazement, Plumer heard Sherburne and other responsible legislators play politics with this barbarism, exalting the Bible in hypocritical speeches, anathematizing those who dared to traduce it, and suggesting that the proposed penalty was not strong enough. Although he was conscious that his deism would arouse prejudice against his cause, Plumer combated the proposal, declaring that it was not in support of, but contrary to, the teachings of true Christianity. Christians, he said, would do well to allow their God to vindicate himself. This argument helped to defeat the motion, but Plumer could not prevent the framing of a new law that punished with a fine of fifty pounds any person who should "wilfully blaspheme" the Trinity or "the canonical scriptures." [16]

The Plumer-Sherburne antagonism flared up at nearly every point of contact. In 1792, when Sherburne, no longer a member, was appearing as counsel to plead for certain petitions before the legislature, Plumer, as speaker of the House, was forced to silence him or "suffer the rules of the House . . . to be grossly violated." The members upheld Plumer's decision on appeal, and Sherburne "left the Court in a great passion." [17] Later, the Langdon-Sherburne group became the nucleus of the Republican party in New Hampshire, and Plumer immediately engaged it in mortal combat.

Before party lines had formed, however, Plumer took an interesting stand on the question of impeaching John Langdon's brother, an associate justice of the Superior Court. Woodbury Langdon's career as a merchant and shipowner had not included much time spent in the study of the law, but Plumer, who practiced before him, insisted that "he had a strong discriminating mind, and great promptness and decision of character." When Woodbury failed several times to attend distant sessions of court and answered the inquiries of a legislative investigating committee with contemptuous defiance, the western delegates obtained

15. *N. H. State Papers,* XXII, 41, 47, 56-57; Plumer, Autobiography, 39; Plumer, "John Samuel Sherburne," Biographies, V, 490, N. H. Hist. Soc.; Plumer, Jr., *Life of Plumer,* 106.

16. Plumer, Autobiography, 46-47; *Laws of the State of New Hampshire* (Portsmouth, 1792), 256-57.

17. Plumer to Jeremiah Smith, Jan. 2, 1792, Letter Book, I, Lib. Cong.

his impeachment. Plumer had worked with the leader of this movement, Colonel William Page of Charlestown, "a bold, assuming, but imprudent, man," in projects of judicial reform, but he voted against the impeachment and refused to become one of the House managers for the trial before the Senate. Not only this, but he scolded his friend Jeremiah Smith for accepting such an appointment. Plumer believed that the persecution of Langdon was "instituted more to gratify personal pique and private resentment than to promote the public interest," and he objected strongly to what he considered unwarranted legislative interference with the judiciary. He was pleased, therefore, as well as vastly amused, when the impeachment trial ended in a complete fiasco after Langdon had resigned in order to accept a federal appointment.[18]

The only group to compare in strength with the Langdon influence was a junto of expert politicians at Exeter, headed by the state treasurer, John Taylor Gilman. They were soon to become the leaders of the Federalist party in New Hampshire, but it was Plumer's misfortune to fall afoul of them as well as of the Portsmouth leaders. The first brush came in 1791 over the question of a state tax. In spite of the fact that annual expenditures had fallen to their prewar level, which was amazingly low, and that the people were still burdened with a large amount of delinquent taxes, the Exeter gentry wished to raise a tax of three thousand pounds for the year. The treasurer insisted that taxes, whether wanted or not, should be collected every year to habituate people to paying them. This was good Hamiltonian doctrine, but Plumer could not agree with it. Since the treasury already contained enough money to pay the expenses of government for two years, Plumer was convinced that Gilman and his cohorts wanted the additional funds only for speculation. He took credit for the defeat of the measure in the House, and came to be regarded as a troublesome person by the Exeterites.[19]

During his tenure as speaker, Plumer split with the Gilman crowd over two other important issues. Since the beginning of the Revolution, state securities, though not by their terms of issue exempt from taxation, had been omitted from the list of taxable property. In the days when they had circulated at a fraction of their face value, this leniency was justifiable, but now that the state's credit was restored and its notes

18. *N. H. State Papers*, XXI, 813, 815; XXII, 76, 81-82, 117; Plumer, Repository, IV, 241, N. H. State Lib.; Plumer, Autobiography, 41-43, 45; Plumer to Smith, July 6, 1790, Letter Book, I, Lib. Cong.; Lawrence Mayo, *John Langdon of New Hampshire* (Concord, 1937), 257.
19. Plumer, Autobiography, 47-48; *N. H. State Papers*, XXII, 177, 231-32, 237.

appreciating in value, it was inequitable that they should not be taxed, particularly when most of them were held by speculators. Plumer introduced a bill to add securities of this character to the list of ratable property. "I thot the holders could better afford to pay a moderate tax on that property than many poor persons could for their polls, or small farmers with large families for their lands, houses & cattle," he explained.[20] As he was walking homeward from the day's session, Plumer fell in with Gilman, who upbraided him severely for his authorship of the bill and complained that it operated chiefly against himself and his brothers, who were holders of a large amount of the notes. Plumer replied that the bill was completely impersonal; that he saw no reason why state securities should escape taxation when money at interest did not; and that if the Gilman brothers had purchased state notes, they had already earned 20 per cent in appreciation and could well afford to pay a small tax. The two men parted in a bad humor, and a few days later Plumer's bill was passed, although the official copy had been stolen from the clerk's file by a speculating state senator in a crude effort to prevent its consideration.[21]

At this session, the legislature also incorporated the first bank in New Hampshire, located at Portsmouth. The proprietors and chief supporters of the corporation were Portsmouth and Exeter men who had long been prominent in commercial affairs. Plumer found himself again at odds with his wealthy friends, for he had no great faith in private banks as financial institutions. "I very much doubt whether the bank will have sufficient applications for loans—or whether the bills will obtain so general circulation as to render the bank profitable to the Stockholders," he wrote to Congressman Smith. He was afraid that New Hampshire's unfavorable balance of trade with Massachusetts would draw the bank's notes, and ultimately its specie, to Salem and Boston. The community was not sufficiently commercial to support a bank—farmers would derive no benefit from it. "Banking is, however, a subject with which I am little acquainted," he admitted. "I therefore am not sanguine as to the correctness of my opinion." [22]

Plumer's opposition stalled the incorporation bill for several days in the legislature. Two of the proprietors, James Sheafe and John Pierce,

20. Plumer, Autobiography, 50.
21. *Ibid.*, 50-51; Plumer to Jeremiah Smith, Jan. 2, 1792, Letter Book, I, Lib. Cong.; *N. H. State Papers*, XXII, 444, 451; *Laws of N. H.* (1792), 191.
22. Plumer to Jeremiah Smith, Jan. 2, 1792, Letter Book, I, Lib. Cong.

conservative, respectable Portsmouth merchants and friends of Plumer, tried to win him over by offering him as many of their own shares as he might wish to take at par, although the bank stock was already selling at a premium. Sherburne tried to discredit his opposition by circulating rumors that it grew out of his fear that the bank would put an end to private moneylending and thus cut off a rich source of his income. Ultimately, the bank bill passed, but Plumer did manage to defeat an attempt of the proprietors to induce the state to purchase part of the bank's stock.[23]

By 1792 Plumer had had his fill of politics. Although still speaker of the House, he had alienated men of power and influence by his stand on public finance. When he was nominated in council to be probate judge in Rockingham County, the office went to Oliver Peabody, one of the Exeter Junto.[24] When his friends backed him for the state Senate in 1790 and 1792, he was defeated. When he was proposed as a candidate for Congress in 1792, he refused to run. "I really wish not to be named as a Candidate," he wrote, "for I declare that if every vote in the State was dependent on my will, no man should vote for me." [25] But, he was neither despondent nor bitter. Despite his differences with the Langdon-Sherburne faction and the Exeter Junto, he protested that he felt "no *party spirit*" and he stated flatly that "there is no office I seek." [26] Increasingly, his thoughts turned toward political retirement.

After four years of experience under the Federal Constitution, politics in New Hampshire still operated, as they had in the 1780's, on a purely personal basis. "Parties" were temporary alliances of office-seekers and their friends put together before each election, as Plumer indicated in 1792 when reporting on political intrigues in the legislature.[27] So rudimentary was political organization that, although William Plumer had become one of the principal Federalists in New Hampshire, he had never made a campaign speech, written a political editorial, drawn up a list of voters, or made any sort of appeal to any part of the electorate outside the bounds of Epping township. Politics was still a gentlemanly occupation, or at least an activity confined to gentlemen, and the average man

---

23. The New Hampshire Bank was the sixth bank chartered in America. James Squires, *The Granite State of the United States* (N. Y., 1956), I, 170 ff.; Plumer, Autobiography, 51-52; *N. H. State Papers*, XXII, 385, 394, 446, 475.
24. *Ibid.*, 249-50; Plumer to Jeremiah Smith, July 6, 1790, Letter Book, I, Lib. Cong.
25. Plumer to William Page, Aug. 1, 1792, *ibid.*
26. Plumer to Jeremiah Smith, Jan. 2, 1792, *ibid.*
27. Plumer to William Page, Aug. 1, 1792, *ibid.*

—even the average voter—pretty largely ignored it.[28] Something more challenging to New Hampshire and Plumer than Hamiltonian fiscal policy was required to set the pattern of politics.

At the moment of his renunciation of political ambition in 1792, William Plumer was just completing one of the most important and enduring labors of his life—a revision of the constitution that remains to this day, in effect, the fundamental law of the state of New Hampshire. Although the constitution adopted in 1784 has technically never been replaced, it was actually so thoroughly modified by Plumer and his colleagues in the constitutional convention of 1791-92 that the state courts have made the mistake of referring to the amendments of those years as a new constitution.[29] In carrying through these sweeping changes, Plumer was consummating the efforts of constitutional architects over a period of sixteen years toward the creation of a workable instrument of government.

Plumer lived in an era of constitution-making and resided in the state that experimented most extensively with this process. In her hastily and crudely constructed constitution of January 5, 1776, New Hampshire demonstrated her reaction against a strong royal governor, swinging abruptly from a well-balanced colonial government to a form of legislative dominance in which executive authority virtually disappeared.[30] When this provisional document was replaced by a more formally considered state constitution in 1782-84, a group of conservatives, led by John Pickering, tried to restore a genuine separation and balance of powers,[31] but their efforts were defeated by the people, to whom the proposed constitution had been submitted for ratification.[32] Although young William Plumer, then a selectman in Epping, had worked hard for the acceptance of the emasculated constitution which was finally adopted, his personal attitude toward it was merely tolerant.[33] He did

28. George Leutscher, *Early Political Machinery in the United States* (Phila., 1903), 4, 122. See also John Morison, *The Life of Jeremiah Smith* (Boston, 1845), 124-25.

29. James Colby, *Manual of the Constitution of New Hampshire* (Concord, 1912), 93.

30. *Ibid.,* 69-72. The record of the adoption of this constitution may be found in the journal of the so-called Fifth Provincial Congress, printed in *N. H. State Papers,* VIII, 1-4. A facsimile of the original printed copy is included in the appendix of vol. XI, opposite p. 738.

31. See "Address of the Convention," *ibid.,* IX, 845-52. According to William Plumer, Jr., this was written by Pickering and Jonathan Sewall. William Plumer, Jr., "The Constitution of New Hampshire," New Hampshire Bar Association, *Proceedings,* 2 (1905), 233*n*.

32. Nevins, *American States,* 175, 183.

33. Plumer, Autobiography, 16.

"not feel hostile to either democracy, aristocracy or monarchy," he wrote. "I am fully resolved to use my power & influence in supporting that form of Government which my country establishes. . . . I am inclined to think the people are much more interested in the good administration than in the theory or form of the government." [34]

Seven years under the constitution of 1784, however, had convinced Plumer and many others that theory and form were important after all. By 1791 conservatives were worried about the innumerable weaknesses which stood revealed, and wished to restore those features that had been rejected by the people in 1784. The Federal Constitution, which had replaced the weak Articles of Confederation, served as a good example of what could be accomplished by determined conservatives. Moreover, the operation of the new federal government rendered anomalous many provisions of a constitution designed for a supposedly sovereign state in a loosely confederated league. Plumer had wrestled vainly with some of the problems raised by this ambiguity, and he was convinced that constitutional prescriptions were necessary to govern such cases.[35]

Eager to participate in the formulation of the state's fundamental law, Plumer secured election in August 1791 to the revisionary convention which had been mandated by the constitution of 1784. This success encouraged him to believe that his community was finally in the mood to consider a stronger government. Other like-minded towns sent such conservative co-workers as John Pickering, William Page, Edward St. Loe Livermore, and Jeremiah Smith, who were able to offset the anarchic tendencies of Nathaniel Peabody and Joshua Atherton.[36] The stage was set for the climax of the counterrevolutionary movement that had begun with the policy of deflation and the first draft of the constitution in 1781.

William Plumer was the most indefatigable worker and perhaps the most influential man in the convention of 1791-92. To the first session he brought a sheaf of amendments which would have established a virtually new constitution, had they all been adopted. Throughout this seven-day session he was in constant attendance, vigilant in debate, and active upon a number of important committees. At the end of the

34. Plumer to Jesse Johnson, Dec. 23, 1784, Letter Book, I, Lib. Cong.
35. For Plumer's attacks on the endemic pluralism in New Hampshire, see above, and Plumer, Autobiography, 39.
36. For biographical sketches of these and other delegates to the convention, see Nathaniel Bouton, ed., *Journal of the Convention to Revise the Constitution of New Hampshire, 1791-1792* (Concord, 1876).

week's discussion, the convention elected a grand Committee of Ten (two delegates from each county), which was to consider all the suggested amendments and any others considered suitable, and report at the next session.[37] Plumer represented Rockingham County, and he was the moving spirit in the committee's deliberations. Throughout the winter of 1791-92, the group met whenever a session of the General Court or of the law courts brought the members together. Much of the labor devolved upon Plumer, who complained but nevertheless complied with the committee's assignments, if only to prevent Peabody and Atherton from obstructing progress.

Early in February the full committee fought its way through a heavy snowstorm to Concord to prepare its final report for the second session of the convention. Plumer feared that Peabody's delays would prevent the report from being made ready, and he denounced Atherton as being "fickle as Proteus." "This has thrown a heavy burden on Page & myself," he grumbled to Jeremiah Smith, who had taken his seat in Congress. "I have drawn all the amendments, & have made out a fair copy of the whole constitution with those amendments incorporated therein." [38] Plumer also prepared the committee's report and the explanatory address [39] which accompanied it. Peabody and Pickering opposed the report on the floor of the convention, but Plumer, Page, Atherton, and Livermore [40] defended the committee's recommendations.

The real work of the constitutional convention was done at this February session of sixteen days. Plumer was placed on all the important committees, drew up a majority of the reports, and probably devised the strategy by which the amendments were finally carried. His influence was so marked that people who disliked the result of the convention's labor called it "Plumer's Constitution." But it was far from being Plumer's ideal.

Plumer's major efforts at reform were directed toward four goals: a separation of church and state, the creation of a genuine executive au-

37. *N. H. State Papers*, X, 57. The committee consisted of Nathaniel Peabody and William Plumer for Rockingham County, Nathan Hart of Moultonborough and Ebenezer Smith of Meredith for Strafford County, Robert Wallace of Henniker and Joshua Atherton of Amherst for Hillsborough County, William Page and Sanford Kingsbury of Claremont for Cheshire County, Elisha Payne of Lebanon and Jonathan Freeman of Hanover for Grafton County.

38. Plumer to Jeremiah Smith, Feb. 8, 1792, Letter Book, I, Lib. Cong.

39. Plumer preserved a copy of this address, probably the only one now in existence, in his Repository, IV, 331 ff., N. H. State Lib.

40. Plumer, Autobiography, 53.

thority, a rational system of legislative apportionment, and a thorough-going reform of the judiciary. As a substitute for the ambiguous statement on religious toleration in the Bill of Rights, Plumer introduced in the first session of the convention a guarantee that "the free exercise & enjoyment of religious profession & worship, without discrimination or preference, shall forever hereafter be allowed within this State to all mankind," and that no person should "ever be obliged to pay tithes taxes or any other rates . . . for the maintenance of any minister or ministry, contrary to what he believes to be right, or had deliberately or voluntarily engaged himself to perform." [41]

Plumer's motion was defeated by a crushing majority of eighty-nine to fifteen on the first roll call vote in the convention.[42] A proposal to expunge the Protestant test for officeholders was also defeated in the convention, but Plumer persuaded the Committee of Ten to reverse that decision and justified the step before the people in the following words: "The Religious test is omitted because it is incompatible with the principles of a free government, and inconsistent with the bill of rights which secures to all the free enjoyment of their Religious sentiments and the right of electing and being elected into office; and because it is not sufficient to exclude the wicked and designing but may prevent the honest and virtuous." [43] Although approved by a majority of the voters, the anti-test amendment failed to receive the necessary two-thirds majority [44] and the Protestant test was not finally stricken from the constitution until 1877.

The convention showed substantial agreement on the necessity of a clearer separation of powers in the state government. It removed the governor, heretofore called the president, from the Senate and gave him a qualified veto over acts passed by the legislature. Although the Executive Council was retained, its members were to be chosen by the people rather than by and from the General Assembly, and the governor could veto nominations made by them.[45]

Plumer and like-minded reformers failed, however, in their proposals for revision of the legislative department. The constitution of 1784 had created an elective Senate of twelve members, in which the wealthier

41. Plumer, Repository, IV, 331, N. H. State Lib. Plumer's proposed article does not appear in the journal of the convention.

42. *N. H. State Papers*, X, 41-42; the journal of the convention is printed, *ibid.*, 23-168.

43. Plumer, Repository, IV, 331 ff., N. H. State Lib.

44. *N. H. State Papers*, X, 141.

45. *Ibid.*, 48, 67-68, 93, 104; Plumer, Repository, IV, 331 ff., N. H. State Lib.

counties were more heavily represented.[46] The House of Representatives was composed of one delegate from every town with 150 male taxpayers (and another representative for every 300 additional voters) ; those with fewer than 150 could be combined with neighboring towns to be jointly represented. Plumer and his friends thought that this awkward and discriminatory concession to wealth in the Senate and to the cherished tradition of town autonomy in the House had resulted in a grossly deformed General Assembly. They therefore recommended that the senators be elected from districts equal in wealth, to be determined by the legislature.[47] The convention approved the proposal. But when the Epping delegate then introduced an amendment that would have given New Hampshire a manageable House of Representatives by limiting the membership to sixty, elected from equal districts,[48] his proposal won only twenty-two favorable votes. Eventually he persuaded the Committee of Ten to bring in a report that the House should never consist of more than 110 members or less than 80, but the convention rejected his proposal without a recorded vote. In the end, the reformers were forced to leave the composition of the House exactly as it stood. The only change was a provision for the payment of representatives' salaries by the state, rather than by the towns—an obvious victory for the rural villages.[49]

Although Plumer and his colleagues failed in their efforts to revamp the House, they took full advantage of their unexampled opportunity to remodel the state judiciary. At its first session the convention decided to abolish the old courts completely and entrusted to the Committee of Ten the task of constructing a new system. During the session of the legislature in December, the committeemen who were also members of the General Court met in Plumer's lodgings every night to carry on this work. Plumer obtained permission from the legislature to examine the dockets of the courts, and there secured valuable data to support his theories.[50] His research revealed that only one of twenty actions entered in the lower court dockets ever reached a trial decision; and that of this

46. Rockingham County was given five senators; Strafford, Hillsborough, and Cheshire, two each; Grafton, one.

47. *N. H. State Papers,* X, 43-44, 51-52.

48. Plumer, Repository, IV, 331 ff., N. H. State Lib.

49. *N. H. State Papers,* X, 48-50, 96, 178. After the latter clause became effective, membership in the House increased until by 1821 it reached 192, out-distancing the national House of Representatives.

50. Plumer to Jeremiah Smith, Dec. 10, 1791, Letter Book, I, Lib. Cong.; Plumer, Autobiography, 50.

twentieth, three-fourths were appealed. By increasing the original jurisdiction of the state's highest court and decreasing appeals from justices
of the peace and county courts, the committee hoped to expedite pro-
cedures and eliminate costly delays. The Committee of Ten proposed to
give the state Supreme Court the power "of granting new trials and
restorations to law and of hearing and determining causes in equity,"
which would deprive the legislature of its excuse for interfering with
the decisions of the courts. "We conceived," boasted Plumer, "that the
proposed Judicial system for administering Justice promises less expence
and much more uniformity and will greatly increase the wisdom dignity
& respectability of the courts of law." [51]

No part of the committee's report caused such stormy debate in the
second session of the convention as did the judiciary section. It was
attacked in print by Thomas Cogswell, the delegate from Gilmanton and
a judge of the Inferior Court that the committee proposed to destroy.[52]
"What . . . can these gentlemen be after!" the angry pamphleteer asked.
"At one stroke [they] level a judiciary system, that has cost the wisdom
of ages to erect!" After warning his readers that they should suspect
the motives of Page and Livermore, he turned to Plumer:

I have a regard for him, not because he was a great zealot in religion,
and through our troubles in the war created a great deal of uneasiness by administering under the appearance of an itinerant preacher the
doctrines of passive obedience and non-resistance. Neither do I regard
him for his changeableness of disposition; but because he often discovers
a goodness of heart, which if genuine, would do honor to human nature.
But I am afraid he will be found as erroneous in politics, as he has been
enthusiastic in religion . . . —how came it about, that these gentlemen
should be so anxious to alter our laws and judiciary system? Is it out
of pure regard to the love of liberty, and the citizens of this State? Or
is it because they once had an antipathy to our government, and still
retain it? [53]

51. Plumer, Repository, IV, 331 ff., N. H. State Lib. The exegesis, which Plumer
prepared as an explanation of the Committee's recommendations, appears nowhere
in print. Plumer's copy of the document is a hasty transcription of the original and
there are obvious errors in spelling and punctuation. In 1813, when the entire judicial
system was actually renovated by Plumer's political enemies, then including Smith,
this pattern of 1792 was followed in its essential parts. Plumer then opposed it. See
chap. 12.

52. Plumer, Biographies, IV, 541, N. H. Hist. Soc.; Bouton, ed., *Journal of the
Convention,* 34.

53. [Thomas Cogswell], *Some Remarks on the Proceedings of the Late Convention*
(n.p., 1791), 12.

Plumer sent a copy of this pamphlet to Jeremiah Smith with the contemptuous comment, "If you have an unusual stock of patience you will read it." [54] Nevertheless, Cogswell gave apt expression to the extremely conservative viewpoint on the judiciary. The new courts, he insisted, would be arbitrary and expensive; they would favor the rich and mulct the poor; the only people to benefit by them would be the pettifogging lawyers and a new train of twenty judges at two hundred pounds each.[55]

These were persuasive arguments, and Plumer soon discovered that since voting at their first session to overhaul the judicial system, the delegates to the constitutional convention had weakened considerably. Reforming zeal had given way to discretion, and the convention decided to dump the entire problem into the lap of the legislature.[56] From the general wreckage, only two specific recommendations from the committee's report were ultimately accepted by the convention and the people.

Plumer was personally responsible for one of these recommendations, an amendment which prevented lawyer-members of the legislature from acting as counsel for parties whose petitions or memorials were under consideration by the General Court. Plumer denounced this practice as "a dereliction of principle, equally degrading & improper," [57] combining the incompatible roles of advocate and judge. The people were inclined to believe that lawyer members even encouraged appeals to the legislature in cases where they were interested, intending to use their influence for a more favorable settlement than could be had before a judicial tribunal.[58] Plumer's motion to prohibit this evil passed in the convention without a recorded vote.[59]

After the convention finished its labors it referred the long list of seventy-two amendments to the people and adjourned to await their decision.[60] The leaders most responsible for these amendments suffered considerable anxiety during this waiting period. From Charlestown, Page wrote to Plumer in alarm that the amendments had not yet reached the towns in Cheshire County, but that the opposition had already de-

54. Plumer to Jeremiah Smith, Dec. 10, 1791, Letter Book, I, Lib. Cong.
55. [Cogswell], *Some Remarks on the Convention,* 26.
56. *N. H. State Papers,* X, 98-100.
57. *Ibid.,* XXII, 47; Plumer, Autobiography, 40.
58. [Cogswell], *Some Remarks on the Convention,* 10.
59. *N. H. State Papers,* X, 53.
60. *Ibid.,* 111-12. A few copies of this document, entitled *Articles in Addition to the Constitution of the State of New-Hampshire* ... (Exeter, 1792), are still in existence. See New York Public Library, *Bulletin,* 8 (1904), 175.

feated his re-election to the legislature.[61] Plumer had qualms of his own about having his reputation at the mercy of the people, whom he considered an erratic tribunal. The best minds in New Hampshire had spent the better part of a year in studying, debating, writing, and polishing a document which the people might destroy overnight by a few votes.[62] "The great mass of the people took no interest in the revision," Plumer admitted. "Many of them felt their inability to decide the questions submitted to them, & refused acting." [63] The highest number of votes cast on May 7 for and against any amendment was 4,987—only a little more than half the vote cast two months earlier in an almost uncontested gubernatorial election.[64]

Small as it was, however, the popular vote in May was sufficient to riddle the structure that the convention had so laboriously erected. When the delegates reconvened to count the votes, Plumer was placed on the committee that announced the result. Forty-six of the seventy-two amendments had been accepted by the necessary two-thirds vote, but the twenty-six rejected articles contained the very heart of the revised system.[65] The people had vetoed the changes proposed in the Senate, had voted against removing the governor and councilors from the legislature and adding to their powers, and had refused to order the legislature to remodel the judiciary. Only the trimmings on the new structure had been accepted; the great internal framework that gave it form was thoroughly demolished.

After a brief period of dismayed indecision, the convention appointed a committee of four, including Plumer, to survey the wreckage and salvage what it could. This group agreed that the amendments which had been accepted were themselves inconsistent without those which had been rejected, and they used these incompatibilities as an excuse for recommending that the convention draw up a new series of amendments. The convention promptly appointed a strong committee, again including Plumer. After two days of discussion, this committee reported "that the

61. William Page to Plumer, Apr. 5, 1792, Letter Book, I, Lib. Cong.

62. Perhaps Concord provided a typical example. The "Freeholders" met on May 7 at one o'clock in the afternoon, decided not to straighten a road, leased part of the school lot to James Walker, and voted upon the 72 amendments to the constitution apparently without previous public debate. *Concord Town Records, 1732-1820* (Concord, 1894), 271-72.

63. Plumer, Autobiography, 54.

64. *N. H. State Papers,* X, 141.

65. *Ibid.,* 141-42.

seeming inconsistency mentioned in the Report of the Committee of Saturday last, may be fairly reconciled," [66] and asked to be discharged. The convention then appointed two more committees, one to reconcile the seeming inconsistencies and another, including Plumer, Smith, and Livermore, to rewrite the amendments dealing with the executive. The two committees submitted reports incorporating minor revisions of the amendments which had originally been sent to the people in February. The revised amendments actually reconstituted the system which the people had flatly rejected.

The convention quickly accepted these recommendations and decided that no opportunity would be given for piecemeal rejection; the reconstituted amendments, of which the sections on the executive were most significant, would have to be accepted or rejected as a whole. This proved to be a successful stratagem. When the convention met again in September, Plumer had the satisfaction of reporting that there had been 2,122 votes cast in favor of the amendments and only 978 against them.[67] Thus, although the efforts made to remodel the legislature and the judiciary had been defeated, Plumer and his friends had made good their attempts to organize a strong and independent executive department. It was a maneuver comparable in decision and daring to the calculation by which the Massachusetts conservatives had made sure of their constitutional victory in 1780.[68]

By the time "Plumer's Constitution" was finally ratified, its alleged author had already carried into action a resolution to withdraw his candidacy for re-election to the legislature. He had, by 1792, become the father of two children and felt compelled to devote more attention to his family and his law practice. His responsibilities as speaker of the House, a leading member of the constitutional convention, and a very busy attorney had kept him almost continuously away from home for two years,

66. *Ibid.*, 144.

67. *Ibid.*, 164. The convention ordered a number of printed copies of the revised constitution. Some of these, entitled *Constitution of New Hampshire as Altered, Approved and Established by the Convention at Concord in September, 1792* (Concord, 1792), survive in various libraries. The full text of the constitution as amended in 1792 may be consulted in *N. H. State Papers*, X, 169-96. Various editions of the *New Hampshire Manual for the General Court* print the current constitution with all amendments clearly marked, so that the changes made in 1792 can easily be discovered.

68. For the story of the Massachusetts convention, See Samuel Eliot Morison, "The Struggle Over the Adoption of the Constitution of Massachusetts," Mass. Hist. Soc., *Proceedings*, 50 (1917), 353-412; Robert J. Taylor, ed., *Massachusetts, Colony to Commonwealth: Documents on the Formation of Its Constitution, 1775-1780* (Chapel Hill, 1961), *passim*.

and had seriously injured his health. "I resolved," therefore, he wrote, "to abandon public life & devote my attention to my professional business, & enjoy the ease & comfort of domestic life, books, & friends." [69] It was a resolution firmly carried out, but destined to be reversed by events in faraway Paris.

69. Plumer, Autobiography, 53.

CHAPTER IV

Lawyer and Federalist

"The true American Spirit prevails in all parts of New Hampshire—the citizens universally determine to resist that french fraternity, which has proved the ruin of Switzerland, Holland and Venice." [1]

FOR five busy years, between 1792 and 1797, William Plumer resolutely stayed out of public office and concentrated upon making money. This was his most active period at the bar; he pressed himself in order to provide for a growing family, build up a competence, and gain enough financial security to allow a more flexible future. Plumer had no intention of spending a long life in the law courts; he hoped that a few years of intensive effort would make him financially independent and able to devote his remaining years to public life or scholarly retirement. "I spent no portion of my time in idleness," he declared, "none in pursuit of pleasure; the hours which were not devoted to business & sleep, were occupied in reading & study." During the months of February and March 1797, for example, Plumer attended the Superior Court in Portsmouth and Dover for seven weeks in succession, arguing cases in two sessions of the court each day, consulting with clients, preparing briefs until midnight, and collecting a generous share of the fees.[2] By such devotion to business, Plumer increased his property in eight short years from less than three to more than fifteen thousand dollars.[3]

In his haste to get rich, Plumer was not content with his professional fees alone, but acquired wealth in ways generally confined today to

1. Abiel Foster to William Plumer, May 28, 1798, Plumer Papers, N. H. State Lib.
2. Plumer, Autobiography, 57, 61.
3. Estimate of the Principal Part of the Property, inventory for Nov. 1, 1787, Plumer Papers, N. H. State Lib.; Estimate for Dec. 31, 1795, Plumer, Autobiography, 59.

bankers and real estate promoters. Like most men with some liquid capital in that period before banks were established, he entered extensively into the practice of making private loans. Although the law limited interest rates to 6 per cent, Plumer frequently made loans at 12 per cent, taking nothing but verbal security for the extra interest in order to protect himself against suits for usury. He not only admitted his law-breaking in this respect, but justified it on the ground that price-fixing laws of any kind were unrighteous.[4]

In the period prior to easy bank credit, such practices were as common as they were necessary.[5] In order to collect a large sum of money which he had lent to the town of Epping, the busy lawyer in 1793 got himself elected to the offices of town agent and auditor. He also accepted the office of tax-collector, which was contracted out by the selectmen to the lowest bidder. Plumer's bid was $1.34. Within five days, he collected all the taxes without resorting to distraints, earned a dollar a day salary, and, as town agent, paid himself the debt which the town owed him. Such sharp practices make it easy to understand why Plumer increased his fortune rapidly and earned a measure of unpopularity in the process. Yet, although Plumer had his full portion of Yankee business shrewdness, he did not live for money. As an attorney, he offered his services freely to the poor, taking many a case without prospect of fee. "I never regretted the sacrifice," he wrote. "It is true it encreased my labor, & made some wealthy unprincipled men my enemies; but even they had more respect & fear for me than hatred; & it interested the feelings of better men in my favor, & was the cause of giving me some profitable business, which, probably, I should not otherwise have had." [6] The portion of Plumer's income annually set aside for charitable purposes was unusually large. If he made money diligently, he did it only as a means to an end. "I am not anxious for wealth," he told a friend in 1796, "competence is my object. I am labouring to make my wants few, that I may easily supply them." [7]

Like many of the capitalists, large and small, of his day, Plumer tried his hand at land speculation. In 1793, and again four years later, he and a few associates proposed to buy all of the ungranted land in New Hamp-

4. Plumer, Autobiography, 80.
5. Equally guilty of this technical violation of the law were such New Hampshire worthies as President Wheelock of Dartmouth College, John Phillips, the noted philanthropist, and several of the politicians who were foremost in criticizing Plumer.
6. Plumer, Autobiography, 55-56, 75.
7. Plumer to Jeremiah Smith, Apr. 25, 1796, Letter Book, I, Lib. Cong.

shire.[8] It was probably fortunate for them that the legislature declined these offers. The 80,000 acres which they would have purchased (for $20,000) included the White Mountain area and the northern tip of the state, beyond Stewartstown and Errol. It was, and is today, entirely unfit for agriculture, and Plumer could never have sold it profitably to farmer-settlers. Nor did the lumber industry or the tourist trade develop early enough to have benefited Plumer as a would-be monopolist.

To a very large extent, the Epping lawyer's industry in this period was a natural response to parental instinct, for he was obliged to support a growing family. "On the 9th of February [1789] I had a son born; to whom I gave my own name," was Plumer's laconic announcement in his journal of his eldest child's arrival.[9] It was characteristic that he neither mentioned his wife's agency in the matter, nor allowed himself to betray paternal pride. The second child was a daughter, born in November 1790 and named after her mother. Little Sarah inherited as much of her father's intellectual capacity as did any of the children, but her promise was blighted by poor health, a series of domestic tragedies, and an early death. Not long after Plumer had finished his labors on the revision of the state constitution and retired from office, a second son, named Samuel after his grandfather, was born.

The short periods of time that Plumer could spend at home with his family were marred by one misfortune. After the birth of their eldest son, his wife became the victim of recurring fits of hysteria, which increased in frequency and duration as she grew older. Plumer characteristically attributed her condition to misguided medical treatment, but his own home remedies, if applied, did not alleviate the trouble.[10] Mrs. Plumer's illness was not only a serious trial to herself and her family but a handicap to her husband in the social responsibilities of his career. Still, it was before the time of "First Ladies," and Sally Plumer was no Abigail Adams; she shared her husband's triumphs only as a silent partner. While Plumer mounted the ladder of political fame, she stayed quietly at home, managing her household, giving orders to the hired men in her husband's absence, and bearing his children.

8. Plumer, Autobiography, 56, 63.

9. *Ibid.*, 38. William Plumer, Jr., was destined to become the most famous of Plumer's children—a congressman, state legislator, reformer, and poet of some merit. He has frequently been confused by librarians and historians with his father, and with some justification, since the two men were virtually indistinguishable in thought and spirit.

10. Entry for July 12, 1808, William Plumer, The Register of Opinions and events (1807-36), Plumer Papers, Lib. Cong. (hereafter cited as Plumer, Diary).

Although Plumer resisted until 1797 the temptation to hold public office again, he maintained a continuing interest in public affairs. It was difficult, in fact, to tell when lawyers were members of the legislature and when they were not. Plumer attended every session of the assembly after 1792 as faithfully as if he had been an elected member, arguing causes in the public hearings and helping to determine party strategy in secret caucuses. It was during these years of so-called retirement that Plumer cast his lot with the Federalist party. Neither political theory, nor economic interest, nor class feeling determined Plumer's affiliation. What made a Federalist of Plumer (and a Republican of John Langdon) was a foreign war that enlisted the sympathies, the interests, and ultimately the weapons of Americans.

The Anglo-French war and its resultant interference with American neutral commerce sharply divided New Hampshire leaders into Francophiles, led by Senator Langdon, and Francophobes, who supported the national administration's policy of neutrality and peace with Great Britain. Plumer identified the former faction with the old Londonderry rioters. "People who expect to acquire property by robbery, alias privateering, & those who are involved in debt, who are anxious for paper money & tender laws—who have much to hope and nothing to fear from desperate measures, these desire war," he assured Congressman Smith.[11] As if to confirm his opinion, news of the signing of Jay's Treaty produced a riot in Portsmouth, in which some of Langdon's cronies were the ringleaders. When these men were tried in Superior Court, with Sherburne as their counsel, Plumer reported, "the tribunal of justice in imitation of the French revolutionists, resounded with loud repeated clapping of hands of the rioters; & for this . . . they received from the Court but a feeble reprimand." [12] The attacks upon Washington in the press, the interference of Congress in the conduct of foreign affairs, the mob outrages and the burnings in effigy—all these affronted the most fundamental instinct in Plumer's politics : his essential conservatism, his respect for law and order and established government.

Like many of his contemporaries, Plumer identified the tactics of this first organized opposition in the nation's history with sedition, and he viewed them with the same alarm that the Exeter rebellion had aroused. He was deeply concerned with the Jacobin "demoniac clubs," which had

11. Plumer to Jeremiah Smith, Mar. 22, 1794, Letter Book, I, Lib. Cong.; Mayo, *Langdon,* 265.
12. Plumer to Jeremiah Smith, Sept. 23, 1795, Letter Book, I, Lib. Cong.

been organized in Portsmouth and a few other villages,[13] and with the way in which the Republican leaders were using the controversial foreign situation to promote their party views at home. Although his attempts to bring about the defeat of Langdon and Sherburne were unsuccessful, he was more fortunate in helping to elevate John Taylor Gilman, a strong Federalist, to the governor's chair in 1794. "As a state we are federal—strictly so," he wrote in a triumphant vein to Smith. "We are ready to go any length that reason can justify in support of the federal government & its administration. The sons of anarchy & misrule in this happy country, like Sisiphus, will find their incessant labour unavailing." [14]

Plumer's perfervid Federalism on national issues was all the more impressive because he was growing increasingly unsympathetic with the Federalist leaders in the state government, including Governor Gilman, whom he had helped to elect. At the very moment when the controversy over Jay's Treaty was threatening to split the state, Plumer obtained evidence which convinced him that the Exeter Junto was guilty of peculation. Exeter politicians had controlled the state treasury almost continuously since 1775. When Gilman stepped up from the exchequer to the governorship, another Exeterite, Oliver Peabody, became state treasurer. Plumer was convinced that the Gilman family, together with Peabody, Benjamin Connor, a clever floor leader in the assembly, and Jonathan Clark, another Exeter politician, not only controlled the treasury, but dictated the fiscal policy of the state.

In 1794, the fiscal junto persuaded the legislature to liquidate the state debt. The larger part of it, in state notes and certificates, was to be redeemed at 75 per cent of face value, and the various issues of state bills were to be called in at an even more unfavorable rate. Creditors were to receive half of their money in specie and the other half in new state notes bearing 6 per cent interest and payable in eighteen months.[15] In order to provide the specie for resumption, the legislature authorized the treasurer and governor to borrow £25,000 ($83,250) at 6 per cent interest. Peabody was also requested to call upon state debtors for immediate payment or to issue writs against them.[16]

13. Plumer to Jeremiah Smith, Dec. 17, 1794, *ibid.* Eugene Link, *Democratic-Republican Societies, 1790-1800* (N. Y., 1942), 13-15, found no evidence in his newspaper sources of such clubs in New Hampshire, but Plumer was certain that they existed.
14. Plumer to Jeremiah Smith, Jan. 1, 1796, Letter Book, I, Lib. Cong.
15. *Laws of New Hampshire* (Manchester, etc., 1904-22), VI, 202-4.
16. *Journal of the Senate, June Session, 1794* (Portsmouth, 1794), 51.

On the face of it, this looked like a partial repudiation of the state's debt, a measure that the country towns might have carried against the conservative east. Actually, the vote on the bill showed the opposite sectional alignment. Plumer thought that he had the key to this puzzle: the scheme was not a repudiation, but a speculation. Since 1792, when securities had become subject to taxation, the Exeter gentry, according to Plumer's belief, had disposed of their holdings to James Greenleaf, the Boston speculator. One-third of the state's debt was said to have been in his hands when the law of 1794 deprived him of at least a fourth of his anticipated gains.[17] If this were true, the Gilmans had nothing to lose by this extraordinary law. On the contrary, Plumer believed that they had everything to gain. Never one to underestimate his own abilities, Plumer later said that "it was fortunate for them I was not then a Member, for had I been the law would not have passed." [18]

The part of this complicated scheme open to the greatest suspicion was the authorization to borrow a large sum of money at a time when the state treasury was in an unusually flourishing condition. It not only contained a large amount of specie, but $300,000 in United States securities gained through the federal assumption of state debts. Its assets also included a block of shares in the New Hampshire State Bank (purchased as soon as Plumer had left the legislature), large sums due from excise masters, tax collectors, and the Masonian Proprietors, and £11,000 ($36,630) on loan at 6 per cent interest to certain individuals.[19] These individuals had been specifically exempted from the demand for immediate repayment made of all the other state debtors.

Plumer regarded these maneuvers with intense suspicion. He knew that the bills which authorized the treasurer to lend the state's money to private individuals had been introduced by Connor, the Exeter representative. He also knew that the £11,000 had been lent to nine men, five of whom were citizens of Exeter, three of the five being brothers of the governor. Clark and Connor themselves were the other two. It seemed absurd to Plumer that the state should have to go into debt when its own reserves were in the hands of speculators. He questioned the partiality that spared the governor's brothers but expected of other state debtors immediate payment. Among those who were embarrassed by the state's sudden demand for a settlement was George Jaffrey, who, as one of the Masonian Proprietors, had given bond for his share of the $40,000

17. Plumer to Jeremiah Smith, Jan. 27, 1795, Mar. 9, 1802, Letter Book, I, Lib. Cong.
18. Plumer to Smith, Mar. 9, 1802, *ibid.*
19. Plumer to Smith, Jan. 27, 1795, *ibid.*

which they had agreed to pay the state in 1788.[20] Plumer had been retained as Jaffrey's counsel in the settlement of this perplexing business and had already assured him that his case would receive fair treatment in the courts "where popular influence and the intreagues of interested men will have little weight." [21] It was probably while acting for Jaffrey that Plumer began to investigate the conduct of the state treasurer.

In November 1794, Plumer was in Boston, "on a scheme of speculation," [22] which may have included visits to Greenleaf and to Nathan Bond, the broker from whom Peabody had borrowed $40,000 of the $83,250 loan that the New Hampshire legislature had authorized. The Epping lawyer soon concluded that Bond had not advanced a cent of money to the state, but had simply given his promise to pay the amount whenever desired, in exchange for Peabody's obligation to repay the sum with 6 per cent interest. Thus, without any money actually changing hands, Plumer believed that the state was pledged to pay $2,400 annual interest on money it had not really borrowed, and that this sum was, in fact, to be divided among the nine public debtors (who would thus be able to pay the interest on their loans from the state with its own money), and a Boston financier (who was being handsomely rewarded for a negligible risk).[23]

It is impossible at this late date to say whether this elaborate speculation actually took place, but Plumer was convinced that it did. He wrote long letters to Smith, stating both facts and suspicions and specifically accusing Peabody, Gilman, and Connor of participating in the plot.[24] He could not believe that the loan from Bond was more than purely nominal because the Boston broker was a commission agent rather than a moneylender, and Plumer doubted that Boston investors, who could earn 12 to 15 per cent on their money in a variety of enterprises at home, would lend $40,000 at only 6 per cent to a state which had just repudiated a quarter of its former obligations. Plumer was sufficiently certain of his ground to risk a libel suit in 1808, by writing and offering to publish a specific narrative of this 1794 speculation.[25] Finally, long after

20. Oliver Peabody to George Jaffrey, July 12, 1794, *N. H. State Papers,* XXIX, 372.

21. Plumer to George Jaffrey, Dec. 1, 1793, Plumer, Repository, IV, 375, N. H. State Lib. See also the long letter from Jaffrey to Plumer, June 5, 1794, *N. H. State Papers,* XXIX, 363-71.

22. Plumer to Jeremiah Smith, Nov. 26, 1794, Letter Book, I, Lib. Cong.

23. Plumer, Autobiography, 58.

24. Plumer to Smith, Jan. 27, 1795, Letter Book, I, Lib. Cong.

25. [Plumer], "Veritas," No. 3, in Plumer, Repository, II (1774-1814), 33-39, Lib. Cong.

his partisan spirit had been softened by age, he repeated the story in his autobiography. While the truth or falsehood of Plumer's charge cannot be determined, Plumer believed it to be true in 1795, and his actions based upon that belief are important.

Plumer's discoveries in Boston coincided with the struggle over the Jay Treaty and posed a puzzling question: the disclosure of the evidence he had against the treasurer might drag down the entire state administration and thus do irreparable injury to the Federalist cause. At the local level the welfare of the party was of little concern to Plumer, but in this period he identified the party with the national administration, and the national administration with righteousness. Washington's foreign policy had no firmer champion in New Hampshire than Gilman, unless it was Plumer; a period of national crises was no time for Washington's supporters to be fighting among themselves. For Plumer it was enough that Gilman had taken a courageous and correct stand on the Jay Treaty; considerations of national policy dictated that Plumer should not attack the governor on purely local issues.[26]

Since Plumer was not a member of the legislature, he was under less compulsion of conscience to proceed in the matter. But in the end he "could not silently consent to have the state imposed on by such peculations," and he decided to follow an oblique course. Nathaniel Peabody, one of the excise masters who felt injured by the law's partiality, moved for a committee to investigate the treasurer's transactions.[27] Plumer was in strange company when he co-operated with his Atkinson antagonist, but he furnished the committee with some of the facts at his disposal. When the treasurer was required to name the nine men to whom the state's money had been lent and the broker from whom the state had borrowed, he asserted that a small part of the $40,000 was deposited in the New Hampshire Bank, and the remainder was in his care. Although the legislature condemned this answer as unsatisfactory, they failed to push their embarrassing investigation. The General Court ordered the treasurer to discharge his obligation to Bond, the Boston broker, and to recover the money borrowed from the state as soon as possible. In order to carry through the redemption plan, it was then necessary to levy a tax of £8,000 ($26,640).[28] A scandal was thereby averted, but suspicion, ill will, and discontent were increased. The people

26. Plumer, Autobiography, 58.
27. Plumer to Smith, Jan. 27, 1795, Letter Book, I, Lib. Cong.
28. *Journal of the House of Representatives, December Session, 1794* (Portsmouth, 1795), 54; *Journal of the Senate, December Session, 1794* (Portsmouth, 1795), 31, 36.

grumbled at the unexpected tax; the handful of Republicans complained that justice had failed; and the gulf widened between Plumer and the Federalist leaders.

As national issues increasingly intruded into state political life, it became more and more difficult to decide local questions on their merits. This was particularly evident in the shifting attitude of the New Hampshire Federalists toward their state judiciary. The problem was complicated, for the Federalist lawyers still struggled between contempt for the fallible men who occupied the bench, and reverence for the bench regardless of its occupants. John Pickering, who had been appointed chief justice in 1791, "brought to the position more law learning than any judge who had sat there before him," [29] and the tone of the judiciary should have improved accordingly, but ill health and nervous disability had made him unpardonably inattentive to his duties. Yielding to a flood of complaints, Governor Gilman recommended an inquiry into the conduct of the judges, a course of action which led Plumer to question his political sanity. The House of Representatives responded by introducing a resolution to address the Governor for the removal of Pickering and another justice, both Federalists, but this blow to adminstrative prestige failed by one vote.[30]

The irony of this narrow escape was that Pickering probably deserved to be removed. Plumer loved and respected the Chief Justice, but thought that he probably should resign.[31] The death of John Sullivan, judge of the federal district court in New Hampshire, however, gave the state leaders an easy way out. New Hampshire Federalists, particularly Plumer and Sheafe, interceded in Pickering's behalf, and President Washington appointed him to the federal court. Plumer had nourished aspirations for this post,[32] but he finally supported a candidate whom he considered unfit for judicial office. Perhaps he explained to himself that a man unable to attend to the strenuous duties of the state Superior Court might easily make a very good federal district judge; the federal post required little effort and no travel. However, the basic fact remains that Pickering's appointment was dictated not by consideration for the proper administration of federal justice in New Hampshire but by Federalist politics.

29. Bell, *Bench and Bar,* 45.
30. *House Journal, Dec. Sess., 1794,* 90; Plumer to Smith, Jan. 27, 1795, Letter Book, I, Lib. Cong.
31. Plumer to Smith, Dec. 23, 1794, *ibid.*
32. Plumer to Smith, Mar. 22, 1794, *ibid.*

For a few months in 1796, Plumer feared that he had overestimated the strength of his own party, and expressed regret that he "did not stand candidate." Although he overcame his personal prejudice against the Governor and voted for him, Gilman's popular majority shrank, and the Republican party grew in the state legislature. While the Federalists were worrying about Republicans in their own legislature, those in Congress gave them a greater fright by opposing the grant of the necessary appropriations for carrying Jay's Treaty into effect. "We are alarmed at the proceedings of your House," Plumer wrote to Smith. "You act as if the Devil had taken full possession & presided over your deliberations." When the appropriation bill finally passed Congress, Plumer could hardly contain his elation. " 'Tis the best news we have had for years," he assured Smith; "anxiety now yields to the pleasing satisfaction that our country is delivered from the machinations of its *Frenchified* representatives." [33]

The Federalist triumph in Congress paved the way for the election of a full slate of Federalists in the first actual party contest for congressmen and presidential electors in New Hampshire. Plumer's friends had urged him to be a candidate for Congress, and his resolution to stay out of political life wavered momentarily. To Congressman Smith he confided, "I hope I shall not have a single vote. But if I was elected, I should consider myself bound to accept, 'tho it would be with much reluctance —but this is in confidence. I intreat you not to name me as a candidate. Should I live four or five years hence, I will, if requested, pursue public life for a season." [34]

The request came much sooner than Plumer had expected. In March 1797, the Epping electorate returned him to the state legislature *in absentia,* and he decided that the state of public affairs required his acceptance. "Hail, not Thane of Cawdor; but Speaker that is to be," his old fellow law student, Congressman Gordon, wrote from Philadelphia after learning the results of the election.[35] As this prophet had predicted, Plumer became speaker of the state assembly in June, defeating the Republican candidate and the former speaker, Russell Freeman, a Hanover Federalist. A further distinction fell to him when the speaker, for the first time, was allowed to present nominations for all committees.[36] Since

33. Plumer to Smith, Mar. 9, Apr. 19, 25, May 11, 1796, *ibid.*
34. Plumer to Smith, Aug. 12, 1796, *ibid.*
35. William Gordon to Plumer, Apr. 26, 1797, Plumer Papers, N. H. State Lib.
36. *Journal of the House of Representatives, June Session, 1797* (Portsmouth, 1797), 13.

the House acceded to every nomination Plumer made, it gave him an authority in the legislative program greater than that of the governor. It also gave a cohesion to party organization that had hitherto been lacking. Plumer claimed to have discharged this part of his official duty "impartially, & to the satisfaction of the house." [37] This was confirmed by the fact that a Republican motion to revoke the rule won only thirty-seven votes.

On national affairs, New Hampshire Federalists were united. They denounced the "piratical conduct of the French" in ordering C. C. Pinckney, the American peace envoy, out of the country and for turning privateers loose on American shipping; and they were outraged when the local Republicans continued to support France and condemn their own government. Plumer therefore saw to it that the House reply to Governor Gilman's opening address, which served in effect as a party platform, was a ringing declaration of support for President Adams's foreign policy; he had the satisfaction of seeing it adopted by a vote of 104 to 27.[38] In state politics, however, Plumer could not reconcile himself to the Exeter Junto, and this fundamental disagreement over domestic policy ran so deep that he failed to be re-elected to the speakership in 1798.

When the mantle of leadership was transferred to the shoulders of John Prentice, his former teacher, Plumer, with peevish magnanimity, conceded that "the change was favorable to the public interest, for tho Prentice could neither read or dispatch business, he was better qualified to preside than to reason." [39] If Plumer was bitter, he sublimated his feelings in a patriotic attack on French aggression. Freed from the restraints imposed on the presiding officer, Plumer was chosen to write the reply to Gilman's annual address at the very moment when excitement was running high over the revelation of the XYZ correspondence: "Although we believe that the blessings of honorable peace are worthy of great sacrifices, yet even peace purchased with the loss of our liberty and independence is a greater evil than war. The unanimity and har-

37. Plumer, Autobiography, 62.
38. Plumer to Jeremiah Smith, Mar. 23, June 11, 1797, Letter Book, I, Lib. Cong,; *House Journal, June Sess., 1797,* 19-21, 35-37. Plumer loaded the committee to compose an answer to Gilman's address with Federalists, and promised Jeremiah Smith that "we shall have an answer the sentiment & composition of which, will not make you blush for New Hampshire."
39. Plumer, Autobiography, 70. Relieved from the responsibilities of presiding, Plumer was able to take a much more active part in the legislature of 1798. He served on 29 committees, was elected speaker pro tem., and presided over the important convention of both houses for the apportionment of taxes. Plumer, Jr., *Life of Plumer,* 135.

mony, the firm, yet steady attachment of the citizens of the United States in general, and of this State in particular to the government of their choice, will be a strong and never failing resource in every event." [40] Plumer's reply was accepted without a division, and to prove that its patriotism was not confined to memorials, the assembly authorized the purchase of artillery for the militia and appropriated $4,000 for the erection of fortifications at Portsmouth if the governor should deem them necessary.

Plumer was thoroughly infected with the virus of Francophobia that swept over the country in 1798. He wore the black cockade of the anti-Jacobins in his high-crowned hat and "embraced every opportunity" in daily conversation to condemn French politics.[41] His fervent Federalism was permanently memorialized in the naming of his children: the first three had all been given family names, but his next two sons, born in 1796 and 1799, became George Washington and John Jay Plumer, respectively. Even his religious liberalism was tarnished by political considerations. It was Plumer, the deist, who took the initiative in dismissing the House chaplain in the June session of the legislature when the rash young preacher prayed for the success of the French armies and neglected to recommend President Adams to divine favor. Plumer was too keenly aware of clerical influence to countenance a preacher who prayed against the administration, even if it meant a whole session without benefit of clergy. "For the Court to live without prayers," he wrote his wife, "will, I believe, be less offensive to Heaven than jacobinical sacrifices." [42]

Ill health forced Plumer to decline election to the legislature in 1799, but he followed Federalist policies both in Concord and in Philadelphia with intense interest. Together with the rest of the "wise and good" majority, he thought that the national government had done well to protect itself against traitors from within by a new Naturalization Act, an Alien Bill, and a Sedition Law; he was even disposed to believe that Congress should have prohibited foreign-born individuals from holding federal offices.[43] Plumer was delighted when the New Hampshire legislature unanimously adopted a report rejecting the Kentucky and Vir-

40. *Journal of the House of Representatives, June Session, 1798* (Portsmouth, 1798), 43.

41. Plumer, Autobiography, 68-69.

42. *Ibid., 72*; Plumer to Mrs. Sarah Plumer, June 14, 1798, Letter Book, I, Lib. Cong.

43. Plumer to Abiel Foster, May 19, 1798, *ibid.; Journal of the House of Representatives, November Session, 1798* (Portsmouth, 1799), 78.

ginia Resolutions and declaring that the Alien and Sedition Acts were "constitutional and in the present critical situation of our country highly expedient." [44] Twenty years later he ruefully admitted that he had acted under the influence of high party spirit without thoughtfully examining the laws in question. "A review of my own conduct in life," he admitted at a time too late to be of much practical benefit, "increases my charity & respect for well informed men, whose opinion differs from my own." [45]

In 1799, neither Plumer nor any other Federalist entertained feelings of charity or respect for their opponents. Experience in party warfare had not existed long enough to have produced civilized amenities, and the partisans of Adams's day were inclined to regard each other as engaging in treasonable rather than legitimate opposition. "The spirit of party ran high," recalled Plumer of that period, "divided families, neighborhoods, towns & states; &, blind to public interest, embittered the sweets of social life, & hazarded the rights of the nation." Although this impartial attitude of thirty years after the event was then colored by membership in the party that he had thought treasonable in 1797, he still condemned its activity. "I could not approve of men who deliberately condemned our government, & justified that of France," he wrote.[46]

The prevalent political hysteria in New Hampshire infected Plumer with an intolerance that expressed itself not only against Republican preachers but against Republican officeholders. As early as 1795, he had warned Congressman Jeremiah Smith against three Portsmouth men with "levelling principles" who held important offices under the federal government—"the very government they wish to destroy. They seek the honors & enjoy the emoluments of office attached to the government," Plumer complained, "yet pursue measures hostile to its exist-

44. *Journal of the House of Representatives, June Session, 1799* (Portsmouth, 1799), 60-61. Frank Anderson, "Contemporary Opinion of the Virginia and Kentucky Resolutions," *American Historical Review,* 5 (1899-1900), 231, assumed that the Republican members refrained from voting, but only three members were absent at the roll call and they had voted for the equally partisan reply to Gilman's address. The three members who had not voted on the reply were present and voted in favor of the response to the Virginia Resolutions. Thus every one of the 140 members of the House of Representatives and every one of the 12 senators had subscribed to one or both of these strongly Federalist resolutions. The nine House members who had dissented from the majority in 1797 and the one Republican senator from the Portsmouth district thus rejected a doctrine enunciated by Thomas Jefferson himself and assented to an unqualified endorsement of the Adams administration. In the realm of national foreign policy, New Hampshire could well be called unanimously Federalist in 1799.

45. Plumer, Autobiography, 374.

46. *Ibid.,* 68, 69.

ence." [47] President Adams dismissed one of these officials as a defaulter, but the other two were efficient and popular, had been firm patriots during the Revolution, and gave no cause for complaint in the way they conducted their offices. But as the French crisis deepened, they indulged in abuse of Adams and lent their weight to the democratic organization growing up in Portsmouth.[48] When these facts aroused critical comment in the Boston *Centinel,* a leading Federalist organ, Plumer wrote to the secretary of the treasury and asked for their dismissal. "Singular indeed," he asserted, "must be the views & motives of that government who finds its interest in appointing & continuing men in office whose talents are employed in weakening & destroying the confidence of the people in that very government. . . . 'Tis giving aid to Jacobinism." [49] Finding the New Hampshire congressmen even more insistent than Plumer, President Adams dismissed the Portsmouth officers.[50]

This whole affair was pernicious in its effect. It placed upon the Federalist party the odium of introducing an element of the spoils system, which was all the justification that Jefferson needed in 1801 to reverse the process. The dismissals, furthermore, gave the Republican party two influential martyrs in New Hampshire. Adams replaced men who had been patriots with men whose loyalism during the Revolution was candidly admitted, and thus substantiated the charge that the Federalist party was even more pro-British than anti-French.

The state Federalists not only followed the example of their national leaders in the matter of intolerance but they strayed into the same fatal tendency toward disunity that characterized the councils of President Adams. In 1797, Speaker Plumer and Governor Gilman had fallen out over the latter's blunt insistence that he would resign unless the legislature raised his salary.[51] When Gilman resorted to the highly irregular expedient of sending a "haughty, acrimonious" message to Plumer, insisting that the legislature withdraw a resolution which it had already passed endorsing the current salary, he placed the speaker between the Scylla of party loyalty and the Charybdis of personal conviction. Party loyalty, which at this juncture was synonymous with patriotism to Plumer, triumphed. He not only communicated the message, but he

47. Plumer to Jeremiah Smith, June 30, 1795, Letter Book, I, Lib. Cong.
48. Plumer, "William Gardner," Biographies, V, 539-40, N. H. Hist. Soc.
49. Plumer to Oliver Wolcott, June 8, 1798, Letter Book, I, Lib. Cong.
50. Morison, *Jeremiah Smith,* 139-40.
51. This was a favorite tactic with Gilman. He had obtained an increase in his salary as state treasurer in 1785 by threatening to resign. See *N. H. State Papers,* XVIII, 750, XX, 219.

appointed a strongly Federalist committee to consider it, and the Federalist majority subsequently voted a two hundred dollar increase. Although this gave the Republicans useful ammunition against extravagance in government,[52] Gilman was not satisfied. He requested from the next legislature two hundred dollars compensation for expenses incurred in reviewing the militia. When Plumer openly opposed Gilman's cause, the friends of the governor took alarm and the matter was quietly dropped. The governor's salary remained henceforth fixed at $1,200 until 1816, when Plumer, then occupying the chair, initiated a reduction to the former level.

The Exeter Junto had also enlivened Plumer's speakership in 1797 by introducing another tax bill. The treasury contained enough money to support the government for two years, but the Exeter men, from the governor down, insisted that an annual tax should be raised as a matter of policy. Plumer thought it a peculiarly inappropriate time to irritate the people with an unnecessary assessment when the federal government was on the point of levying its first direct tax. The Exeter leaders, however, with that curious indifference to public opinion that brought about the final downfall of the Federalist party, continued to agitate for their tax against Plumer's vigorous opposition. With some help from shrewd Republican leaders willing to saddle their opponents with responsibility for an unpopular measure, they secured passage of their bill and the rocky farms of New Hampshire were soon hosts to a double set of assessors and collectors.[53] When the fervor of patriotic defiance of France had burned out and nothing remained but a Federalist legacy of expensive new establishments and heavy taxes, Republicanism increased by leaps and bounds in the back regions of New Hampshire.

Oliver Peabody's burning desire for a state tax which Plumer considered unnecessary confirmed the Epping Federalist in his old suspisions of the treasurer's integrity. When he was appointed to draft the annual resolution for the auditing of the treasurer's accounts, therefore, he phrased it in such a way as to grant authority actually to count the money in the treasurer's possession, but his language was so guarded that it did not betray his design. The unsuspecting legislature passed the resolution, and placed Plumer himself on the auditing committee.[54] In May, the investigators inspected the treasurer's books and vouchers and

52. Plumer to Peleg Sprague, Feb. 21, 1798, Letter Book, I, Lib. Cong.; Plumer, Autobiography, 64.
53. Plumer, Autobiography, 65.
54. *Ibid.*

found them faultless. When they asked to count the money in his possession, however, the startled official refused, claiming that the demand
was unprecedented, ungentlemanly, and unnecessary; he had good bonds-
men and would produce the money whenever bills were to be paid.
Plumer made out his report to the legislature, stated the facts of the
interview without drawing conclusions, and politely sent a copy to the
treasurer.[55] He even delayed submitting the committee report until the
legislature had re-elected Peabody treasurer. On the penultimate day of
the session, however, at a time when Plumer was absent in a committee
meeting, a letter was received from Peabody in which he complained of
the unjust suspicions cast upon him and declared that the state's money
was on deposit in the New Hampshire Bank.[56] The legislature adjourned
the next morning before Plumer learned about the letter, and nothing
more was said of the matter.

Between them, Peabody, Gilman, and Connor (Exeter's representative) had managed the vindication so carefully as to remove suspicion
without arousing debate. When Plumer later examined Peabody's letter,
he noticed that although the treasurer stated specifically that the money
was "now" on deposit, he had carefully avoided stating where it was on
May 10 when the committee examined his accounts. Plumer believed
that the money had actually been in the hands of various members of the
Exeter Junto or invested in private speculative ventures.[57]

The Federalist leaders not only quarreled over fiscal policies but they
worked at cross purposes in the regulation of the state judiciary. In the
decade after 1792, the Federalist legislators enacted a series of measures
which accomplished many of the judicial reforms that Plumer had tried
to write into the state constitution. These changes were readily made
because the bulk of the country members thought that they "would lessen
the business & influence of lawyers." [58] Even when they worked together,
however, it became evident that the Federalist lawyers and such non-
professionals as Gilman and the Federalist speaker, Russell Freeman,
were animated by different motives. The difference became obvious in
Governor Gilman's judicial appointments.

During the decade of Plumer's principal practice before the Superior
Court (1789-99), its entire personnel changed at least twice; fourteen
men received commissions as judges, and a round dozen of them actu-

55. Plumer, "Oliver Peabody," Biographies, V, 513, N. H. Hist. Soc.
56. *House Journal, June Sess., 1798*, 62, 71.
57. Plumer, Autobiography, 71-72.
58. Plumer to Jeremiah Smith, Jan. 25, 1797, Letter Book, I, Lib. Cong.

ally occupied the bench for at least one term. The highest court in the state suffered in eleven years the indignity of ten resignations, one impeachment, and innumerable threats of removal. The responsibility for this woefully unstable condition rested in part with judges who sometimes accepted positions for which they soon found themselves to be unqualified, and in part with governors who tended to select judges on the basis of military or genealogical records rather than legal attainments. The ultimate censure, however, fell upon the legislature, which refused to provide judges with the "honorable salaries" that the constitution authorized. In the face of opposition, which came from the conservative Senate as well as the rural constituencies, the reformers in 1797 pushed the remuneration of the chief justice to $850 and of the associates to $800 each,[59] but Plumer's repeated efforts to obtain further increases were unavailing.[60] "When will the legislature," he wrote in disgust, "be convinced that doing justice to their public officers is necessary to insure the prompt & due administration of justice to the people? And that rigid parsimony defeats the object it pursues, & augments, instead of diminishing the expence?"[61]

This theorem should have been demonstrated in 1798 when Governor Gilman and his council tried to fill two vacancies in the Superior Court by offering commissions to Paine Wingate, who had no legal training, and Ebenezer Smith, an utterly undistinguished lawyer. So dismayed was the legal profession by the latter appointment, especially, that Plumer took the extraordinary step of persuading Smith not to accept it.[62] He then urged upon the executive officers the appointment of Arthur Livermore, the son of a former chief justice.[63] Since the Livermores and the Gilmans were not friendly, Plumer's suggestion was received without enthusiasm by the council. Instead, one of the councilors made overtures to Plumer himself, but was promptly rebuffed. In September, Prentice was appointed to the vacancy and received his commission but he delayed a decision, neither accepting nor declining the office. He was

59. *House Journal, June Sess., 1797*, 48.
60. Edward Livermore to Plumer, June 3, 1797, William Plumer Letters, III (1791-1817), Plumer Papers, Lib. Cong. (hereafter cited as Letter Book, III) ; Plumer, Autobiography, 65-66.
61. Plumer to William Gordon, Feb. 22, 1798, Letter Book, I, Lib. Cong.
62. Plumer, Autobiography, 66, 68; Plumer to Arthur Livermore, May 1, 1798, Letter Book, I, Lib. Cong.
63. Ezra Stearns, "Hon. Arthur Livermore, a Biographical Address," Grafton and Coös Counties Bar Association, *Proceedings* (1892), 445.

hopeful of succeeding Samuel Livermore in the federal Senate, but wished to have the judgeship to fall back on if his election failed. As a result, the vacancy on the Superior Court bench continued unfilled from March until December.[64]

Election of a United States senator in 1798 was also postponed from June until December because of a multiplicity of candidates. Since the Gilmanites opposed the re-election of Samuel Livermore, they fell in behind John Prentice.[65] Plumer was advanced by some of his friends, but he himself favored James Sheafe, a Portsmouth merchant and an acknowledged loyalist during the Revolution. Prentice's indecision between judgeship and senatorship had caused the failure of a court session in Grafton County for lack of a quorum, and the Concord *Courier* printed a violent attack upon his conduct.[66] Taking advantage of this situation in the December session, Republican representatives gave their votes to Livermore, the least popular of the Federalists, and the old senator was renominated in the House by a majority of one vote. Prentice, realizing now that his temporizing was likely to influence the Senate adversely as it had already injured him in the House, hastened to return his judge's commission to the governor. His decision came too late. Wearied with the struggle, the Senate concurred in the election of the elder Livermore, and on the same day the governor and council appointed his son Arthur to the position that Prentice had relinquished.[67]

This double defeat was too much for the equanimity of John Prentice. On the last day of the session, from the speaker's chair, he made a violent and bitter personal attack upon William Plumer, naming him as the author of the *Courier* libel and challenging him to deny it. Plumer sat quietly in his chair and ignored the insults. He had not written the article, but such was his self-command that he refused his former teacher even the small satisfaction of an angry denial.[68] This election quarrel,

64. Plumer to William Gordon, June 26, 1798, Atherton Papers, N. H. Hist. Soc.; Plumer, Autobiography, 74, 77-78.
65. When the federal judiciary was established during the first session of Congress, Livermore had opposed holding any terms of court at Exeter, "alledging that it had little or no commerce, & that its river was a *mud creek*." Such slanders could never be forgiven by the proud squires of the Revolutionary capital. *Ibid., 77.*
66. *Courier of New Hampshire* (Concord), Dec. 1, 1798. It was discovered later that this article had been written by Edward Livermore. See Plumer, Jr., *Life of Plumer,* 135.
67. Plumer, Autobiography, 78; Stearns, "Arthur Livermore," Grafton and Coös Counties Bar Assoc., *Proceedings* (1892), 432, 446.
68. Plumer, Autobiography, 78.

coming upon the heels of treasury suspicions, executive doubts, and geographical antagonisms, left few important men in the Federalist party on friendly terms with each other.

In spite of dissension, New Hampshire Federalism stood at the pinnacle of success in 1799, when the Republican element in the legislature was virtually wiped out. This unanimity reflected the voters' reaction to the XYZ excitement and their horror at the bloody excesses of French republicanism. "We must consider France as an ambitious, faithless & perfidious nation with whom we have no treaty," wrote Plumer in 1798,[69] five months before the treaty was abrogated officially. Governor Gilman anathematized France in a speech to the legislature as a nation "contemning all moral and religious obligation." [70] Newspapers denounced the "terrible Republic," the home of "confusion and impiety," while humble farmers shuddered at monsters who seemed to "make no more Difficulty in Cutting off their great Mens Heads, than we do of a Sheeps Head." [71]

To these sentiments, the Congregationalist clergy added their powerful voices. "Would it afford you pleasure to see the *guillotine* erected in our land," thundered the Reverend Noah Worcester of Thornton. "Would it be to you a delightful employment to be the managers of this deadly machine, or to be the carriers of human blood, in buckets, from morning to evening?" [72] William Plumer estimated the services of the orthodox clergy so highly that his prejudice against their sermons underwent a notable relaxation. He began attending once more the services of the Reverend Peter Holt, successor to Josiah Stearns in the Epping meetinghouse.[73] Indeed, he even took charge of the campaign for building a new church and expended two hundred and twenty-two of his own dollars for two family pews.[74] "Political considerations induced me to undertake this business," he frankly admitted.[75] Three years later, Plumer exerted himself to obtain a more adequate support for Holt, subscribed liberally to the fund, and spoke in town meeting in favor of

69. Plumer to William Gordon, Feb. 5, 1798, Letter Book, I, Lib. Cong.

70. *House Journal, Nov. Sess., 1798,* 13 ff.

71. *Courier of N. H.* (Concord), Apr. 3, 1798; Charles Hanson, ed., *A Journal for the Years 1739-1803 by Samuel Lane of Stratham, New Hampshire* (Concord, 1937), 58.

72. Noah Worcester, *Election Sermon, 1800* (Concord, 1800), 26.

73. Plumer, Autobiography, 55; Plumer, Register, I, 62-64, Lib. Cong.

74. Stearns, "Congregational Church in Epping," in Hurd, ed., *Rockingham and Strafford Counties,* 216.

75. Plumer, Autobiography, 100. Plumer even went so far in 1798 as to submit again to church taxes.

a more generous contract for his maintenance, which would necessarily involve higher ecclesiastical taxes.[76] Plumer excused this extraordinary concession to "law religion" "on account of the support [Holt] gave to the civil government." Many Republicans were undoubtedly guilty of equal hypocrisy in their cultivation of the Baptist vote, but they erred at least on the side of religious liberty, while the Federalists allied themselves with a doomed institution.

The strong Federalism of New Hampshire and of William Plumer in 1799 did not proceed from a unity of economic interest, an absence of class consciousness, nor a general agreement upon the issues of national or state policies. Federalism in the Granite State had achieved the close union of upper and lower classes upon the single paramount issue of foreign policy, and this union was founded upon social and religious conservatism. Once the immediate foreign danger that had induced this solidarity seemed to have diminished, the underlying antagonisms came to the surface and gave rise to lively political battles in staid, old New Hampshire.

76. *Ibid.*, 158. Plumer succeeded in obtaining a contract for only $400 annual salary and 15 cords of wood. Half the population of Epping by this time belonged to dissenting sects.

CHAPTER V

The Decline of Federalism

"All, all came down, a motley nation—
As tho' in hell there were vacation,—
Burning with Jacobinic zeal
To overturn the public weal." [1]

EVEN with unanimous votes behind them, the Federalists could never quite believe in their own popularity, and in 1799 William Plumer had strong premonitions of disaster to come. Determined to fight, even in a losing cause, he campaigned successfully for election to the legislatures of 1800 and 1801, only to see his own party disintegrate while the tides of Republicanism crept inexorably forward, finally engulfing Epping. In 1802, Plumer retired again from politics—permanently, he said —only to be thrown into the national vortex itself by election to the United States Senate.

The Federalists fought against the stars in their course, but their reign might have been longer had they fought less strenuously. During ten years of political dominance, they managed to convince the people of New Hampshire that their continued control of the state would stifle any change toward democracy, deny religious toleration, maintain an expensive administration in favor of speculators, and subject the entire state to the political and financial domination of the Exeter Junto.

The Federalists increased their unpopularity by clinging to Exeter as a state capital and county seat, thus feeding the flame of sectional animosity, which had almost died out during the French crisis. In the County Court of Sessions Plumer opposed the plan to have a courthouse built at Exeter when there was already one just ten miles away at Portsmouth and when the western towns were struggling to establish a new county in the Merrimack Valley.[2] But the Exeter politicians were strong

1. Quoted from the *Village Messenger* (Amherst) in Daniel Secomb, *History of the Town of Amherst* (Concord, 1883), 103-4.
2. Plumer to Jeremiah Smith, Mar. 9, 1802, Letter Book, I, Lib. Cong.

enough to get their courthouse, to keep the state offices in their narrow circle, and to postpone the formation of a new county.

The issue upon which Federalists in general, and William Plumer in particular, were most vulnerable was that of religious freedom. The legislatures of 1800 and 1801 received many petitions from Baptist and other dissenting groups for incorporation as local societies in order to obtain a portion of the ecclesiastical taxes for their own preachers. Plumer voted against most of these petitions, even though many Federalists supported them. The paradox of a deist who championed the cause of religious liberty in the courts against judges of his own party but displayed more bigotry in the legislature than even the orthodox Federalists can only be explained by politics. "I was against these sectaries because they were hostile to the federal interest, & opposed to the congregational & presbyterian clergy, who in general were zealous federalists," Plumer admitted. He soon learned that suppression was a more powerful incentive to growth than tolerance might have been. "I ought to have advocated their cause," he later acknowledged, "& . . . given full liberty to all sects to think & worship as they pleased." Fortunately, Plumer balanced this record to some extent by suppressing in committee a bill "for the support of public teachers of religion and morals," which an overly-zealous member of the House had introduced.[3]

Perhaps the Federalists' greatest mistake in state politics was to allow their opponents to maneuver them into a position in which they appeared as the party of ruthless capitalism. In 1799, John Langdon and the other wealthy "Jacobins" at Portsmouth had organized the Union Bank and applied to the legislature for an act of incorporation. Langdon's bank was obviously a political machine, but the Federalist leaders encountered irresolution in their own ranks when they decided to deny it a charter and prohibit it from issuing notes.[4] Although Plumer was not a member of this legislature, he was, as usual, attending its December session in Exeter when Governor Gilman invited him to a Federalist caucus to consider the problem.[5] Plumer realized that anything the Federalists did would arouse opposition, but he advocated firm adherence to the strong policy which Gilman and Peabody had proposed. The Exeter politicians,

3. Plumer, Autobiography, 88; *Journal of the House of Representatives, November Session, 1800* (Portsmouth, 1801), 16. The legislative record of these petitions may be found scattered throughout the journals, particularly in *ibid.*, 22-26.

4. William Robinson, *Jeffersonian Democracy in New England* (New Haven, 1916), 29-30.

5. Plumer, Autobiography, 81; *N. H. Gazette* (Portsmouth), Feb. 26, 1805.

however, persuaded the legislature not only to cripple the Union Bank, but to authorize the purchase of still more shares in the New Hampshire Bank (their own), even though taxes had to be raised as a consequence.[6]

The Federalists could scarcely have handled this issue in a more disastrous fashion. Their renewed purchase of New Hampshire Bank stock was indefensible, and Plumer questioned its propriety, as he had questioned the first attempt to commit the interests of the state to a private corporation.[7] In his unyielding opposition to the Union Bank, however, he, like other leading Federalists, could not escape the charge of protecting personal interests, for he had become the owner of $2,000 in New Hampshire Bank stock.[8] With both their personal and their social fortunes endangered by this new "diabolical" invention of the Jacobins, it was inevitable that the Federalists should crush it with their customary arrogance, and equally inevitable, perhaps, that they carried their counteroffensive too far. The Republicans could not only pose as martyrs to their tyranny but could persuade the common voter that he too was being sacrificed to the Moloch of Exeter.[9]

These difficulties led Plumer in 1800 to decide that the times required "the aid of every friend of his country," and he therefore "condescended once more" to accept election to the legislature.[10] Unfortunately for the full effect of his condescension, Plumer lived in a town where the Union Bank had many friends, and its agents were understandably opposed to his candidacy. Some of his neighbors asked for a pledge that he would not vote against the new bank, but the forthright lawyer declared that, if elected, he would act according to his convictions and would vote against incorporating the Union Bank, or any other bank. He won election only on the second ballot, by a scant majority of two votes, running far behind Gilman at the head of the Federalist ticket.

The Republicans sent a strong contingent to the legislature and opened a vigorous offensive with a memorial from the proprietors of the Union Bank, praying either for an act of incorporation or for the repeal of the law prohibiting unincorporated institutions from issuing notes. Because of illness, Plumer appeared in the House a week late, on the very day when the committee appointed to consider this memorial brought in an

6. *Journal of the House of Representatives, December Session, 1799* (Portsmouth, 1800), 100.
7. Plumer, Autobiography, 82.
8. Entry for July 1, 1800, Plumer, Property Book, N. H. State Lib.
9. *Political Observatory* (Walpole), Feb. 2, 1805.
10. Plumer to George Thatcher, Mar. 11, 1800, Letter Book, I, Lib. Cong.

unfavorable report. John Goddard, a Portmouth merchant, a leading Republican politician, and a heavy stockholder in the Union Bank, was extremely angry at this second rebuff, and in the ensuing debate, according to Plumer, "discovered much malignity . . . abounded in personal reflections . . . never appeared so small and contemptible." Despite their ignoble character, Plumer felt that Goddard's arguments should not go unanswered. Unfortunately he had not been informed that the bank memorial was on the day's calendar and was caught without his notes on the subject. Nevertheless, he plunged into the debate extemporaneously and delivered one of the major speeches of his career.[11]

Plumer began with impersonal considerations of economics. He opposed another bank at Portsmouth, he said, for the same reasons, now even more pertinent, that he had opposed the first one—that it was poor business. Seven-eighths of New Hampshire traded, not with Portsmouth, but with Massachusetts and Connecticut, obtaining their circulating medium in the course of this business, not by borrowing Portsmouth bank notes. One bank was more than enough. Plumer declared that he would rejoice to see but one bank in the Union, the property of the United States, with its profits paying the expenses of government. He viewed the increase in private banks, "speculating institutions," with alarm.

Plumer then shifted boldly to a frontal attack on the proprietors of the proposed Union Bank—Langdon, Sherburne, and Goddard, who had "for eight years waged implacable & incessant war against the administration. . . . If we incorporate these men as [a] Banking society," he continued, "we give them the mean of extending their political poison with more certain success." If you want to arm your internal enemies, Plumer said, incorporate their bank, but "if the administration of your country is to be preserved, adopt the report of your Committee."

What effect this mixture of politics, economics, and prejudice had upon the convictions of the legislators is not recorded. The debate continued for another four hours and then the committee's report was accepted, eighty-six to fifty-nine. The Union Bank was defeated. Nevertheless, there had been an ominous increase of nine votes in favor, all from the new members of the House.

The Federalists, however, had an irreducible majority of some thirty votes, and they used this bludgeon to impose their will upon the state. First, with Plumer's enthusiastic participation, they elected James

---

11. Plumer to Jeremiah Smith, June 14, 1800, *ibid.;* Plumer, Autobiography, 84.

Sheafe, a Portsmouth merchant and ex-Tory, to replace John Langdon, the Portsmouth merchant and ex-Federalist, in the United States Senate. Plumer took part in the Federalist caucus to compose a congressional ticket and was asked to be a candidate. Because of his poor health, he refused, although he found serious objections to Dr. Samuel Tenney of Exeter, who was chosen in his place. In order to make doubly certain that they would control the presidential election in New Hampshire the Federalists then decided to take the choice of electors away from the people and vest it in the legislature.[12] Plumer defended this action as constitutional, which it certainly was, but the Republicans complained that it was undemocratic and a step backward in New Hampshire.[13] Certainly, it was another evidence of the Federalist inability to trust the people.

Among other duties given to Plumer as soon as he returned to the legislature was that of writing the replies to Governor Gilman's speeches. Within the traditional formula, Gilman and Plumer managed to play a lively Federalist duet; in fact, their speeches and answers from 1797 to 1802 form an interesting antiphony of high Federalist doctrine. Plumer was the better writer, although he was handicapped by the convention which required that his answer be a mere echo of the Governor's melody. Sometimes, however, he introduced a strain of counterpoint which must have startled the prosaic Gilman. In 1800, for example, the governor chose to proclaim the virtues of conservatism by using Napoleon as a whipping boy: "To contemplate the causes, by which nations once free have lost their liberties . . . [to] view them in the extremes of Democracy in name, while tyranny in all its horrid forms, was actually exercised . . . —such considerations might tend to rouse our endeavours for avoiding such calamities." [14]

Plumer, arriving a week late, was asked to revise a bombastic and ill-

12. Virginia changed in 1800 from district elections to a general ticket; Georgia and Pennsylvania from the general ticket to choice by their legislatures. Only two states, Maryland and North Carolina, retained the democratic method of popular election by districts. See Charles Paullin, *Atlas of the Historical Geography of the United States* (Baltimore, 1932), 89, 93.

13. This speech is abstracted from Plumer's own report of it in a letter written, but not sent, to Jeremiah Smith, June 14, 1800, Letter Book, I, Lib. Cong. In that letter, Plumer said of Dr. Tenney: "He is a man of strong prejudices—of feeble intellect; indolent and unacquainted with men. I do not say I will oppose him; but it will require a great effort to reconcile my mind to vote for him." The reconciliation was undoubtedly made. See also Plumer, Autobiography, 84, 85.

14. *Journal of the House of Representatives, June Session, 1800* (Portsmouth, 1800), 26-29.

digested repetition of this theme; he sat down in his lodgings that night to dash off a state document embodying the necessary dignity and force.[15] Ignoring Napoleon, he found his text in the fact that the people of New Hampshire had just voted not to revise the 1792 constitution.

This event affords clear evidence of the stability of our citizens, of their attachment to a Constitution and form of Government, well adapted to secure their invaluable rights and privileges, and of their opposition to a spirit of innovation, dangerous at all times to the rights of freemen. . . . we assure your Excellency that the great body of our citizens are firmly attached to the administration of our State and Federal Governments— and that they are unitedly resolved to support the government of their own choice against the machinations of foreign and domestic enemies, and transmit the same inviolate to their latest posterity.[16]

Unfortunately, the harmony between Gilman and Plumer in their oracular capacities seldom extended to more practical matters. The Exeter leaders, with some reason, regarded the member from Epping as erratic, and he reciprocated by pushing his own legislative program. Considering the government too expensive, he introduced a resolution that it would be expedient for the next year's legislature to have but one session. In contrast to earlier practice, when the legislature met three and sometimes four times every year, Plumer's resolution paved the way for the single annual sessions which soon became normal.[17] Another of Plumer's pet bills, however, ran into serious opposition from the governor. New Hampshire law allowed the former owners of property sold for unpaid taxes a year in which to redeem it by paying the new owner his purchase price plus 6 per cent interest. Plumer proposed raising this interest rate to 12 per cent in order to make delinquency more unpleasant and tax sales more profitable. His bill passed with little difficulty but was vetoed by Gilman because it seemed inconsistent with the law limiting regular interest rates to 6 per cent. Plumer disposed of this argument in the devastating style which he could command when his contempt was aroused, and the bill was passed over Gilman's veto by heavy majorities

15. Plumer, Autobiography, 83.
16. *House Journal, June Sess., 1800*, 50-52.
17. *Ibid.*, 103; Plumer, Autobiography, 90. Single sessions were held in 11 of the 18 years that followed Plumer's resolution. Special sessions were required by emergencies in two of the remaining years, and the other five double-session occasions were years in which a new apportionment of taxes—always a long and tedious business—had to be made.

in both houses. "The governor was mortified and offended, but said nothing to me on the subject," Plumer wrote.[18]

Having antagonized the governor, Plumer proceeded to irritate the lesser Federalist leaders by one of those periodic displays of independence which faithful ward politicians can neither understand nor forgive. The original division of the state into senatorial districts, made in 1792, had taken on the character of a slight Federalist gerrymander. The Republicans, therefore, introduced annual resolutions to redistrict the state and the Federalists annually buried them in committee. In 1800 they made the mistake of placing Plumer in charge of the obsequies. Benjamin Connor, the second Federalist member of the committee, made the conventional proposal that the resolution be postponed, but Plumer decided that it should be investigated. Discovering that the districts actually were disproportionate, he drew a new map and summoned his committee. Connor, seeing that Exeter was in the same polluted district with Portsmouth, hurriedly voted against it. But Plumer and the delighted Republican committeeman formed a majority and reported their bill to the house. Before it got to a third reading, the Federalist tacticians called Plumer aside and begged him to support a postponement; he finally agreed, although he insisted that the division was just and did not create Republicans; if the people were actually Republicans, they had a right to elect Republican senators. The motion to postpone failed in the House but the reapportionment was killed in the Senate.[19] "On that occasion," wrote Plumer thirty years later, "I then thot, & still think, the rights of the people were sacrificed to party considerations. I then informed some of my political friends that I could not support the claims of party against those of justice & equity." [20]

In 1800 Plumer spent a month in actual attendance in the legislature at considerable loss of time and money, but as the year drew to a close he was inclined to think that his sacrifice was in vain, particularly after John Adams was beaten in November. "Our political hemisphere gathers blackness," wrote Plumer during the subsequent March elections, "the prospect is alarming. . . . Wild democracy is gaining ground in New Hampshire." [21] It gained ground particularly in Epping where the annual town meeting was unduly boisterous and Plumer was "frequently interrupted" when he spoke in Gilman's favor. His own vigorous de-

18. *House Journal, Nov. Sess., 1800,* 81; Plumer, Autobiography, 90.
19. *House Journal, Nov. Sess., 1800,* 74, 105.
20. Plumer, Autobiography, 89.
21. Plumer to John Norris, Mar. 16, 1801, Plumer Papers, N. H. State Lib.

nunciation of the Union Bank in the previous legislature had marked him for proscription. Knowing this, and influenced by private considerations, Plumer had determined not to return to the legislature, but Jefferson's victory shook his decision. "Considering the state of the nation, the importunity of my political friends, & the vanity, natural to man, that my individual efforts would aid the cause of my country, I again consented to be a candidate for representative," he asserted. This time it required three ballots for his election. "It is a humiliating circumstance," Plumer wrote, "when a man is conscious he has devoted his time, talents, & money to the public service, & faithfully discharged his duty, to find it difficult to obtain a re-election to an expensive & laborious office." [22] Then he drew the inevitable moral lesson. "It is easy to make men uneasy with their rulers; but difficult to convince the ignorant of the propriety & necessity of the most important measures of government. I think public opinion is progressing to a change—democracy will eventually triumph in New Hampshire." [23]

Plumer's pessimism was somewhat premature. The Federalists won a comfortable majority in the General Court but again encountered difficulty in electing a senator, this time to fill the vacancy caused by Samuel Livermore's resignation. Although Plumer agreed to accept the appointment if no other suitable person could be found, he willingly supported Simeon Olcott, the honest but inept chief justice.[24] Olcott's election left a vacancy at the head of the New Hampshire bench which could be filled by a better man and Plumer urged Jeremiah Smith to fill it in the almost certain event that Congress should abolish the circuit court to which Smith had been appointed by President Adams.[25] A dependable judiciary, Plumer insisted, would be "a formidable check to the many wanton abuses that a Legislature, dependent upon annual elections, & too often influenced by popular passions, may commit." [26]

Plumer had good reason to speak feelingly of legislative abuses, for things had not gone at all well during the single session of 1801. The Union Bank proprietors had returned to the attack, and some of the chief Federalists, convinced that their opposition would soon be unavail-

22. Plumer, Autobiography, 91.
23. Plumer to Jeremiah Smith, Mar. 10, 1801, Letter Book, I, Lib. Cong.
24. Plumer to Jeremiah Smith, June 13, 1801, Letter Book, III, *ibid.; Journal of the House of Representatives, June Session, 1801* (Portsmouth, 1801), 6, 14, 64; Plumer, Autobiography, 92.
25. Morison, *Jeremiah Smith,* 150-54.
26. Plumer to Thomas Thompson, July 13, 1802, Plumer Papers, N. H. State Lib.

ing, were for extracting what advantage they could out of granting what they felt would ultimately be obtained anyway without their consent. But Plumer and some others advocated war to the bitter end, and the issue was fought all over again in the legislature. A bill of incorporation passed the House eighty-four to sixty, but was defeated by the adverse vote of seven senators.[27] Near the end of the session, the Union Bank men presented a bill to exempt their institution specifically from the restraining act of 1799. This proposal elicited an angry rebuttal from Plumer: "Under this exemption, they may hold property to any amount, issue bills to any extent, establish branches in every town in the State if they please, & that without being subject, as the New Hampshire bank is, to the visitation and control of the legislature. I think a legislature which has refused to incorporate them, cannot, with propriety, give them greater authority & more extensive priveledges, than an act of incorporation." [28]

In spite of Plumer's remonstrance, this bill passed in the House with a twenty-eight vote majority, but went to its rendezvous with death in the Senate, where the faithful seven again administered the *coup de grâce*. These actions caused Plumer to repent of his backsliding from party regularity in the matter of senatorial reapportionment, and he voted against the annual Republican bill, which passed the House, seventy-nine to sixty-three, but failed in the Senate, four to seven.[29] The onslaught of the Jeffersonians was causing some strain to Plumer's nerves. His reply to Gilman's address contained a warning "against the efforts of party, and the spirit of imprudent innovation" in the national government. His committee on printing transferred the state account from the office of the *New Hampshire Gazette*, which had just been bought out by Republicans, to the printer of the *Courier of New Hampshire*, a staunch Federalist organ. A letter from the Maryland legislature was laid before the House proposing that the Federal Constitution be amended to designate electoral votes for President and Vice-President, in order to prevent a repetition of such dangerous episodes as Burr's tie with Jefferson in the recent election. Such an amendment had been proposed by the New Hampshire legislature itself in 1798 after Jefferson had come uncomfortably close to winning the presidency from Adams, but the shoe was now on the other foot, and the Federalists postponed consideration.

27. Plumer, Autobiography, 93; *House Journal, June Sess., 1801*, 36-38; *Journal of the Senate, June Session, 1801* (Portsmouth, 1801), 27.
28. Plumer, Autobiography, 93.
29. *House Journal, June Sess., 1801*, 60-62; *Senate Journal, June Sess., 1801*, 47-48.

In spite of these minor victories, however, three important bills, vigorously opposed by the strongest men in the Federalist party, had passed this House of Representatives by majorities of twenty-eight, twenty-four, and sixteen.

A year of Jeffersonian democracy had persuaded Plumer that, even if the heavens had not fallen on March 4, 1801, they were still supported only by the slender pillar of New England Federalism. A terrible blizzard in February 1802, which blocked the roads with four-foot snow drifts, provided him with the text for a political sermon:

The decisive course that is now pursuing, on the *tempestuous sea of liberty,* by the pilot who now presides at the helm of Government, will, I fear, prove more fatal to our prosperity & safety, as a nation, than the winds & snow have to our present ease & convenience. . . . I know it is our duty not to dispair of the Commonwealth; & I feel a strong disposition quietly to submit to *the powers that be;* but I fear their measures have an inevitable tendency to anarchy. And anarchy must necessarily produce despotism; for the world is agreed, that even a bad government is preferable to no government.[30]

Some of the Jeffersonian measures struck close to home. Plumer heard that Postmaster Granger had recommended cutting off the Epping post road, which had been in operation only eighteen months after it had taken four years of effort to get it established.[31] Edward St. Loe Livermore, like William Marbury, had failed to receive his commission from the new administration; when Plumer inquired about the matter from his old family friend, Henry Dearborn, he received the disturbing information that John Samuel Sherburne, not Livermore, was appointed district attorney for New Hampshire.[32] Jefferson also cleaned out the old Tories whom Adams had installed in the customs at Portsmouth and reinstated the partisans of France whom Plumer had helped to remove.[33] To account for all these aberrations, Plumer sought the primary infection, and since French influence could hardly now be blamed, he found it in the excess of democracy. "Every popular assembly," he wrote, "is to a certain degree, a mob, influenced either by their passions & prejudices, or what is more fatal, by unprincipled designing dema-

---

30. Plumer to George Upham, Mar. 1, 1802, Letter Book, I, Lib. Cong.
31. Plumer to Upham, Mar. 23, 1802, *ibid.*
32. Plumer to Henry Dearborn, June 1, 1801, Letter Book, III, *ibid.;* Dearborn to Plumer, June 13, 1801, Plumer Papers, N. H. State Lib.
33. Plumer, Autobiography, 69.

gogues. . . . In a government thus constituted & organized can you rationally expect stability?" [34]

In September 1801, while he was attending the Superior Court at Dover, Plumer was seized with an intestinal disorder, "the Illiac passion," which left him unable to attend to business for many weeks. The physical shock of this illness crystallized an intention that had been half-formed for several years—to retire not only from public life but from legal practice as well. Part of this intention was due to personal reasons. Plumer had a sincere, if prosaic, affection for his family, and the long absences from home necessitated by his career were distasteful. He had accumulated a sufficient property to make retirement possible, but only if he devoted all his time for a few years to securing and investing it. That done, however, he looked forward eagerly to a life devoted entirely to reading, study, and literary production. [35]

At the same time, for some reason which he does not make altogether clear, the antagonism between Plumer and John Taylor Gilman became intolerable in 1802. It may have been partly due to the fact that Gilman decided to give up resistance to the Union Bank and carried the party with him, contrary to the convictions of William Plumer, who predicted that instead of reconciling their opponents by this concession, the Federalists would merely accelerate their own defeat. [36] "Under these circumstances," he wrote just before the March elections, "I could not, with honor to myself, accept a seat in the House, & support their principal measures." [37]

If, however, the evidence of an extraordinary letter that Plumer wrote to Jeremiah Smith on March 9, 1802, is to be credited, the major reason for his retirement was an unconquerable aversion to further association with the Exeter Junto. He complained bitterly of Gilman's base and ungenerous attitude toward himself, which was shared by the other citizens of the little town. "There seems to be something in the air at Exeter that makes men bitter against me," he declared, and then added with

34. Plumer to George Upham, Mar. 15, 1802, Letter Book, I, Lib. Cong.

35. Plumer, Autobiography, 94-95. As part of his retirement program, Plumer wrote to his wealthy friend, John Norris, of Salem, Mass., for advice on investments in banks and insurance companies. Plumer to Norris, Mar. 16, 1801, Letter Book, I, Lib. Cong. In 1803 he bought 20 shares in the Portsmouth Bank and 20 shares in the Fire and Marine Insurance Company of Portsmouth. Entries for Apr. 1 and Sept. 1, 1803, Plumer Account Book, N. H. State Lib.

36. Plumer, Autobiography, 97. This Federalist legislature did incorporate the Union Bank, and, as Plumer predicted, the party lost control of the state.

37. Plumer to Jeremiah Smith, Mar. 9, 1802, Letter Book, I, Lib. Cong.

prophetic pessimism, "I will not be surprised if you become armed against me—but you will have no more reason than the others." With a depth of rancor unusual for him, Plumer found the basis for all his failures and disappointments in the hostility of the Exeterites. They had been afraid of his talents and influence and had therefore barred his political advancement whenever possible. They had never consulted him on legislative programs until opposition to their favorite measures had driven them to seek his aid. This was because "they considered me as an obstinate person, incapable of being bound in leading strings," Plumer insisted. In spite of all this and in spite of Gilman's personal ill treatment, he had supported the Governor as the only man who would uphold the national administration. "I did what I shall ever do, I sacrificed my personal resentment to the interests of my country," Plumer declared.[38]

Having relieved his pent-up emotions by writing this philippic, Plumer had the good sense to file it away, rather than send it to a man who resided in Exeter and was the social and political intimate of the Gilman family. It is a curious psychological document. Much of it was petty jealousy, which Plumer unquestionably felt but was usually strong enough to suppress. Much of it was deliberately exaggerated to produce a picture of persecution that did not actually exist. Gilman had appointed Plumer solicitor for Rockingham County and had consulted him on more than one occasion when united party action was necessary. From the Governor's viewpoint, to be sure, Plumer must have been deemed an undependable ally. What this unsent letter clearly reveals is that both Gilman and Plumer recognized, subconsciously, that their political views were fundamentally different; that—to put it into language which they would never have employed—Gilman was a Hamiltonian Federalist while Plumer was actually a Madisonian Republican. They agreed completely upon the importance of the federal Union and resistance to French domination; on nearly every other subject they were at opposite poles. When questions of foreign relations lost their overwhelming importance, and when the two men broke on a major domestic and local issue—the Union Bank—Plumer felt no obligation to support Gilman any longer.

Plumer had, however, postponed his break with Gilman until it could be made without disaster to the party. One more strong pull, to bring the ship of state into the deep waters of Federalism where the Jacobin shoals could do her no harm, and Plumer could retire with a clear

38. *Ibid.*

conscience. John Langdon was the Republican candidate for governor in 1802, and his genial personality had captivated many a wavering Federalist.[39] The Democrats were active and in high spirits; the Federalists slept at their posts; if something were not done to awaken the friends of government from their apathy, Langdon would carry the election. Spurred by the prospect of this disaster, Plumer began a tremendous campaign of correspondence to party leaders and friends in every quarter of the state. "If we act with that prudence & firmness, the occasion requires," he exhorted, "we shall succeed, & the blessing of a good administration will be *our reward*." [40]

During the winter months of 1802, at the very time that his resentment against the Exeter Junto was growing to fever heat, Plumer loyally continued his correspondence. The frauds and deceits of the "Demo's" could be overcome only by eternal vigilance, he piously asserted. "The use of poisoned weapons are forbid to us. . . . The shield of truth, & the helmet of rational argument are sufficient to support our cause." Plumer's chief concern was that these legitimate weapons should be wielded with sufficient force. His conception of strengthening the shield of truth was to vilify Langdon, while portraying the character of Gilman in glowing colors. "You know Govr. Gilman to be a man of integrity & firmness," he wrote to a local politician. "It becomes an object of importance to re-elect [him]." [41]

Duly impressed with the necessity of maintaining New Hampshire's Federalism, Benjamin Gilbert of Hanover suggested that Plumer should have written a history of Gilman's administration for the newspapers to show that all the calumnies spread against the governor were false. The suggestion contained unconscious irony, for in his unsent letter to Smith, Plumer had indeed written such a history. If published, it would have damned the Federalist administration more effectively than any Republican propaganda. Gilbert, however, unaware of this irreconcilable conflict in the Federalist party, ended his letter with an exhortation to Plumer to remain in harness. "I hope the obstacles to your re-election to represent Epping next year, are only imaginary; & that neither your own health nor the politics of your constituents, are in so crazy a state as you represent them—you cannot be spared—you must be well enough

39. Plumer to Jeremiah Smith, June 18, 1801, Letter Book, III, Lib. Cong.

40. Plumer to David Hough, Jan. 30, to George Upham, Jan. 27, 1802, Letter Book, I, Lib. Cong.

41. Plumer to Benjamin Gilbert, Jan. 30, to David Hough, Jan. 30, 1802, *ibid.*

and willing to legislate one year more—and your constituents must not advise you otherwise." [42]

The politics of Epping were indeed in a crazy state. As March approached, Plumer stuck to his resolution to avoid a personal political contest and gave his support to another Federalist candidate for representative. Even though this man was a Baptist,[43] he lost the election, as did many another Federalist in Rockingham County and the Merrimack Valley. The excitement produced by Langdon's entry into the contest brought out more than twenty-five hundred new voters, and Gilman was barely re-elected.[44] Even President Jefferson took grateful notice of this sudden rush toward democracy in New Hampshire.[45]

The Federalists, however, retained majorities in both houses of the legislature. This proved to be a fact of extreme importance to Plumer, for this General Court of 1802 had a piece of business not originally on the agenda—the election of a senator to Congress. This was occasioned by the resignation of James Sheafe, who had succeeded Langdon only fifteen months previously. One winter in the mud and rain of Washington had apparently given him an incurable nostalgia for the Piscataqua.

Plumer knew nothing of Sheafe's resignation, for he had taken his own retirement seriously and, for probably the first time since 1785, had remained completely absent from a meeting of the legislature. On the last day of the session, however, Plumer was elected to fill the vacant Senate position. When he was notified two days later, it came to him as a complete surprise. Since the legislature had already adjourned, Plumer was presented with a *fait accompli* that canceled his plan of retirement. His friends immediately wrote their congratulations and urged him to accept the appointment. "I feel myself placed in a situation that is truly embarrassing," he replied to Thomas W. Thompson, young Daniel Webster's law tutor in Salisbury. Plumer spoke with some exaggeration of suffering "almost daily . . . the ravages of disease & the signals of dissolution." The unsettled state of his business affairs, the youth of his children, and the illness of his wife weighed heavily on his mind. Yet if he should not accept, the legislature would have to be reconvened for another election or the state be only partially represented in the Senate.

42. Benjamin Gilbert to Plumer, Feb. 17, 1802, Plumer Papers, N. H. State Lib.
43. Plumer to Jeremiah Smith, Mar. 9, 1802, Letter Book, I, Lib. Cong.
44. Parker Lyon, ed., *The New Hampshire Register and United States Calendar for the Year 1860* (Concord, 1859), 40-41.
45. Thomas Jefferson to John Langdon, June 29, 1802, Jefferson Papers, CXXIV, Lib. Cong.

"Unpleasant as my situation is," he concluded, "I do not think I am at liberty to decline the appointment." [46]

There were other considerations which made Plumer's reluctance to go to the United States Senate in 1802 more intelligible than it would be today. He would be in the disagreeable position of belonging to a hopeless minority engaged in a bitter and savage struggle with a ruthless majority. Political antagonisms confined within the narrow limits of the raw new town of Washington had become as uncomfortable as village church feuds in New England. The mere prospect of having to live in Washington for five years was physically and socially unappealing —no less than five New Hampshire congressmen had been driven to resign since December 1799. There was, therefore, genuine regret behind Plumer's decision. "But for many years," he wrote, "I have beleived the nation has a just claim to the services of all its citizens, & when the nation commands, it's the duty of the individual to render a prompt obédience. I wish I was better qualified, but such talents as I have I will devote to the service." [47]

Plumer's elevation to the United States Senate, after repeated failures to be elected to minor positions or even appointed to a petty judicial office, was a strange turn of events which calls for an explanation. According to the story which Plumer himself put together after learning the facts from his friends, a caucus of the Federalist members of the legislature had agreed upon his nomination without a division. The Republicans thereupon abandoned the candidate they had originally chosen and nominated Nicholas Gilman, one of whose brothers was governor, another a state senator, and who had himself served four terms in Congress. This was a shrewd maneuver, for Gilman was a hybrid in politics and commanded some support in both parties. Torn between party loyalty and his natural feelings, Governor Gilman had finally advised his followers to vote for *"a federalist,"* but in such equivocal terms as to leave some doubt whether he meant brother Nicholas or Plumer. Oliver Peabody and Benjamin Connor were equally "paralized, embarrassed, & confused" but finally had decided in favor of party regularity and worked for Plumer's election. Nathaniel Gilman, however, had remained loyal to his brother, quarreled with his Exeter friends, and entered his vote against Plumer in the Senate journal. In the end, although the Gilman gambit had succeeded well in creating Federalist dissension, it failed to

46. Plumer to Thomas Thompson, June 23, 1802, Plumer Papers, N. H. State Lib.
47. Plumer to Jeremiah Smith, June 23, 1802, Letter Book, I, Lib. Cong.

defeat Plumer. He had been elected by a majority of fourteen in the House and by seven to five in the Senate.[48]

Plumer's reconstruction of events was corroborated by an article that appeared in the *New Hampshire Gazette* in August, written and signed by Nicholas Gilman. He had been absent from the state when the election occurred, but he was ambitious to return to national politics and extremely angry at this setback. He claimed in this article that Plumer's election was fraudulent since it had been achieved by propaganda to the effect that he, Gilman, was not a resident of the state. Connor and Peabody, he said, should have denied such false statements, but instead they had played leading parts in an intrigue which outraged public opinion, especially in Plumer's own county. He quoted earlier remarks by Connor and Peabody to the effect that Plumer had no honor or integrity and said that by their recent action they had either defrauded the public or made restitution to a much injured reputation.[49]

Except for this outburst of private resentment, Plumer's election did not seem to have caused much excitement. His own friends were convinced that New Hampshire was honored by the selection;[50] but the Federalist press announced it without comment. Two brief letters in the same issue of the *Republican Gazette* of Concord, June 22, constituted the entire complaint of the opposition. "It cannot escape the notice of the Citizens of New-Hampshire, (who are nearly all republicans)," said one writer, "that this is the second or third anti-revolutionary character which has been elected by a small majority in the General Court, to the Senate of the U. States, within the space of one short year!"[51] Sheafe, Olcott, and Plumer were the "characters" referred to in this inaccurate notice. In another column, religious prejudice was added to patriotic bias. "The 'Federal republicans', it is hoped, will not harp anymore about their *Religion,* when it is found that none but Old Tories & Deists can gain preferment."

The most interesting comment on the Federalists' choice, however, came from within the party. In a letter written from Washington, February 18, 1803, Congressman Samuel Tenney of Exeter, whom Plumer had felt reluctant to support in 1800, apologized for the election by doubt-

---

48. Plumer, Autobiography, 97-99.
49. *N. H. Gazette* (Portsmouth), Aug. 10, 1802.
50. According to the mellow recollections of Daniel Webster fifty years later, the "leading men" at Concord had agreed "that the new Senator was by all odds the ablest man in the Federal party" and "that it was thought a great object to have secured his election." See Plumer, Jr., *Life of Plumer,* 147.
51. *Republican Gazette* (Concord), June 22, 1802.

ing "whether any gentleman of talents sufficiently respectable to entitle him to a seat in the Senate of the U. States could have been induced to stand a candidate for the appointment, whose principles are federal & whose reputation was unblemished." As between Plumer and Gilman, however,

Could there be any question whether they should send into [the senate] a man of decided principles, upon whose conduct his friends could always depend, or one who would vote with one party today & the other tomorrow? a man of talents for business or a mere gallant for the city Belles? For myself, altho I have been in habits of intimacy and friendship with Mr G—more than twenty years, while I have so fully entered into the popular prejudices against Mr P—that I have avoided all friendly intercourse with him, had I belonged to the legislature, I am persuaded I should have given the latter a decided preference. I am very sensible that Mr Plumer is an usurer—that he has been considered as an oppressor of the poor—& that he has taken advantages of the embarrassed debtors, who have been obliged to put themselves into his power, as a moneylender, which you & I should have disdained—These practises have arisen out of 'his haste to be rich'—& I know he has carried them so far as to have excited the odium of many who were disposed to respect him for his talents. But I do not recollect that I ever heard him accused of any acts of downright dishonesty. . . . I travelled with Mr Plumer from Exeter to this place & we have lodged together ever since. This has given me an opportunity of becoming acquainted with him : & I declare to you that had I never before heard of the man, I should have formed an opinion of him highly favorable to the benevolence of his heart, the purity of his mind & the correctness of his morals. For myself I am free to acknowledge a full conviction that my prejudices against him have been illfounded—& that I believe him to be a much better man than he has been generally considered.[52]

Plumer also acquired a better opinion of Tenney upon closer acquaintance.

Having been drawn abruptly back into the current of political activity, Plumer resumed his vigorous habits and prepared for the great adventure in Washington. He resigned his office of county solicitor and wound up most of his law business. In October, he visited Dr. Benjamin Waterhouse at Harvard College and was inoculated with "the kinepox." His important office gave him a keener sense of party responsibility; he en-

52. Samuel Tenney to Josiah Bartlett, Feb. 18, 1803, Bartlett Papers, Lib. Cong. The Bartletts were not so easily reconciled to Plumer's elevation. See a letter from Levi to Ezra Bartlett, June 18, 1802, Bartlett Papers, N. H. State Lib.

tered into the congressional campaign with zeal, buying large lots of political pamphlets for distribution and writing his customary letters. He had the satisfaction of seeing Epping vote for the Federalist ticket, and the state maintain its Federalist delegation intact. Before he left for Washington in November, he knew that Jeremiah Smith had accepted the office of chief justice. Correct principles seemed to be entrenched in every department of New Hampshire's political life. It was with implicit faith in his political creed, and some assurance of its continued predominance in New England, that he went southward to tilt with the Virginia Democrats.[53]

53. Plumer, Autobiography, 100.

CHAPTER VI

United States Senator

"We shall, I presume, do little business in Congress this session. The ruling party, tho desirous of further innovation, are fearful lest they should interrupt the *successful tide of experiment.*" [1]

O N the eve of his departure for the United States Senate, at the halfway point in his career, Plumer was forty-three years of age. His hair was still black, his figure erect, and his eye keen. His one hundred and fifty pounds were distributed with necessary sparsity over a frame nearly six feet in height, but there was no appearance of awkwardness or lack of strength. His portrait engraved at Washington in 1803 by the French artist, Charles Fevret de Saint-Mémin, shows, in profile, a strong, intelligent, and not displeasing face, unsmiling, it is true, but nevertheless generous and friendly.[2] Plumer was more noted for a puritan gravity of demeanor than for a sense of humor. His long lean face and dark skin would have given him a perpetually somber appearance had it not been for the jet-black sparkle of his eyes.[3] "His eye was, perhaps, his most expressive feature," wrote his son. "It seemed on fire when he was engaged in debate, or in earnest conversation. Yet there was a gentleness about it, which made it as attractive in his milder moods as it was terrible in his anger." [4]

Success in his profession and in politics had not made Plumer pretentious. He dressed well and not too much at variance with the prevailing mode, but he was willing to sacrifice style to patriotism, and occasionally wore suits of American cloth to encourage domestic manu-

1. Plumer to John Taylor Gilman, Jan. 16, 1803, Plumer Papers, N. H. State Lib.
2. See frontispiece.
3. George Thatcher to Plumer, Feb. 9, 1800, Plumer Papers, N. H. State Lib.
4. Plumer, Jr., *Life of Plumer,* 541.

factures. In an age when ownership of a carriage was the distinguishing mark of wealth and aristocracy, Plumer was content to travel in a simple chaise.[5] The sturdy farmhouse which his father had purchased for him in 1784 continued to serve as his "seat" after he became a senator and, indeed, as executive headquarters in the years when he was governor. Sitting in dignity at the top of a gentle, grass-covered slope, the old house was furnished simply, for its owner had a true Yankee horror of ostentatious display. The mere rumor that his children planned to give their mother a carpet caused him to write peremptorily, "purchase none at present. A turkey carpet I never owned, & probably never shall. My money I had rather lay out for books, or to releive the poor. I will not pay tribute to other people's eyes." [6] The household revolved about a room which William Plumer used as a law office, library, and scriptorium. It was stacked high with neatly arranged documents and books, which were his only luxuries, and here, on the rare occasions when he could snatch time from his engagements, Plumer could usually be found, happily buried in a volume of history or classic prose.

Plumer had an abiding love of the soil, and he remained by preference in Epping rather than move to a metropolis such as Portsmouth where his business might have been enhanced. Unlike many gentleman-farmers, he made a profit from his farm. He enjoyed working on his land at the side of his sons and laborers, and considered himself a progressive practitioner of the science of agriculture. He valued his country home even more, however, as a rural retreat from the busy life of court and legislature.

It was difficult for Plumer to wrench himself away from this home and his family. Leaving a wife and five young children "produced feelings I never before experienced," he recalled. William, Jr., now aged thirteen, was a student at Phillips Exeter Academy, but the other children—Sally, aged twelve; Samuel, ten; George, six; and Jay, three— were still at home and would have to be left to the care of an invalid mother and nearby relatives. Plumer hesitated to be absent from them for so long a period because he had a strong sense of parental responsibility and ideas about child training far in advance of his time. "I have never had occasion to inflict a blow on one of them, & seldom to use a severe expression," he declared. "I have treated them more like companions than children, accomodating my language & conduct to

5. *Ibid.*, 89-90.
6. Plumer to William Plumer, Jr., May 20, 1817, Plumer Papers, N. H. State Lib.

their years, . . . always preferring reason & persuasion to parental authority." [7]

On the eighteenth of November, the Epping lawyer, who had never before been farther away from home than Holderness or Boston, began his five-hundred-mile journey to Washington. At Exeter, he tarried briefly to visit his oldest son, then joined his traveling companion, Dr. Tenney. As they journeyed southward, Plumer was surprised to find the experience agreeable; new scenes and new acquaintances delighted him; pleasant weather made the discomforts of stage coaches endurable; and his appetite was so stimulated that, for the first time in his life, he enjoyed eating. In New York he renewed pleasurable acquaintance with his old fellow law student, William Coleman, now editor of the *Evening Post*.[8] The efficacy of his inoculation was agreeably proven when he met there a man "who had the smallpox broke out full upon him" but was not infected. On the second of December, after fifteen days of travel, he arrived safe and well in the capital of the United States.

Senator Plumer found satisfactory lodgings on the third floor of Frost's boarding house on Capitol Hill, whence he could easily walk to the Senate chamber. Frost's housed a purely Federalist company, consisting of seven New England congressmen who generally lived a communal life of enforced bachelorhood. Plumer paid ten dollars a week for "half a chamber and victuals" and furnished his own wood and liquors.[9] This was a high price for ordinary lodgings, but Plumer did not, at first, complain. He received without cost the privilege of association with some of the most distinguished Federalists in America.

As soon as his domestic arrangements were made, Plumer looked up General Varnum, a Republican acquaintance from Massachusetts who agreed to accompany him on a ceremonious visit to President Jefferson. Plumer described his first encounter with the great democrat in a spiteful letter to Jeremiah Smith: "In a few moments, a tall highboned man came into the room; he was drest, or rather *undrest,* with an old brown coat, red waistcoat, old corduroy small clothes, much soiled—woolen hose —& slippers without heels. I thought this man was a servant; but Genl Varnum surprised me, by announcing that it was the President. Never, never rally me again upon my inattention to dress—I certainly dress as

7. Plumer, Autobiography, 101, 235-36.
8. Plumer, "William Coleman," Biographies, V, 463, N. H. Hist. Soc.
9. Plumer to Samuel Plumer, Dec. 7, 1802, William Plumer, Letters, 1802-7, Lib. Cong. Unlike the Letter Books, this small collection of family correspondence, stitched together with some of Plumer's historical notes, is unnumbered.

well as the first officer of the nation. I tarried about 20 minutes—he is easy of access, & conversed with great ease & freedom." [10]

Plumer was not the only competent observer who has left a record of Jefferson's unkempt appearance, but there is more of party rancor than of straight reporting in this letter. Plumer went to Washington as a Federalist, with an ingrained prejudice against Jefferson which yielded only partially to the President's generous hospitality. Even after he became a Republican, Plumer never wholly overcame his suspicions of the philosopher President.[11] But he was a man to whom politics were usually secondary to human intercourse. In contrast to some of the more bitter Federalists, he maintained a cordial social relationship with the President and even thought that Jefferson acted unwisely in asking members of only one party at the same time to his dinners, since "the more men of liberal minds & good hearts are acquainted, the more they respect & esteem each other, tho they may differ upon particular subjects." [12]

For a decade the city of Washington had been gradually rising from the swamps and forests of the federal district. It had been occupied by the government only two years when Plumer first arrived, and was as yet more distinguished for the breadth of vision evident in its plan than for anything in its appearance. Plumer was particularly struck by the great gaps between the standing buildings, a consequence of the "error" involved in starting houses in every part of the city at the same time. Few of the roads or gardens were fenced and Plumer complained especially about the absence of trees. He admired the road built straight from the "presidential House" to the foot of Capitol Hill, however, and the flagstone footwalk on its northern border called the Appian Way. The Capitol, which then consisted only of the north wing (where the Supreme Court later sat), also elicited his admiration, "particularly the

10. Plumer to Jeremiah Smith, Dec. 9, 1802, Letter Book, I, Lib. Cong.

11. William Plumer, Jr.'s tendency to give his father's phrases a more epigrammatic quality than they actually possessed has led to some misconception about the relations of Plumer and Jefferson. His *Life of Plumer,* p. 246, contains a purported quotation from a letter written by his father to his mother on Christmas Day, 1802, which has been widely copied: "I wish his [Jefferson's] French politics were as good as his French wines; but to me, at least, they have by no means so exquisite a flavor." See William Robinson in *DAB* s.v. "Plumer, William." The nearest thing to this delightful invention in the actual letter is the following sentence: "His wine was truly the best I ever drank, particularly his champaign—It is delicious indeed." Nothing was said about French politics. Plumer to Sarah Plumer, Dec. 25, 1802, Plumer Papers, N. H. State Lib.

12. Plumer, Autobiography, 103. Plumer's changing attitude toward Jefferson is treated in Lynn Turner, "Thomas Jefferson Through the Eyes of a New Hampshire Politician," *Mississippi Valley Historical Review,* 30 (1943), 205-15.

senate chamber." But the dilapidated condition of the temporary brick "Oven" in which the House of Representatives then met, before the south wing (now the Statuary Hall) was completed, gave Plumer a chance to draw a moral lesson: "Some of the members of the House are alarmed, least the roof & craked walls of their building should bury them beneath its ruins. It would be a severe judgment if those walls, that witnessed the prostration of the Judiciary, & the demolition of the internal revenue, should punish the temerity of the destroyers." At the other end of the Appian Way stood the cluster of buildings in which the executives offices were housed. Those sheltering the Treasury, Navy, War, and Post Office departments were "of brick, elegant & convenient . . . The Presidents house is of free stone—large & very elegant . . . The fence around [it] is a rough, unhewn rail fence five feet high. The house is . . . a palace, but the fence is not fit for a barn yard; but perhaps, it is [as] much in unison with the house as its theoretic tenant is with the dignified office he holds." Plumer, who, after all, was only a provincial lawyer, viewed Washington more favorably than did other observers, but he did not have much faith in the future of the city: "There is but little commerce. The inhabitants calculate upon spunging their living from the members of Congress, & not from business. I think the city will not for a century rival New York, Philadelphia, Baltimore or even Boston." [13]

If living in Washington was uncomfortable, Plumer could make no complaint on the score of the company assembled within its confines. During the five years he spent in the national capital, Senator Plumer encountered leaders from every section of the country, and the effect of this association in rubbing off his Yankee provincialism is easily discernible in his letters and his diary.[14] He was, however, to enjoy only a

13. For Plumer's observations on Washington, see his letters to Jeremiah Smith, Dec. 9, 1802, to Nicholas Emery, Jan. 6, 1803, Letter Book, I, Lib. Cong.; to William Plumer, Jr., Feb. 22, 1803, Plumer Papers, N. H. State Lib. See also Wilhelmus Bryan, *A History of the National Capital* (N. Y., 1914), I, 142, 339, and Hans Caemmerer, *Washington, the National Capital* (Wash., 1932), 249 ff.

14. The interesting light which Plumer's observations throw upon these famous acquaintances deserves wider recognition than it has generally received. In a letter to his friend, Jeremiah Smith, for example, Plumer discloses the fascination which the personality of the Vice-President exercised even upon a glacial Yankee: "If A. Burr had the reputation of as much integrity & virtue as his *good sense* actually imposes on him, we should not live under the feeble, nerveless administration of a dry dock & indissoluble salt mountain philosopher. The Vice President was formed by nature to command; but tho his personal friends are strongly attached to him, his influence is limited." Plumer to Jeremiah Smith, Dec. 18, 1803, Plumer Papers, N. H. State Lib.

brief acquaintance with such Federalist giants as Gouverneur Morris and James Ross, who were serving the last of their terms in the Seventh Congress.[15] Federalism seemed to be a dying cause in the United States Senate. Already reduced to a minority of fourteen to eighteen when Plumer appeared, the Federalist contingent shrank to nine after the elections of 1802, while in the House of Representatives its numbers were relatively even smaller. What they lacked in quantity, however, the Federalists tended to offset by strong leadership and arrogant pugnacity.[16] Plumer's accounts of the canings, challenges, and duels to which the Federalist bravos were compelled by their minority complex amused Jeremiah Smith, and prompted him to suggest that the best contribution New Hampshire could make to the cause would be to send five bullies to assail Republicans at the next Congress.[17]

The period of Plumer's participation in the national government was short, but one of almost unparalleled importance. During that half-decade Napoleon almost succeeded in his attempt to dominate the world, the United States unwittingly doubled its territorial extent, the Federalists plotted to detach New England, Aaron Burr conspired to detach the West, and Jefferson tried to crush the Supreme Court. Plumer was keenly interested in these momentous events, but his own connection with them was merely peripheral. Their effects upon the little world in which he moved, however, were profound. During the five years that Plumer spent in the Senate, defeat and repudiation turned the Federalist party into a states' rights, anti-federal, pro-foreign remnant, while responsibility and experience made nationalists and constitutionalists of the Republicans. The psychological revolution wrought by these facts in Plumer's mind, when he began to understand them, presents a fascinating study.

Plumer had at first so little insight into this transition that it baffled him, and he reacted by clinging stubbornly to long-accustomed loyalties. By the time he understood what was happening, the opportunity for action in the national sphere had already slipped away. Plumer, in fact, was dwarfed by the expansion of his stage-setting when he came to Washington. A veteran legislator and a skilled debater, he suddenly discovered himself in the company of still more experienced and more

15. Plumer to Jeremiah Mason, Nov. 19, 1803, *ibid.*

16. Plumer, Autobiography, 118; Plumer, "Jonathan Dayton," Biographies, V, 322-24, N. H. Hist. Soc.

17. Plumer to Jeremiah Smith, Dec. 28, 1802, Letter Book, I, Lib. Cong.; Smith to Plumer, Jan. 28, 1804, William Plumer Letters, IV (1804-7), Plumer Papers, Lib. Cong. (hereafter cited as Letter Book, IV).

readily articulate men. The result was that he played an almost silent role in the public proceedings of Congress.

Soon after Plumer entered the Senate there occurred an incident which impaired his self-confidence. To Washington came news of a disastrous fire that had swept over Portsmouth, consuming 114 buildings and causing damage estimated at $200,000.[18] Jeremiah Smith, with macabre humor, ascribed the tragedy to the vengeance of a righteous God upon the Sodom of Jacobinism, but the effect of his joke was spoiled by the fact that the fire had broken out early on a Sabbath morning and in the New Hampshire Bank building.[19] At any rate a Republican administration sympathized with the sufferers, and Plumer was made chairman of a committee in the Senate to consider an appropriation bill for their relief. In reporting and defending an amendment, however, he found himself so self-conscious that he could not state the principles on which it was made. "This circumstance surprized & mortified me," he reported, "for I had long been in the habit of speaking freely in public." [20] Plumer's mortification was so deep that for the remainder of his Washington sojourn he avoided committee work and took almost no part in the framing of legislation. Yet he felt that he was not without influence. "I speak none," he wrote, "yet my influence on many subjects is not confined to my own vote. I am industrious in all private circles. . . . And I have frequently plenary evidence that my brother senators, of all parties, have much confidence in my opinion." [21]

As a faithful husband absent from his wife and children, Plumer could not participate largely in the new capital's social life, nor did the ordinary amusements of a Southern city appeal to him. Horse racing and card playing were the only available means of breaking the monotony in a constant male society, and Plumer's Puritan frugality revolted at every form of gambling. "Before I reached Washington," he told his son many years later, "I resolved not to play cards for even a cent . . . I was aware that if I played for small sums, I must necessarily sometimes be compelled to play for larger, or be taxed with meaness. . . . I therefore wholly

18. Nathaniel Adams, *Annals of Portsmouth* (Portsmouth, 1825), 324-25.

19. Jeremiah Smith to Plumer, Dec. 28, 1802, Plumer Papers, N. H. State Lib.

20. Plumer, Autobiography, 108.

21. Everett Brown, ed., *William Plumer's Memorandum of Proceedings in the United States Senate, 1803-1807* (N. Y., 1923), 449. This is a printed, annotated edition of three manuscripts preserved among the Plumer Papers in the Library of Congress and entitled respectively Memorandum, 1803-1804; Memorandum, 1804-1805; and Register, I, 1805-1807 (hereafter cited as *Plumer's Memorandum*).

avoided cards—alike the enemy of time & of mental improvement." [22]
Plumer was even more opposed to the horse races, held annually in
November, since they practically suspended the sitting of Congress for
two weeks. Grave senators invented the most childish expedients for
adjournments in time to place their wagers, and congressmen occasionally
rode their own entries. The effect of such behavior upon public opinion
in New England may be estimated by a sarcastic paragraph from one of
Jeremiah Smith's letters to Plumer: "You do not mention anything of
the races—Now that our rulers have turned Jockies we are anxious to hear
who has lost and who has won—We have been told that Randolph rode
one of the Horses—did it come out first? It must mortify him sadly if
he is less successful on the Turf than in the House." [23] Plumer, however,
was in no position to answer his friend's inquiries. "I have never attended the horse-races," he noted coldly in his journal.[24]

Plumer's recreation was intellectual. While other congressmen wrote
out speeches or gambled on their favorite mounts, he haunted the Congressional Library, temporarily but spaciously housed in the completed
north wing of the Capitol.[25] It "contained a valuable collection of books
on law, political subjects, & history," he recalled. "The members of each
house could take out books, giving a receipt to return them at a time
specified. I . . . availed myself of this liberty, & read books I had not
seen before." [26] For Plumer, the library was an oasis in this "desert-
city." He was sufficiently farsighted to suggest the present requirement
that all authors securing copyrights furnish copies of their works to the
library. "It would exhibit at one view the state of literature & science
in the United States—an object very desirable," he wrote.[27] But there
were congressmen who grumbled at the library's expense and withheld
their patronage, except when the spicy *Secret History of St. Cloud*
happened (much to Plumer's disgust) to be purchased through a book-
seller's mistake.[28]

In the lumber room above the Senate chamber, Plumer discovered
another treasure such as would appeal only to a man afflicted with schol-

---

22. Plumer to William Plumer, Jr., Dec. 7, 1819, Plumer Papers, N. H. State Lib.
23. Jeremiah Smith to Plumer, Dec. 4, 1803, *ibid.*
24. *Plumer's Memorandum,* 195.
25. William Johnston, *History of the Library of Congress* (Wash., 1904), I, 34.
26. Plumer, Autobiography, 103.
27. William Plumer, Notes on the History of North America, 48, Plumer Papers,
Lib. Cong.
28. *Plumer's Memorandum,* 541, 559.

arly kleptomania. Here, in the midst of baskets of glass, piles of lumber, dust, and mildew, were thrown the documents that had been printed for the use of former congressmen and carelessly left in their desks at session's end. Although hampered by the hostile attitude of John Beckley, the Republican clerk of the House and Librarian of Congress,[29] Plumer hastily began collecting sets of these documents for himself, his friends, and the Massachusetts Historical Society. "It is to the tedious days that I spent in that cold & damp chamber," he wrote in 1827, "that I am now indebted for a larger & more complete sett of those public papers than any other private individual in the nation possesses." [30]

On the whole, Plumer enjoyed his senatorial experiences. His health was better in the mild climate of Washington than in the rigors of New England winters. Contact with great minds was stimulating. After accustoming himself to the leisurely Southern routines, he found more than enough business to occupy his time. He described his daily schedule to his son as follows: "I usually rise myself—dress, make a good fire, & read half an hour, every morning by candle light. Breakfast at half-past nine—read or write an hour—At 11, go to the Senate—adjourn at one P.M.—converse half an hour or more in the hall—return to my chamber read or write—dine at three—walk, visit, or receive visits— read, at 7 OClock drink tea—spend an hour with the company—return to my chamber read & write till 11 OClock—rake up my fire lock my chamber door & go to bed." [31]

No senator was more punctual and constant in his attendance than Plumer, and when the Senate was busy he spent four to seven hours in the chamber, rather than two. He also devoted two hours a day to answering the letters he received.[32] Much of his correspondence was published in newspapers, and it probably had a considerable effect on public opinion in New Hampshire. "Your letters are much talked of by those who are so happy as to receive them," wrote Smith.[33] If Washington's political atmosphere had only been as serene as it was stimulating, Plumer would have been a happy man.

Plumer's major contribution as a senator was not to his own generation but to posterity. During the last four of his five sessions he kept a

29. *Ibid.*, 537-39.
30. Plumer, Autobiography, 108.
31. Plumer to William Plumer, Jr., Jan. 5, 1807, Letter Book, IV, Lib. Cong. The routine described in this letter was established later—after Plumer had moved to another boarding house and was living alone.
32. Plumer to Thomas Thompson, Feb. 18, 1803, Plumer Papers, N. H. State Lib.
33. Jeremiah Smith to Plumer, Feb. 14, 1803, *ibid.*

voluminous journal, which, in print, runs into more than six hundred pages. Assiduous industry and acute observation make this journal in many respects a more detailed and accurate record of what was actually said in the Senate chamber than either John Quincy Adams's diary or the *Annals of Congress*. It contains much important material not recorded elsewhere, such as the Senate debate on the Breckinridge Bill for the government of Louisiana. Written hastily at night from notes scribbled during the day, it is marred by errors of grammar and composition as well as errors of opinion, but Plumer frequently insisted that whatever he recorded as a fact was true.[34] Shorn of its prejudices and its inevitable nearsightedness, Plumer's Memorandum becomes an indispensable commentary upon Jefferson's administration.[35]

The immediate effect of Plumer's transfer from New Hampshire to Washington was to make him even more fanatically Federalist than he had been in 1798. He had never seen so many Democrats in one place before; and these were not only numerous but domineering. "I can do little good here," he wrote to the Federalists at home. "I am, as I expected, in the minority, & all the service I can perform for my country, is of the negative kind." [36] Few administration measures met with his approval, chiefly because he had previously determined to oppose them. Jefferson's message of December 14, which reported a full treasury, a diminishing debt, increased revenues, and widespread prosperity, brought no satisfaction to Plumer.[37] To John Norris, a wealthy Salem merchant, he wrote that "the mass of the people have not talents or information to discover that our flourishing condition is the result of Federal measures. It is, to us, a humiliating consideration that whilst the present administration are reaping what we sowed, they should employ themselves in censuring those measures, & receiving applause from the populace that they do not merit." [38]

---

34. *Plumer's Memorandum,* 313-21.

35. Unfortunately, posterity was virtually unaware of the existence of the three bulky manuscripts in which Plumer kept this journal until Professor Everett Somerville Brown of the University of Michigan edited and published the major portion of it in 1923. Henry Adams and Edward Channing could have made good use of this treasure. Still more unfortunate, however, has been the tendency of many writers since 1923 to ignore Brown's easily accessible edition and to depend, as Adams was forced to do, upon William Plumer, Jr.'s biography, which contains very little of the Senate journal and misquotes much of what it does include.

36. Plumer to Oliver Peabody, Dec. 22, 1802, Letter Book, I, Lib. Cong.

37. James Richardson, *Messages and Papers of the Presidents* (Wash., 1896-99), I, 342-46.

38. Plumer to John Norris, Dec. 20, 1802, Letter Book, I, Lib. Cong.

In some respects Plumer even exceeded his party in opposing the administration. Jefferson, the reputed Anglophobe, had suggested a mutual abolition of discriminatory duties between Great Britain and the United States, but Plumer, supposedly an Anglophile, fearing that Jefferson's actual purpose was to injure the commercial states and destroy the merchant marine, opposed the conciliatory gesture. Plumer also took it into his head to contest the administration's Indian policy, although even his brother Federalists considered him eccentric in this respect. His idea was that Jefferson's friendly purchases were pretexts for exterminating the unfortunate red men, although he subsequently changed his mind and decided that they were doomed to extinction anyway.[39] He voted regularly, and usually alone, against all Indian treaties.

On the other hand, Plumer voted with the Republicans for the repeal of the Bankruptcy Act. This law had been enacted by the Adams administration and was a favorite measure with the Hamiltonian Federalists. Plumer, however, had himself lost more than a thousand dollars in the operation of the law and he was as bitter against it as any Virginia planter.[40] He believed that it was defective, lacked adequate penalties, and was so vague as to baffle the courts, an opinion with which Judge Smith heartily agreed.[41] But Plumer's chief criticism, in which the Virginians concurred, was that the law was written solely for the benefit of merchants, and did nothing to aid hard-pressed farmers, land speculators, or industrialists. In discussing the merits of a repeal, Gouverneur Morris suggested to Plumer that, since it had been a Federalist measure, Federalists were bound to defend it. Plumer could not see that it had any connection with party politics and refused to be thus guided in his decision. On the final vote in the Senate, Republican merchants joined with seaport Federalists against repeal, while Plumer, of Federalist, agricultural New Hampshire, stood with Virgina planters and Kentucky frontiersmen to carry it.[42]

39. Plumer to Edward Livermore, Dec. 21, 1802, *ibid.;* Plumer, Autobiography, 102. A recent biographer of Jefferson confirms Plumer's opinion of the President's Indian policy. "While paying lip service to peace, justice and friendship," he says, "Jefferson's graduated steps for dealing with the Indians envisaged a cynical and effective procedure for getting rid of them that held little of these abstract principles and had only expediency to commend it." Nathan Schachner, *Thomas Jefferson, a Biography* (N. Y., 1951), II, 731-32.

40. Plumer, Autobiography, 124-25.

41. Jeremiah Smith to Plumer, Feb. 14, 1803, Plumer Papers, N. H. State Lib. See also Charles Warren, *Bankruptcy in United States History* (Cambridge, 1935), 19-20.

42. Plumer to Edward Livermore, Dec. 24, 1803, Letter Book, III, Lib. Cong.; Plumer, Autobiography, 125; *Plumer's Memorandum,* 86.

Plumer's continual letter-writing in Washington was an exercise in conscious propaganda. He later admitted that too many of his letters "were declamatory, & written with a view to support the interest of party," but he felt that the principal service he could render his country was to thwart the measures of the majority.[43] This is rather a mild apology for the persistent skill with which Plumer sounded the tocsin of alarm. The Republicans can do nothing but destroy, he wrote. They repeal tax laws and boast of economy, but they have not brought a single cent into the treasury. Congress is kept idle at enormous expense so that the southern Episcopalians can celebrate a pagan holy day on December 25.[44] The administration will exterminate the Indians "under the friendly pretence of *protecting & providing for them, by treaties,* as Bonaparte does of Switzerland." Jefferson tells the people that they have the quiet enjoyment of religion, yet he invites an impious blasphemer to quarter himself in the White House. "Heaven grant him as much of *Payne* as he justly merits," mis-punned Plumer.[45] Fortunately for the country, a Federalist minority, with "the weight of talents, respectability & application to business," prevented the destroyers from doing greater mischief.[46] "The Ministerialists now see, that tho' a rude hand may demolish the wisdom & labour of ages, it requires skill & superior genius to support the administration of a government, whose base is public opinion." [47] The Republicans feared superior Federalist talent on the one hand and the wrath of the people on the other; that is why they had apparently declared a moratorium on their revolution. But this inaction, of itself, was ominous, Plumer believed. "The prospect of public affairs is gloomy to a federalist. Of many things of which I was informed in New England *the one half was not told me.* The federalists have the weight of talent and property; but unless they are more attentive & industrious their talents & wealth will not save them from the ravages of demoralizing democracy." [48]

The most amazing thing about this alarmist propaganda is that it was written, as Plumer acknowledged, at a time when there was almost

---

43. Plumer, Autobiography, 103.
44. Plumer to David Lawrence, Dec. 27, 1802, Plumer Papers, N. H. Hist. Soc. This is a small collection of letters, chiefly to members of the family. Plumer to Mrs. Sarah Plumer, Dec. 25, 1802, Plumer Papers, N. H. State Lib.
45. Plumer to Jeremiah Smith, Dec. 28, to Edward Livermore, Dec. 21, 1802, Letter Book, I, Lib. Cong.
46. Plumer to John T. Gilman, Jan. 16, 1803, Plumer Papers, N. H. State Lib.
47. Plumer to Nicholas Emery, Jan. 6, 1803, Letter Book, I, Lib. Cong.
48. Plumer to Edward Livermore, Dec. 21, 1802, *ibid.*

nothing to disturb the prosperity and calm of public affairs. A Federalist had to exercise all his ingenuity to find an issue upon which to quarrel with the administration, and he was usually forced to resort either to the memory of crimes already committed or to vague forebodings of evil. The only cloud appearing upon Jefferson's horizon was the rumor, of which Plumer had obtained confirmation on December 14 from the lips of Jefferson himself, that the Spanish Intendant of Louisiana had closed the port of New Orleans against American commerce.[49] Since it was generally known that Spain had retroceded Louisiana to France, Plumer assumed that the Intendant's order had originated with Napoleon. It was obvious to Plumer that if the Emperor were to occupy the western bank of the Mississippi and seal up the mouth of the river, "he might then become a dangerous neighbor; & make a grant of such exclusive priviledges to the western states as might detach them from the union, or what would be nearly as fatal to our repose, make them dependent on him, & hostile to us." [50] Yet in spite of this imminent catastrophe, President Jefferson had notified Congress only of the Spanish order, which he called an "irregular proceeding." "Gracious Heaven," Plumer exclaimed to Smith, "is this the dignified language of the President of the United States, to the representatives of the nation, upon the subject of Spain's violating its solemn treaty engagements!... Is your pride flattered, or your ambition raised by being a citizen of a free country governed by such choice spirits?" [51]

President Jefferson fully appreciated the perils of this critical situation and undoubtedly felt more sincere interest in the Westerners' plight than did New England Federalists. Yet, sincere or not, the congressional minority, in this crisis, had a program that seemed to conform more nearly to the hard realities of international politics than did Jefferson's hopeful idealism. Plumer explained and justified their policy in a letter to the Reverend Peter Holt, his clerical ally in Epping.

Your ideas of the infraction of the Spanish treaty are correct. That infraction is an evil of great magnitude. The population of the western states is increasing with astonishing rapidity. There is now near half a million of people who reside west of the Allegheney mountains. Their soil is luxuriant & is in fact the Eden of the United States. The Mississippi is the only practicable highway they have for near 300 miles in which they can carry their immense produce to market. The boats in

49. Plumer to Jeremiah Smith, Jan. 9, 1803, *ibid.*
50. Plumer, Autobiography, 105.
51. Plumer to Jeremiah Smith, Jan. 9, 1803, Letter Book, I, Lib. Cong.

which they freight it down the river are incapable of proceeding to a foreign market; this renders it necessary that they should have a place of deposit near the mouth of the river. This place Spain was bound to provide, but regardless of its plighted faith, that nation has not only shut up New Orleans, but have prohibited their people in that country from having any trade or connection with us. We ought to have seized that city & held it as a place of deposit. This we could have done with ease, as the Spaniards are now incapable of resisting us. This would have been a spirit worthy of an independent, but injured nation, & would have given aid to negotiation. It is a moment favorable to such an enterprise. There is no doubt Bonaparte owns that country; and while his ambition is aiming to humiliate the pride & destroy the opposing power of Great Britain, he would not willingly pursue a line of conduct that would compel the United States to become his enemy. But if we lose this opportunity, I fear he will take posession, erect his triumphant standard, & extend his settlements on those shores.[52]

In spite of its chauvinism, this program seemed logical and realistic. A similar show of spirit had succeeded against the same power in 1799. In dealing with such unscrupulous persons as Napoleon, a *fait accompli* would be more convincing than a protestation of outraged innocence. President Jefferson, however, rejected a forcible solution of the problem and staked the security of his country upon Napoleon's cupidity. Fortunately for him and for the United States, there occurred an unforeseen miracle which triumphantly vindicated his judgment and placed the obloquy of obstructionism upon the Federalists.

Senator Plumer joined his Federalist friends in attempting to block virtually every step of Jefferson's program. He and they opposed the appointment of James Monroe as a special envoy to France on the specious ground that, as a former Jacobin sympathizer, he would be "obnoxious to Napoleon." Plumer then vigorously supported the inflammatory resolutions in which the Federalists insisted upon the immediate seizure of New Orleans.[53] During the debate on these resolutions, however, he again displayed his characteristic independence of party discipline. Senator Mason of Virginia, who was seriously ill, asked for an adjournment in the late evening, and Plumer supported him, even though the Federalist caucus had decided to continue the session until

52. Plumer to Peter Holt, Feb. 24, 1803, Plumer Papers, N. H. State Lib.
53. Plumer, Autobiography, 105, 106. Arthur Whitaker, in *The Mississippi Question, 1795-1803* (N. Y., 1934), maintains that Federalist chauvinism was merely an insincere attempt to embarrass Jefferson, but however it may have been for some Federalists, Plumer supported the Ross resolutions in good faith.

a vote was taken. Since Plumer's defection carried the motion for adjournment, he was severely censured by Gouverneur Morris, and a sharp exchange between the two men ensued. Morris ended by warning Plumer that no politician could follow such an independent course and remain in office. "Then, as a politician I shall fail, & return to private life again," answered the forthright Yankee.[54]

The Federalist gambit was ultimately defeated by the disciplined Republican majority, and President Jefferson was given a free hand and a $4,000,000 appropriation to negotiate a settlement.[55] In later years, blessed with the knowledge that all had ended well, Plumer admitted the superior wisdom of the President's policy. "I thot the conduct of the president & house were timid & pusillanimous, & frankly condemned it. I did not then perceive that was the only course to open the door for reconciliation, without wounding the pride of either nation; & that after we requested Spain to disavow the conduct of her officers & restore our rights, if she should refuse, that would be an effectual mean of uniting our citizens in resorting to war." But he also believed that Federalist bluster and belligerence had been useful. "These proceedings had a salutary effect both at home & abroad. They afforded conclusive evidence to our executive, & to the governments of France & Spain that both parties would unite in war to defend our rights against the encroachments of other nations." [56]

Plumer approached the end of his first senatorial session in a state of deep depression. It was discouraging to be defeated on every roll call by the same exasperating margin, and Plumer did not fail to notice that the victorious majority came from the South and West. Jefferson's success was gall and wormwood to the unyielding Federalist partisans, and it was all the more bitter because it seemed to be sectional. Plumer was infected with the prejudice and pessimism of his New England boardinghouse companions. Thus his letters began to take on a cutting edge. "The profligacy of manners, & the vices, of the southern people, in general far exceed my expectations," he wrote to a friend in Epping.[57] Hence it was easy to conclude that a Southern administration's popularity proceeded from vice rather than virtue. "How contemptible and

54. For an interesting example of progressive elaboration, compare this account with those of the incident in Plumer, Jr., *Life of Plumer,* 254, and in Claude Bowers, *Jefferson in Power* (Boston, 1936), 180.

55. *Debates and Proceedings in the Congress of the United States, 1789-1824* (Washington, 1834-56), 7th Cong., 2d Sess., 103-4 (hereafter cited as *Annals of Congress*).

56. Plumer, Autobiography, 106, 107.

57. Plumer to Joseph Sheppard, Jan. 3, 1803, Letter Book, I, Lib. Cong.

wretched," he declaimed to Smith, "is the man, who, at the expence of honor & conscience, obtains an office, & cannot then pursue his own opinion, but must adopt such measures as will please the unthinking populace! From such a disposition, & from such an office thus obtained, *Good Lord, deliver me!*" [58] In a letter to Livermore, lately displaced by the fervently hated Sherburne, Plumer waxed sarcastic. "Are you so unreasonable as to expect an impure fountain will send forth sweet water! If the head is sick, & the heart corrupt, can you expect health & soundness in the members?" [59]

From this fixation in regard to Southern wickedness, Plumer proceeded to the logical inference that virtue resided only in the other end of the Union. "The good sense & steady habits of those [New England] States will be the mean of preserving our liberties, if they are to survive the violence of party," he assured his constituents. Another letter added party to sectional prejudice: "I consider the steady habits & federalism of the eastern States as the sheet anchor & political salvation of the nation." Such reasoning led to a conclusion that, in the face of Federalist contempt for democracy and Republican faith in the people, was startling. "If a free elective government is to be maintained for any length of time, it will owe its support to the federalism of New England." [60]

As the new year dawned and the March elections drew near, Plumer determined to do all that he could to preserve at least the Federalism of New Hampshire. On January 3, he wrote to Joseph Sheppard of Epping, urging him to offer himself as a candidate for the legislature. "I am more fully confirmed in the necessity of electing federalists into office in New England," he said, and explained carefully how a determined minority could be the saving remnant in a composite nation.[61] There followed letters to his brothers and prominent citizens in Epping, urging support for Sheppard. One to the Reverend Peter Holt is particularly interesting as a specimen of a communication from a deistical senator to a Calvinist divine on topics of mutual political interest. After explaining the particular reasons why it was imperative for Epping to have a Federalist representative, Plumer said: "I think it would be sound policy to sit up Mr. Sheppard; Quakers & Baptists would unite for him, & if the Congregational federalists would join, he would be chosen.... I do not wish you to do anything that should in the least affect your use-

---

58. Plumer to Jeremiah Smith, Jan. 9, 1803, *ibid.*
59. Plumer to Edward Livermore, Jan. 13, 1803, *ibid.*
60. Plumer to David Lawrence, Dec. 27, 1802, to Joseph Sheppard, Jan. 3, 1803, *ibid.*
61. Plumer to Sheppard, Jan. 3, 1803, *ibid.*

fullness with the people. But, perhaps, you may with safety communicate your opinion to some confidential friend, say Major Sanborn." [62]

Plumer had also turned his attention to the gubernatorial contest in New Hampshire. On January 16, he wrote a long letter to his "friend," John Taylor Gilman, enjoining the Governor, for the sake of New England Federalism, to remain the candidate of his party. Jefferson, he warned, had endorsed John Langdon as "a true '76 patriot," and he urged Gilman to see that the state militia was kept at full strength, since "our military strength & preparations will have an influence upon the measures of the Southern States." [63] But Plumer really opened his heart on this subject to Oliver Peabody, whom, five years previously, he had accused of gambling with the state's money. "You may be assured the Administration are anxious for the destruction of New England federalism. . . . Tis not a change of men only but of measures that they seek; their System . . . is directed not only agt. public, but private, virtue. . . . It is impossible to say how far the Republicans would proceed in their wild measures were it not for their fear of uniting New England agt. them." [64]

Plumer's fears for New Hampshire were well founded, but premature. Leaving Washington early on the morning of March 4, he reached Epping before the annual meeting had taken place, but his interest in politics was effaced by a family sorrow. His father died early in the morning following his homecoming. It is therefore unlikely that he attended the town meeting, where his candidate failed to be elected to the legislature. But he could take satisfaction in the general results of the state elections. Although John Langdon had assured Jefferson that the Federalists "sicken at the sight of our prosperity" and had promised great things, Langdon's time had not yet come. [65] Gilman was re-elected by a greater majority than in 1802, [66] and the Federalists won both branches of the legislature, which held a deliberately short and innocuous session in June. Plumer spent a pleasant summer in Epping reading, receiving visits, and collecting his debts. It was an interlude of serenity. On the national scene, however, tensions were mounting, for war was momentarily expected in Europe and the fate of New Orleans was still unknown. Each party girded itself for the inevitable struggle when Congress would assemble in November.

62. Plumer to Peter Holt, Feb. 24, 1803, Plumer Papers, N. H. State Lib.
63. Plumer to John T. Gilman, Jan. 16, 1803, *ibid.*
64. Plumer to Oliver Peabody, Jan. 31, 1803, *ibid.*
65. Langdon to Jefferson, Jan 26, 1803, Jefferson Papers, CXXIX, Lib. Cong.
66. Lyon, ed., *New Hampshire Register . . . 1860*, 41.

CHAPTER VII

Constitutional Issues

"My fears, for the fate of New England, are quieted only by my unshaken confidence in that Divine Providence that has done so much for her." [1]

O N Independence Day in 1803, President Jefferson startled the infant republic by announcing that it had suddenly doubled its territorial extent. Senator Plumer and his colleagues were summoned to special session in October for the ratification of the treaty by which Louisiana had been purchased. Federalist policy in regard to this incredible piece of diplomatic luck was immediately laid down in the party press; it was to be determined opposition, a fight to the death at each barricade against the combined power of a political majority and public opinion. It seems impossible to modern Americans, fully cognizant of what the trans-Mississippi area has contributed to the nation, that men who opposed the annexation of this territory could have been either honest or patriotic. The Federalists were both, even though they may have been mistaken. For the impartial consideration which their position deserves, the contemporary opinions of Plumer are particularly instructive.

The President had moved with almost reckless assurance after the treaty came to his hands. He had allowed the Senate only thirteen days in which to ratify. These were more than sufficient at a time when the majority was thoroughly disciplined, the minority reduced to a mere handful, and the filibuster not yet invented. [2] Three days after the treaty had been laid before it, the Senate advised its ratification, twenty-four to seven, with one Federalist, Jonathan Dayton of New Jersey, voting yes. That night, Plumer recorded the reasons for his vote against the

1. Plumer to Jedediah Morse, Nov. 28, 1803, Gratz Collection, Historical Society of Pennsylvania.
2. "Congress is not so respectable as ... last year," wrote Plumer to Jeremiah Mason, Nov. 19, 1803, Plumer Papers, N. H. State Lib.

treaty. He found an impressive array of defects in this memorable document.

Plumer noted that the stock created for the purchase of Louisiana increased the national debt by 50 per cent, and he questioned whether value had been received for the money. "In the course of debate," Plumer wrote, "it was confidently affirmed that the vacant unoccupied lands, to which the United States would acquire the right of sail, were of much greater value than the purchase sum. But on that point, opinions were formed more from conjecture than knowledge. We were ignorant of what grants of land, & to what extent, had been made to individuals, during the different periods which that country was in the possession of France, Spain, & Great Britain." [3]

Even more disturbing than the uncertainty of value was the uncertainty of title. Whether France had owned the territory she ceded to the United States, Plumer noted, depended altogether upon the terms of the secret treaty of "St. Idelphonso" by which Spain had retroceded it in 1800, but "the Senate were not indulged with a view of that treaty." The Spanish minister, the Marquis d'Yrujo, had entered a caveat in the name of his king against ratification by the United States, alleging that the stipulations of San Ildefonso had never been carried out by France, "& that this treaty is founded in the *breach* of faith on the part of that nation." Since the Spanish minister presumably knew the terms of San Ildefonso while Plumer did not, the Senator might be excused for believing that his country had merely purchased a "simple *quit claim*" from France, and that "if Spain has not given a good title to France, this treaty has given none to us." [4] Coupled with the fact that the Spaniards were still indubitably possessed of Louisiana and that Napoleon was in no position to drive them out, d'Yrujo's protests sounded rather grim to the Federalists—and to some Republicans as well.[5] It would have been unfortunate for Jefferson's reputation if the administration, after spending $15,000,000 for it, had been forced to seize New Orleans after all, as the Federalists had advised the previous winter.

These objections, although weighty, would not have troubled the Federalists if they had themselves negotiated the treaty. They were rationalizations that grew out of a sectional inferiority complex and merely

3. Plumer, Autobiography, 111. Plumer was in error, of course, in naming Great Britain as a possessor of Louisiana.

4. *Plumer's Memorandum,* 4, 5.

5. Gallatin had suggested in September that forces be prepared to seize New Orleans in case Spain refused to surrender it. Henry Adams, ed., *The Writings of Albert Gallatin* (Phila., 1879), I, 152-53.

bolstered that fundamental grievance. "Admit this western world into the union," wrote Plumer candidly, "& you destroy with a single operation the whole weight & importance of the eastern states in the *scale* of politics. That portion of your *present* Union is inhabited by a hardy brave race of men. They know their importance, . . . and they have too much pride tamely to shrink into a state of insignificance. Adopt not the ruinous measure that will precipitate them to erect a separate & independent Empire." [6]

Plumer thought the eastern states would, by the contractual principles upon which the Union was founded, be entirely justified in secession if the terms of the treaty were carried out. The Union, he said, was like a company in trade, consisting of several partners. "And with as much propriety might a *new* partner be admitted, & the *firm* of the old company changed, without the consent of each of the old partners, as to admit a new State, formed from without the limits of the original territory, into the Union, without the previous consent of each State." [7]

What would the South say to an arbitrary annexation of Canada and Nova Scotia? Even without Louisiana, the country was too large and the settlements too sparse for security. A republican government depends upon close communication between the people in every part; the farther it is extended the more its energies are dissipated. "A piece of our coin, an eagle, may be extended to the size of a coach wheel, but its beauty & use will be destroyed." [8] History and reason showed that a republican government could not be maintained long over such a vast territory.[9] It would inevitably break up, and the moment of dissolution might precipitate civil war or dictatorship.

Plumer's strongest, if not his most sincere, argument against the treaty was that it was unconstitutional. In an hour's conversation with Plumer, Jefferson himself had declared that the treaty could not be made legal until an amendment admitting Louisiana to the original Union had been added to the Constitution. The majority of the Republicans, however, considered this a metaphysical argument and proceeded

6. *Plumer's Memorandum,* 9. It is obvious that Plumer prepared these notes for a speech in the Senate but decided not to deliver it.

7. *Ibid.,* 8. Josiah Quincy repeated this argument against the actual admission of Louisiana into the Union in 1812.

8. *Ibid.,* 6.

9. The man sent to purchase Louisiana had written in 1786 to the man who sent him that even the eastern part of the Mississippi Valley would never be inhabited. James Monroe to Thomas Jefferson, Jan. 19, 1786, Stanislaus Hamilton, ed., *The Writings of James Monroe* (N. Y., 1898-1903), I, 117-18.

on the principle that the treaty-making power transcended constitutional limitations. The Federalists in general took their stand somewhere between these two extremes. Plumer had no doubt that the United States could acquire new territory by conquest or purchase and establish a military or colonial government therein, but not state governments, as the treaty had stipulated.[10]

These were abstruse and partisan concepts, but Plumer also had explicit objections to the treaty on constitutional grounds. The Constitution authorized Congress to establish a uniform rule of naturalization, and it had done so; but the treaty, without regard to that rule, naturalized "a whole people by a single operation." [11] The Constitution declared that duties should be uniform throughout the United States and that no preference should be given one port over another, yet the treaty exempted French and Spanish shipping in New Orleans from foreign port duties for twelve years. Of course, New England Federalists feared the effect of this provision upon their section's commerce, but their argument had a general validity since it had been to prevent such jealousies that the Constitution forbade preferential treatment of one port over another. In November, Plumer explained his vote against the treaties to his brother on the ground that he "considered a ratification of those instruments as a direct violation of that Constitution [he] had bound [himself] by the strongest obligations to maintain." [12]

While much of Plumer's argument was defensible, a great deal more was mere partisan spite. He thought that the American envoys had been gulled by clever Frenchmen, but at the same time accused Monroe of having willingly paid an inordinate sum to Napoleon for use against England. He complained because all the expense of keeping Louisiana would be drawn from the commerce of the Eastern states, while any benefits derived would accrue to the South. He perceived a diabolical scheme of some kind in Napoleon's insistence upon the incorporation of the inhabitants into the United States—what did he care for the Creoles? —perhaps he wished to embroil the country with Spain, or introduce his spies into its councils, or leave an excuse to reoccupy the territory or pick a fight with the United States sometime in the future. If the President could *purchase* new states without the consent of the old, what

10. Plumer to John Quincy Adams, Apr. 4, 1829, William Plumer Letters, VIII (1817-33), Plumer Papers, Lib. Cong. (hereafter cited as Letter Book, VIII) ; Everett Brown, *A Constitutional History of the Louisiana Purchase* (Berkeley, Cal., 1920), 23-25; *Plumer's Memorandum,* 12.

11. *Plumer's Memorandum,* 10.

12. Plumer to Daniel Plumer, Nov. 22, 1803, Letters, 1802-7, Lib. Cong.

was to prevent him from *selling* an old state without its consent? How could the inhabitants of Louisiana *"enjoy all* the rights . . . of citizens," if none of them could be elected to the presidency? No demand had been made upon Spain for the treaty violation in withdrawing the right of deposit at New Orleans. "We have an Executive whose measures are better calculated to invite insults than to resent them . . . to drain our Treasury than to maintain the honor & glory of the nation." [13] There was much more in this strain of rambling invective, which only emphasized the helpless despondency that seized Plumer as he saw Virginia's influence extend to the Rocky Mountains.

Plumer's gloom was projected in the face of well-nigh universal satisfaction over the purchase of Louisiana. His vote against ratification earned him no plaudits from the Federalists in New Hampshire, and he was forced to defend it against the criticism of his own brother. After two decades of experience had proved that Jefferson had gambled shrewdly, Plumer finally confessed that "the purchase of Louisiana, has proved thus far beneficial & of great importance to the United States, & that it was a fortunate circumstance that we obtained peaceable possession of that vast territory. But was the business to be again decided, I could not vote for the treaty. I consider the constitution as obligatory, & that I am not [at] liberty to dispense with its injunctions, or from motives of expedience, or public interest infringe its principles." [14]

The actual struggle over Louisiana in Congress began after the treaty was ratified in the debate over legislation necessary to implement its provisions. On October 26, the Senate passed a bill authorizing the President to take possession of Louisiana, with the six Federalists from New England offering the only opposition. This act gave Jefferson dictatorial power in the new territory until Congress established a permanent government. Plumer considered it unconstitutional. "Had such a bill been passed by federalists, the Democrats would have denounced it as *monarchal*," he grumbled, "but when enacted by the *exclusive friends* of the people, it is pure *republicanism*." [15]

In November, the House bill creating the necessary bonds for the purchase came to the Senate. Federalist leaders fought savagely against it, but Plumer, influenced perhaps by John Quincy Adams's strong stand, joined him and the Republicans in voting for the appropriations. It was the first time Senator Plumer had dissented from his party in a

13. *Plumer's Memorandum*, 11, 13.
14. Plumer, Autobiography, 114-15.
15. *Plumer's Memorandum*, 27.

really important issue, and it gave him much uneasiness. Some of his Federalist friends delicately suggested that he should be guided by their more extensive experience, but Plumer remained obdurate.[16] "A large majority of the Senate have, contrary to my opinion, declared the Instrument a treaty," he reasoned. "I think I am not at liberty to withhold my vote upon the ground either that the treaty is unconstitutional, or its a bad bargain. . . . Perish the eleven millions of stock; but preserve the *faith* of the nation." [17]

The final act in the drama of the Louisiana Purchase was the organization of the region into territorial governments, and the only substantial record of the long Senate debate on this issue is the one that Senator Plumer jotted down each night in his journal.[18] Since the bill provided a government for the first foreign colony acquired by the United States, it established important precedents, but little was known about the conflicts and compromises from which these precedents emerged until Plumer's account was published. The debate proceeded with reckless inconsistency and conflict along geographical lines, often in defiance of political loyalties. Frontier democrats bitterly assailed the "system of tyranny, destructive of elective rights" which the administration proposed for Louisiana. New Englanders and Georgians quarreled rancorously over slavery in the new territory. Senators from the upper South voted against the foreign importation of slaves into Louisiana but stoutly defended the treaty rights of the Creoles to retain their slave property. John Quincy Adams said that their motives were as clear "as if they had had the window in the breast," [19] but Plumer spelled it out more specifically: "It is obvious that the zeal displayed by the Senate [sic] from the Slave States, to prohibit the foreign importation of Slaves into Louisiana, proceeds from the motive to raise the price of their own slaves in the markett—& to encrease the means of disposing

16. *Annals of Congress,* 8th Cong., 1st Sess., 65-73; Plumer, Autobiography, 116.

17. *Plumer's Memorandum,* 31-32.

18. Neither the *Annals of Congress* nor the *Memoirs of John Quincy Adams* (see below, n. 19) contain anything like an adequate report of this debate. Henry Adams, who knew nothing of Plumer's Memorandum, wrote that "Few gaps in the parliamentary history of the Union left so serious a want as was caused by the failure to report the Senate debate on this Bill." Henry Adams, *History of the United States During the Administrations of Jefferson and Madison* (N. Y., 1890-91), II, 123. Plumer's long report of this debate shows that it was fully as important as Adams supposed. Professor Everett Brown printed this portion of the Memorandum in the *Amer. Hist. Rev.,* 22 (1916-17), 340-64. It appears in *Plumer's Memorandum,* 107-40.

19. Charles Francis Adams, ed., *Memoirs of John Quincy Adams* (Phila., 1874-77), I, 293 (hereafter cited as *Adams's Memoirs*).

of those who are most turbulent & dangerous to them." [20] The much-amended Breckinridge Bill for the government of Louisiana finally passed with only one Republican, and four New Englanders, including Plumer, voting against it.[21] The Federalists, in spite of their vociferous opposition to the bill, did not suggest a better one. Only John Quincy Adams seemed to sense that the conflict of cultures in New Orleans would require an adjustment more delicate than rough-and-ready Americanism. The fundamental Federalist objection was revealed by Plumer in a letter written for publication in a Newburyport paper: "This [bill] gives an encreased weight of patronage to the Executive; & lays a foundation to make new States. These new States, if we may judge from those lately made, will prove so many satellites moving round & subordinate to Virginia. The weight & influence of New England, in the councils & legislation of the Union, will soon be reduced to a cypher." [22]

What seems now to have been a disproportionate amount of time was spent by both the Seventh and Eighth Congresses on the subject of the Twelfth Amendment to the Constitution. It was obvious even to contemporaries that the rise of political parties had rendered nugatory the principle of judicious selection upon which the founding fathers had based the electoral college. Yet the introduction of an amendment designed to eliminate such accidents as Burr's near-election to the presidency touched off an interminable debate and revived a quarrel that had almost wrecked the Constitutional Convention. It aroused Plumer's interest more than any of the momentous questions debated in the Senate during his five-year attendance, and it elicited the one great oratorical effort of his career. No matter how trivial the struggle over the Twelfth Amendment may seem in retrospect, it was regarded as fundamental by contemporaries.

The Republicans were eager to push the amendment through Congress and have it ratified in time for the November elections in 1804, yet they could not safely introduce the measure until the autumn of 1803, when they finally had the essential two-thirds majority in the Senate. No sooner was Congress assembled in October than resolutions for the amendment were introduced in both houses. The Senate resolution was written by DeWitt Clinton, who insisted that he had given it much

20. *Plumer's Memorandum,* 11-12, 115-16, 130. Professor Brown has an excellent analysis of this debate over the extension of slavery in his *Constitutional History of the Louisiana Purchase.* His discussion is based chiefly on *Plumer's Memorandum.*
21. *Annals of Congress,* 8th Cong., 1st Sess., 256.
22. Plumer to John Park, Dec. 10, 1803, Plumer Papers, N. H. State Lib.

study. After a brief discussion, the Senate discovered that Clinton's resolution involved an absurdity in supposing that two candidates for the presidency might each have a majority of the electoral votes and that it was defective in not requiring a majority vote for the Vice-President. These errors gave the Federalists good grounds for urging reference of the resolution to a committee, and although the motion was vigorously opposed as a needless delay by senators whose legislatures were then in session, it prevailed by a single vote.[23]

The Republican majority now sought immediate acceptance of a new committee report, and the Federalist minority shrewdly protested against such unseemly haste. Senator Plumer said he had heard much complaint against the omnipotence of the British parliament, but he was now actually seeing "the overbearing precipitate spirit of a triumphant majority" in action. In the midst of this debate, DeWitt Clinton suddenly deprived his party of its two-thirds majority by resigning in order to take office as mayor of New York. Republican urgency thereupon turned into glacial deliberation, and for nearly a month, until another senator arrived to restore their dominance, the majority suffered the humiliation of Federalist taunts at their unwillingness to introduce their own resolutions.[24]

On November 22, the committee finally reported resolutions for an amendment requiring that electors should designate their votes for President and Vice-President respectively and that the House of Representatives should choose from the three highest candidates, rather than from five, on occasions when an electoral majority was lacking. The report precipitated an eight-day wrangle, which a reporter characterized as "tedious, intricate, and desultory . . . very difficult to follow, and often to comprehend." [25] To some extent, division followed small state versus large state lines rather than political affiliation. Senator John Quincy Adams of Massachusetts had originally favored the designating principle,[26] but he came to believe that the amendment was unfair to the small states and asked if they could produce no champion to vindicate their rights. It may have been the stimulus of this challenge that brought

23. Plumer to Peter Holt, Feb. 24, 1803, *ibid.; Annals of Congress,* 8th Cong., 1st Sess., 16, 372; *Plumer's Memorandum,* 15-16.

24. *Plumer's Memorandum,* 22, 26, 32-33.

25. *Annals of Congress,* 8th Cong., 1st Sess., 81.

26. Much to the disgust of his New Hampshire colleague. "Federalism as well as Religion, is sometimes *wounded in the house of its friends,*" Plumer complained with pretended piety to the Reverend Jedediah Morse, Nov. 28, 1803, Gratz Coll., Pa. Hist. Soc.

Plumer to his feet on December 2 to make the most complete statement for the opposition that appeared in the debate.[27]

The senator from New Hampshire, prosaic as usual, opened with a full investigation of the methods prescribed by the Constitution for its own amendment. The object of the founding fathers, he believed, had been to make amendment as difficult as possible in order to preclude dangerous innovations. Yet, in the present case, these wise restrictions were being ignored by a ruthless majority. The Constitution stated that amendments might be proposed by two-thirds of both houses of Congress. Such an amendment had been introduced, but its form had been changed and the proposition robbed completely of its original character by simple majority vote. Now that the deformed resolution was approaching a final vote, Plumer insisted that a two-thirds majority of the entire Senate, not simply of the senators present, was required for passage. If this were not the proper construction of the Constitution, he said, it would be possible for twelve senators, representing only six states, but being a two-thirds majority of a quorum, to carry an amendment actually opposed by the remaining twenty-two, constituting two-thirds of the Senate. Plumer's argument on this point was mathematically correct, but ingenuous. The Senate consisted of nine Federalists and twenty-five Republicans, but two of the Republicans were absent and one was voting against the amendment. Preliminary calculations had indicated that the final vote would be twenty-two to ten; hence, if the Federalists could make good their contention that a two-thirds majority of the entire Senate (twenty-three) was necessary, the amendment could be blocked.[28]

Plumer had been particularly annoyed because several senators, especially from small states, had expressed personal doubts as to the desirability of the amendment but declared that they were bound in its favor by instructions from their state legislatures.[29] Plumer now vigorously attacked the entire theory on which this position rested: "If these instructions are obligatory, we are mere machines—& our votes on this important question must be governed not by the propriety of the measure, or the conviction of our own judgments, but by the sovereign

27. Plumer's speech is greatly condensed in the *Annals of Congress*, 8th Cong., 1st Sess., 153-56. He gives it in full in his own *Memorandum*, where it occupies 27 printed pages.
28. *Plumer's Memorandum*, 46-50.
29. Plumer, Autobiography, 123-24.

mandates of State Legislatures." [30] Thinking, possibly, of former occasions, when, as a member of the New Hampshire legislature he had voted to instruct senators, Plumer admitted that the practice was sometimes permissible, but certainly not in the present instance. The legislatures were now demanding the submission of a question to themselves; as if a petit jury were to demand from a grand jury the indictment of a certain individual and then were to condemn him. The Constitution provided that amendments should originate in Congress and be ratified by the state legislatures, but this measure had been intiated by the ratifiers and had left the proper originating body nothing to do but rubber-stamp the proposal. Plumer suggested, rather vaguely, that this case required the alternative process of amending by convention rather than by Congress and legislatures.

Proponents of the resolution had made much of the New Hampshire legislature's demand for this very amendment in 1798. Plumer met this challenge explicitly. Neither New Hampshire, he declared, nor any other state in the Union had asked for such provisions as had been added to this resolution. Then Plumer added that his state had acted too hastily in 1798, and that he himself had not understood what he was doing when he voted for that resolution. "I think it more noble and dignified for a man, when convinced of his errors to renounce them, than to persist in them against the conviction of his own judgment," he added grandly.[31]

Plumer denied not only the senator's responsibility to the state legislature that elected him but to public opinion as well. He questioned whether "the noisy declamation of a few restless turbulent scribblers" actually represented public opinion; but "had the great mass of the people clearly & unequivocally expressed their opinion in favor of this resolution," there would still be no obligation upon the Senate to pass it. The whole debate, Plumer said, resolved itself into a single question. "Are *two-thirds* of the Senate convinced that the peace prosperity & security of the Union renders these amendments *necessary*. If we are not thus convinced we are bound to reject the resolution." [32]

The natural inference from this argument was that if the senators were so convinced, they would be bound to accept the resolution, yet Plumer promptly went on to say that they could not, for this amendment would destroy the Constitution. The basis of his argument was again the compact theory, requiring the agreement of all the partners to a

30. *Plumer's Memorandum,* 51.
31. *Ibid.,* 52-53.
32. *Ibid.,* 53.

change in any part of the Constitution that had been a compromise essential to the original union. "A change in the *principles* of the constitution, either by abolishing particular parts of it, or by introducing *new principles* into that important instrument, may operate as a dissolution of the Union," he warned. Could the fourth article be amended to create a new state out of Massachusetts and New Hampshire without their consent? And what "would the gentlemen from Virginia, say, if an Eastern senator should move to expunge from the Constitution the parts of it that related to slavery?" [33]

Plumer at last reached the climax of his speech. This amendment destroyed one of those subtle arrangements by which states small and large, Eastern and Southern, commercial and agricultural, free and slave, had been induced to submit to a common government. His argument merged all of these diverse elements into two great opposing parties, the small, Eastern, commercial, free states against the large, Southern and Western, agricultural, slave states. This analysis ignored the fact that the senators from Vermont and Rhode Island, small Eastern free states, favored the amendment, and those from the Southern slave states, Delaware and South Carolina, opposed it. His mind reduced the whole complex scene to a deadly rivalry between New England and Virginia, and he finally burst out into an extraordinary attack upon a compromise far more necessary to the existence of the Union than any between small and large states.

By this resolution, you destroy the *complex system* of election,— a principle which gives weight & influence to the small states, & to the eastern portion of the Union, & still retain the right, in consequence of your slaves, to the extra number of Electors & Representatives. Why should property (for such you consider *slaves*) give an increase of Electors to one portion of the Union, but in other states property is not all considered. . . . Why should the four states of Maryland, Virginia, North & South Carolina be entitled for their slaves to more than thirteen Electors & Representatives, while all the wealth of New England does not give them a single vote, even for the choice of one of those officers? . . . With propriety & truth it may be said that a constitution establishing such *unequal rights* was the work of *compromise*. And will honorable gentlemen who enjoy these *unequal priveledges* by their votes here, & those of their State Legislatures at home, render this *inequality* still greater? There is a point in *sufferance* to which men will submit; but

33. *Ibid.,* 55, 56.

beyond *that,* even cowards, will be desperate, if not brave. What the effect this inequality—this change in our constitution, will produce in New England time alone will unfold. The people of the eastern states are a brave hardy race of men—they are not insensible of their rights— and they have too much pride to be reduced tamely to a state of insignificance.[34]

Plumer's forensic tour de force was rambling, discursive, and probably dull. He spoke for two hours, at a time when the issue had already been settled, and rehearsed many an argument that the Senate had heard repeatedly. "I was much agitated & embarrassed, & pronounced [my observations] badly," he admitted. "It was the first & last set *speech* I made in the Senate." [35] Plumer had only succeeded in occupying time, and the resolution subsequently passed by more than a two-thirds majority, twenty-two to ten. Six days after leaving the Senate, the amendment was approved by the House, eighty-five to forty-two, with all four representatives from New Hampshire voting against it.[36] The transfer of a single vote in either house of Congress would have defeated the resolution.

Plumer went down fighting. On the evening before the final vote in the lower house, he wrote to Governor Gilman advising him, if possible, to adjourn the legislature before the proposed amendment reached New Hampshire. If this were not feasible, Plumer advised that a postponement until the June session would be preferable even to a hasty rejection, since the latter act would be decried as arbitrary by the opposition and could not in any case prevent the next legislature from reconsidering the amendment. His letter reflects a sincere conviction that the amendment was fatal to the state's interest and that the people would realize it to be so if they were given plenty of time to reflect. It closed with a significant statement. "If we could take from the House of Representatives the negro representation, that rotten part of the constitution, the resolution would not tomorrow pass." [37] Gilman agreed with some reluctance to Plumer's second proposal, and consideration of the amendment was postponed in New Hampshire.[38] But there were enough Republican states to provide the necessary three-fourths margin, and the amend-

34. *Ibid.,* 66-68.
35. Plumer, Autobiography, 123.
36. *Annals of Congress,* 8th Cong., 1st Sess., 776.
37. Plumer to John T. Gilman, Dec. 7, 1803, Plumer Papers, N. H. State Lib.
38. *Journal of the House of Representatives, November Session, 1803* (Concord, 1804), 122.

ment became a part of the Constitution in time to operate in the election of 1804.

In 1823, surveying the two decades since he first stated his arguments against the Twelfth Amendment, Plumer believed that he had been vindicated by experience. In the first election under the new scheme, Jefferson had chosen a political relic, the sixty-five-year-old George Clinton, as his running mate, in order to hold the Northern Democrats in alliance. Except for one term, Virginia and New York had monopolized the executive offices, and no small state had broken into the charmed circle. The office of vice-president had become a sinecure which the incumbents did not even fill; Daniel D. Tompkins had been absent from Washington during four-fifths of his term.[39]

The verdict of history has indeed been kind to the ten senators who opposed the Twelfth Amendment, necessary though it may have been. With a few notable exceptions, the vice-presidents since Aaron Burr have verified the dismal predictions of 1804.[40] The office, as Plumer foresaw, immediately became an object of political jobbery, with some tragic results in American history. Nor can it be denied that Plumer's fundamental objection to the Twelfth Amendment has been verified. In the years since 1804, very few candidates for either executive office have actually come from a small state.[41] It so happened that New Hampshire furnished one of these, but Plumer did not live quite long enough to see his own state purchased by slave-holding votes. Franklin Pierce was one of only seven New Englanders who have been elected to either of the executive offices since 1804. If the Union had indeed been, or remained, a compact between sovereign states as Plumer conceived it to be in 1804, almost every national election since that time would have justified his forebodings in regard to New England. The development of nationalism, however, rendered his statistics academic and his fears sterile. The Twelfth Amendment was in itself a strong influence toward nationalism and centralization. The paradox of the amendment is that it was sponsored by the champions of states' rights, and bitterly fought by the party of centralization and loose construction.

39. "Cincinnatus," No. 97, Plumer, *Essays,* III, 18-22, N. H. State Lib., publ. in *Literary Journal* (Concord), Jan. 1824.

40. The vice-presidency is currently undergoing a vital change which may render many of Plumer's predictions invalid.

41. In the forty elections held under the provisions of the Twelfth Amendment, from 1804 to 1960, all but 35 of the 169 candidates of the principal parties have come from the larger states of the Union. All but nine of the men elected to the presidency have come from the six largest states.

Having had what he considered sufficient evidence of Republican disposition to undermine the Constitution, it was logical in Plumer's opinion to expect an attack upon the federal courts. Plumer had come to the United States Senate convinced that "the removal of the Judges, & the destruction of the independence of the judicial department" was a cardinal point of Jeffersonian policy.[42] This program of demolition had begun, he believed, with the repeal in 1802 of the Judiciary Act by which the Adams administration had tried to preserve Federalism in the only branch of the national government not lost to it through the elections of 1800.[43] Although the Constitution decreed that judges should hold their offices during good behavior, sixteen of them were deprived of their benches by the repeal. The Federalists took the position that removing an office from a judge was as effective a method of intimidating the judiciary as removing the judge from the office, and equally unconstitutional.[44] Plumer considered the repealing statute of 1802 "a direct & palpable violation of the constitution"—an opinion which the vicissitudes of two decades did not cause him to change.[45] His friend, Jeremiah Smith, shared this conviction in 1802.[46]

Plumer sensed that the Jeffersonians would not be content with trimming the national judiciary back to its original size, and he informed his friends at home that attacks on the older judges were being planned in Democratic caucus.[47] Even he was surprised, however, when the first blow fell upon the distant head of John Pickering in New Hampshire rather than upon a judge in Washington. This was logical enough, since the Portsmouth lawyer had become an insane drunkard, clearly unable to perform his duties as a federal judge. Unfortunately, the

42. *Plumer's Memorandum,* 101.

43. In Jefferson's metaphor, the Federalist judiciary was a "battery" from which "all the works of republicanism are to be beaten down and erased." See his letter to John Dickinson, Dec. 19, 1801, Andrew Lipscomb and A. L. Bergh, eds., *The Writings of Thomas Jefferson* (Wash., 1903), X, 301-3.

44. The constitutional issues are discussed more fully in Lynn Turner, "The Impeachment of John Pickering," *Amer. Hist. Rev.,* 54 (1948-49), 485-507. Permission to use parts of the article is gratefully acknowledged.

45. Plumer to Jedediah Morse, Jan. 6, 1804, Gratz Coll., Pa. Hist. Soc.; "Cincinnatus," No. 130, in Plumer, Essays, III, 156, N. H. State Lib., publ. in *Portsmouth Journal,* May 13, 1826.

46. Morison, *Jeremiah Smith,* 148-49. See chap. 12 below for Smith's later inconsistency.

47. Plumer to Jeremiah Smith, Feb. 14, 1803, Jan. 10, 1804, Plumer Papers, N. H. State Lib.

Constitution guaranteed that federal judges should "hold their Offices during good Behaviour," and provided no other means for removing them than "Impeachment for, and Conviction of, Treason, Bribery, or other high Crimes and Misdemeanors." [48] Therefore, in order to get rid of Pickering, the strict constructionist Republicans had either brazenly to violate the Constitution or to give the term "misdemeanors" a connotation far more inclusive than its ancient common-law meaning. In either case, they enabled their loose construction opponents to pose as defenders of the Constitution in its pristine purity. The Pickering case thus became a political rather than a legal issue. Instead of standing in American history as the correct precedent for future cases of judicial impeachment, it became a tragic blunder reflecting little credit upon those connected with it.[49]

For a man like William Plumer, the Pickering impeachment posed two serious problems, neither easily susceptible to categorical solutions. The first problem was personal; Pickering had been one of New Hampshire's leading citizens and was a long-time friend.[50] Plumer had been partly responsible in 1795 for securing Pickering's appointment to the federal court. Relieved of the necessity of riding circuit and crossing ferries, the former chief justice had, for about five years after his appointment, performed his federal duties competently. His eccentricities, however, gradually sharpened into mental derangement until, by

48. Article III, Sec. 1, and Art. II, Sec. 4.
49. "So confused, contradictory, and irregular were these proceedings," declared Henry Adams, "that Pickering's trial was never considered a sound precedent. That an insane man could be guilty of crime and could be punished on *ex parte* evidence, without a hearing, without even an attorney to act in his behalf, seemed such a perversion of justice that the precedent fell dead on the spot." Adams, *History of the United States,* II, 158.
50. Historians have generally ignored Pickering's earlier career and judged him unfavorably on the basis of the partisan testimony given at his impeachment trial. John Morse, for example, in the first edition of his *Thomas Jefferson* (Boston, 1883), 259, called Pickering "a worthless fellow morally and mentally." Upon being called to account by his fellow members of the Massachusetts Historical Society, Morse added an appendix to his book which grudgingly admitted that he had done "an unintentional injustice to the memory of a worthy man." See 1897 edition, p. 345. More recent writers, such as Bowers, *Jefferson in Power,* 270-71, Fletcher Pratt, *The Heroic Years* (N. Y., 1934), 29-31, and Samuel Eliot Morison, *The Growth of the American Republic,* 3d ed. (N. Y., 1942), I, 397, have failed to profit by Morse's mistake. Pickering's friends, on the other hand, testified strongly to his intellectual prowess, sobriety, and moral integrity in the years before his mental decay. See Plumer's biographical sketch in the *N. H. State Papers,* XXII, 839-43; Adams, *Annals of Portsmouth,* 332-34; communication by Dr. Andrew Peabody, Mass. Hist. Soc., *Proceedings,* 1st Ser., 20 (1882-83), 333-38.

the turn of the century, he was not only incapable of exercising judgment but had become an alcoholic.[51]

Even personal friendship could not justify the retention of a lunatic upon the federal bench, and Plumer admitted, at least in later years, that Pickering ought to have resigned. That he was not encouraged to do so was largely a matter of politics. His resignation would create a vacancy for a Republican president to fill, and his prospective successor, Republican district attorney John Samuel Sherburne, was, as Plumer reminded his Portsmouth friends, "a man whom we cannot approve."

This remark indicates Plumer's second problem and he did not face it well. Although in 1827, he declared it wrong for Pickering to have remained in office, in 1802 he urged Sheafe not to allow the unfortunate judge to resign. Political prejudice and personal dislike for Sherburne sadly warped Plumer's perspective. He could take refuge, however, in a defect in the Federal Constitution. Had it provided for removal of an incompetent judge by address, as did the constitutions of New Hampshire and at least six other states, Plumer believed that every senator would have agreed to address the President for Pickering's dismissal.[52] In the absence of any process of removal except by impeachment, however, Plumer found it possible to justify the dispensation of federal justice in New Hampshire by a mental incompetent under the shelter of a constitutional technicality.

President Jefferson was fully conscious of his party's dilemma in relying upon the uncertain process of impeachment. He had expressed his belief to Plumer that the Constitution should be amended to provide for the removal of judges by address, and Pickering's case gave him the strongest grounds for urging such an amendment. Neither the President nor his opponents, however, were in a mood to subordinate partisan advantage to statesmanship in 1803. As in the case of the Louisiana Purchase, Jefferson condoned an almost certain violation of the Constitution rather than risk the uncertainty of an amendment. Plumer himself asked the President if he considered Pickering's insanity a good cause for impeachment and removal. Jefferson replied, "If the facts ... stated in the impeachment are proven, that will be sufficient cause of removal without further enquiry." [53]

51. See above, p. 62; *N. H. State Papers*, XXII, 843.
52. Plumer, Autobiography, 130; Plumer to James Sheafe, Dec. 13, 1802, Letter Book, I, Lib. Cong.
53. *Plumer's Memorandum*, 100, 102.

Against this loose doctrine, the Federalists held to the opposite extreme: acts justifying impeachment had to be indictable.[54] "In an impeachment," wrote Plumer, "it is requisite to allege & prove crimes & misdemeanors in the accused; otherwise a judicial officer will hold his office not by the tenure of *good behavior,* but the *pleasure of the legislature*—a tenure fatal to the independence of an important department in the government." This was to be the first line of defense in nearly every subsequent impeachment trial, and it rests upon the further argument that the word "misdemeanor," as employed in the Constitution, is a "term of art" borrowed in unchanged significance from English parliamentary law wherein it had always signified gross misbehavior.[55] Whatever the merits of this particular argument may be, poor Pickering, *non compos mentis,* stood beyond its scope. For his acts, as Robert Goodloe Harper later remarked, he was not amenable to any earthly tribunal.[56]

Although William Plumer was more intimately connected with developments in the Pickering case than with almost anything else he encountered in Washington, he played a passive role in the actual trial. His propensity for note-taking, however, makes possible today a far more thorough understanding of this important bit of history than could ever have been obtained from official documents alone. In general outline the Pickering case was accurately described in Henry Adams's monumental history, but Plumer's journal throws a merciless light upon the twistings and contradictions into which the politician-judges were betrayed in adapting their principles to their interest in prosecuting the trial.

The action against Pickering began with a report from the Secretary of the Treasury, which President Jefferson transmitted to the House of Representatives on February 3, 1803. Plumer examined this interesting document and discovered that the evidence it contained consisted entirely of affidavits from Republican officeholders and hangers-on in Portsmouth, swearing to the misbehavior of Judge Pickering during

54. Albert J. Beveridge treats this doctrinal question fully, but naturally from a pro-Federalist point of view in *The Life of John Marshall* (Boston, 1916-19), III, chap. 4, *passim.* For a modern statement in harmony with the Jeffersonian doctrine, see Westel Willoughby, *The Constitutional Law of the United States* (N. Y., 1910), 1124.

55. See the very learned argument prepared for the use of defense counsel in the Swayne trial, Asher Hinds, *Precedents of the House of Representatives* (Wash., 1907), III, 322-25.

56. Plumer, Autobiography, 130; *Annals of Congress,* 8th Cong., 1st Sess., 342.

a case tried in his court the previous October.[57] It was clear, even from biased testimony, that in this particular trial Judge Pickering had been thoroughly intoxicated, and that in this condition he had threatened spectators, bullied witnesses, silenced the district attorney, rendered an arbitrary decision in favor of his Federalist friends, and refused to grant an appeal.[58] Even if his verdict were just, his behavior had been scandalous. The smarting Republicans who had suffered by it blamed everything upon the judge's inebriation—not a single reference was made, in any of the affidavits, to the possibility that his maudlin reactions were those of a lunatic.[59]

On the basis of these hostile statements, the House of Representatives impeached Judge Pickering,[60] and drew up articles which virtually proclaimed in writing that he was to be sacrificed to political expediency. The authors made no appeal to the Senate to give the impeachment clause of the Constitution such liberal construction as to permit the removal of an unfit judge from the bench. On the contrary, their whole effort, until forced into another position by the defense, was to exclude the idea of insanity, and construe Pickering's behavior as criminal misdemeanor.[61] Plumer found it difficult to recognize in this partisan accusation the eminent jurist whom he had "loved and respected" for twenty years.

The evident reluctance of some Northern Republicans to condemn an insane man led Plumer, unfortunately, to believe that the impeachment might not succeed. Fearing that the Federalists at home were not sufficiently exerting themselves, he wrote to Jeremiah Mason that the

57. *Message from the President enclosing Documents Relative to John Pickering*, printed by order of the House of Representatives (Wash., 1803), 3. These documents are the message of President Jefferson to the House, Feb. 3, 1803, and the depositions against Pickering, gathered from Portsmouth witnesses by order of the Secretary of the Treasury. The deponents were Thomas Chadbourne, Jonathan Steele, John S. Sherburne, John Wentworth, Richard Cutts Shannon, and others—all Republicans and present or would-be officeholders under the administration.

58. See Turner, "Impeachment of John Pickering," *Amer. Hist. Rev.*, 54 (1948-49), 489-90, for a full account of this affair.

59. Deposition of Edward Livermore, *Annals of Congress*, 8th Cong., 1st Sess., 337-42; Plumer to James Sheafe, Feb. 12, 1803, Plumer Papers, N. H. State Lib.

60. *Annals of Congress*, 7th Cong., 2d Sess., 460, 544, 642.

61. *Extracts from the Journal of the United States Senate in All Cases of Impeachment* (Wash., 1912), 20-22. Henry Adams was for once too generous when he stated in his *History of the United States*, II, 156, that "This ground was fairly taken by the impeachers, though not formally expressed." The very opposite was true. In order to have an impeachable case, the managers strained every nerve to prove the commission of criminal acts *on the bench*, without regard to possible causation.

"ruling party" counted upon frightening Pickering's friends into effecting his resignation. Since Pickering's removal would lead directly to the condemnation of the remaining federal judges, Plumer felt that it should be contested to the last ditch. Whether his advice ever reached the immediate friends of Pickering is not revealed by the correspondence. At any rate, the local Federalist leaders showed no disposition to make Pickering's case their own. His defense was left entirely to his relatives, who were poorly equipped to match the small army of witnesses for the prosecution whose expenses were paid by the federal government.[62]

The opening day of the impeachment trial in the Senate was marked by two interesting events; the expected absence of John Pickering, the defendant, and the unexpected appearance of Robert Goodloe Harper as an attorney for the defense. Harper, a brilliant Baltimore attorney and persistent baiter of Republicans, appeared, not as counsel for the defendant whose insanity made him incapable of employing counsel, but as agent for Pickering's son. Invited within the bar by the Vice-President, Harper offered to give evidence of Pickering's insanity and added that the judge's disability and "narrow circumstances" had made it impossible for him to appear or to send witnesses to Washington. At this point, the House managers objected to hearing Harper any further in his anomalous capacity. Burr referred the question to the court, and the senators retired to their committee room for a decision, leaving the indignant managers to cool their heels in the Senate chamber.[63] Many hours later, Plumer wrote to Edward Livermore: "Complaints have often been made against our Common Pleas, but what think you of a court, able to judge the president himself, who sits five hours on the question of whether Harper can be heard as attorney for Pickering's son and not yet decided?"[64]

It required not five hours but three days for the Senate to settle this question. A three-cornered debate raged between the Federalists, who had already determined to vote for an acquittal, those Republicans who

62. Plumer to Jeremiah Mason, Jan. 14, 1804, Letter Book, I, Lib. Cong.; Jeremiah Smith to Plumer, Feb. 10, 19, 1804, Letter Book, IV, *ibid.*

63. *Plumer's Memorandum*, 151-55; *Annals of Congress,* 8th Cong., 1st Sess., 330-32. The appearance of Harper in the trial, whether so designed or not, added immeasurably to its political character. Hardly another Federalist leader was so thoroughly hated by the Republicans, since Harper had deserted their ranks to become the majority floor leader during Adams's administration. James Bayard to Robert Harper, Jan. 30, 1804, Elizabeth Donnan, ed., *Papers of James A. Bayard,* American Historical Association, *Annual Report for the Year 1913* (Wash., 1915), II, 150-61.

64. Plumer to Edward Livermore, Mar. 4, 1804, Letter Book, IV, Lib. Cong.

were equally determined to vote for a conviction, and the moderate Jeffersonians who were troubled by Harper's evidence. The efforts of each group to place its predetermined action upon a legal footing gave rise to the most fantastic interpretations of law. The Federalists were determined to admit the evidence of insanity, which if proved, they said, would prevent any further proceedings. For precisely this reason, the administration Republicans made "the most persevering and determined opposition" to hearing such evidence. The moderates wanted to avoid the appearance of arbitrary persecution: "I trust we are not *yet* arrived to that state of things in which it is necessary to suppress evidence or refuse to hear counsel," said Senator Stephen Bradley of Vermont.[65] Moderation finally prevailed, and on late Monday afternoon the court voted, eighteen to twelve, to hear Harper's evidence.

This decision enraged the managers for the prosecution, who immediately stalked out of the Senate chamber, but Harper was admitted to the bar and allowed to proceed with his statement. He read a number of depositions and extracts from court records (to one of which Plumer had been a witnessing attorney), which testified to Pickering's insanity and the doubtful character of the statements in the articles of impeachment. Harper closed his appearance with a short but forceful protest against regarding insanity as criminal, and asked that the court grant a postponement of the trial.[66] He then withdrew.

Now that the evidence to prove insanity had been heard, the Senate decided to do nothing about it. Having salved their consciences, the moderate Republicans swung back into line, and without debate carried a vote to proceed immediately with the trial. "This had evidently been settled by the members of the ruling party out of Court," decided Senator Adams.[67]

On March 8, the managers returned and began the proof of their indictment. They did little more than call up witnesses, who, in Plumer's opinion, were "well chosen & prepared for the purpose to which they were called," and who "discovered a great forwardness in testifying against the accused." [68] All seven of them were Republicans, and five had been appointed to federal offices by the Republican administration. Two of the witnesses, John Samuel Sherburne and Jonathan Steele,

---

65. *Plumer's Memorandum,* 156-59, 166. Plumer recorded the only circumstantial account of this debate.

66. *Annals of Congress,* 8th Cong., 1st Sess., 334-43.

67. *Ibid.,* 345; *Adams's Memoirs,* I, 300.

68. Plumer to Jeremiah Smith, Mar. 11, 1804, Letter Book, IV, Lib. Cong.

aspired to Pickering's place.[69] Since no representative of the accused was present to cross-examine, the witnesses reveled in a freedom that would certainly have been denied them in a regular court.[70] They ascribed Pickering's misbehavior to intoxication, and carefully avoided any mention of insanity until they were questioned on that subject by the court; they then declared that the judge's insanity had been produced by habitual use of ardent spirits. In attempting to establish this point, the witnesses were permitted to relate hearsay stories and to contradict each other without reproof.

After the prosecution rested, it was suggested that the two senators from New Hampshire be asked to give evidence in the case.[71] Olcott had been Pickering's associate in the state Superior Court, and was able to refute expressly the random assertions that Pickering had been a drunkard before he was appointed to the federal bench. Plumer established Pickering's excellent character prior to his insanity, which he believed to have been "about four years since." He stated his explicit belief that Pickering's insanity was the cause of his intemperance and added the common-sense observation that the two maladies had increased by reciprocal effect.[72] Some of the senators seized upon Plumer's statement as evidence that Pickering had drunk himself insane, in spite of the specific denial.[73] After Olcott and Plumer's damaging statements, the prosecution felt compelled to recall the witnesses whose testimony had been impugned. Sherburne excused himself on the plea of illness, but the others reappeared, to give the lie direct to the honorable senators from New Hampshire. The managers then closed their case, declaring that the testimony was so conclusive as to render further argument unnecessary, and that they would retire, "entertaining no doubt of full justice being done by the decision of the Senate." [74]

The Federalist senators then strove to secure a postponement in order to compel Pickering's appearance.[75] Senator Samuel White of

---

69. There was an unfortunate element of personal ingratitude in the testimony of these two witnesses. Sherburne had been a student in Pickering's law office and had frequently been befriended by the older man. Steele, clerk of the court, of course owed his appointment to Pickering.

70. *Annals of Congress,* 8th Cong., 1st Sess., 355.

71. This resulted in another bizarre feature of the trial, with two men becoming both witnesses and judges.

72. *Annals of Congress,* 8th Cong., 1st Sess., 359-61.

73. For example, Israel Smith of Vermont. See Plumer, Biographies, IV, 529, N. H. Hist. Soc.

74. *Annals of Congress,* 8th Cong., 1st Sess., 362.

75. *Adams's Memoirs,* I, 302-3.

Delaware insisted that there had been no summons, no appearance, no plea, no defense, and that their proceedings scarcely deserved the name of a mock trial.[76] Republican senators were driven again to declare that technical niceties did not concern them; their object was to get rid of Pickering. A day was consumed in acrimonious debate before White's resolution was finally defeated, nine to nineteen. A motion to pronounce judgment on the following Monday was then passed by a vote of twenty to nine. These votes demonstrated that the issue was already settled.

Plumer occupied a part of the Sabbath day, which followed, in writing a bitter description of the trial to Jeremiah Smith, then added: "Tomorrow, no doubt, an insane man will be convicted of high crimes & misdeamers [*sic*]; & probably the next day John Samuel Sherburne will be announced as his successor—for it is not yet necessary to enquire whether the Candidate *is honest, or attached to the constitution.* . . . There is nothing here to induce me to tarry much longer, either as it respects myself or my country. I fondly hope I shall live to see the righteous separated from the wicked by a geographical line. True policy demands it." [77]

On Monday, after brushing aside a Federalist proposal that each senator be required to decide whether Pickering was guilty "of high crimes and misdemeanors," the majority adopted a form of vote that would merely declare Pickering guilty or not guilty "as charged." "Whether this motion was made to evade the fair question . . . without deciding the question of law, let the impartial decide," was Plumer's press comment upon this action.[78] The final roll calls found only twenty-six men, out of a total membership of thirty-four, willing to place their names on the record in relation to this precedent-forming impeachment. These voted strictly according to party: the nineteen Republican senators found Pickering guilty on every charge; the seven Federalist senators pronounced him not guilty. A resolution to remove Pickering from office passed immediately, twenty to six, with all but the six New England Federalists in its favor.[79] Thus, after a so-called trial of charges based upon ex parte evidence, in which the absent defendant was morally unaccountable for his alleged crimes and mentally incapable either of

76. White silenced an objection to this remark from Senator Nicholas of Virginia by inviting him to challenge. See Plumer, Biographies, IV, 493, N. H. Hist. Soc.

77. Plumer to Jeremiah Smith, Mar. 11, 1804, Letter Book, IV, Lib. Cong.

78. Plumer to John Park, 1804, *ibid.*, publ. in the *Repertory* (Boston), Mar. 27, 1804.

79. *Extracts in Cases of Impeachment,* 34.

pleading or of defending himself, a partisan body of judges gave to poor, crazy John Pickering of New Hampshire the distinction of becoming the first victim of a judicial purge in our national history.

On the day following Pickering's conviction, Plumer wrote a long, circumstantial, and skillfully partisan account of the trial for publication in the Boston *Repertory*. "How far these proceedings will form a precedent to establish the doctrine, That when requested by a majority of the House, two thirds of the Senate can remove a Judge from office without a formal conviction of high crimes and misdemeanors, time alone can develop," he editorialized. "I really wish those in New England who are boasting of the independence of our Judiciary would reflect on what a slender tenure Judges hold their offices whose political sentiments are at variance with the dominant party." [80] Events which occurred during the remaining fifteen days of the session fitted perfectly into Plumer's preconceived pattern of Republican villainy. Only ten days after Pickering's removal, Jefferson asked the Senate to confirm his nomination of John Samuel Sherburne to the vacant judgeship and of Jonathan Steele to the district attorney's office vacated by Sherburne. "Thus is the man who advised & promoted as far as he was able the impeachment of Judge Pickering, rewarded by being appointed his successor," wrote Plumer.[81] Unfortunately for Republican harmony, Steele returned his commission to Secretary Madison, saying that he had been made a contributing instrument in creating vacancies, and a due regard for his reputation forbade his profiting by that achievement. This scarcely-veiled criticism of both Sherburne and the administration was followed soon by Steele's withdrawal from the Republican party. Sherburne's appointment excited a considerable degree of hostility in New Hampshire, where Pickering had been generally popular. When Sherburne himself became insane, after some twenty years on the bench, many devout people of Portsmouth considered it to be the judgment of God visited upon him for his part in Pickering's removal.[82]

The Pickering case offers one of the best available lessons in the hypertension of politics. The Federalists, believing that all the law, justice, and constitutionality had been on their side, could regard Pickering's removal as nothing less than an act of tyranny by a ruthless

80. Plumer to John Park, Mar. 13, 1804, Letter Book, IV, Lib. Cong.
81. *Plumer's Memorandum*, 178-79.
82. Plumer, Biographies, V, 327, N. H. Hist. Soc.; Mass. Hist. Soc., *Proceedings*, 1st Ser., 20 (1882-83), 333-38.

majority. John Quincy Adams called it a "degrading and deforming sentence upon one visited with the heaviest of human calamities," [83] and Plumer assumed that the remaining Federalist judges would also be the victims of impeachments in which "conviction and punishment will follow the accusation as certainly as it did in Revolutionary France." Republicans, of course, were quite willing to fulfill Plumer's prophecy and considered Pickering's misbehavior only the most flagrant but not necessarily the most guilty case of judicial tyranny. An unbiased observer could only regard these furious passions with the frank amazement of the unknown person who penciled on the envelope of one of Plumer's alarmist letters to Jedediah Morse—"breathing dis-union because a Judge Pickering is dismissed *tho insane;*—regarding it as proof of the dominancy of Virginia." [84]

83. John Quincy Adams to John Adams, Mar. 8, 1805, Worthington C. Ford, ed., *The Writings of John Quincy Adams* (N. Y., 1913-17), III, 106-14.
84. Plumer to Jedediah Morse, Mar. 10, 1804, Gratz Coll., Pa. Hist. Soc. The note is penciled on the back of this letter.

CHAPTER VIII

The Secession Plot

"I hope New England will retain her federalism,
& be ready at the favorable moment to embrace a
better state of things." [1]

A MERICAN history affords few instances in which a proud and determined minority has been so humiliated as were the New England Federalists in the first session of the Eighth Congress. Within six months, Plumer and his colleagues had suffered what they felt to be three successive disasters, any one of which alone would have been hard to bear. The purchase of Louisiana had thrown an illimitable expanse in the scales against New England; the Twelfth Amendment had deprived her of even a remotely accidental chance to control the national executive; the condemnation of Pickering had broken down the judicial barrier that alone remained to protect her institutions. A revival of national Federalism seemed hopeless. "Its sun is set to rise no more," mourned Plumer. "It is a principle too pure to govern." [2] Each time Plumer cast his vote with an unavailing minority, he felt that the blessings for which he had urged the adoption of the Constitution were becoming Southern curses. What then remained but to make a fresh start, and establish in New England a separate confederation, founded upon the pure principles of the Constitution?

Separation was not a new idea. It was inherent in the American experiment, had been seriously discussed by Virginia between 1794 and 1800, and was plotted by the people beyond the Alleghenies whenever they felt themselves neglected. Congressmen often used a threat to dissolve the Union as a clinching point in debate without arousing more than perfunctory protest. Familiar with all this talk, Plumer was probably not surprised when he read the following strong words in a

1. Plumer to Jeremiah Smith, Dec. 4, 1803, Plumer Papers, N. H. State Lib.
2. *Ibid.*

letter from Jedediah Morse, the Massachusetts geographer, written just after the Louisiana treaty had been ratified:

I have long been of the opinion that a division of the States would become indispensable to the preservation of our dearest interests. . . . If the States east of the Patowmack & Allegany Mts could be peaceably erected into a separate government, under the present constitution, without the Amendments which have been made since its adoption, I should hope that the reign of New England liberty wd be prolonged— but connected as we now are with—I will not say what,—I fear we shall be by degrees drawn into a vortex, in which our religious, political & literary institutions & all the principles and habits which are their fruits, & wch. are our glory and happiness, will be ingulphed & lost.[3]

Plumer received similar communications, in more guarded language, from other Federalist friends, and he read editorials of like import in Federalist newspapers.[4] Listening to these whisperings from the North, he was easily converted to the scheme of secession hatched in the bold Federalist heads in Washington during the winter of 1803-4. "How mutable is the State of things!" he wrote to Edward Livermore. "But a few years since our fairest hopes rested on the wisdom and integrity of the General Government, to protect us against the ignorance & frauds of State legislatures!"[5] How sadly now was the situation reversed! Plumer had come to believe, with Fisher Ames, that "State justice and State power" were the sole remaining "shelter of the wise, and good, and rich, from the wild destroying rage of the southern Jacobins."[6]

Senator Plumer was by no means a ringleader in the plot to establish a Northern Confederacy. "The subject at the first, filled me with horror & disgust," he claimed many years afterward. But he soon became a willing conspirator. It was a New Hampshire congressman, Samuel Hunt, who first initiated Plumer into the plot.[7] Hunt belonged to an important Connecticut Valley family, but he was a small-scale Aaron Burr rather than a typical Yankee. A few years spent abroad had filled him with contempt for democratic, plebeian America and had stirred within him restless dreams of adventure. The Constitution and the government were ridiculously feeble, he told Plumer. It was necessary for

3. Jedediah Morse to Plumer, Nov. 18, 1803, *ibid.*
4. See *Connecticut Courant* (Hartford), Aug. 17, 1803, and *Salem Gazette,* Nov. 18, 1803, for examples.
5. Plumer to Edward Livermore, Mar. 4, 1804, Letter Book, IV, Lib. Cong.
6. Seth Ames, ed., *The Works of Fisher Ames* (Boston, 1854), I, 310.
7. Plumer, Autobiography, 132, 397.

the commercial states north of Maryland to separate from the tobacco planters and establish an authoritarian regime more favorable to a mercantile aristocracy.[8] Plumer expressed skepticism as to whether such a plan could gain wide support in New England and asked Hunt to name a single prominent sympathizer. Hunt answered promptly that he could depend upon his uncle, Governor Caleb Strong of Massachusetts.[9]

Presently, Plumer was hearing definite details of the separation scheme from the Connecticut congressmen, notably Roger Griswold. When the New Hampshire senator expressed fears that the conspirators were exposing themselves to personal danger, Griswold reassured him. The Connecticut leader outlined to Plumer a well-matured technique of secession. The first essential was to gain firm control of the state governments in New England. These should repeal the laws which authorized the election of representatives to Congress and recall their senators. Thereafter, they might gradually set up their own customs collections, sever all further relations with Washington, and eventually establish a Northern Confederacy. If New England united in the measure, it could be done peacefully, but even if Virginia resorted to arms, there would be little to fear.[10]

Plumer conversed frequently with Hunt, Griswold and Uriah Tracy, senator from Connecticut, until he came to believe that their plan was feasible. But the plotting, if these dialogues can be so denominated, was cautious and bilateral. There were no secret conclaves where all the malcontents gathered to perfect their plans, at least none in which Plumer was concerned. He almost never conversed with more than one person at a time on this subject. In later years, he recalled Calvin Goddard and James Hillhouse of Connecticut, Simeon Olcott of New Hampshire, and Timothy Pickering, senator from Massachusetts, as other men who talked knowingly with him on the subject.[11] These were far from comprising all of the New England Federalists in Congress. Tracy had sounded Adams on the proposition, but so cautiously as to make the Massachusetts senator believe that he opposed the plan.[12]

8. Plumer, "Samuel Hunt," Biographies, IV, 419, N. H. Hist. Soc.
9. Plumer to John Quincy Adams, Jan. 16, 1829, Letter Book, VIII, Lib. Cong.
10. Plumer to John Quincy Adams, Dec. 20, 1828, *ibid.* This letter was published by Adams in Washington in 1829, but can be consulted most readily in Henry Adams, *Documents Relating to New England Federalism, 1800-1815* (Boston, 1877), 144-46. It was supplemented by a detailed and circumstantial account written to Adams on Jan. 16, 1829.
11. Plumer, Autobiography, 132, 396-97.
12. Plumer, Jr., *Life of Plumer,* 303-4.

How many other members of Congress were approached or involved it would be impossible to say. Plumer was obviously not admitted to the full confidence of the chief conspirators. He did not know they had gone so far as to plan an army for the defense of the new confederacy and to solicit aid from the British minister at Washington.[13] Nor did Plumer know that Timothy Pickering was endeavoring to interest the Essex Junto in the conspiracy. John Quincy Adams was astonished, twenty-five years later, to learn that Plumer had even been involved in the plot.[14]

Although Plumer did not know it, Timothy Pickering was the actual ringleader of the cabal. In a letter to George Cabot, January 29, 1804, he outlined more explicitly the scheme that Griswold had explained in general terms to Plumer. "Perhaps the violation of the Constitution in the arbitrary removal of the judges may hasten such a crisis," wrote Pickering. "The signal, a bold but safe step by members of Congress." [15] This plot came within a hair's breadth of execution when the six Federalist senators from New England decided to boycott the final vote in John Pickering's trial.[16] With Machiavellian cunning, Pickering asked his personal enemy, Senator Adams, to prepare a statement of justification for their contemplated step, and Adams did so. This was the "signal," which, had it been given, might have drawn not only Plumer, but even Adams, into public association with a secession plot. At the last minute, however, Pickering abandoned the idea.[17]

Plumer was sufficiently interested in the scheme to sow seed for it in New Hampshire. He began to burden the mails with intrigue devoted to the first step in the secession, the election of a Federalist administration in March. This necessarily involved rapprochement with his doubtful friends of the Exeter Junto. Both John Taylor Gilman and Benjamin Connor were urgently warned against abandoning their candidacies and every important Federalist in the state was exhorted to act quickly.[18] Jeremiah Mason read: "I hope the great necessity of

13. Beveridge, *Marshall*, III, 281-83.
14. The statement that "Plumer guaranteed New Hampshire" in Pratt, *Heroic Years,* 62, is pure melodrama. Even if Plumer had been the head of the conspirators, his influence in New Hampshire was not such as to warrant his making any guarantees. See his letters to John Quincy Adams, Letter Book, VIII, Lib. Cong.
15. Adams, *New England Federalism,* 338-42.
16. Pickering to John Q. Adams, Mar. 10, 1804, Pickering Papers, XIV, Mass. Hist. Soc.
17. Ford, ed., *Writings of John Q. Adams,* III, 34-38; *Adams's Memoirs,* I, 303-7.
18. Plumer to John T. Gilman, Dec. 7, 1803, Plumer Papers, N. H. State Lib.; Plumer to Benjamin Connor, Jan. 26, 1804, Letter Book, IV, Lib. Cong.

preserving our *State governments* as a security against the approaching storm which may *rend* the Union will induce men of sound minds, who have property as well as reputation & life at hazard, to exert themselves at the March elections." [19] Even Plumer's humble neighbors in Epping were urged to preserve "the federalism of New Hampshire one year more," and to be "industrious in & out of town." [20]

Plumer's correspondence campaign, however, went deeper than mere electioneering—its chief purpose was to explore public opinion on the question of secession. By January 25, he had already written four hundred letters since leaving Epping in October, and nearly all of them sounded the persistent tocsin of alarm.[21] The reasoning in his correspondence with Edward St. Loe Livermore, now resident in Newburyport, can serve as an example of what Plumer continued to write throughout the session.

All the great measures of Congress are tending to one point—to build up & aggrandize Virginia in particular, & the States south of the Potomac in general. The weight, influence & votes of New England will soon be of little avail in the national legislature. The negro votes made Mr Jefferson president, & those votes carried through the House of representatives the resolution of what is called an amendment, but in fact what destroys one of the first principles of our constitution. The measures pursued in the South will, I hope, unite the eastern States. I cannot beleive New England will long approve a system of measures by which their votes will be swallowed up in those of slave-holders. From the States east of the Potomac almost the whole of the revenue is collected to pay the national debt, & to support a government in which they have not an efficient & equal voice. To render this state of things still more injurious, new territorial governments are forming in the west, then will soon become States, & will have senators & representatives in Congress, who it is to be feared will be subservient to the views & interests of the South. What portion therefore can New England have in Jefferson, & what inheritance in the *ancient dominion*? [22]

Succeeding letters played interesting variations on this main theme, introducing new discords as they appeared in Congress and adapting each passage cleverly to the tastes of its recipient. To his friend Bradbury Cilley of Nottingham, a rich, conservative, patriotic country

19. Plumer to Jeremiah Mason, Feb. 15, 1804, Letter Book, IV, Lib. Cong.
20. Plumer to David Lawrence, Jan. 22, 1804, Plumer Papers, N. H. Hist. Soc.
21. Plumer to Mrs. Sarah Plumer, Jan. 25, 1804, Letter Book, IV, Lib. Cong.
22. Plumer to Edward Livermore, Dec. 24, 1803, Letter Book, III, *ibid.*

squire, Plumer inveighed against executive aggrandizement and the prospect of a Jacobin judiciary. "My hopes rest on the union of New England. . . . The abolishing the loan offices is again under consideration. I have done purchasing public stocks; & what I own are now ready for sale." Oliver Peabody, the state treasurer, was treated to a jaundiced view of the finances, purporting to show that the money drawn from New England into the national treasury was sufficient to "support the government of . . . [our] States, maintain our Clergy, schools, poor, make our roads, & pay our town and country charges." [23] Writing to Benjamin Hathorne of Salem, Plumer skillfully touched on a seaman's prejudices. The administration's bill to protect sailors, he argued, was simply a measure to hide foreign deserters in the American marine so that the West and South could be freed of dependence upon Yankee ships. James Sheafe, who loved trim vessels, was probably horrified to read that "the *wasting œconomy* of Administration is such that the ships [to be sent to the Mediterranean theater of war] are destitute of rigging & not a single ship has the necessary cables for a voyage." For publication, Plumer wrote that the new duties, levied ostensibly to prosecute the Tripolitan war, were deliberately made high enough to pay the interest on Louisiana stock as well. "Thus early, & in this deceptious manner, must the commerce of the eastern States, be taxed for the purchase of the useless wilds of Louisiana." [24]

Plumer's correspondence campaign was all-inclusive. An inquiry from a Republican constituent in regard to military bounty lands in Ohio gave Plumer an opportunity to demoralize the opposition. Your lands are not salable, he informed his correspondent, because the government has opened the vast wilds of Louisiana to settlement. "Our interests are variant; & I wish the eastern people were more cordially united in support of our rights." [25] As time went on, Plumer's hints grew broader and his tone more insistent. At the beginning of February, he sought a definite response from T. W. Thompson, the leader of Federalism in the Merrimack Valley. "What is to be done? Do you wish this State of things to continue?—a state, if it progresses, in which the rights of person & of property cannot be secure; a situation which every year will add power & influence to the south & to the west at

23. Plumer to Bradbury Cilley, Jan. 15, to Oliver Peabody, Jan. 19, 1804, Plumer Papers, N. H. State Lib.
24. Plumer to Benjamin Hathorne, Mar. 8, to James Sheafe, Mar. 22, to John Park, Mar. 24, 1804, Letter Book, IV, Lib. Cong.
25. Plumer to Thomas Cogswell, Feb. 7, 1804, *ibid.*

the expence of the east. . . . must New England support & submit to a government directed by *slaveholders*?"[26] A few days later, Plumer sounded out Chief Justice Smith: "I think New England must soon feel its degraded condition; & I hope will have energy to assert & maintain its rights. And it certainly will be of infinite importance that the necessary changes should be effected *under the forms & by the authority of the existing governments.* What think you of this—must the inheritance be severed?" Just before the election in New Hampshire, Plumer reached an extraordinary depth of bitterness in a letter to Livermore: "It is of importance that the Legislatures of New England should be composed of well-informed firm honest federalists. We must, if we wish for security to person, property, talent or reputation, introduce a *new order of things.* The *aristocracy* of *talents,* of *reputation,* & of *property,* in the eastern States, are viewed by the idols of the day not only with jealousy but rancour. If there was a Marat in the House, & a Robespeire in the Senate, the *rights* of many would soon be the *halter* and the *block.*"[27]

The seditious congressmen of 1804, however, elicited no enthusiasm from their constituents. Pickering received only morbid sympathy from the Essex Junto.[28] Some encouragement came from Connecticut, but Plumer's seed fell upon stony ground. Only Jedediah Morse, among all his correspondents, displayed any zeal for secession. Thompson was in accord with Plumer's spirit of revolt, but he was not infected with the naively sanguine temper of the Washington *émigrés.* On February 27, he wrote that the time was still far distant when New Englanders could be aroused to active rebellion. "At present," he reported gloomily, "you know that nine tenths, if not nineteen twentieths of our people make no further inquiry than the State of the markets & the amount of the taxes & so long as the balance is much in their favor they will not feel for the honor of their country." The most remarkable answer Plumer received was from his friend, James Sheafe, who as a merchant, Federalist, and old Tory might have been expected to favor a pro-British secession. His correspondence, however, shows a strong sense of practical patriotism contrasting with Plumer's temporary hysteria. "On the subject you hint at of separation, as a commercial man I should dread such an event," he protested. "I am writing on a subject that

26. Plumer to Thomas W. Thompson, Jan. 28, Feb. 3, 1804, *ibid.*
27. Plumer to Jeremiah Smith, Feb. 10, to Edward Livermore, Mar. 4, 1804, *ibid.*
28. Hervey Prentiss, *Timothy Pickering as the Leader of New England Federalism, 1800-1815* (Salem, Mass., 1934), 26-27.

you have the means of understanding a great deal better than I have and from your habits of close thinking and observing I know your opinion is well formed and I do not think on the whole however that you will believe that a Sep' can be made before a half century is past without consequences ruinous to all the States." [29]

Smith was the most disappointing of all Plumer's correspondents, for although his strictures on Jefferson and democracy far outdid Plumer's, his only remedy was mock resignation. He answered Plumer's questions with an oblique rebuff, saying, "At present I do not see much reason to despair of the republic for this year." The truth was, he pointed out, that Federalist leaders were apathetic or too busy reaping a large share of Jeffersonian prosperity to be concerned with the fate of the nation or even of the party, whereas the Republicans were straining every nerve to grasp the visible prize of victory. They had held a general caucus during the winter session of the legislature and agreed upon candidates for every office. This step had been followed by the creation of a formidable political machine, complete from a "grand committee of election & correspondence" to a local chieftain for every town in New Hampshire. It had been organized at a secret night meeting in the office of Philip Carrigain, a young Concord lawyer whose enthusiasm, according to Smith, often outran his discretion. The announced purpose of the organization was to promote the cause of republicanism and of pure and undefiled religion. "Did you believe 15 years ago that a thing of this kind could happen in New England?" Smith inquired of Plumer. "What think you of pure & undefiled religion under the care of Carigain & French—are you willing to confide your temporal concerns to these worthy citizens? They have leisure and I presume inclination to superintend the management of *your* property—neither of them are much embarrassed or cumbered with any of their own." [30]

An ironic footnote to Plumer's disunionist schemes was the fact that his own brother Daniel was appointed Republican agent for Epping by this same committee which Smith thought so dreadful. At the very moment when lawyer William was plotting secession in Washington, farmer Daniel was laboring for Jefferson in Epping, and each of the brothers was ignorant of the other's activity. In January the Senator wrote to his brother, expressing a hope that the true New Englanders

29. Jedediah Morse to Plumer, Feb. 3, Thomas W. Thompson to Plumer, Feb. 27, James Sheafe to Plumer, Mar. 7, 1804, Letter Book, IV, Lib. Cong.
30. Jeremiah Smith to Plumer, Feb. 19, 22, 1804, *ibid.*

of Epping would unite to elect the right men at March meeting, else they would be ruled by slaveholders.[31] Daniel frugally used the back of this very letter to draft a report to his state chairman: "I am fully of the Opinion that if proper diligence is used by the Republicans throughout the State, that we shall gain the election. from present appearances I feel pretty confident that in Epping we shall make a gain of 20 or 30 votes from March last."

Daniel's organization proved to be more effective than William's propaganda. At the March meetings the Republicans gained firm control of the state legislature [32]—a victory which struck a decisive blow at the schemes of Pickering and Griswold and made the fruition of a secessionist plan virtually impossible. The secessionists, however, unwilling to concede defeat, were already launched on a far more ambitious undertaking—to gain control of New York by electing Aaron Burr to the governorship.[33] This scheme was never revealed in full to Plumer, but he happened to be present during some of the preliminary negotiations. One evening in Washington the Vice-President had invited a select company, including Pickering, Hillhouse, and Plumer, to an excellent dinner. The conversation drifted toward the Federalists' favorite topic, and Hillhouse stated unequivocally that the separation must soon take place. With exquisite tact, Burr agreed that New England was shabbily treated; he also mentioned that New York had grievances which he hoped, as governor, to rectify. In the heady atmosphere of free talk, intrigue, and good wine, Plumer received the distinct impression that Aaron Burr favored a Northern Confederacy. Yet upon reflection that night in his lodgings, he realized that Burr had created the impression without at all committing himself to secession.[34] Forthright James Hillhouse had not been so perceptive. Still excited from the evening's conversation, he had said emphatically to Plumer on the way home, "The eastern States must, & will, dissolve the Union, & form a seperate government of their own—& the sooner they do this the better." [35]

At the end of the long congressional session of 1803-4, Tracy informed Plumer that further plans would be perfected at a meeting of Federalist leaders in Boston early in the autumn. Alexander Hamilton, he said, had promised to attend, and Plumer himself was to be invited

31. Plumer to Daniel Plumer, Jan. 24, 1804, Letters, 1802-7, Lib. Cong.
32. Lyon, ed., *New Hampshire Register . . . 1860*, 41.
33. Prentiss, *Pickering*, 28-29.
34. *Plumer's Memorandum*, 517-18. Plumer recorded this incident some years after it had occurred.
35. Plumer, Autobiography, 397.

when the details were arranged. Plumer therefore went home with the impression that Hamilton was one of the plotters. The idea of Burr and Hamilton working in double harness was, of course, fantastic, as Timothy Pickering learned in New York on his way home from Washington.[36] Samuel Hunt, on the other hand, visited his uncle, the governor of Massachusetts, on his homeward journey with more encouraging results. He was soon writing to Plumer *"that governor Strong was decidedly in favor of forming a new confederated government in New England."* [37] It became apparent that the only real strength of the secession movement lay in the Connecticut Valley, where Hunt, Olcott, Strong, Tracy, Hillhouse, Goddard, and Griswold—all the planners except Pickering and Plumer—lived.

Plumer spent April and May in New Hampshire, expounding his secessionist views to the leading Federalists and meeting with a general lack of enthusiasm. His immediate reaction was to become even more radical. Writing to Samuel Hunt, he declared that he was now prepared, *"maugre all consequences, to dissolve the present partnership, & establish a new firm with four partners."* [38] He also reported, rather too optimistically, that he had found *"a considerable number of good men who were of the same opinion,"* but added *"that much time was necessary to make arrangements."*

To anyone not suffering from the persecution complex developed by the Washington Federalists, it must have been obvious that no support for a secession scheme existed among the New England people. As Thompson had pointed out, New Hampshire basked in Jeffersonian prosperity, made even more lush by the war boom in the carrying trade. When the Republican legislature of New Hampshire met in June, it passed a resolution endorsing Jefferson's administration, ratified the Twelfth Amendment, and divided the state into congressional districts.[39] Gilman assured his own defeat at the next election by vetoing these acts, while Langdon won increased popularity by his conduct as speaker of the House.

Meanwhile, the project of disunion was receiving discouraging set-

36. Adams, *New England Federalism,* 147-48.

37. Plumer to John Quincy Adams, Jan. 16, 1829, Letter Book, VIII, Lib. Cong. Plumer told Adams that he had destroyed Hunt's original letter.

38. Plumer, Autobiography, 133. Plumer certainly had this letter before him when he wrote this portion of his autobiography in 1827, but it has not been found among his preserved papers.

39. Robinson, *Jeffersonian Democracy in New England,* 77.

backs in more important quarters. Burr had been defeated for the governorship of New York in April, in spite of Federalist support, and was soon to make himself anathema to the Federalist party by his fatal duel with Hamilton.[40] Hamilton's death also caused the secessionists to postpone their convention in Boston. Plumer waited in vain during the summer for a summons to the meeting that would have been at least as treasonable as the Hartford Convention, which he was to condemn so bitterly ten years later. Burr's well-aimed bullet killed not only Hamilton, but the Boston convention, and may have saved Plumer's reputation from irreparable damage.

The common tendency of Federalist leaders, in consonance with their aristocratic aloofness and dislike of democracy, was to retire from the field of combat and sulk in their tents when the struggle became too severe. Heretofore they had managed without political organization. With social prestige, economic dominance, legal acumen, and the means of information generally at their disposal, they had not been compelled to recognize politics as an art in itself. But the Republican machine had proved its effectiveness in the March campaign so thoroughly as to impress and depress the Federalist leaders. Judge Smith's attitude was typical, although couched in his own ironic style. "I am glad to find that federalism is at a low ebb with you. It is dead, and I sincerely wish it buried out of my sight. Don't flatter yourselves that it is ever to have a resurrection. Federalism can suit only a virtuous state of society. These times demand other principles and other systems." [41]

Plumer was not so easily disheartened. He reasoned that the machine idea, perfected by the Republicans, might be equally well developed by the "virtuous," provided they were willing to mix sweat with virtue. Two important elections, both by general ticket, were yet to be held, the choice of four congressmen in August, and of six presidential electors in November. Even though Plumer had not the slightest hope that Jefferson would be defeated, the electoral votes of New Hampshire and a solid Federalist delegation in Congress were essential to any possible survival of the Northern Confederacy dream.

Another practical Federalist who saw eye to eye with Plumer in this matter was Thomas W. Thompson of Salisbury. This shrewd and affable Harvard graduate had made a tidy fortune as a country lawyer and was

40. Samuel Wandell and Meade Minnigerode, *Aaron Burr* (N. Y., 1925), I, 258 ff.
41. Jeremiah Smith to Plumer, Nov. 21, 1803, Plumer Papers, N. H. State Lib. Also quoted in Morison, *Jeremiah Smith*, 213.

now prepared to devote his energies chiefly to politics. He and Plumer accordingly celebrated the Fourth of July, 1804, by meeting with four other men in strictest secrecy at Concord to organize a party machine.[42] Five of these six men were lawyers, but none of them had any close relations with either the Exeter Junto or the Portsmouth aristocracy. They were eminently practical men, not too deeply concerned with the protocols of eighteenth-century politics and willing to learn from their adversaries.

These self-constituted bosses devised a more potent and more highly centralized machine than the Republicans had created. Under Plumer's chairmanship, each man was assigned the task of organizing a county committee, which was to appoint agents in each town within its jurisdiction. The town agents were further requested to appoint lieutenants for each school district. Every man in the organization was required to (1) "use great industry to support federalism . . . & confirm its disciples," (2) "procure as many subscribers for federal newspapers as [he] could," (3) make special efforts to enlist new voters, (4) hire occasional laborers just before elections, (5) be industrious in personal work and correspondence, and (6) contribute toward the expense. In addition, the six leaders undertook to write for the newspapers and to organize their distribution, while the town agents were expected to make up classified lists of all voters, see that all the Federalists attended town meetings, furnish them with ballots, and, if the result was propitious, make sure that the town clerk duly reported to the secretary's office.[43]

The central committee voted to request Jeremiah Smith and Plumer to combine their talents in the production of a campaign pamphlet. A compendium of Plumer's logic and Smith's wit would have made excellent reading, but the Chief Justice demurred and Plumer agreed to perform the task alone. Although he had written occasional pieces for the newspapers since 1782, Plumer had never before ventured into the field of major propaganda, and he distrusted his own abilities as a pamphleteer. Ten days of assiduous labor, however, resulted in a composition entitled *An Address to the Electors of New Hampshire by Impartialis* that vindicated the judgment of the committee. Six thousand copies of this address were printed and distributed to the voters a few

42. Plumer, "Thomas W. Thompson," Biographies, V, 276, N. H. Hist. Soc. The four other men were Roger Vose, Oliver Crosby, William Kent, and William H. Woodward.

43. Plumer, Proceedings of the Federalists in New Hampshire in 1804, in William Plumer, Repository, I (1801-7), 264-68, N. H. State Lib.

days before the election in August.[44] It added immeasurably to Plumer's political reputation and launched him upon a life-long career as a newspaper pundit.

"Impartialis" retailed his arguments in a businesslike manner which betrayed his identity to discerning readers. His announced purpose was to contrast the Federalist and Republican administration of national affairs. He prefaced his argument with the assumption that the Federalists were those who, under Washington's leadership, had saved the country from its "degraded situation" at the close of the war, written and adopted the Constitution, and established a national government, while those who were first Antifederalists, then Democrats and Jacobins, "have now assumed to themselves the specious name of REPUBLICANS." Plumer denied the "cruel insinuation" that Washington's administration had been monarchical and pointed to the arbitrary acts of Jefferson's congressional majority as far more autocratic. "But," he mourned, "what reason had you to expect that those, who were *opposed* to the Federal Constitution, would administer your government under that Constitution, agreeably to its principles?"

"Impartialis," however, was really less interested in comparing records than he was in denouncing Virginia and the South. "Virginia is almost wholly exempt from taxes, yet she is using the whole weight of her influence to encrease the duties on the commerce and navigation of the north." Taxes on ardent spirits, which the South and West distilled from their own peaches and corn, were abolished, while the duty on New England's molasses remained. The President who had boasted of a great surplus at the beginning of Congress's last session, had to ask for additional duties at the end of it. The Virginians, he wrote, declaimed constantly on their devotion to liberty, yet they lived under an aristocratic state government and from the labor of slaves. Life in New Hampshire was actually more democratic and free. "Can you therefore believe that the former are the real friends of liberty and equality, and the latter its enemies?"

The climax of Plumer's pamphlet came in an open attack on Southern institutions, slavery, and the three-fifths compromise in the Constitution. With its artful wording, its mixture of historic foresight and demagoguery, this final appeal contained too much dynamite to have been designed simply for blasting a handful of Republican candidates out of the path to Congress. Under cover of an explicit denial, Plumer un-

44. Plumer, *Autobiography*, 134-35.

doubtedly intended to undermine New Hampshire's attachment to the Union by these words:

In the Southern States slavery is established by law—and ... every FIVE of these NEGRO SLAVES are accounted equal to THREE OF YOU. ... Those slaves have no voice in the Election; they are mere property; yet a planter possessing a hundred of them may be considered as having SIXTY VOTES, while one of you who has equal or greater property is confined to a SINGLE VOTE. ... THESE ARE STUBBORN FACTS and they imperiously demand your serious attention. They are urged not with a view to weaken, much less, dissolve the Union; but to point the danger to which you are now exposed from the overbearing influence of Virginia.[45]

Altogether, it was a remarkable pamphlet and a remarkable campaign. For the first time in their history, the Federalists of New Hampshire acted as if the common man's vote was worth soliciting. They went about their work, however, with a sense of guilt and took elaborate pains to escape detection, Plumer met his Rockingham County committee at Brewster's Hotel in Portsmouth on the theory that they would attract less attention in a large town than anywhere else—it was announced that they were holding a proprietary meeting for a new township. Money was raised to allow the printer of the *Portsmouth Oracle* to hire a postrider to keep the coastal leaders in touch with those in the Connecticut Valley.[46] The energetic Federalist campaign surprised and enraged the Republicans. Granger wrote to Jefferson that the Federalists were "making astonishing exertions," and the result was eloquent testimony to the effectiveness of their tactics.[47] The Federalist candidates won by an average majority of eight hundred votes, but even more remarkable was the fact that the total vote cast was almost double that of the 1802 congressional election. A further tribute to the efficiency of the new machine was the fact that the man who stood lowest on the list of five candidates received only sixteen fewer votes than the man who stood highest.[48]

45. [William Plumer], "Impartialis," *An Address to the Electors of New Hampshire* (Portsmouth, 1804), 3-14.

46. Plumer, Autobiography, 135. Treadwell, the printer, hired Daniel Blaisdell, a Grafton County councilor, whose sons made the weekly horseback journeys. Blaisdell was afterwards prosecuted by the federal government for carrying letters without postal authority.

47. Robinson, *Jeffersonian Democracy in New England,* 64. Gideon Granger to Thomas Jefferson, Sept. 2, 1804, Jefferson Papers, CXLIII, Lib. Cong.

48. Lyon, ed., *New Hampshire Register ... 1860,* 31.

Plumer had reason to congratulate himself on the results of his first major venture into the field of political propaganda. "IMPARTIALIS ... has had his day of triumph," growled a Republican writer; "he has robbed you of your votes, and your State is to be for two years more, represented by men, who hate a Republican government, and who will employ all their time in Congress to check its operation." [49] The Federalist state committee was tremendously elated by its first victory, and met immediately afterward at Thompson's home in Salisbury to prepare for the presidential contest in November. It was decided at this meeting that propaganda efforts would be made by each member of the committee in the leading newspaper of his own county, and Plumer was consequently assigned to write for the *Portsmouth Oracle*. The result was a series of six articles under the signature of "Cato," which were published in September and October.

Plumer's literary strategy, in these articles, was to ridicule Jefferson's inconsistency by comparing extracts on the same subject taken from his *Notes on Virginia,* his reports as secretary of state, his presidential messages and other public documents. It was easy to show by this method that Jefferson the Secretary contradicted Jefferson the historian, and that Jefferson the President denied them both. Plumer not only concluded from these discrepancies that the President was untrustworthy but he ridiculed the most extreme of Jefferson's ideas on each topic with petty malice. [50] He quoted Jefferson's attacks on the Virginia laws requiring profession of Christianity (nearly identical with Plumer's own criticism of the New Hampshire constitution in 1782), his statement that his neighbor's religious opinion did him no harm, his blaming Christianity for the shedding of much innocent blood, and his approval of religious noncomformity in Pennsylvania. "Cato" expressed sanctimonious horror at these impious ideas. Then he delivered a philippic against Jefferson's friendship for Paine and quoted such extracts from *The Age of Reason* as were best calculated to roil New England tempers.

This article marked one of the lowest ethical points in Plumer's career. In the light of his own beliefs, the attack on Jefferson's deism was hypocritical, designed with malignant skill to arouse the very passions and prejudices that Plumer himself condemned. Years later, he regretfully admitted that his remarks had been "too personal. The pen was too often dipped in gall, & there was too much of declamation, & address

---

49. *A Republican Address to the Electors of New Hampshire* (Walpole, 1804), 3.
50. [William Plumer], "Cato," Nos. 1-3, 5-6, Plumer, Repository, I, 214-39, 244-61, N. H. State Lib., publ. in *Portsmouth Oracle,* Sept. 21, 24, 28, Oct. 13, 22, 1804.

to popular prejudices & feelings." [51] Yet these articles contained a kind of eccentric sincerity. From Plumer's point of view, it was safe enough for a Puritan, who understood the necessity of order and restraint, to indulge in deistic philosophy, but it was a very different matter for a Virginia aristocrat with a mob following to countenance attacks on religion. Plumer's tolerance did not extend to a man whose deism was tinged with approval of assignats and the guillotine.

The New Hampshire Republican machine recovered from its surprise defeat in August and demonstrated a clear superiority in the propaganda department. Its major effort was a pamphlet entitled *A Republican Address to the Electors of New Hampshire,* which devoted itself exclusively to a refutation of "Impartialis." Its most effective argument was the title page, on which quotations from "Impartialis" and Washington's Farewell Address were arranged in parallel columns. Opposed to Plumer's inflammatory denunciations of Virginia and fervid appeals to New England provincialism stood the words of the man he pretended to venerate, earnestly warning his fellow citizens against "every attempt to alienate any portion of our country from the rest," and begging that no "ground should be furnished for characterizing parties, as northern and southern." The remainder of the *Address* was an anticlimax, but it served to emphasize the growing weakness of the Federalists. "Your self-styled disciples of Washington, can do no more for you at the seat of government for the ensuing two years, than to sit or stand as monuments of the ease, with which an honest people may be defrauded of their votes," it said with brutal frankness. "Impartialis" was plainly accused of misrepresenting the administration's policies, of which "he cannot plead ignorance since he holds a station that enables him to discern the truth." The most effective argument of the *Address,* however, was simply that the Federalists were disunionists. The writer drove this point home with telling sarcasm, suggesting that Senator Plumer return to the national capital and, as a self-proclaimed disciple of Washington, read those sections of the pamphlet by "Impartialis" in which he denounced the first President's native state. "His voice will be heard with contempt & execration," declared the writer. [52]

Plumer read the *Address* after his return to Congress and declared it unworthy of a reply, [53] but its effectiveness in New Hampshire was abundantly evident at the town meetings in November. The electorate

51. Plumer, Autobiography, 136-37.
52. *Republican Address to Electors,* 1-2, 7, 14.
53. *Plumer's Memorandum,* 202-3.

that had swung from Republican to Federalist between March and August sprang back again in even less time.[54] Not only New Hampshire but even Massachusetts chose Republican electors, and only Connecticut and Delaware among all the seventeen states refused to help re-elect Jefferson. It was the first political landslide in American history, and it buried beyond any hope of resurrection the secessionist plot of 1804.

As Plumer packed his bags in October to return to Washington, not yet aware of the disaster that was to come in the November town meetings, but suffering a premonition of it, he wondered if the game was worth the candle. The most strenuous efforts had succeeded only momentarily in stemming the revolutionary tide. The news from Europe, where Napoleon was busily engaged in liquidating the only republics which had grown in that soil, suggested a terrifying interpretation of the trend of events in New England. "Perhaps I have been in error," thought Plumer. "I may have considered the existence of the government as depending on the being of federalism. If in this I have erred, it proceeds from the heart not the head—my motives have been just, if my conduct has been improper. . . . The United States are the only Republic of consequence on earth—must we fall as our predecessors have—must monarchy eventually swallow up all other forms of government?" [55]

In such a mood Plumer met his secessionist friends again in Washington and reported that their plot had no chance of success in New Hampshire. Tracy assured him that, although the death of Hamilton had prevented the meeting in Boston as scheduled, "the plan was not, & would not be abandoned." [56] It was apparent, however, to Tracy and his friends that Plumer's heart was no longer in the conspiracy. Timothy Pickering made a last effort to rekindle his zeal. One afternoon the two senators took a long walk towards the forests north and east of the straggling capital city. Plumer's change of spirit made it difficult for Pickering to open the subject, but at length, he plunged into it with his usual abruptness. Was Plumer not still convinced that the country was too large for union and that New England and New York must form a separate government? Pickering stopped and faced the New Hampshire senator squarely, awaiting his reply. The title page of the *Republican Address to the Electors of New Hampshire* may have flashed into Plumer's mind, for he answered simply, "Was not the disunion of the

54. Lyon, ed., *New Hampshire Register . . . 1860,* 22.
55. Plumer, Proceedings of the Federalists in 1804, Repository, I, 264-68, N. H. State Lib.
56. Plumer to John Quincy Adams, Jan. 16, 1829, Letter Book, VIII, Lib. Cong.

States the object which General Washington most pathetically warned the people to oppose?" "Yes," admitted the General's former Quartermaster and Secretary of State. "The fear of it was a ghost that for a long time haunted the imagination of that old gentleman, & excited fears which alarmed him." Pickering continued with disparaging comments on Washington's judgment and military ability until the two walkers returned to the outskirts of the city. Then the conversation changed to another topic.[57] This was the last mention of secession that Plumer heard from the lips of its advocates. When the plotting rose to the surface again in 1808, he was on the other side of the fence.

Few intrigues have ever fizzled out so ingloriously as the secession plot of 1804, but few plotters have ever built upon so flimsy a foundation. It requires some discontent to arouse a people against their government, and the only dissatisfaction with Jefferson's regime in 1804 existed in the imaginations of the Federalist leaders. The defeat of Burr, the defection of New Hampshire, and the re-election of Jefferson demonstrated the unreality of their visions. This was enough for Plumer. He had, thanks to the good sense of his New Hampshire friends and his own innate caution, narrowly escaped a plunge which would have destroyed his political character. Never again was he to make such a near-fatal mistake. Twenty-three years after the events of 1804, Plumer frankly acknowledged in his autobiography the part he had played in them and closed his account with a characteristic paragraph in which confession, remorse, and profound gratitude are equally blended. "This was, I think, the greatest political error of my life: & would, had it been reduced to practise, instead of releiving, destroyed New England. . . . Fortunately for my own reputation the erroneous opinion I formed produced no bitter fruits to myself or my country.[58]

57. Plumer, Autobiography, 397-98.
58. *Ibid.*, 133-34. See Appendix A for comment on the secessionist movement in New England.

CHAPTER IX

Farewell to Washington

"I part with the honors and emoluments of office without regret or disgust. I have done my duty—I have acted according to the convictions of my own heart." [1]

THE collapse of the Northern Confederacy bubble had an immediate psychological effect on Plumer, comparable to the fading of his religious enthusiasm in 1780. His first reaction upon awakening to reality was a deep sense of discouragement. The fatal weakness of the Northern Federalists, he thought, was their inability to dramatize the insidious danger of Jacobinism. "The only rallying point we have is against the abuses of power & the ruinous measures of the general government." These, however, were deep and fundamental evils which only statesmen could discern, but to which the mass of people, gulled by "the unblushing assurance with which a democrat retails lies," were blind. It was hopeless to expect New England to present any kind of opposition to the administration's iniquity until unity was restored. "In this state of things, what measures ought the Federalists in Congress to pursue, what line of conduct ought they to observe?" asked Plumer of himself. His answer was a strange one for a politician—"to observe *a total silence upon politics.*" Opposition only emphasized the success of the Democrats and abetted their attack upon New England's institutions. "I am still a federalist," insisted Plumer, but "I believe federalism is too pure a government for the people—That it presupposes more knowledge & virtue in the mass of the people than they really have." [2]

The first step, then, in Plumer's political metamorphosis was a change from active to passive Federalism. The alteration was immediately noticeable in his correspondence. Although he had promised the editor

1. *Plumer's Memorandum,* 640.
2. *Ibid.,* 198-99.

of the *Portsmouth Oracle* a weekly newsletter from Washington, he stopped writing for this or any other newspaper after November.[3] The energy formerly expended in partisan propaganda he now devoted to transcribing government documents and writing to members of his family. To William, Jr., whose schoolboy politics were rabidly Federalist as a result of his father's letters, Plumer outlined his new views and advised the exercise of similar caution. He had no immediate intention of breaking with the Federalist party, but the resolution to investigate and reflect before forming an opinion had an excellent effect. It stripped the scales of partisan blindness from Plumer's eyes, prevented him from making hasty judgments that pride would afterward compel him to support, and allowed him to assume an intelligent rather than a merely obstructionist attitude of opposition. "It produced," he wrote in his autobiography, "by insensible degrees, a change in my political opinions & conduct on many subjects." [4]

In line with his new policy of passive resistance, Plumer did what he could to moderate party strife in Washington. The Federalists had always celebrated Washington's birthday with an elaborate and snobbish dinner intended to perpetuate the myth that Washington was the founder and patron saint of their party. Plumer believed that the banquet was politically inexpedient, and he agitated so effectively against it that it was abandoned. He also continued to do what he could to break down the self-erected social barriers between men of opposite political creeds. Although such bitter partisans as Tracy and Griswold never visited the President, Plumer invariably presented himself at the Executive Mansion each time he arrived in Washington, at the New Year's levees, and whenever he was invited to dine. "These are visits & dinners of ceremony," he reminded himself. "Beside, I have a curiosity, which is gratified, by seeing & conversing with him. I gain a more thorough knowledge of his character, & of his views, & those of his party—for he is naturally communicative." Plumer found the President more attentive to his dress and table than he had been in the winter of 1803, but also apparently less sure of himself and in lower spirits.[5] The wars of Europe, which had rendered Washington's and Adams's hours in

3. Plumer to Daniel Treadwell, Nov. 6, 1804, Letter Book, IV, Lib. Cong.; Plumer, Autobiography, 140.
4. Plumer to William Plumer, Jr., Nov. 20, 1804, Letter Book, IV, Lib. Cong.; William Plumer, Jr., Autobiography (1789-1819), N. H. State Lib. (hereafter cited as Plumer, Jr., Memoirs, I, to distinguish it from his father's autobiography); Plumer, Autobiography, 140.
5. *Plumer's Memorandum*, 193, 212-13, 299.

office so unhappy, were beginning to cloud the fair horizon of Jefferson's success.

Plumer was not yet able to view Jefferson and his works with impartiality. He accepted invitations to the President's excellent dinners with alacrity, only to come home and fill his diary with petty criticism of his host. In the carping and malicious style that had become a literary convention among the members of the Essex Junto, he deprecated Jefferson's state papers in letters to his family. "Never let any of your composition resemble that of the President's message of the 8th of November," he admonished his son. "You justly say it is not english. And I will add it is intricate, perplexed, & enveloped in obscurity." [6] Plumer allowed Jefferson's dry docks, gun boats, salt mountains, fossil skeletons, and mixed metaphors to obscure an appreciation of the President's genuine political skill and linguistic artistry.

The second session of the Eighth Congress, held during the winter of 1804, corresponded perfectly to Plumer's mood of watchful waiting. It was an indecisive, puzzling session, marking the transition from the confidence and success of Jefferson's first administration, to the doubts, difficulties, and failures that beset his last four years in office. The familiar guideposts to legislators, particularly those erected along the party line, seemed to point the wrong way, or to have disappeared altogether, leaving to them the unaccustomed labor of making independent decisions. The resultant confusion grew so great toward the end of the session that Plumer could write: "The Senate are less divided by the party spirit of Feds & Demos than I ever knew it before . . . our divisions arise from other sources—from *Free* States & *Slave* states—from Commercial states & anti-commercial states." [7]

Such conditions were favorable to Plumer's newly determined independence, but he had the uncomfortable feeling that many of his brother-legislators were equally untrammeled. It is one thing to be independent in a world of dependents, but it is quite another matter to be a free spirit among men and principles jarred loose from their moorings. An air of mystery, of intrigue, of impending disaster, which Jefferson's vague messages and tortuous policy did little to dispel, hung over the Senate chamber, and Plumer found it peculiarly oppressive. Small groups of Republican senators would leave the chamber and engage in anxious conversation in the lobby, breaking off awkwardly when Plumer or

6. Plumer to Plumer, Jr., Dec. 5, 1804, Letter Book, IV, Lib. Cong.
7. Plumer to Jeremiah Smith, Feb. 7, 1805, *ibid.*

another Federalist walked by.[8] Plumer complained that he had no information beyond rumor on the most important issues pending in the Senate. He had to wait until the majority had reached a caucus decision before he could learn the facts on any question, provided that the majority decided to reveal them at all.

Plumer was particularly puzzled and fascinated by the sinister figure of Aaron Burr. Both his partisan veneration for Hamilton and his moral attitude toward dueling were outraged by the unprecedented appearance of the Vice-President, under indictment of murder, on the first day of the 1804-5 session. "The high office of the President, is filled by an *Infidel,* & that of the Vice President by a *Murderer,*" indignantly wrote Plumer. "When such men are in office we may say with propriety *we have fallen on evil times.*" [9] By the end of the session, however, Burr had exercised his personal charm to such good effect that nearly all his past sins were forgotten. On Saturday, March 2, he took leave of the Senate and of public office in a remarkable speech, full of righteous retrospection and undying love of country, and delivered with such consummate skill as to remove even the suspicion of hypocrisy. Several senators were moved to tears and a resolution of thanks to Burr for the ability and impartiality with which he had conducted his office was passed unanimously. Plumer tried to explain his own conflicting emotions to his wife by saying that he condemned dueling as much as any man, but he could not deny that Burr's official conduct had been highly admirable.[10] He could not shake off the extraordinary influence of the man's personality, and on the way home to Epping, he wrote a letter to his son which shows how vividly Burr could impress even a prosaic Puritan. "This man, but for his vices, might have held the first office in the gift of the nation. . . .—But he is fallen, & I much doubt if he can ever rise again. . . . Of all things in life nothing is more valuable than integrity. To loose office is trifling but to loose the esteem & confidence of mankind, & what is infinitely worse, to forfeit the esteem of oneself, & of high Heaven is a state of extreme wretchedness; & to which I hope your conduct in life will never lead." [11]

The administration's most bitter and humiliating defeat in this session resulted from the defection of six Republican senators in the impeachment and trial of Judge Chase. The judge's exoneration was certainly

8. *Plumer's Memorandum,* 218-19.
9. Plumer to John Norris, Nov. 7, 1804, Letter Book, IV, Lib. Cong.
10. *Plumer's Memorandum,* 312-13; *Adams's Memoirs,* I, 365-67; Plumer to Mrs. Sarah Plumer, Mar. 2, 1805, Letter Book, IV, Lib. Cong.
11. Plumer to Plumer, Jr., Mar. 10, 1805, Letter Book, IV, Lib. Cong.

not expected by Senator Plumer, who assumed that President Jefferson intended to sweep the entire bench clean of Federalist judges. "The judges of the Supreme Court must fall," he wrote to Jeremiah Mason. "They are denounced by the Executive as well as the House. . . . Men of more flexible nerves can be found to succeed them." [12]

Plumer was not alone in believing that the Pickering case had established a precedent which the Republicans would not fail to employ in removing Judge Chase. If the impeachment process could be used to effect the removal of a man mentally incapable of criminal intent, it could easily be made effective against a judge who willfully and wittingly used the bench as a soap box for political speeches. "It was impossible to establish by a stronger case than . . . [Pickering's], the principle that *criminality* was not an essential ingredient of impeachable offenses," wrote John Quincy Adams to his father.[13] Judge Jeremiah Smith drew out the inescapable connection between the Pickering and Chase cases on a thread of humor: "If you convict Judge Chase you can at least claim the merit of being impartial—treating all alike—the men of sound mind & the distracted—This is a degree of impartiality few Judges can pretend to—You will pardon me but I suspect (forgive me if this suspicion's rash) that you have men among you better qualified to try Pickering than Chase—a non compos—than a reasonable being—I fear Chase, whatever may have been the case with the N H Judge, will not be tried by his Peers." Then, having professional cause to be apprehensive of impeachments, Smith ended with a prayer that he had composed especially for judges. "From lightning and tempest, from plague pestilence & famine, From battle (Mr Jefferson will join me in this) & murder (and Burr in this) and from impeachment, Good Lord deliver us." [14]

Except for its final and unexpected result, the Chase trial followed the pattern set by the Pickering case. The Republicans made the same effort to represent impeachment as an inquest into fitness for office rather than as a criminal trial, endeavoring, as Senator Giles put it, to avoid being "entangled with the *rules* of Courts." [15] In marked contrast

12. Plumer to Jeremiah Mason, Jan. 14, 1804, Letter Book, I, Lib. Cong.

13. Ford, ed., *Writings of John Q. Adams,* III, 106-14.

14. Jeremiah Smith to Plumer, Jan. 7, 1805, Letter Book, IV, Lib. Cong.

15. *Plumer's Memorandum,* 141-42, 230, 239; Plumer, Autobiography, 141. The best accounts of the Chase trial are to be found in Adams, *History of the United States,* II, 218-44, and Beveridge, *Marshall,* III, 157-222. Both are too anti-Jeffersonian. Beveridge is one of the few historians of this period who has used the Plumer manuscripts.

was the Federalist position on this legal controversy as stated by Plumer: "There can be no principle of law better known, or that is more clearly founded in the reason & fitness of things, than That a Judge is never to be punished for an error of judgment—To impeach convict and remove a judge from office, for having formed an erroneous opinion, & honestly acting agreeably to that opinion, is a doctrine pregnant with ruin to the Judiciary. . . . the constitution authorizes the one house to impeach, & the other to try, civil officers *only* in case they have committed *high crimes & misdemeanors.*" [16]

This was the argument which determined that senators who had condemned Pickering would acquit Chase in spite of consistency and precedent. The extremists on either side might insist that there was no technical difference between removing a demented drunkard or an obnoxious partisan by the only constitutional means which had been provided, but the moderates allowed conscience and reason rather than consistency to guide them. The highest vote secured by the managers on any of the eight articles of impeachment was nineteen to fifteen, four short of the two-thirds necessary for conviction.[17] The six Republicans who deserted their party on this ballot came from Vermont, New York, Ohio, and South Carolina. In New England, only the Rhode Island senators voted with Virginia. Plumer's Northern Confederacy had made its appearance, not as a result of Federalist senators plotting to destroy the Constitution, but of Republican senators voting to defend it.

The acquittal of Chase came so near the end of the session and in the midst of such a flurry of last-minute business, that Plumer did not have time to recover from his surprise until he was in the stagecoach on his homeward journey. At Baltimore, he visited Judge Chase in his home, where the members of the family were "pleased to greet him who had been a righteous judge of their father," and a warmly sentimental evening ensued.[18] Although Plumer was to change his mind about many things, he never repudiated his attitude toward the Chase impeachment. "Tho I considered judge Chase as having, in a few instances, been guilty of intemperate feelings & language, & of imprudence not becoming the character of judge," he declared long afterward, "yet I did not in any instance consider them of such a nature as ought to have prevented me from voting for his appointment as a judge, much less to remove him on impeachment, & being satisfied he was not guilty of

16. *Plumer's Memorandum*, 232-33.
17. *Extracts in Cases of Impeachment*, 55-60.
18. Plumer to Plumer, Jr., Mar. 10, 1805, Letter Book, IV, Lib. Cong.

high crimes & misdemeanors as charged, my vote on each article was *not guilty*. The propriety of those votes I have never seen cause to question." [19]

After this fiasco, the Virginia leaders had perforce to accept their defeat and reconcile themselves to the federal judiciary with its nationalist potentialities unimpaired. Their abandonment of the attack on the judiciary did much to reconcile moderate Federalists like Plumer to the Republican regime; if there were enough conservative Northern men in the Republican party to curb its democratic rashness, the nation might not necessarily crumble in its hands. Plumer did not rationalize his feelings in this manner, but they are apparent in all of his writing. He stopped talking about Virginia tyranny and New England secession. Another ground of reconciliation emerged in the fact that the administration gave every evidence of having forgotten about states' rights and the curtailment of national powers. Plumer and Jefferson, coming from opposite directions, had turned into the same street.

Plumer was undoubtedly influenced in coming to terms with the administration by the political transformation of his constituency. Encouraged by their triumph in the national elections in 1804 and led by a newly-created partisan press,[20] the New Hampshire Republicans conducted the state campaign of 1805 with the assurance of victory already achieved. The Federalists, on the other hand, virtually conceded their own defeat. Plumer dutifully wrote to the members of his old state committee, expressing a hope that his fellow partisans had "recovered from the panic & [would] punctually attend the meetings at the hour, and act manfully," but he offered no concrete encouragement. He betrayed his own apathy by assuring his brother Daniel that he wished only for the election of the men best qualified both in town and state.[21] From

19. Plumer, Autobiography, 146.
20. Robinson, *Jeffersonian Democracy in New England,* 68-69; Richard Purcell, *Connecticut in Transition, 1775-1818* (Wash., 1918), 310-11; *Political Observatory* (Walpole), Feb. 2, Mar. 9, 1805. Until 1801, when the Republicans purchased the *New Hampshire Gazette* (Portsmouth), they had had no journalistic voice in the state. In 1805, they established their second journal, the *Political Observatory,* in Walpole on the Connecticut River and in the center of an overwhelmingly Federalist area.
21. Plumer to William Kent, Dec. 31, to T. W. Thompson, Dec. 23, 1804, Letter Book, IV, Lib. Cong.; Plumer to Daniel Plumer, Feb. 5, 1805, Letters, 1802-7, Lib. Cong. Plumer did not write for this campaign the pamphlet *An Appeal to the Old Whigs of New Hampshire* (n.p., 1805) which has sometimes been attributed to him. It was written by young Daniel Webster in a vain effort to animate the leaders in his party. See Claude Fuess, *Daniel Webster* (Boston, 1930), I, 125.

Daniel's point of view, this is exactly what happened in the March elections. John Langdon beat John Taylor Gilman by a decisive majority, while the Republicans won majorities in the council and in both houses of the legislature.[22] Plumer viewed the results with resignation. "Democracy has obtained its long expected triumph in New Hampshire," he wrote to Uriah Tracy, "and [its] success is not owing to snow, rain, hail, or bad roads. It is an incontravertible fact that the federalists in this State do not compose the majority. . . . Many good men have grown weary of constant unremitted exertions to support a system whose labors bear a close affinity to those of *Sisiphus*. They therefore feel disposed to tend to their own affairs, & leave those of the State to the discretion of *philosophers*. These good men are thoroughly persuaded that those who can dissect the wing of a butterfly, or the proboscis of a musquitoe, are well qualified to give & administer laws." [23]

Senator Plumer himself was one of the good men who had grown weary of ineffectual well-doing. The long dreaded triumph of democracy in New Hampshire, coming upon the heels of the puzzling congressional session he had just attended and the vindication of the federal judiciary, seemed very much like an anticlimax rather than the clap of doom. He shifted another degree on the political scale, and admitted that Langdon's election appeared less alarming to him than he had expected—that it would not "convulse the State." "Indeed," he wrote, "I feel a greater degree of indifference on the subject than I thought for." [24] During the placid summer of 1805, Plumer lost interest in politics very rapidly. He canceled his subscriptions to partisan newspapers and spent his time pleasantly reading history and working on his farm. Domestic interests engrossed much of his attention. "On the *fifth* day of the *fifth* month in this *fifth* year of the nineteenth century," Plumer recorded the birth of his fifth son, and he could not resist the temptation to name the baby Quintus. Thus burdened, the little chap lived only "*five* times *five* days." [25] In September, Plumer accompanied his eldest son to Cambridge and saw him safely through the entrance examinations at Harvard. There had been some trepidation about this

22. Lyon, ed., *New Hampshire Register . . . 1860*, 41. Everett Stackpole, *History of New Hampshire* (N. Y., 1916), III, 6, makes the amazing declaration that Plumer organized this Republican landslide.

23. Plumer to Uriah Tracy, May 2, 1805, Letter Book, IV, Lib. Cong.

24. *Plumer's Memorandum*, 317-18.

25. Plumer, Autobiography, 158. The baby's tombstone, in the private burial yard on Plumer's estate, is inscribed with a recital of these curious facts, and has consequently received much notice from antiquarians.

event, for young William had acquired something of his father's aversion to the study of dead languages. Headmaster Abbot of Phillips Exeter admitted that the Senator's son could not parse Greek or Latin verbs but nevertheless gave him a letter of introduction and recommendation. The examinations were creditably passed, and the elder Plumer, muttering something about the greater importance of being "acquainted with the *spirit & import* of the ancients than with their *literal meaning*" felt vindicated.[26]

One result of Plumer's recovery from partisan obsession was that he returned to an intermittent practice of law between sessions of the Senate. In one case, he acquired a substantial increase in reputation by advocating successfully "the claim of a poor friendless girl against the son of a wealthy father for the maintenance of an illegitimate child." [27] Plumer's renewed legal practice had, however, the regrettable effect of finally alienating him from Jeremiah Smith. In spite of earlier disagreements, beginning with the Langdon impeachment, the two gifted men had maintained cordial relations for seventeen years. But Smith's conduct on the bench grew increasingly arrogant, in Plumer's opinion, and led to inevitable clashes of personality. A judgment rendered against Plumer's brother, Samuel, as plaintiff, brought on harsh words and mutual accusations. "Smith seems to think that he has engrossed all the legal knowledge, & *that wisdom shall die with him*," complained Plumer, and decided to break off their friendship. A year later, Smith proposed a reconciliation, saying that "he thot men of science & liberality were so few in the state that they were bound to visit each other," [28] but since he refused to apologize, Plumer rejected the overture. The precise assignment of responsibility for this unfortunate quarrel was too difficult a task even for William, Jr., but in gathering information for his father's biography, he discovered that most of Smith's friends had found the judge's ambition, opportunism, and sarcasm hard to endure.[29] For Plumer, the quarrel meant the dissolution of one of the few personal links that had bound him to the Federalist party.

During the three years following its stunning defeat in 1805, the

26. Benjamin Abbot to Eliphalet Pearson, Sept. 23, 1805, Plumer Papers, N. H. State Lib.; Plumer, Autobiography, 158.
27. William Plumer, Register, I, 34, Lib. Cong.
28. *Ibid.*, 58; Autobiography, 197. Plumer, Register, I, 34-38, contains a long and detailed account of this quarrel, and the case of *Plumer* v. *Crockett,* which occasioned it.
29. William Plumer, Jr., Notes for a Life of William Plumer, N. H. State Lib., 24. Also a letter from William Plumer, Jr., to an unidentified resident of Exeter, Apr. 11, 1851, Plumer Papers, *ibid.*

Federalist party of New Hampshire virtually retired from activity.[30] To a certain extent its apathy corresponded with Plumer's mood; he welcomed the abatement of party zeal and felt that it had a moderating effect on the Republicans. "The federalists are silent," he wrote to Calvin Goddard, "& as good men should be, they are perfectly submissive to the powers that be." [31] The fall of the Federalists from the seats of power, however, sharpened the antagonism between Plumer and the Exeter Junto. In 1801, young Daniel Webster had first met Plumer at a convivial dinner party in Exeter at the home of Oliver Peabody, and had been impressed by the deference paid by the prominent New Hampshire Federalists to their visitor. The scene contrasted significantly with one which occurred in the fall of 1805, when Plumer, on his way to Congress, stopped at Tenney's home in Exeter to pay his respects to his colleague. Peabody and two other Exeter Federalists came in while Plumer was conversing stiffly with the doctor and his wife. The atmosphere grew increasingly chilly, until Plumer left to spend the night in a tavern, not even troubling to call upon ex-Governor Gilman. A few weeks later he wrote to William, Jr.: "The Exeter gentry were never partial to me—& as its now low tide in their affairs on the political sea—they feel splenetic & vexed with every man who dares to differ from their *unthinking unfledg'd Minds*." [32] From this time Plumer virtually severed relations with the Exeter Junto.

John Langdon proved to be even less interested in "convulsing" the state than Plumer had expected him to be. He recommended no revolutionary measures, and his legislatures did nothing more radical than to incorporate the Baptists and Universalists as religious sects, thus exempting them from compulsory church taxes.[33] Neither did the Republican legislature of New Hampshire imitate Congress by setting up a little theater of impeachments as Chief Justice Smith had sarcastically predicted. Instead, in answer to Smith's fervent prayers, it granted

30. The *Farmer's Museum* (Walpole), formerly the *Newhampshire and Vermont Journal,* Mar. 14, 1806, has an interesting explanation of this collapse. The Federalist leaders retained their old allegiance "unmoved by the violent and temporary gusts of party," as the editor loftily put it, but they were content to wait until their less enlightened fellows would "again embrace their former sentiments which they have been deprived of by the deceptive arts of demagogues."

31. Plumer to Calvin Goddard, Aug. 31, 1805, Letter Book, IV, Lib. Cong.

32. Plumer, Jr., *Life of Plumer,* 233; *Plumer's Memorandum,* 325; Plumer to Plumer, Jr., Feb. 23, 1806, Letter Book, IV, Lib. Cong.

33. Sanford Cobb, *The Rise of Religious Liberty in America* (N. Y., 1902), 516-17; Robinson, *Jeffersonian Democracy in New England,* 147. These bills passed without division, which means that the Federalists did not contest them.

him an annual bonus of $500 as long as he remained in office, thus
making him the highest paid official in the state government.[34] Only
a few months after their party friends in Washington had impeached
Judge Chase, the Republicans in the New Hampshire legislature voted
down a resolution to remove Judge Livermore by address.[35] They
permitted the state judiciary to remain solidly Federalist, although
with their majorities they could easily have purged the entire system.
Senator Plumer, with irony more delicate than he customarily employed, congratulated Governor Langdon on the legislature's conservatism and declared solemnly: " 'Tis certain that a people had better
submit to some inconvenience, & even to partial evils, than encounter
the more substantial ones that necessarily follow innovation. Not that
I think our Courts, or system of laws perfect; but great & material changes ought not to be made but from necessity & with great
caution." [36]

In the realm of national affairs, the Republicans acted more like
"New England men" than Plumer himself. Unwilling to wait even
until 1807 to begin redressing the black balance against the North, the
legislature in 1805 instructed New Hampshire congressmen to support
an amendment to the Constitution prohibiting immediately the further
importation of slaves.[37] When Senator Plumer later received this instruction from Governor Langdon, he was compelled to point out that
the amending clause itself rendered obedience impossible, and that even
if it were possible it would probably not be expedient.[38]

Thus Plumer returned to Washington in the autumn of 1805 with
a lighter load of Federalist prejudice than he had ever carried before.
This does not mean, however, that he had any confidence in Jefferson's
policies. "We merit the approbation of the country for having done as
little as we have," he later reported. "For at this critical juncture I think

34. Smith's long letter of appeal to the legislature is printed in Morison, *Jeremiah
Smith*, 156-65. The resolution for granting his request passed the House by a vote
of 101-54, which meant that not less than 28 Republicans voted for it in spite of
Smith's avowed partisanship. See *Journal of the House of Representatives, June
Session, 1804* (Portsmouth, 1804), 45. Plumer assumed that Republicans wanted to
keep Smith on the bench to prevent his becoming the Federalist candidate for governor.

35. *Journal of the House of Representatives, December Session, 1805* (Portsmouth,
1806), 93.

36. Plumer to John Langdon, Jan. 18, 1806, Letter Book, IV, Lib. Cong.

37. *House Journal, Dec. Sess., 1805*, 36. See Herman Ames, "Proposed Amendments to the Constitution of the United States," Amer. Hist. Assoc., *Annual Report
for the Year 1896* (Wash., 1897), II, 327 (No. 372).

38. Plumer to John Langdon, Feb. 3, 1806, Letter Book, IV, Lib. Cong. The
reversal of roles effected by this incident requires no comment.

we shall find more security in standing still than in action." His uncertainty was increased by the frequent evidence of dissension in the Republican ranks, by John Randolph's inexplicable attacks upon the administration, and by Jefferson's unwillingness to assume a straightforward foreign policy. "I think Administration is not only embarrassed, but divided, on the measures requisite for us to adopt," he wrote at one time. On another occasion he wrote, "What course our Government will adopt is enveloped in mystery." [39]

Thrown upon his own resources, Plumer added to the general chaos by frequently voting with undisciplined independence. On the Yazoo Bill to compensate the purchasers of land from the corrupt land companies whose contracts had been canceled by the Georgia legislature, Plumer found himself in unexpected agreement with John Randolph not only against the Jefferson administration but against his New England colleagues. Investors in his state were among the Yazoo purchasers, and one of them, Robert Fletcher, the plaintiff in the celebrated case of *Fletcher* v. *Peck,* had been associated with Plumer himself in earlier New Hampshire speculations. [40] The Yazoo Act was a favorite measure of Plumer's party and of his most admired friend within that party, John Quincy Adams. On the other hand, its defeat was the favorite project of John Randolph, who represented everything that Plumer disliked in Virginia democracy. Under these circumstances, his opposing vote was a personal declaration of independence—from Federalism, from New England separatism, even from the suspicion of seeking the favor of the administration. He later asserted: "Though deserted by every man in New England & by every Federalist in the Senate, I never gave a vote with more thorough conviction of its propriety." [41]

As Plumer lost his conviction that a Jacobin revolution was imminent, he relaxed considerably, and his personality underwent a subtle change. When he first arrived in Washington in 1802, he was more strait-laced than a Congregationalist minister, with no time for the horse races, the Christmas celebrations, or the card playing which enlivened the dull existence of most congressmen. But although horse-racing was too distinctively Southern to attract his interest, he did venture during

39. Plumer to Edward Livermore, Feb. 11, 1806, to Plumer, Jr., Jan. 29, 1806, to Jeremiah Mason, Dec. 21, 1805, *ibid.; Plumer's Memorandum,* 339.

40. Beveridge, *Marshall,* III, 584 ff.; Plumer to William Gordon, June 18, 1797, Letter Book, I, Lib. Cong.; Plumer to Gordon, Feb. 5, 1798, Atherton Papers, N. H. Hist. Soc.

41. *Plumer's Memorandum,* 462-63, 483.

his last winter in Washington, to attend the theater one evening "to see Manfredi., his wife, daughters & son dance on the tight rope— ballance—& perform other feats—price one dollar." It was probably the first time he had ever been inside a theater, but he soon went to see the Manfredis again. "They were very nimble," he wrote apologetically. "I do not think my time or money mispent." [42]

The chief source of amusement and innocent gossip in the "desert city," however, was the diplomatic corps. General Turreau, Napoleon's ambassador, was a rough, gross man who rode publicly through the streets to visit a prostitute. The sensation created by this spectacle was heightened by the beatings he administered to his wife until the neighbors had to intervene and rescue her from his hands. Even more fascinating than the domestic difficulties of the Turreau ménage was the person of Soliman Melemelli, the ambassador sent by the Bey of Tunis to Washington in the winter of 1805-6. This Arabian Nights creature with his retinue of brightly dressed domestics was carried to the Potomac by an American frigate and supported in the capital by the federal government. Plumer was greatly intrigued by his appearance, and described a visit to his exotic quarters with undisguised delight.[43]

Such diversions indicate that Plumer's mood was mellow during his last two years in Washington. His communication with William, his oldest son, evolved from expressions of paternal pride in schoolboy translations of Latin phrases to man-talk about Senate debates and foreign treaties. Father Plumer scolded his son, Samuel, for bad spelling (making the usual mistakes in his own during the process), enjoined domestic economy upon his daughter (citing his Washington landlady as a sterling example), and wrote a movingly tender letter to nine-year-old George on the day before Christmas, sending him a song book as a New Year's gift. The correspondence also reveals unexpected traits of compassion in Plumer's character. He spent the whole of New Year's Day nursing a younger brother of Arthur and Edward Livermore who had fallen ill during a visit to Washington.[44] These are illuminat-

42. *Ibid.*, 534.
43. *Ibid.*, 345, 358, 521.
44. See Plumer to Mrs. Sarah Plumer, Jan. 1, 1805, to Plumer, Jr., Feb. 8, 1805, Mar. 15, 1806, to Samuel Plumer, Feb. 20, 1805, to Arthur Livermore, Feb. 20, 1805, to Sally Plumer, Dec. 13, 1805, to George Plumer, Dec. 24, 1805; Plumer, Jr., to Plumer, Feb. 14, 1805, Jan. 4, 1806; George Livermore to Plumer, Mar. 22, 1805, Letter Book, IV, Lib. Cong. Unfortunately, the young man died in Concord on his return journey.

ing glimpses of the human being who lived behind the façade of the politician.

Even the façade grew gayer, however, as Plumer began to discard nearly every trace of party spirit. In visiting Republican colleagues, he now discovered that his former opponents were, for the most part, patriotic gentlemen whose continued opposition to his point of view did not prevent mutual esteem. Such men as William Giles of Virginia and James Jackson of Georgia, who represented the very antithesis of New England Federalism and who marshaled that slave power against which Plumer had been so bitter in 1804, became his personal friends. When Jackson died in Washington during the spring of 1806, Plumer was deeply affected. The funeral service was held on a cold, rainy day, and Plumer was ill, yet he was one of only three Federalists who attended. "Cursed be the spirit of party!" he wrote. "Its blind baleful malevolent degrading effects ceases not with the grave." [45]

Among the factors that aided Plumer's reconciliation to Republicanism was a gradual dissolution of his prejudices against Thomas Jefferson. He found it much easier to discuss questions of state with the head of the nation when he himself was not bound by party obligations to function in the opposition. He was also better fitted to enjoy Jefferson's unequaled hospitality. In a letter to his daughter, he described an excellent dinner with the President, at which an illuminating little incident occurred. Jefferson begged Plumer to take "a few of his Illinois nuts" and plant them on his estate.

"After twenty years, they will bear," continued the President.

"I shall, then, despair of eating of them," replied Plumer (who lived for forty-four years afterward).

"Your children will eat with pleasure the fruit of your industry," declared the courtly Jefferson.

Plumer, not to be outdone in etiquette, rejoined: "I will teach them to bear in remembrance to whose politeness they are indebted for the nuts that produced these trees of fruit." [46]

Here is a very different picture from the monster of political and moral infidelity which Federalists had painted in 1800. But Plumer was still puzzled by the contradictions in Jefferson's character. He regarded as tragically premature the President's announcement in the spring of 1806 that he would not serve a third term, for *"Most men*

45. *Plumer's Memorandum,* 352, 460-61.
46. Plumer to Sally Plumer, Dec. 27, 1806, Letter Book, IV, Lib. Cong. This is a free version of the conversation, but the words have not been changed.

shun—but all seek the rising sun." [47] Nevertheless, he was impressed by the voluntary renunciation of power, and he sat down one Sunday evening to analyze his mingled feelings toward this strange man. "The more critically & impartially I examine the character & conduct of Mr. Jefferson the more favorably I think of his integrity.... He is a man of science. But he is very credulous—he knows little of the nature of man—very little indeed.... He is a closet politician—but not a practical statesman. He has much *fine sense* but little of that *plain common sense* so requisite to business—& which in fact governs the world.... An infidel in religion—but in every thing else credulous to a fault! Alas man is himself a contradiction!" [48]

As Plumer grew more friendly with the Republicans in Washington, he became more critical of the Federalists. "Rigid Federalists I think are bad members of Congress," he concluded. "Their prejudices govern more than their reason." After listening to one of Senator Pickering's bitter and abusive speeches, Plumer wrote resignedly, "If he advocates an opinion he generally does it fatally." [49] When the handful of Federalists in the House of Representatives refused to support a Massachusetts Republican for speaker against the Southern candidate, Plumer wrote: "I think the eastern States have an interest different from that of the southern, & I really wish we might support that interest—not indeed in such a way as would endanger the peace & happiness of the Union. In Virginia a federalist is still a Virginian; but in New England a federalist does not feel or act as a New Englandman." [50] Plumer had conceived a very different, and much more promising, formula for solving his section's political difficulties than the one he had advocated less than two years before.

Plumer also became increasingly irritated with the social snobbery of his fellow partisans. During his last winter in Washington, he accordingly left the Federalist den at Coyle's and took a single room in a newly finished hotel on Capitol Hill. It was more expensive, but the company was better.[51] The agreeable mixture of Federalists and Republicans at their table was enlivened, during the term of the Supreme

47. *Plumer's Memorandum,* 453.
48. *Ibid.,* 453-54.
49. *Ibid.,* 428, 437-39.
50. *Ibid.,* 337. Cf. Plumer, Jr., *Life of Plumer,* 335.
51. *Plumer's Memorandum,* 523, 570, 622; Plumer to Sally Plumer, Dec. 1, 1806, to Mrs. Sarah Plumer, Dec. 28, 1806, Letter Book, IV, Lib. Cong. The company included young Henry Clay, who made a vivid impression on Plumer, and Thomas Mann Randolph, Jefferson's son-in-law.

Court, by a group of the most brilliant lawyers from every part of the United States. It was an appropriate environment for a man who had almost ceased to be a Federalist but had not yet become a Republican.

A similar transformation took place in Plumer's relations with New Hampshire politicians whom he had frequently condemned in unqualified language.[52] There was certainly an element of appeasement in this correspondence, for Plumer congratulated the Republican administration on many of its achievements and spoke critically of former Federalist officeholders. These ideas, however, were expressed in Plumer's usual boldness of language, not in the circuitous manner of a wily politician trimming his sails. He criticized Jefferson as freely to Republican correspondents as to Federalists. If he meant to conduct negotiations for transferring his allegiance to the Republicans in order to stay in office, he began extremely late and spoke with tactless independence. His correspondence reads more like that of a man winding up his public affairs and seeking peace with all his neighbors before he retires.

There is no evidence in Plumer's correspondence, unless his friendly letters to Republicans be so considered, that Plumer made the slightest effort to secure a re-election to the Senate. In June 1806, the Republican legislature chose Nahum Parker of Fitzwilliam, the councilor from Cheshire County, to succeed him.[53] "I felt no anxiety for a re-election," wrote Plumer upon receiving the news. "No doubt much of this indifference proceeded from a full persuasion that a man so moderate in his politic's as I am could not be elected.—I am too much of a federalist to have republican votes, & too much of a Republican deeply to interest federalists in my favor." [54]

Plumer's capitalization of the "R" in "Republican" may have been an unconscious revelation of the state of his politics, although he certainly made no open declaration of a change. A better indication was the fact that in August, he voted for a congressional ticket of his own, made up of three Federalists and two Republicans (neither of whom was on the regular Republican ticket). But he had no illusions. "The Democratic list will prevail," he wrote, "feeble as they are. . . . I regret

52. For example, Plumer to John Langdon, Jan. 18, 1806, to Philip Carrigain, Jan. 24, 1806, to Amos Cogswell, Jan. 27, 1806, to John Goddard, Apr. 14, 1806, Letter Book, IV, Lib. Cong.

53. *Journal of the House of Representatives, June Session, 1806* (Portsmouth, 1806), 48.

54. *Plumer's Memorandum,* 506.

that men devoid of talent, information, & respectability, should be called to represent the State in the Supreme legislature of the Nation." [55]

Plumer spent the summer of 1806 preaching his new gospel of political moderation. Soon after his return from Washington, he called on Governor Langdon, who treated him with great civility. In June, he visited Boston where the Massachusetts Republicans had just won control of their legislature for the first time but had failed by a few votes to elect their candidate for governor. "Boston is now a Vast pile of combustibles," [56] he reported, and used his influence with friends in both parties to counsel acceptance of the new political balance. Plumer found a troubled atmosphere also at Salem, where religious fanaticism added to the bitterness of party struggles. "They croud into [houses of worship] with zeal to serve the Lord," he wrote, "but with hearts full of bitterness and hatred against those who do not subscribe to their creed." Plumer spent one evening with William Gray, a prominent Federalist and the greatest merchant in New England. Plumer expounded his new doctrine of nonpartisan moderation and believed that he made a strong impression on the merchant.[57] Within two years, both of these men had withdrawn from the Federalist party to support Jefferson's embargo.

Meanwhile, Plumer had been thinking about his own future. The most obvious course was to return to the practice of law, but this was a prospect that he did not relish. "I dislike the drudgery & fatigues of the business," he confessed. "And I am not ambitious of wealth." [58] There remained the second possibility that he might continue in the public service in some capacity other than that of a senator. Hearing in December 1806 that a vacancy was likely to occur in the Court of Common Pleas for Rockingham County, he wrote to Governor Langdon: "Will you permit me, in confidence, to say, That if you judge me qualified for that office, I shall, if appointed, accept it." [59] The vacancy

55. *Ibid.*, 512-13.

56. *Ibid.*, 500-1. For a full account of this election, see Edward Stanwood, "The Massachusetts Election in 1806," Mass. Hist. Soc., *Proceedings*, 2d Ser., 20 (1906-7), 12-19.

57. *Plumer's Memorandum*, 501; Plumer, Autobiography, 195. See Edward Gray, *William Gray of Salem, Merchant* (Boston, 1914), 34, 38, 41.

58. *Plumer's Memorandum*, 511. Plumer's disinclination toward further practice did not arise from fear of failure. He did some business at the Rockingham Court of Common Pleas after his return from Washington, with eminent success. Plumer, Diary, 30, Lib. Cong. He succeeded in obtaining an acquittal in a famous murder trial which attracted nearly a thousand spectators. Plumer to Samuel Plumer, Mar. 22, 1808, to Plumer, Jr., Feb. 21, 1809, N. H. State Lib.

59. Plumer to John Langdon, Dec. 17, 1806, Letter Book, IV, Lib. Cong.

that Plumer anticipated did not occur, however, and nothing came of his application.

Plumer's economic position was sufficiently secure that he did not feel compelled to seek an additional income. He owned $50,000 worth of property, much of it in wild and unproductive lands, but the remainder invested in securities that produced a steady revenue.[60] He lived a temperate, frugal life on his country estate, so that his annual expenditures, even including the maintenance of a son at Harvard, did not exceed $1,500. It was entirely feasible for him to retire from active life and devote the remainder of his years to a project that had long attracted him—the writing of a history of the government of the United States.

It was characteristic of Plumer that on July 22, 1806, he retired to his study and drew up the arguments for and against the pursuit of this new career. He considered first the question of desirability. There existed many state histories and histories of the Revolution, but the field was clear for such a general comprehensive work as Plumer contemplated. He decided that this history would be highly useful as a revelation of many facts unknown to most Americans and as a guide to future statesmen. Nor was the earnest New Hampshire senator blind to the personal rewards to be derived from such a book. "If well executed it would be an imperishable monument that would perpetuate my name more effectually than anything I could do," he considered. "If ill executed, it would tarnish & destroy much of the little fame I have acquired." [61] Plumer had collected in his own library an excellent set of documents, but he would need to consult many more. His researches would require indefatigable industry and patient application which would be difficult in the face of his poor health, his remote situation, and his growing family. Finally, Plumer had the honesty to admit his own disqualifications for the task. "I am no scholar—I am not even master of the English grammar—& I cannot read any other language. It requires much time to express my ideas on paper so as to satisfy myself—Tho' I find I compose with more & greater facility than formerly. I am greatly deficient in geography and subjects of general science. This will prove a great impediment to my progress in this contemplated work." [62] At the end of his day of contemplation, Plumer found his credits and debits too nearly balanced to reach a decision. Nevertheless,

60. Summary for July 1, 1807, Plumer, Property Book, N. H. State Lib.
61. Plumer, Autobiography, 196; *Plumer's Memorandum*, 508, 509.
62. *Plumer's Memorandum*, 511.

the project had seized his imagination, and from that day forward he regarded himself a disciple of Clio.

During his last two sessions in Congress, Plumer attended to his duties as conscientiously as ever, but in some subtle way, he had doffed the statesman's toga and assumed the historian's mantle. He recorded the debates and votes in less voluminous but more revealing detail. With some degree of detachment, he noted the ludicrous conflict within the Republican party itself over retention or repeal of the extraordinary revenues created to finance the war with Tripoli. Federalist congressmen were inclined to exploit these divisions. Plumer, however, ignoring the maneuvering that produced strange contradictions in the records of many senators, voted consistently for retaining the special duties.[63] He could write with a certain sense of superiority: "And tho' it is right, as it respects the administration, if they adopt measures meerly to gain popularity that they should be taken in their devices & reap the fruit of their own doings—Yet it will be wrong for me to adopt such a line of conduct as will punish them; but at the same time injure my country." [64]

From the time that Aaron Burr had taken his leave of an admiring Senate and Plumer had predicted that he would never rise again, his recurrent rising had been a subject of fascination to the New Hampshire senator. Soon after Plumer returned to Washington in November 1806, President Jefferson issued a proclamation against the Burr conspirators, based on the assumption that they planned to attack Mexico. From other sources, however, Plumer heard that Burr and General Wilkinson, probably financed by Yrujo, had combined their talents for intrigue and planned to detach the western states from the Union. Senator Bradley assured him that all these stories were lies and that Burr's only purpose was to take possession of the Bastrop grant in Louisiana. Rumors subsequently reached Plumer's ears that the governor of Ohio had seized Burr's boats and that the conspirator himself had been arrested and acquitted in Kentucky, but still no information of what had developed was given to Congress. Plumer wrote indignantly: "This state of incertitude is painful, & to the government disgraceful. If Burr has treasonable designs agt the United States, they ought to have been known, & crushed in embryo. If it is private speculation in lands—the public ought to know it—& be quiet." [65]

63. *Ibid.*, 572-74, 622, 638; Plumer, Autobiography, 205-6.
64. *Plumer's Memorandum*, 573-74.
65. Thomas P. Abernethy, *The Burr Conspiracy* (N. Y., 1954), 190-91; *Plumer's Memorandum*, 530-32, 536.

On the twenty-seventh of December, Plumer took advantage of a dinner with the President to learn from Jefferson himself that Harman Blennerhassett, the wealthy Irish immigrant, had been duped by Burr, and that Wilkinson was busily fortifying New Orleans against a combined land and naval attack, led by Burr and Francisco Miranda, the South American revolutionist. The President insisted "there was no room to doubt of the integrity, firmness & attachment of Wilkinson to our government," and that "the conspiracy would be crushed, extensive as it was, with little trouble & expense to the United States." [66]

Not until January 22, however, did the President transmit a message and documents to Congress with positive information that a conspiracy existed. Up to this point, Plumer had been somewhat skeptical, but the President's message, coupled with the arrival in Washington that same night of Burr's lieutenants, Erick Bollman and Samuel Swartout, who had been arrested by Wilkinson in New Orleans and brought under guard to the capital, gave him a sudden moment of panic.[67] It was shared by his fellow senators. The next day, in secret session, Plumer and all of his colleagues, "except 3 or 4," voted for a bill to suspend habeas corpus in order to keep the apprehended conspirators safely in jail.[68] The House of Representatives, however, contemptuously rejected the measure by an overwhelming margin. "It was a singular circumstance, that on such a subject, the two houses should be so unanimous, the one in passing, & the other in rejecting the bill," wrote Plumer.[69] Even more singular was a fact unnoticed by Plumer; that the Senate, designed to serve as a conservative balance wheel against the impulsive House, had been the irresponsible party in these proceedings, while the representatives had refused to be frightened into frantic gestures. Most singular of all, perhaps, was the fact that Senator James A. Bayard of Delaware, who had so lustily defended the Sedition Act in 1798, was

66. *Ibid.,* 543-44.
67. *Ibid.,* 585. Walter McCaleb, *The Aaron Burr Conspiracy,* 2d ed. (N. Y., 1936), 248-49, erroneously states that Bollman and Swartout did not arrive until after January 31. The Senate's bill to suspend the writ of habeas corpus, passed on January 23, would have been pointless, had its immediate purpose not been to prevent the release of Bollman and Swartout. Dr. McCaleb's chronological error led him to misinterpret the action of the Senate. See pp. 246-47. Plumer's chronology is confirmed by Jefferson's message to Congress on January 26. See *Annals of Congress,* 9th Cong., 2d Sess., 45.
68. *Plumer's Memorandum,* 585-90. Cf. *Annals of Congress,* 9th Cong., 2d Sess., 44. Plumer's account of the debate on this bill is the only extended one in print.
69. Adams, *History of the United States,* III, 339-40; Plumer, Autobiography, 212.

the man who cautioned his fellow senators in 1807 to "remember that in such moments legislatures have been hurried on to enact laws that have formed precedents dangerous to freemen." [70]

Plumer soon repented of his panic and rejoiced that the suspension of habeas corpus had not been effected. He became convinced that Burr had not contemplated treason, but that Wilkinson, who had "done more to destroy our little feeble military establishment, than its bitterest enemies have been able for years to effect," had himself created a reign of terror in New Orleans and was now extending it to Washington. It was apparent that the government meant to stake its entire case upon the shifting sands of Wilkinson's loyalty. When Plumer had his last interview with the President, on March 4, 1807, Jefferson was depending upon Wilkinson to arrest Burr, and gloomily contemplating the hazards of trying the traitor before John Marshall. The relations among Burr, Jefferson, and the Republican party presented a fascinating drama, but as a mere spectator, Plumer could never quite decide whether the play was burlesque, mystery, or Greek tragedy.[71]

Burr's treason, however, presented a less serious threat to the United States than the situation in Europe. France and England were locked once more in mortal combat and American commerce was being harassed by both belligerents. Plumer's first reaction to this familiar peril, conditioned by his old Federalist hatred for republican France, was to blame everything upon Napoleon and to regard England as "the only barrier of the civilized world" against tyranny. His willingness to excuse British depredations grew in part out of correspondence from merchants and shippers in Portsmouth who insisted that "the noise respecting Impressment of our Seamen is louder than the real evil requires," and that "the most remote danger of war, for this extended carrying trade is absurd & ridiculous to the last degree." [72] Plumer had no economic sympathy for the mushroom commerce that moved under the American flag from one foreign port to another, and his early distrust of merchants in general was revived by the deceptions to which

70. *Plumer's Memorandum,* 588.
71. *Ibid.,* 618-19, 623, 641. Historians are in the same dilemma. The two most extensive monographs on the Burr conspiracy, those by Walter McCaleb and Thomas P. Abernethy, take diametrically opposite points of view. Dr. McCaleb reached the same conclusion to which Plumer finally came but did not make use of the Plumer papers. Professor Abernethy consulted *Plumer's Memorandum.*
72. John Pierce to Plumer, Apr. 7, 1806, Plumer to John Pierce, Apr. 17, 1806, James Sheafe to Plumer, Mar. 2, 1806, Letter Book, IV, Lib. Cong.

they resorted in order to avoid British capture. Of one such case, then being argued in the Supreme Court, he wrote, "The whole transaction is an attempt, in which is unveiled a series of iniquitous measures to stamp on belligerent property [Spanish] the character of *neutral*, to protect it from British capture. That nation has too much cause to complain of the frauds of our merchants." [73]

In 1806, Jefferson attacked this problem in a characteristically subtle fashion by maneuvering a Senate committee headed by John Quincy Adams into reporting resolutions condemning English seizures, requesting the President to demand redress, and advocating trade restrictions until the grievances were removed. The Federalists, with the sole exception of Plumer, were enthusiastic friends of these resolutions, hoping that they would force Jefferson into the same embarrassing position that Washington had occupied in 1795, and that the negotiation would result in an even more unpopular treaty than Jay's. Plumer, however, believed that the President was as eager to negotiate as the Federalists had been in 1794, but that he was trying to throw responsibility for a venture of doubtful popularity upon the Senate. "This business," Plumer wrote, "has been by Mr. Jefferson, & his friends in the Senate, managed with great address." [74] The New Hampshire senator could not suppress his admiration for a man who had induced his own enemies to relieve him of an unpopular duty, without even asking them to do so. [75]

The resolution condemning Great Britain's spoliations passed the Senate unanimously, but Plumer joined six scattered Republicans in a minority vote against requesting the President to demand indemnities. Plumer was seriously opposed to establishing a precedent for senatorial intermeddling with a properly executive function. In the meantime, the situation in England had materially changed with Pitt's death, and Jefferson himself assured Plumer that the prospects for an understanding with England were "very flattering indeed." [76] Yet Congress, much to Plumer's disgust, applied the irritant of a nonimportation act, which hung like a dead weight around the necks of Monroe and Pinckney, as

73. Plumer to Plumer, Jr., Feb. 23, 1806, *ibid.* The case was probably *Manella, Pujals & Company* v. *James Barry.* See Benjamin Curtis, *Reports of Decisions of the Supreme Court of the United States,* 5th ed. (Boston, 1870), I, 624.

74. *Plumer's Memorandum,* 393, 398, 429, 433; *Adams's Memoirs,* I, 390-400. See also Schachner, *Jefferson,* II, 809-11.

75. Plumer to Jedediah Morse, Feb. 24, 1806, Letter Book, IV, Lib. Cong.

76. *Annals of Congress,* 9th Cong., 1st Sess., 112; *Plumer's Memorandum,* 432-33, 462, 470.

they tried to negotiate with the British government, and had to be suspended by Congress as soon as it assembled again in the autumn of 1806.[77]

On the very day on which the Senate agreed to suspend nonimportation, news reached America of Napoleon's conquest of Prussia, an event which rendered any hope of maintaining neutral commerce completely visionary. "The Emperor of France is the wonder & astonishment of the world," exclaimed Plumer. Napoleon's dazzling success began to dislodge the old Federalist stereotypes from Plumer's mind. During a visit to the President, Plumer agreed with Jefferson that Napoleon would conquer all Europe including England, and that the change of masters would probably be a good thing for the mass of people.[78] Even in his correspondence with Federalists, Plumer indicated his belief that America's interest lay in appeasing the conqueror of Europe, rather than in submitting to the insults of the crumbling "barrier of the civilized world." [79] This opinion measures at once the degree to which Plumer had receded from Federalism, the awe imposed by Austerlitz and Jena, and the growth of irritation over the British cruisers infesting American harbors and despoiling American commerce.

That the administration was committed to this policy of appeasement could hardly be doubted. Jefferson admitted to Plumer that there was no prospect of obtaining Florida from Spain without the aid of Napoleon and that France expected a continuation of America's self-imposed embargo against trade with her rebellious colony, Haiti.[80] The President complained that British ships were carrying American supplies to the island, and that "the prohibition would injure us, the allies of France, & benefit Great Britain, their enemy," but he did not suggest defiance

77. Plumer to Edward Livermore, Apr. 5, 1806, to John Goddard, Apr. 14, 1806, Letter Book, IV, Lib. Cong.; Richardson, *Messages of the Presidents,* I, 411; *Plumer's Memorandum,* 520-21.

78. *Ibid.,* 528, 546.

79. Plumer to Edward Livermore, Feb. 12, 1807, Plumer Papers, N. H. State Lib.

80. *Plumer's Memorandum,* 335-435 *passim,* contains detailed and revealing accounts of the Senate debates on the "Two Million Bill" for the prospective purchase of Florida, and the Logan Bill to interdict American commerce to Haiti. Discussion of these measures has been omitted in this work for lack of space. Henry Adams gives the story in vol. III of his *United States,* and good recent accounts, both based in part on *Plumer's Memorandum,* may be consulted in Morton Borden, *The Federalism of James A. Bayard* (N. Y., 1955), and Schachner, *Jefferson,* II. An interesting example of different conclusions drawn from the same evidence may be seen in these works. Plumer is charged by Borden, pp. 149-50, with "incredible" ignorance for not having divined Jefferson's strategy on these measures, while his perspicacity in "reading Jefferson's maneuvers aright" is cited by Schachner, II, 806.

of Napoleon.[81] If Plumer's ears did not deceive him when he heard the President call France an ally, he at least made no protest.

In the meantime, the entire first session of the Ninth Congress had passed without the submission of a treaty from London, and Congress adjourned on March 3 with no assurance that war with England would not be the first item of business on their calendar in the fall. On the following morning Plumer called to take his last leave of the President and received confirmation of the rumor that a copy of the treaty had been sent to Jefferson by the British ambassador. The President was forced to admit that the document was entirely unsatisfactory and that the prospect was for even greater restrictions on American trade as England and France tightened the screws of their economic warfare.[82] Whatever their sympathies might have been, Americans seemed unable to purchase even a grudging friendship with either of the great European belligerents except at the price of alliance and war.

During his last session in Congress, Plumer turned with relief from current intrigues to his preparations for recording those of the past. By dint of his own exertions in the Capitol lumber room and subsequent begging from his friends, he ultimately acquired a collection of government documents extending to nearly "four or five hundred bound volumes." Not content with this published material, Plumer also began the tedious process of copying the executive journals of the Senate, but was asked to desist by Samuel Alleyne Otis. The timorous old secretary of the Senate had held his post since the organization of the federal government but had been mortally afraid of losing it ever since the Republicans had come into power. So Plumer had to give up his copying and confine himself to taking sketchy notes from the journal.[83]

The would-be historian also read extensively, copied private letters shown to him by his influential friends, and began an acquisitive correspondence with scholars and antiquarians all over the country. In January, Plumer dispatched a letter to Jeremiah Mason which, in view of the position that Mason held among the Federalists, was an informal notice by Plumer of his withdrawal from the party: "It was my intention to have written you long since; but I have had no leisure. When the Senate was not in session my whole attention has been directed in pursuit of documents & information to aid me in my contemplated *history of the United States.* A work that every day, with me, assumes

81. *Plumer's Memorandum,* 545-46.
82. *Ibid.,* 641, 643.
83. Plumer, Jr., *Life of Plumer,* 357; Plumer, Autobiography, 138-39.

more importance—& to the prosecution of which, I shall, I think, relinquish the prospect of offices of honor & profit. . . . This week I intend to unfold my views to the President, & to the Secretary of State, & request access to the arcana of government." [84]

On the fourth of February, Plumer gained his desired audience with Jefferson and, in much the same language that he had used with Mason, announced his purpose to devote the remainder of his life to history. He took particular care, however, to deny any partisan purpose and declared it his "intention to state facts & delineate characters fairly & impartialy." Jefferson appeared disconcerted by this announcement and inquired particularly as to the period at which Plumer intended to begin his work. It is possible that the President had read "Impartialis," and that a New Hampshire friend had sent him the excoriations of "Cato" as they had appeared in the *Portsmouth Oracle*. Even if this were not the case, he must have known Plumer well enough to realize that the best of intentions could never neutralize the acid impregnating his ink. It was probably clear to Jefferson that if Plumer's history should by any chance go down to posterity as the principal account of his period, the third President of the United States would not become a folk hero. However, Jefferson promised all the aid within his power, particularly after his retirement, and offered to open the archives for such material as did not need to remain secret.[85]

It was a compliment to Plumer that many distinguished gentlemen took his historical intentions seriously. Gallatin offered his aid upon any question in regard to the Treasury Department, and Samuel Harrison Smith, the editor of the *National Intelligencer,* gave him friendly warnings about possible rivals. John Quincy Adams was gratified at Plumer's announcement of his purpose, probably because the two men regarded the world with equally censorious eyes. The two acidulous Yankees agreed that neither Jefferson nor Madison could wish success to an impartial historian; there were traits in their characters that they would not wish "delineated, & transmitted to posterity." [86] It is doubtful if any fledgling historian in America ever had more imposing support than the trio that backed Plumer—Jefferson, Gallatin, and Adams.

Engaged in these pleasant preparations, Plumer moved toward the end of his senatorial career without regrets. He had thoroughly enjoyed

84. Plumer to Jeremiah Mason, Jan. 4, 1807, Letter Book, IV, Lib. Cong.
85. *Plumer's Memorandum,* 600-2.
86. *Ibid.,* 606, 607, 632.

his years in Washington. "This is, for me, a charming winter country," he wrote his daughter, "& was I not so far advanced in life & had so much property in New Hampshire that I cannot dispose of to advantage—I would never spend another winter in that northern inclement world." [87] On the last crowded day of the session, Plumer remained in the Senate chamber until a few minutes before adjournment, then slipped away, his heart too full to permit farewells to friends whom he would never see again. He had a final, and most cordial, interview with President Jefferson, a last look at Washington, which still bore the appearance of a ruined city, and at seven o'clock on the morning of March 5, took his seat in the stage for New Hampshire. He had written to his brother-in-law: "I was called to this high office without being consulted—I accepted it to serve my country—and now I return again with cheerfulness & content to private life." [88]

87. Plumer to Sally Plumer, Dec. 27, 1806, Letter Book, IV, Lib. Cong.
88. Plumer to Phillip Fowler, Feb. 15, 1807, Plumer Papers, N. H. State Lib.

CHAPTER X

The Apostate

"Our two great parties have crossed over the valley
and taken possession of each other's mountain." [1]

THE spring of 1807 was a gloomy season in New England. Wretched
roads delayed Plumer for two weeks on a homeward journey ordinarily accomplished in ten days. At New Haven, fifteen inches of snow
fell during the night and forced the stage passengers to continue their
journey by sleigh. Snow and unseasonable cold continued until the
middle of April, detracting from the natural pleasure of Plumer's homecoming and increasing the difficulty of the readjustments facing him.
"The fatigues of my late journey are still felt," he noted near the end of
March. "My mind as well as body requires the balmy aid of sleep &
repose." [2]

Plumer did not find conditions at home restful. His wife's nervous
condition had become seriously aggravated, and in September, he himself suffered two successive illnesses, which he treated with a minimum
of medicine and a maximum of philosophy. His children, to whom he
expected to devote much of his future, were an immediate source of
anxiety. In June, he took his only daughter, Sally, now an intelligent
girl of sixteen, to Salem, Massachusetts, to place her in school. Before
the year was out, she was being courted by no less a personage than
Henry Gray, son of the merchant prince whom Plumer had already
made his friend during the previous summer. The courtship ripened
quickly into a request from the young man to Plumer for his daughter's
hand, and after making the proper investigations, the proud father gave
his consent. He playfully chided his daughter for wishing, in the bloom
of youth, soon to become Gray. Unfortunately, the pun took on an implication he had not intended, for Gray "afterwards basely broke off the

1. John Adams to William Plumer, quoted in Plumer, Jr., *Life of Plumer,* 403.
2. Entry for Mar. 21, 1807, Plumer, Register, I, Lib. Cong.

connexion." The young man asserted that Sally did not return his affection, but Plumer considered the claim an evasion, supposing that the true explanation was a prejudice against his own religious unorthodoxy.[3] Whatever the cause, it was obvious that poor Sally had been the principal sufferer in the affair. It was the first of a series of tragedies in the life of the unfortunate girl.

Plumer had attempted to provide for the education of his sons by planning, as early as 1799, to raise subscriptions and found an academy in Epping.[4] Since he and his brothers had been the only subscribers, he had been forced to send his two older children to Exeter and Salem for their secondary education. Perhaps it was indicative of his changing politics that he now placed two of his younger sons, Samuel and George, in the Atkinson Academy, founded by his old political associate, Nathaniel Peabody, and conducted by John Vose, an excellent instructor. He entertained high hopes for them in the world of scholarship but they had small taste for academic pursuits.[5] Eventually, he placed them both with merchants in Portsmouth and looked solely to his eldest son to perpetuate the family name in the fields of statesmanship and literature.

For a few weeks in the spring of 1807, it appeared that even William, Jr., might disappoint his father. Plumer had hardly unpacked his trunks from Washington before his son also arrived in Epping, having left Harvard as a consequence of one of its periodic student uprisings. The "Rotten Cabbage Rebellion" of 1807 grew out of a chronic cause of complaint—the inedible stuff served up as food at commons. Virtually the entire student body had been involved; the "government" had demanded humiliating acts of submission, and William, unwilling to degrade himself, had come home to seek his father's advice.[6] Plumer was fairly certain that the notably stiff-necked college officials were much to blame for the difficulty, but he also recognized the necessity of submission to their discipline. He persuaded William to return to Cambridge with letters of dignified apology, which secured re-admission to

3. Entry for July 12, 1808, Plumer, Diary, Lib. Cong.; Plumer, Autobiography, 233, 235; Plumer to Sally Plumer, Dec. 15, 1807, to Henry Gray, Dec. 28, 1807, May 28, 1808, Plumer Papers, N. H. State Lib.

4. The subscription list may be seen in Plumer's Repository, IV, 391, *ibid.*

5. William Cogswell, "History of Atkinson," N. H. Hist. Soc., *Collections*, 6 (1850), 66-70; Plumer to Samuel and George Plumer, June 6, 27, Sept. 5, 1808, Plumer Papers, N. H. State Lib.

6. Plumer, Jr., Memoirs, I, 93-117, *ibid.;* Samuel Batchelder, *Bits of Harvard History* (Cambridge, 1924), 138-41, contains an interesting account of this incident.

his former standing.[7] Both father and son were more willingly reconciled to this step because Professor John Quincy Adams advised it.[8] Nevertheless, the incident must have been disconcerting to an ambitious parent.

Plumer's equanimity was not long disturbed by domestic mishaps. In the midst of family distractions, he wrote a letter to Thomas Jefferson which reveals his conception of what his own future was to be. After thanking the President for some documents just received, and reminding him of his intention to devote the remainder of his life to history, Plumer pledged himself again to objectivity and rejected any idea of political bias. He planned to begin work immediately by arranging and indexing his notes, to start writing within a year, and to spend another winter in Washington seeking further information. Then Plumer inserted an interesting digression into his letter. "In New Hampshire we are peculiarly happy," he declared. "We are literally *all republicans, all federalists*. The bitter, intolerant spirit of party is extinct; the slight shades of difference that exist are every day becoming less, & I trust the time is not distant when not a vestige of them shall remain." Plumer had heard a rumor that the collector of customs at Portsmouth was to be removed. If this were to happen, he wrote:

I should feel myself under great obligation to you in being appointed his successor. I would immediately remove to Portsmouth, from which I am now distant only 18 miles. With good clerks, I could in four hours in each day fully & faithfully discharge the duties of that office. This would not derange my prime object, that of *history*. It would furnish me with funds to prosecute the work more effectually; for I am now neither poor nor rich. It would afford me more & better society; & conversation, as well as reading, is requisite to enable a man to write well. *I write this paragraph in perfect confidence.*[9]

Naive and hypocritical as this letter might have appeared to Jefferson, it contained a certain amount of truth. If the nation was, as Plumer supposed, returning to that golden age when a capable man did not have

7. Plumer to President Samuel Webber, Apr. 30, 1807, Plumer, Jr., to Plumer, May 3, 1807, Plumer Papers, N. H. State Lib.

8. Young Plumer admired John Quincy Adams in "Rhetoric and Oratory" more than any other professor. "No one ever missed his eloquent lectures." Plumer, Jr., Memoirs, I, 118, *ibid.*

9. Plumer to Thomas Jefferson, May 1, 1807, Plumer Papers, *ibid.* This letter is not mentioned in Plumer, Jr.'s *Life of Plumer.*

to carry a party label to receive a public appointment, he saw no moral perfidy in asking for an office from a president to whom he had been opposed. Giving an appointment to Plumer would have been an easy and efficacious way for Jefferson to encourage the arts, and it would probably have been approved by people of both parties in Portsmouth.[10] Plumer, however, was somewhat premature in his vision of the political millennium. Jefferson did not answer his letter, Plumer did not move to Portsmouth, and before the year was out the embargo had closed the ports and revived the bitter animosities of 1798.

In becoming an historian, Plumer did not altogether cease being a politician. Letters combining business and flattery were dispatched from Epping to cabinet members and prominent congressmen, nor did Plumer neglect his contacts in his own state. In June he visited the legislature sitting at Hopkinton and gave his advice freely on the little business that transpired.[11] He was also liberal with his criticism, particularly after his proposal for buying all the public land north of the forty-fifth parallel was rejected.[12] The legislature testified to its respect for his character, however, by placing him upon the annual committee to examine the treasurer's accounts, a trust always confided to the foremost men in the state.[13] In advance of any accomplishment Plumer also began to acquire the status of an historical scholar. In June he carried a trunk full of congressional journals and documents to Boston and presented it to the Massachusetts Historical Society. His reward came in August, when, by Josiah Quincy's nomination, he was elected to a corresponding membership in the society.[14] If his domestic arrangements were not all that he could have wished, he at least held an honorable position in society and looked forward to a cherished career of scholarly seclusion.

Less than two months after Plumer wrote his idyllic description of future expectations to President Jefferson, word reached New Hampshire of the attack by the British warship *Leopard* upon the unarmed American naval vessel *Chesapeake*. In this crisis, William Plumer expressed forcefully the ideas of virtually all Americans in a letter to his son at Harvard: "If the British refuse or neglect to do us prompt &

10. Mason and Sheafe, at any rate, supported Plumer in his request. Plumer, Autobiography, 228.
11. Entries for June 7-27, 1807, Plumer, Diary, Lib. Cong.
12. *Journal of the House of Representatives, June Session, 1807* (Portsmouth, 1807), 51.
13. *Ibid.*, 94.
14. Mass. Hist. Soc., *Proceedings*, 1st Ser., 1 (1879), 193-94; John Eliot to Plumer, Aug. 31, 1807, Plumer Papers, N. H. State Lib.

full justice, I would then cut off all intercourse with that kingdom & her dependencies. I would go further, I would declare war ... we must avenge the insult & injury, or renounce the idea of being a nation." [15] He was convinced that this new outrage was the culmination of a policy of deliberate hostility, pursued for several years by the British government, and it removed whatever traces of Anglophilia that may have remained from his high Federalist days. Henceforward, he became almost as suspicious of England as he had been of France in 1798. "The haughtiness of that nation induces me to think, she will not make those concessions, or that reparation which we are bound to demand, & therefore I judge it probable we shall have war," he wrote in August.[16]

Plumer's determined stand against England rendered him as unpopular with the Exeterites in New Hampshire as Adams had become with the Essex Junto in Massachusetts.[17] After the first hot flame of anger had cooled, the extreme Federalists began not only to criticize the administration but to excuse and justify Great Britain. This attitude appeared as improper to Plumer as the Republican defense of Talleyrand in 1798. "In times like these," he wrote to John Quincy Adams, "we ought to feel as Americans, rise superior to the interest of party, & decide on men & measures by their merits, not their names." Because Senator Adams had so decided, his conduct "had given mortal offence" to the New Hampshire Federalists, who now turned their wrath upon Plumer. "In several of these companies," he reported, "I have not only found myself alone, but have suffered a portion of that abuse and calumny which they have so illiberally vented against you." [18] Before the summer expired, Plumer had virtually read himself out of the Federalist party, and his former colleagues were eager, as he admitted, to "condemn and censure my conduct." [19]

For all of his belligerent talk, Plumer was not a warmonger. Canning's disavowal of the *Leopard*'s attack, the appalling military weakness of the country, and the apparent hopelessness of maintaining neutral commerce in the face of English orders and French decrees soon convinced him that the time was not yet ripe for taking up the sword. He

15. Plumer to Plumer, Jr., July 18, 1807, Plumer Papers, N. H. State Lib.
16. Plumer to Thomas Cogswell, Aug. 3, 1807, Letter Book, III, Lib. Cong.
17. Adams's joining with the Boston Republicans in their public indignation meeting is a well-known incident in American history. *Adams's Memoirs,* I, 468-69.
18. Plumer to John Quincy Adams, Dec. 22, 1807, Feb. 12, 1808, Plumer Papers, N. H. State Lib. See also Worthington C. Ford, "The Recall of John Quincy Adams in 1808," Mass. Hist. Soc., *Proceedings,* 45(1911-12), 357.
19. Plumer, Autobiography, 230.

was in unison with the Old Republicans in believing that the carrying trade was not worth a war.[20] On the other hand, Plumer still agreed with the Federalist merchants that the issue of impressment did not require a trial by battle. "Neither justice or policy will justify us in a war to defend the fugitives & outcasts of other nations from British impressment," he wrote. "I should not feel much confidence in settling a controversy in the *tented field* unless both justice & necessity obliged me to appeal to that sanguinary tribunal." [21]

In this frame of mind, Plumer was well prepared for Jefferson's embargo, although he doubted at first its efficacy against the British. "I fear while we are chastising them with *whips,* we shall be scourging ourselves with *scorpions,*" he wrote.[22] Like all New Englanders, Plumer considered the embargo at best a necessary evil, and he had none of the nearly fanatical faith in its success which inspired Jefferson to resort to totalitarian enforcement. The embargo was useful, in Plumer's view, because it gave the nation time to prepare for war if war was necessary. Yet he saw the administration making little more than empty gestures in that direction. Jefferson depended upon the militia to defend the country, but Plumer, dourly witnessing the quarterly routs called "muster days" in New Hampshire, decided that the standing army had better be increased. "I abhor that love of popularity that shrinks from the responsibility of measures necessary for the defence & security of the nation," he wrote to Senator Nicholas Gilman.[23]

William Plumer anxiously surveyed the growing opposition to the embargo during the spring and summer of 1808. In July he assured President Jefferson of his own allegiance but admitted that the outcome of the congressional elections in New Hampshire was doubtful.[24] The Federalists, suddenly awakened from their somnolence, had become "bitter, malignant, & misrepresented the proceedings of the administration." These were the accusations Plumer had made against the Republicans in 1798. It was not as an apostate, therefore, but as a steady champion of civic righteousness that he spoke at the Epping town meeting in favor of the administration candidates. "I made an animated address for twenty

20. Plumer to Stephen Bradley, Nov. 28, 1807, Plumer Papers, N. H. State Lib.
21. Plumer to Samuel Taggart, Feb. 3, 1808, *ibid.*
22. Plumer to Samuel Mitchill, Jan. 26, 1808, Letter Book, III, Lib. Cong.
23. Plumer to Nicholas Gilman, Mar. 28, 1808, *ibid.*
24. Plumer to Thomas Jefferson, July 22, 1808, Jefferson Papers, CLXXIX, Lib. Cong. Schachner has somewhat exaggerated the significance of this letter in his *Jefferson,* II, 876.

minutes, but I do not think it changed a single vote," he admitted rue-fully.[25] Plumer's part in the congressional election of 1808 established him beyond all shadow of doubt as a Republican. His open transfer of allegiance stemmed from motives of exalted patriotism, yet the means he employed to accomplish it were almost sordid in their pettiness. It was necessary, of course, for Plumer to become friendly with, and perhaps even to flatter, men whom he had formerly despised, since they were now united in the same cause. But his approach seemed overeager, and the passion with which he attacked his former friends was hardly justified, even if his belief in their villainy was sincere.

The least defensible aspect of Plumer's metamorphosis was his per-sistent effort to become even a petty officeholder under the Republican administration. After failing to elicit the President's interest in his ap-pointment to a post in Portsmouth, Plumer addressed him again to solicit a much humbler office—that of postmaster at Epping. Plumer explained to Jefferson that, though the emoluments were trifling, the office would be a great convenience to him in his researches. The frank-ing privilege would save him from a tax that was rapidly becoming burdensome as his scholarly correspondence increased. "This is my *only object* in wishing this small office," he assured the President.[26] But Jeffer-son again neglected his opportunity to patronize the arts, and Plumer had to bide his time until a stronger motive presented itself. It came in the autumn, when Plumer wrote a letter to Governor Langdon, praising him for his support of the embargo laws, but warning him that the post-rider and postmaster in Epping had been subversive influences in the last election. They were "very industrious in their opposition to repub-licanism," he declared, "not content with eating the bread of government, they revile & abuse it & its officers." [27] Plumer suggested that the Gover-nor use his influence with Postmaster General Granger to end this in-tolerable situation, then, without any mention of the boon it would be to scholarship, simply stated that he would "if appointed, accept it, & en-gage that republicanism should not suffer from my conduct."

Thus did William Plumer announce his conversion to Republicanism, not in a strain of noble renunciation, but with petty disparagement of his former allies and a plea for a trifling office. Langdon welcomed him

25. Plumer, Autobiography, 239.
26. Plumer to Thomas Jefferson, Mar. 25, 1808, Jefferson Papers, CLXXVI, Lib. Cong.
27. Plumer to John Langdon, Oct. 15, 1808, Plumer Papers, N. H. State Lib.

to the ranks and promised to clean up the situation in Epping. Before the end of November, the post office was transferred from the Stearns store in Epping village to the home of the former Senator a mile distant.[28] Plumer did not mention the political angle to this story in his autobiography, but insisted that the franking privilege and the opportunity to read newspapers to which he did not subscribe were the chief inducements to his acceptance of the office.[29] Whatever his reasons may have been, Plumer was not content with a postmastership, but looked for another office to augment his income. A vacancy had again occurred on the bench of the Rockingham County court in 1808, and Plumer asked Langdon for the place, assuring him that it was the only office he wished, and adding slyly that the Federalist lawyers would probably oppose his appointment.[30] This would undoubtedly have been the case, not only because of Plumer's apostasy, but because he announced his intention of cutting the red tape and slashing the fees that made those courts so irritating to suitors and so profitable to lawyers. The prospect of displeasing Federalist lawyers must have tempted Langdon, but not sufficiently to induce him to appoint Plumer. He gave the office to one of his councilors, a good Republican farmer. Plumer was told that the Governor had said he would have made him a judge if the party had not needed to reserve him for a higher office.[31]

If Plumer's change of allegiance had been inspired solely by a desire for the loaves and fishes of office, he had chosen a poor time to make his move. While he was drawing toward Jefferson and Langdon, the embargo was driving the majority of his fellow citizens away from them. In August, the long-dormant Federalists returned to the polls in droves and swept their congressional ticket into office by an average majority of thirteen hundred votes. Evidence mounted on every hand to indicate that they were equally determined to win the presidential elections in November.[32] Impelled, perhaps, by the imminence of this disaster and by inclination to demonstrate his usefulness to his newly adopted party, or

28. Gideon Granger to Plumer, Nov. 14, 1808, *ibid.* William Stearns was a son of the former Epping minister, Josiah Stearns.

29. Plumer, Autobiography, 241.

30. Plumer to John Langdon, Nov. 7, 1808, Plumer Papers, N. H. State Lib.

31. Plumer, "Richard Jenness," Biographies, V, 194, N. H. Hist. Soc.; Plumer, Autobiography, 234. Plumer related this incident as having taken place in 1807, but the evidence of his letter to Langdon shows that it was much more likely to have been in 1808.

32. Lyon, ed., *New Hampshire Register ... 1860,* 31; Plumer, Autobiography, 239; John Langdon to James Madison, Nov. 3, 1808, James Madison Papers, XXXV, Lib. Cong.

by desire to settle accounts with the party he had rejected, Plumer now took up his pen in the Republican cause.

In the early part of October, two articles by "Veritas" appeared in the *New Hampshire Gazette.* Their style, if not their subject matter, bore a remarkable resemblance to that of "Impartialis." [33] Although these pieces were designed to influence the presidential elections, they contained no reference to the issues of the campaign, but consisted entirely of personal animadversions upon the characters of two Federalist electoral candidates, Jeremiah Smith and Oliver Peabody. Plumer thus became guilty not only of stabbing former friends in the back but of condemning what he had formerly commended in their conduct. The "Veritas" articles did little to enhance his reputation for consistency, and they seemed to win little credit for him with his new political friends. The *Gazette,* in fact, refused to publish the third "Veritas" essay, which was a savage indictment of the Exeter Junto's fiscal manipulations during the nineties. Plumer supposed at first that the printers were too timid to print this bold exposure, although he promised to indemnify them against any possible libel suits. But he learned later from Richard Evans, the Republican boss in Portsmouth, that the article had been rejected by a secret committee of the party, which censored everything that went into the Republican newspapers.[34]

Plumer's propaganda in the Republican cause availed nothing against the popular discontent. New Hampshire followed all her sister New England states except Vermont in choosing Federalist electors, who cast their votes for Charles Cotesworth Pinckney of South Carolina.[35] Plumer found it ironic that a party which had vociferated so strenuously against the Southern views of the Virginia presidents, should go four hundred miles farther south for a man of their own choice. This afforded him another melancholy proof that "neither honesty or consistency is a trait in the character of *party."* Plumer found nothing inconsistent, however, in his own votes for the Republican electoral ticket, although he actually approved of neither Madison nor Clinton. The fact that the people's inconsistency went counter to his own discouraged him again

33. [William Plumer], "Veritas," Nos. 1, 2, Plumer, Essays, I, 45-48, Lib. Cong., publ. in *N. H. Gazette* (Portsmouth), Oct. 11, 18, 1808. A person unknown to Plumer added derogatory remarks to the second article about Smith's brief career as a "midnight judge."

34. Plumer, Repository, II, 33-39, 40; Richard Evans to Plumer, Nov. 7, 1808, Plumer Papers, N. H. State Lib.; Plumer, Autobiography, 240.

35. Robinson, *Jeffersonian Democracy in New England,* 82. Even Vermont's Republican electors were chosen, not by the people, but by a rotten borough legislature.

with democracy, which, he thought, had "a direct & powerful tendency to vitiate & corrupt the great mass of the people, the source of power." [36]

If Plumer had any doubts as to the ethical implications of the means by which he turned himself from a Federalist to a Republican, he did not record them. If he had not been politically sophisticated before, he had by now become a hardened politician. He soon discovered that his new friends were not much better than he had believed them to be when he was their enemy, but by the logic of necessity he felt it his duty to defend what he had formerly condemned. Plumer accepted these evils stoically, without protest or comment. He recognized them as part of the game, and he continued to proclaim his own integrity with complete composure. There is nothing in his writing to indicate that he felt remorse over the compromises necessitated by practical politics. Plumer appeared to believe that his genuine and unquestioned patriotism was a solvent that absorbed and rendered unimportant all his minor imperfections. He retained always the supreme self-righteousness of the Puritan.

Federalist opposition to the embargo, which Plumer anxiously saw mount to rebellious proportions during the winter of 1808-9, justified his conscience in the employment of every weapon of defense. Taking note of the extent to which Timothy Pickering was responsible for stirring up this excitement, Plumer could but suspect that the secession plot of 1804 had been dragged out again and polished for immediate use. During the early months of 1809, in fact, Plumer experienced the strange sensation of witnessing the outward evolution of a destructive plan, the inner details of which he had helped to organize. The obstructionist tactics of the Federalist majorities in New England seemed to him an obvious revival of the scheme of creating a Northern Confederacy under the simultaneous action of the state legislatures.[37] "At no period of my life have I felt more anxiety for my country than the present," he wrote to Senator Gilman. "Numbers who, a few months since, would have revolted with horror at the fatal idea of the dissolution of the Union, now converse freely upon it, as an event rather to be desired than avoided. Such a measure, to me, appears the most unfortunate & serious that can happen to our Country—It must produce civil war, & eventually

36. Plumer, Autobiography, 240-41; Plumer to John Randolph, Mar. 22, 1808, to Daniel Durrell, Oct. 25, 1808, Plumer Papers, N. H. State Lib.

37. Plumer, Autobiography, 242-44. For the resolution adopted by the Massachusetts and Connecticut legislatures, see Louis Sears, *Jefferson and the Embargo* (Durham, N. C., 1927), 186-87, and Samuel Eliot Morison, *The Life and Letters of Harrison Gray Otis* (Cambridge, 1913), II, 12.

subject us to foreign domination. The spirit of party is always blind and hostile to order and security but there is no state of parties I so much deprecate as those marked with *geographical* lines." [38]

This reversal of the very expressions Plumer had used in 1804 was the testimony of a converted sinner. Five years of sober reflection had taught him the value of intangibles that he had temporarily forgotten. The situation of 1808-9 found its real parallel, not so much in the fantastic plot of 1804, as in the far more dangerous internal divisions of 1798-99. Plumer undertook to elucidate this point to his son when he wrote that "The leading federalists, are practising upon Napoleon's maxim of *dividing the people from their government.*" [39]

As he had been in 1798, Plumer became again a symbol of support for the government's policies. The *American Patriot* of Concord, a newly established Republican journal, listed him together with John Quincy Adams, William Gray, and William Smith of South Carolina as patriotic Federalists who had deserted their party over the embargo.[40] In order to encourage the domestic manufactures that had sprung up to supply the lack of imported goods, Plumer wore homespun garments. His most interesting gesture, however, was his break with the Congregationalist clergy. "I joined the society in 1798," he wrote, "because I thot it would afford some aid to the civil government; but I find the clergy in general, & Mr Holt in particular, are hostile to the government & administration of the nation." Plumer accordingly severed his relations once and for all with Mr. Holt's society. He had no inclination to join a sect, but he recognized the political advantages of cultivating such Republican preachers as the zealous Elias Smith, to whose *Herald of Gospel Liberty* he subscribed.[41] These moves brought about a final reconciliation between Plumer's religious beliefs and his politics, making him henceforward an unwavering champion of religious liberty.

The embargo was finally repealed in the spring of 1809, but it was replaced by a non-intercourse act and the Federalists continued what Plumer called their "indiscriminate censure of all the just & prudent measures of the government." [42] This propaganda heated the people of

---

38. Plumer to Nicholas Gilman, Jan. 24, 1809, Plumer Papers, N. H. State Lib.
39. Plumer to Plumer, Jr., Mar. 28, 1809, *ibid.*
40. *American Patriot* (Concord), Nov. 29, 1808. In 1809 this paper became the *New Hampshire Patriot.*
41. Plumer, Autobiography, 245, 246; Plumer to Elias Smith, Jan. 31, 1809, Plumer Papers, N. H. State Lib. For the interesting career of this remarkable evangelist, see his own *Life of Elias Smith* (Boston, 1840).
42. Plumer to William Giles, Dec. 23, 1809, Letter Book, III, Lib. Cong.

Epping, who had been Republican since 1802, to such passionate reversal of their sympathies that in the March meeting, they turned out even the hog reeves and hay wardens in order to reward "designing or ignorant zealots the devoted tools of [the Federalist] party." A similar political revolution swept the state. When the votes were counted, the Federalists were overjoyed to find that they had elected a governor and a majority in both houses of the legislature. Jeremiah Smith had been persuaded to resign his seat on the bench, where by indefatigable labor he had for seven years been reforming the jurisprudence of the state, in order to become the Federalist candidate for governor. Plumer ascribed his decision to the worst of motives, vanity and the *"love of . . . vulgar popularity."* [43] Smith's victory, however, soon led to frustration and early defeat.[44] In the curious parallels that marked many features of the careers of Jeremiah Smith and William Plumer, Smith usually won the earlier honors, but Plumer displayed the greater staying power.

Although William Plumer had observed these political upheavals with minute attention, had changed his own party allegiance, had donated the services of his pen to the new cause, and had even asked for minor offices from his new political friends, he had done it all essentially as a bystander rather than a participant. There is no evidence in Plumer's papers that he had any intention or desire at this time to re-enter politics. Had he harbored political ambitions, they would have been better served either by his remaining a Federalist and sharing in that party's renaissance in 1808, or by his having been converted to Republicanism at an earlier date, when its sun was ascendant. One must either grant that Plumer's motives in changing parties were largely free of sordid ambition, or admit that he had a very poor sense of timing.

The fact is that Plumer considered himself during these years not a politician but an historian. He spent most of his time reading, and nearly every letter he wrote was primarily a request for documents or historical information. Even his applications for office were motivated by his scholarly ambitions. But the great national crisis and the triumph of the Federalists—men whom Plumer now considered enemies of their country—virtually ensured that he would not be content to remain a sedentary scholar. The political balance in New Hampshire was so precarious that a man of Plumer's conscience and conceit could not refuse public service

43. Plumer, Autobiography, 245, 248. Smith's biographer insists that his motive was a desire to reform the judiciary, but ambition was not wholly absent from his mind. See Morison, *Jeremiah Smith*, 244.

44. Lyon, ed., *New Hampshire Register . . . 1860*, 41.

—service which was about equally divided between fighting the Federalist obstructionists and trying to elevate the performance of the Republican nationalists.

Governor Langdon and his councilors spent their last hours in office filling up vacant posts with deserving Republicans, including each other.[45] Richard Evans, the Rockingham County councilor, was placed on the Superior Court bench, although his knowledge of the law was confined to what he had learned as a rough-and-tumble political boss in the Portsmouth town meeting.[46] As he had done with Ebenezer Smith in 1798, Plumer took it upon himself to warn Evans against accepting his appointment, but without success. The new judge soon had reason to regret his rejection of Plumer's advice, for he had not ridden his first circuit before the *Portsmouth Oracle* carried a strong attack against him and against former Governor Langdon's appointments in general. Believing (incorrectly) that Daniel Webster had written this tirade, Plumer felt called upon to answer his supposed arguments. The result was a series of articles signed "Aristides," published in the Republican press during June and July 1809.[47]

These articles reflect no credit on Plumer. In attempting a defense of what he himself believed to be indefensible, Plumer was forced to resort to evasion and insinuation rather than rebuttal. The reversal of his former zeal for a trained judiciary which these articles denote should be interpreted, probably, as a reaction against Judge Smith's presumed tendency to sacrifice the "merits of suits . . . to *forms*, to quirks, & to the subtleties of nice distinctions." Plumer's flattery of Langdon and Evans, however, cannot even be excused by a genuine change in his earlier sentiments, for he later criticized both men in private for the part they played in this affair. "I thot the interest of my country, tho not [Langdon's] conduct, demanded my services," he explained.[48] It is difficult,

45. Some of the vacancies were actually created by the arbitrary removal of sheriffs and judges who were reputed to have reached retirement age. See Wingate, *Wingate,* II, 476; Plumer, "Paine Wingate," biographical sketch in *N. H. State Papers,* XXI, 827-30; Plumer, Autobiography, 247. This was a "course of conduct improper & impolitic," wrote Plumer.

46. Plumer, "Richard Evans," Biographies, V, 103, N. H. Hist. Soc. The Walker Papers in the New Hampshire Historical Society contain a printed letter of instructions sent by Evans as "Chairman of the Conventional Committee" to Timothy Walker, the Concord Republican leader in 1809. See Walker Papers, fol. 1, 162.

47. Plumer, Autobiography, 246-47; Bell, *Bench and Bar,* 67-68; "Private Note on the Oracle Man," in Plumer, Repository, II, 99, Lib. Cong.; [Plumer], "Aristides," Nos. 1-4, Plumer, Repository, II, 46-98, Lib. Cong., publ. in *N. H. Gazette* (Portsmouth), July 4-25, 1809.

48. Plumer, Autobiography, 249.

however, to see how his country stood to benefit nearly so much as Plumer's political future by these purely partisan productions. Such was the interpretation which the Federalists inevitably gave to his conduct. "How far this surrender of himself, *soul and body,* to the cause, will go towards reconciling *Aristides* to the Democratic party, we cannot tell. . . . We have half a mind to give the name of *Aristides,* in capitals, and to send it round the United States, accompanied by this instance of his *regard to truth.* He would at once, we think, receive letters of *fraternization* from the editors of the Aurora and the Chronicle." [49]

Plumer's avowal of Republican partisanship, however, earned him an initial loss. Although in June Governor Smith had delivered an eloquent address disclaiming party feeling and pleading for political unity, the Governor subsequently became deadlocked with the Republican majority in his council over a vacancy in the Superior Court. At one point the council proposed the name of William Plumer, whose abilities they were reported to have thought adequate but whose "other qualifications" they considered doubtful. Smith was undoubtedly in complete agreement regarding the "other qualifications," but he vetoed the Epping lawyer on the ground that his legal knowledge was deficient. Plumer never referred to this incident, but it was undoubtedly known to him, and it could not have diminished his rancor against his former friend.[50]

In the meantime, Plumer made progress in the Republican party organization. He had attended the June session of the legislature as a spectator, and made it clear to everyone that he had changed his political affiliations. The Republicans apparently invited him to join their caucus, where they overhauled their political machine, and gave him the chairmanship for Rockingham County. The December meeting of his committee had to be held in a tavern within the limits of the gaol yard in Exeter, to accommodate old Nathaniel Peabody, who, although imprisoned for debt, was still active in Republican politics. At this meeting, Plumer persuaded his committee to abandon Henry Butler, senator from the second district (which included Exeter and Epping), and nominate Nathaniel Gilman, who had lost his state treasurer's job in June. Only Peabody, as fractious as he had been in the eighties, opposed both Butler

49. *Portsmouth Oracle,* July 29, 1809.
50. *Journal of the House of Representatives, June Session, 1809* (Concord, 1809), 40-59; Morrison, *Jeremiah Smith,* 246-47, 252. Plumer subsequently criticized the appointment of Jonathan Steele to this vacancy; Plumer to Samuel Bell, Apr. 6, 1810, Letter Book, III, Lib. Cong. Bell defended the appointment as Republican; Bell to Plumer, Apr. 18, 1810, Plumer Papers, New-York Historical Society. See also Plumer, "Jonathan Steele," Biographies, V, 327, N. H. Hist. Soc.

and Gilman. "Peabody is an intriguing dangerous man," wrote Plumer, "he injures the republicans more than he benefits them, & his character is a reproach to us." [51]

Plumer now called upon Nathaniel Gilman to offer him the senatorial nomination, but after some hesitation Gilman declined.[52] At this juncture, Judge Levi Bartlett, whom Plumer had once called "a malignant democrat," urged him to allow his own name to be used, suggesting that he would be an ideal compromise candidate to unite the factions among the Republicans.[53] Plumer wrote that: "After maturely considering the subject, I observed to the judge & the other gentlemen, I did not wish to be senator, & I thot it was not sound policy to nominate me, for as I had within a few years relinquished federalism, there was no republican in the district who was so obnoxious to federalists as I was, or against whose election such strenuous opposition would be made ... I doubted whether I could be elected; yet if they considered it necessary to be their candidate I would, tho reluctantly consent." [54]

This was the regular formula for an acceptance speech, and it does not seem that Plumer was really loath to buckle on his political armor once more. In February, he called a district convention, which unanimously nominated him for the Senate. This combination of circumstances carried so strong a suggestion of unscrupulous intrigue that Plumer could hardly have expected to escape recrimination on all sides. Butler's friends assailed him on the one hand and the Federalists on the other, while many Republicans regarded his metamorphosis with suspicion. His old Federalist associate William Kent wrote to Webster, "can it be possible that the *apostate* will find a majority for *him?*" [55]

Although Plumer may not have behaved with scrupulous rectitude, he had been more the victim than the planner of circumstances. There was

51. Plumer, Autobiography, 251. That Plumer's suspicions were well founded is shown in a letter from Levi to Josiah Bartlett, Jan. 1812, Bartlett Papers, Lib. Cong., which reveals an intrigue by Peabody against Plumer's nomination for governor.

52. Plumer had already written to Senator Nicholas Gilman, urging that his brother should be persuaded to replace Butler; Plumer to Gilman, Nov. 25, 1809, Letter Book, III, Lib. Cong.

53. Plumer, Autobiography, 252. Plumer's statement is confirmed by a letter from Levi to Ezra Bartlett, Feb. 11, 1810, Bartlett Papers, N. H. State Lib., which mentions several possible candidates in the district who might cause internal dissension "unless we should pitch upon Mr Wm Plumer or some prominent Character to whom the other Candidates would willingly yield."

54. Plumer, Autobiography, 252; Plumer to Nahum Parker, Mar. 2, 1810, Letter Book, III, Lib. Cong.; *N. H. Patriot* (Concord), Feb. 20, 1810.

55. William Kent to Daniel Webster, Feb. 28, 1810, Daniel Webster Papers, Lib. Cong.

general agreement in the party that Butler was a liability, and Plumer's effort to secure Gilman's nomination had been sincere. Nevertheless, external appearances were against him, and Plumer could hardly complain when a Federalist writer charged that "the true design of all is, and all along has been, to *put down* Gen. Butler, and introduce William Plumer into his place." This critic claimed that Butler's discredit with the Republicans had arisen from his politeness to Governor Smith. "For this his party never will forgive him, and they have taken care now to make such a selection of a candidate as exposes them to no *danger of that sort* for the future." [56]

So far as party service was concerned, Plumer deserved a solid reward in 1810, for he had entered the journalistic arena again with a series of five articles against "the pretensions of Gov'r Smith" to re-election. The articles were signed once more by "Aristides," published originally in the *New Hampshire Patriot,* and copied by other Republican papers. Even his enemies admitted that they were adroit and able, and the outcry that they raised in the Federalist press proved their effectiveness. Much of Plumer's criticism was valid, although petty and unnecessarily personal. Not until he reached the middle of the last article did Plumer discuss the only important fact which could have justified an attack on a former friend—the fact that Smith "for a series of years had been uniformly *hostile* to the administration of the government of the United States." Even this assertion would have been difficult to prove from Smith's public utterances and conduct, but as the candidate of a party that consistently hampered the policies of the federal government and even toyed with treason, the Governor could not escape responsibility for its conduct. A statement constantly made in the Federalist newspapers, to the effect that Smith would protect New Hampshire against the usurpations of the federal government, elicited the best part of Plumer's literary effort:

This singular circumstance *alone* is of itself a conclusive reason why Mr Smith ought *not* to be your Governor. For at a time when your country's rights are invaded, & you in imminent danger of having war declared against you without any just cause, by one or both of the great belligerent powers of Europe, can anything be more imprudent or more dangerous, than to elect a man for your Governor, who is himself at war with the measures of the administration of your country! Would not the election of Mr Smith be a declaration to those very belligerents, that you

56. *Portsmouth Oracle,* Feb. 24, 1810.

are a *divided people,* & more actively engaged in *opposition* to the government of our own choice, than we are *united in resisting* the alarming encroachments of foreign powers? [57]

These sentences, in vivid contrast to Plumer's language of 1804, were essentially words of contrition for errors of the past, and justification for the pettiness of the present. A contributor to the *Patriot* wrote better than he knew when he said, "No man in this state is more capable of exposing and defeating federal intrigue and stratagem than Mr. Plumer." This writer's conclusion was exalted: "New-Hampshire never produced a greater statesman. The people know him to be a man of integrity and pure patriotism, and will most cheerfully give him their suffrages." [58]

Plumer was not modest about the value of his services to Republicanism in 1810. He assured John Langdon, as early as January 27, that he was devoting two days each week to the campaign and that victory was certain. "Had each republican in the State done one tenth as much as I have done, & am doing, we should [have] ensured success," he wrote to Parker, his successor in the United States Senate. His new friends did not disagree in this estimate of his prowess. Isaac Hill, the new and formidable editor of the *New Hampshire Patriot,* assured him that "Aristides is unanswerable as you will perceive by the federal gazettes. Go on, dear Sir, in doing good, and new England may have occasion to thank you for a deliverance as Vermont did the venerable Stark." [59] In response to requests from other Republican editors, he continued to write short paragraphs denouncing the Essex Junto until the very eve of the election. "I rejoice that in you the republican cause has found a most able advocate," wrote Judge Evans. John Langdon was

57. "Aristides," "The Pretensions of Governor Smith Examined," Nos. 1-5, Plumer, Repository, II, 100-77, Lib. Cong., publ. in the *N. H. Patriot* (Concord), Feb. 6-Mar. 6, 1810. Plumer was careful to verify the facts which he used in these articles. See Plumer to Nahum Parker, Feb. 10, 1810, Letter Book, III, *ibid.*

58. "C. S." in *N. H. Patriot* (Concord), Feb. 20, 1810. The language of hyperbole and of savage denunciation was standard fare in the first decades of the 19th century, and dispensing it cleverly was the accepted high road to political preferment. Young William Plumer, Jr., now graduated from Harvard College and reluctantly reading law with his father, took his first public steps in this campaign with a series of articles, signed "Decius," which were published in the *Patriot* and republished in Portsmouth. (Entries for Jan.-Feb. 1810, Plumer, Jr., Memoirs, I, N. H. State Lib.) They were mistaken for his father's work, although they had considerably less bite. The Plumers' journalism simply conformed to the ethical standards of the time.

59. Plumer to John Langdon, Jan. 27, 1810, to Nahum Parker, Mar. 2, 1810, Letter Book, III, Lib. Cong.; Isaac Hill to Plumer, Feb. 20, 1810, William Plumer Letters, VI (1809-15), Plumer Papers, Lib. Cong. (hereafter cited as Letter Book, VI).

genuinely grateful. He would use his influence, he assured Plumer, to make him president of the state senate. Then Langdon announced his intention of retiring at the end of his year's term. His successor, he said, would have to be one of four or five men, "of whom," he continued, looking earnestly at Plumer, "you are one, & to this you must make no objection." [60]

Plumer's status among Federalists declined in direct proportion to the rise of his reputation with the Republicans. After the bitter campaign was finished, Nahum Parker wrote to him from the Connecticut Valley, "Go on, sir, in the ways of truth, do your duty, be not in fear of curses, for if you are not yet injured, you need fear nothing, for you have had as many curses as a scape goat could wag with." [61] A few excerpts from a long article in the *Portsmouth Oracle* on March 3 show that Senator Parker did not exaggerate. "Mr. P's political history is short," said the *Oracle* writer, "and like the journey of a traveler over cross roads, consists of little else than *an account of the corners he has turned.*" According to this writer, Plumer's election to the national Senate in 1802 was the "most thoughtless and ill-judged act" the Federalists had ever committed and grievously had they paid for it. The *Oracle* advised Governor Langdon to put on his spectacles and read "Impartialis," noting what Plumer had said about him in 1804. In 1806, said the editorialist, Plumer had made frantic efforts to be re-elected, only to realize that the Federalists would no longer support him. "Here was one of Mr. P's *corners*. No race-horse ever wheeled round the distance post so short, as Mr. P. turned here. From that moment he sought to make friends of the mammon of unrighteousness. The residue of his Congressional life was a series of turning. . . . He now *censures* all whom he once *praised* : *believes* everything he once *denied,* and *discards* everything he once *practiced.*" The *Oracle* then tossed Plumer into the discard with lofty disdain : "The Democratic party are welcome to him, if they can make anything of him. But we will give them a word of *advice*—and we will not charge them anything for our advice neither—(and that is what Mr. P. never did.) Our advice is that they *watch* him, or he will tack round some point, and be out of sight in an instant." [62]

When Plumer accepted the nomination for state senator from district two, he appealed for the first time in his long career to the voters of an area larger than his own home town. The result proved that he could

60. Richard Evans to Plumer, Mar. 10, 1810, *ibid.;* Plumer, Autobiography, 255.
61. Nahum Parker to Plumer, Apr. 14, 1810, Letter Book, VI, Lib. Cong.
62. *Portsmouth Oracle,* Mar. 3, 1810.

win votes. In the March elections, 1810, he defeated the Federalist candidate, George Sullivan, while Langdon sent Smith into bitter retirement and the Republicans recaptured the legislature.[63] In 1811, when the Republicans gained another general victory, Plumer repeated his success, this time against Oliver Peabody. These two triumphs over the Exeter Junto in its own domain proved to be the preliminaries to a new career of leadership in the Republican party.

Plumer's brief sojourn in the New Hampshire senate was relatively uneventful. By prearrangement, his fellow Republicans elected him to the presidency of the senate in both years, and he performed his duties easily.[64] Nothing occurred to test his powers of leadership, but he had opportunities to display that rugged individualism which had formerly exasperated his Federalist colleagues and was now to irritate his new Republican friends. "I cannot consent either to acquire or hold office by so base a tenure as the sacrifice of my opinion," he wrote, "& those who expect it from me will be disappointed." [65]

Although the political horizon was unnaturally clear in 1810, a few small clouds remained from the storm of the embargo. One of these was a series of bank failures, which threatened some embarrassment to the state administration, particularly since Samuel Bell, president of the defunct Hillsborough Bank, was a prominent Republican.[66] Legislative committees exonerated the bankers from intentional wrongdoing, but the necessity for state regulation had been painfully demonstrated, and the lesson was gradually applied.[67] "Our numerous banks are now beginning to be *felt* to be, what I long expected they would prove, public nuisances," grumbled Plumer, who estimated that the risk in accepting their notes averaged 20 per cent.[68]

The aftermath of the embargo was also discernible in Governor Langdon's recommendations for aid to domestic manufacturers.[69] Both Langdon and Plumer, however, were cautious about granting corporation

63. Plumer, Jr., *Life of Plumer*, 378. This author's statement on page 382 that John Taylor Gilman was Langdon's opponent in 1811 is incorrect.

64. *Journal of the House of Representatives, June Session, 1811* (Concord, 1811), 95.

65. Plumer, Autobiography, 262.

66. Eli Brown, *True Account of the Defalcation of the Hillsborough Bank* (Concord, n.d.). Brown, a director of the bank, made grave charges against Bell.

67. *Journal of the Senate, June Session, 1811* (Concord, 1811), 32, 43. For a summary of early banking laws in New Hampshire, see Joseph Walker, "Banking and Currency in New Hampshire," in William T. Davis, ed., *The New England States* (Boston, 1904), III, 1645-46.

68. Plumer, Diary, 54-57, Lib. Cong.

69. *Journal of the Senate, June Session, 1810* (Concord, 1810), 13.

charters. In 1811, Plumer used his vote and influence to prevent John L. Sullivan of Boston and his partners from acquiring exclusive rights to canalize the Merrimack River all the way from Concord to Lake Winnepesaukee.[70] In that same year, Sullivan organized the "Merrimack Boating Company" to secure a monopoly of the commerce from Concord to the Middlesex Canal, and petitioned for a charter. His bill passed both houses, but was vetoed by Governor Langdon.[71] Plumer and Langdon objected, not to the contemplated improvements in transportation, but to the poorly guarded grants of extensive powers to an out-of-state corporation.

Plumer's autobiography gives the impression that the legislators of this period spent most of their time, not in passing laws, but in holding caucuses. No sooner had Plumer arrived in Concord in June 1810 than the Republicans summoned him to a conclave to determine state officers. The logical candidates were those whom the Federalists had removed, Nathaniel Gilman for treasurer and Philip Carrigain for secretary; but many Republicans including Plumer, opposed the latter as "destitute of that stability & weight of character which were requisite." Plumer eventually persuaded the Republicans to give the secretaryship to Samuel Sparhawk, an "honest, capable" man, who would "perform the duties of that office with fidelity, & in return support republicanism." The difficulties of the Republicans in filling minor offices, however, proved to be considerably less than their embarrassment in finding a prospective governor. John Langdon, so weary of the bustle of public life that he spurned offers of the vice-presidency, insisted at the beginning of the 1810 session that either Plumer or Nicholas Gilman must be his immediate successor. The latter, however, preferred re-election to the federal Senate and thus eliminated himself as a gubernatorial candidate.[72] The Republican caucus then nominated the veteran John Goddard, and when he declined, named Nathaniel Gilman. Although the treasurer told the notifying committee that he was not qualified for the office, his statement was accepted as a modest assent.[73] It appears that although Plumer might have been John Langdon's second choice for the governorship, he was somewhere below fourth place in the calculations of the other party leaders.

70. Plumer, Autobiography, 262. Sullivan had made his bid in secret, using New Hampshire lawyers and legislators as the ostensible petitioners.
71. *Senate Journal, June Sess., 1811,* 89.
72. Plumer, Autobiography, 256, 257; *Senate Journal, June Sess., 1810,* 66.
73. John Parrott to Plumer, July 18, 1810, Letter Book, III, Lib. Cong.

It was obvious to Plumer, after his experience as a Republican legislator, that the Federalists still commanded most of the wealth, talent, and respectability in the state. "The republicans suffered from the want of an efficient active leader," he wrote; "they want energy & decision of character. . . . The inordinate love of office is the bane of republicanism." [74] He had been thoroughly disgusted by the shameless intrigues that were the chief concern of the legislators at Concord, and he constantly expressed a longing to return to his literary work.[75] In July the Republican state chairman wrote to him, assuming that he would continue to act as county chairman and giving directions for the August campaign. Plumer sent back a refusal in language that was frank to the point of rudeness. "I am from principle a real republican—& will support the election of republicans for the next Congress at the August election —But I now frankly give you explicit notice that if the man, *of feeble talents & doubtful politic's,* whom I have heard named as the Republican candidate for Govr is to be supported next March for that office, I will not support but *oppose* his election." [76]

Plumer could not be moved from this position, although Judge Evans pleaded with him, for the sake of party unity, to support Gilman. In October, John Langdon called Plumer to Portsmouth and insisted that he accept the nomination for governor. Both of the Gilmans, Langdon said, were time servers; the party was weak in capable men, and the state demanded Plumer's services. Plumer in turn assured Langdon that no Republican other than Langdon himself could win an election and that he must consent to one more year of service. In December, when Nathaniel Gilman explicitly told the state committee that he would not run for the governorship, it became imperative that the party quickly unite upon another candidate. Plumer again drove to Portsmouth to urge Langdon to stand just once more. Langdon was reluctant; he promised to contribute two thousand dollars to a campaign fund if Plumer would consent to run; he threatened, if elected, to resign, so that Plumer as president of the senate might succeed him. But none of these stratagems could release him from his responsibility as the virtual founder of the Republican party in New Hampshire. He was in the extraordinary posi-

74. Plumer, Autobiography, 258.
75. Entry for June 1810, Plumer, Jr., Memoirs, I, N. H. State Lib. William, Jr., had obediently followed his father into the Republican party and voted their ticket in the March elections for the first time, but confessed that he had "never approved all their measures."
76. Plumer to John Parrott, July 25, 1810, Letter Book, III, Lib. Cong.

tion of being unable to refuse what other and more eager men could not be offered. Eventually, Langdon had to submit, as Plumer advised, "to the will of the Republicans." [77]

Langdon's obvious grooming of William Plumer as his successor began to bear fruit, however, during the winter of 1810. In December, the Senator received a letter from David L. Morrill, a preacher-politician who had been born in Epping and was now a Republican leader in Hillsborough County. Morrill said he had conversed with many prominent Republicans in his county in regard to a candidate for governor. "Being fully convinced of your abilities," he told Plumer, "& believing your administration would be decisive & efficient . . . I have taken the liberty to mention your name, which, I find, meets with general acceptation. . . . A line from you, suggesting your feelings, wou'd . . . induce us to act with more energy." Plumer's answer to this tempting proposal observed the etiquette of eighteenth-century politics: "I prefer private to public life . . . but if my fellow citizens should think me qualified for that trust I shall not decline their invitation." [78] He went on to say, however, that he thought Republican success depended on Langdon's accepting another nomination.

Plumer was destined to succeed Langdon at the next general election. During the 1811 session of the legislature, he roomed at the same house with Governor Langdon and became his chief adviser, although he did not attend the Republican caucuses. The first of these "nocturnal conclaves," held on June 15, unanimously nominated Langdon, who sent back an unequivocal refusal. Four nights later, a second meeting unanimously nominated Plumer and appointed a committee, headed by the speaker of the House, General Clement Storer, to obtain his answer. Plumer made the conventional demurrers, but after he had stated his inability to decline in the face of such unanimity and in the existing state of national affairs, he added frankly that the gentlemen could not have selected a candidate more obnoxious to their political opponents. He declared that his change of party was no sham; he "was formerly a real federalist, & a zealous supporter of their measures," but had left them when "their opinions & measures" became "erroneous & injurious to the country." He knew that his political enemies could not appreciate his motives, but he was prepared to bear their calumny and "thot the republicans had nothing to fear but their own divisions." After the

77. Plumer, Autobiography, 258-60.
78. David Morrill to Plumer, Dec. 12, 1810; Plumer to David Morrill, Dec. 24, 1810, Letter Book, VI, Lib. Cong.

committee had retired, Plumer sat down to search his conscience. The result of his introspection was not unfavorable; to his diary he confided:

When I received information of the vote of the republicans to support me, a consideration of the effect an election will necessarily produce in my family, my mode of living, the frequent interruptions it will occasion in my literary pursuits, the high responsibility of the office, the raised expectations of my friends—the inveterate opposition of my political enemies, & the anxiety I must feel in office, depressed my spirits, & induced me to regret that my name had been mentioned; but sufficient for the day is the evil it produces. If a Langdon & a Gilman had sufficient abilities to perform the duties of a governor, I may perform the task, in case I am elected.[79]

Plumer was not deceived in his estimation of what the governorship would cost him in personal loss and suffering. The first and most immediate sacrifice was the completion of his "History of North America," which had occupied a large proportion of his time since 1807. The trip to Washington that he had mentioned to Jefferson had not materialized, but the former President continued to manifest an interest in Plumer's enterprise. "I am happy to hear you have entered on a work so interesting to every American," Jefferson had written from Monticello in 1810. The history of the last forty years, he told Plumer, had not been treated with justice; "whenever it shall be written with truth and candor, and with that friendship to the natural rights of man, in which our revolution and constitution are founded, it will be a precious work." [80]

Another friendly sponsor of Plumer's intellectual labors, a kindred soul who had great influence upon him, was John Quincy Adams. From the deck of his ship, bound for St. Petersburg as American envoy to the Czar, Adams had written a highly complimentary letter to Plumer, whom he saluted as a "congenial spirit, . . . which can perceive a very distinct shade of difference between political candor and political hypocrisy. It affords me constant pleasure," continued Adams, "to recollect that the history of our country has fallen into the hands of such a man. . . . I know not another man with whom I have ever had the

79. Plumer, Autobiography, 263.
80. Quoted in Plumer, Jr., *Life of Plumer*, 379. Few letters with a President's signature remain in the Plumer collections at either the Library of Congress or the New Hampshire State Library. A copy of Plumer's letter to Jefferson, dated Apr. 27, 1810, to which Jefferson had replied as quoted above, appears in Plumer, Letter Book, III, Lib. Cong., and is printed in *Jefferson Papers*, Mass. Hist. Soc., *Collections*, 7th Ser., I (1900), 137-38.

opportunity of forming an acquaintance, on the correctness of whose narrative I should so implicitly rely." The experiences that Plumer and Adams had shared since they first met in 1803, and still more significantly, those that they had not shared, gave a peculiar meaning to the following words:

I hope, that the *moral* of your history will be the indissoluble union of the North American continent. . . . The plan of a New England combination more closely cemented than by the general ties of the federal government, a combination first to rule the whole and if that should prove impracticable, to separate from the rest, has been so far matured, and has engaged the studies, the intrigues and the ambitions of so many leading men in our part of the country, that I think it will eventually produce mischievous consequences, unless seasonably and effectually discountenanced, by men of more influence and of more comprehensive views. . . . To counteract the tendency of these partial and foolish combinations, I know nothing so likely to have a decisive influence as historical works, honestly and judiciously executed.[81]

In spite of these exalted expectations, Plumer did not complete his "History of North America." Indeed it is doubtful whether the task lay within the practical limits of his time and abilities. He had trouble deciding upon its organization, being strongly inclined at one time to make it a co-operative venture, and at another to write it in the form of letters to his son.[82] After finally settling upon orthodox narrative, he spent all his moderate store of skill upon the introduction, leaving nothing with which to prosecute the main body of his work. On November 18, 1808, he began his history as far back as the invention of "hyroglyphics" and in 1810 ended his first chapter with the decay of feudalism.[83] He ultimately managed to finish five more chapters, bringing the narrative up to the exploits of Captain John Smith. A few weeks before he returned to the gubernatorial chair in 1816, he wrote a few lines in chapter eight and finally stopped forever in the middle of page 264.

This uninspired fragment was painstakingly constructed, but it consisted entirely of snatches from secondary sources and would have been

81. John Quincy Adams to Plumer, Aug. 16, 1809, Ford, ed., *Writings of John Q. Adams,* III, 339-41.

82. Plumer to William Findlay, Dec. 9, 1811, Letter Book, III, Lib. Cong.; Plumer, Jr., to Plumer, June 25, Plumer to Plumer, Jr., Aug. 1, 1808, Plumer Papers, N. H. State Lib.

83. William Plumer, History of North America, 1-63, Plumer Papers, Lib. Cong.

of little value, even as an introduction to Plumer's original researches. Of these, the brief sketch that he had made in the spring of 1807, before he left Washington, indicated that his treatment of American history after 1789 would have been topical rather than chronological, and that it might have become a series of departmentalized and moralizing essays such as he actually produced later in his "Cincinnatus" articles.[84] Such a work would not have established Plumer as an historian; it might well have been useful, however, to later students of history. It would have dealt with events he had witnessed, in many of which he had been an actor. It would have been buttressed, furthermore, by documents which have since disappeared and by the personal observations of one of the most inquisitive minds in contemporary politics. Thomas Jefferson frequently expressed his fear that future generations would misunderstand completely the struggles through which the young republic had passed in his lifetime, and as late as 1818, he expressed regret to a visiting historian that Plumer had not "begun at the close of the revolutionary war, as he might then hope to see a history of a period concerning which the public know even less than that of the preceding one." [85]

The New Hampshire lawyer, however, had convinced himself after much labor that he had no more of a mind for history than for poetry, and he did not return to his "History of North America" manuscript until, in old age, he made the last rearrangement of his papers. In a shaky hand he then wrote, on page 264, an epitaph to his historical ambitions—"The undertaking I have abandoned." [86]

84. Plumer, Notes on the History of North America, *ibid.*
85. Salma Hale (writing from Charlottesville, Va.) to Plumer, May 8, 1818, Dartmouth Manuscripts, D808308, Baker Memorial Library, Dartmouth College. Jefferson told Hale that Plumer might "afterwards go back as Homer did" to cover the earlier years of our history. He lamented the lack of a good history of the Revolution, but thought that Botta's was the best of those which had been written.
86. Plumer, History of North America, 264, Plumer Papers, Lib. Cong.

CHAPTER XI

War Governor

"WILLIAM PLUMER is at this moment the
man of the people; and he will yet be the choice of
the people, when delusion and error and party
venom shall have been dispelled by the all-powerful
influence of REASON and TRUTH." [1]

I F, in 1812, Plumer's sole motive in leaving his literary pursuits long
enough to become governor of New Hampshire was the prospect of
serving his country, he chose an appropriate time to make the sacrifice.
The nation was backing into war through sheer inability to find any
other course of action. The times demanded unity as never before, yet
the administration, which had allowed itself to be tricked into abandonment of neutrality, was hampered by a malevolent partisan opposition
and embarrassed by divisions within its own ranks. In such an atmosphere of strife, Plumer had little reason to expect courtesy from his
political opponents. Some of the superior intellects among the Federalists, notably Jeremiah Mason and Daniel Webster, assured him that
they had high hopes for his good influence on the judiciary, but Mason
would not promise him to accept an appointment.[2]

The Federalist newspapers, however, "opened the flood gates of low
vulgar abuse & calumny agt me," as Plumer wrote to a friend in Washington.[3] The *Portsmouth Oracle* greeted the first announcement of his
candidacy with the declaration that "if anything was necessary to stimulate the patriotism of the Federalists, we think they would find it in
this nomination. New-hampshire may be very far departed from her
primitive political character, and yet *not far enough* to acquiesce in this
decree of the Democratic Caucus." Threats were subsequently made to
disqualify Plumer because of his supposed agnosticism, and he was

1. *N. H. Patriot* (Concord), Apr. 13, 1813.
2. Plumer, Autobiography, 264.
3. Plumer to John Harper, Mar. 2, 1812, Letter Book, VI, Lib. Cong.

subjected to increasingly violent attacks upon his apostasy in religion as well as in politics, sprinkled liberally with hints upon the subject of usury.[4]

Plumer was also the object of an intra-party intrigue which he chose to ignore. Some of the older Republicans could not forget the savage blows he had dealt them when he was on the other side, and many of the younger ones resented his stepping in to reap where they had sown. Early in the winter, a plot to replace Plumer with Nicholas Gilman was set on foot, supported chiefly by old Nathaniel Peabody and the restless Bartlett brothers.[5] They believed that Senator Gilman could be elected if the papers would support him. In any case, wrote Levi Bartlett, he and "other *consistent* republicans [would] give their votes for a man of principle." [6]

Publicly, however, Plumer was supported with flattery that compensated for the rough treatment he received in the Federalist press.[7] The Republicans, in fact, displayed more visible unanimity in supporting their new candidate than did the Federalists in choosing between their old ones. Smith had failed in two successive elections, and the older Federalists demanded the return of their popular favorite, John Taylor Gilman.[8] For a time, the confused party press endorsed both men, but a rumor that Smith had indignantly refused the nomination when he learned that Plumer was to be his opponent soon gained currency.[9] The palace revolution, it appeared, had been successful, for the Federalists ultimately gave their united support to Gilman, and Plumer found himself a direct rival of the man who, he believed, had always refused to recognize his true worth.

National issues played a larger part than usual in the campaign. The Republicans harped upon Federalist opposition to the general government and tenderness toward Britain, both of which they interpreted as

4. *Portsmouth Oracle,* Feb. 8, Mar. 7, 1812.

5. Plumer does not mention this affair in his papers, nor does William, Jr., in his biography of his father, but he does notice it in his entry for Feb. 13, 1813, Journal, I (1811-13), N. H. State Lib. (hereafter cited as Plumer, Jr., Journal, I).

6. Levi Bartlett to Josiah Bartlett, Jan. 1812, Bartlett Papers, Lib. Cong.; Josiah Butler to Josiah Bartlett, Nov. 16, 1811, Bartlett Papers, N. H. State Lib.

7. *N. H. Patriot* (Concord), Feb. 11, Mar. 7, 1812. Plumer appreciated the importance of the *Patriot.* "In this State much will depend upon your paper," he wrote to Hill. Plumer to Isaac Hill, Nov. 13, 1811, Hill Papers, N. H. Hist. Soc.

8. Plumer, Autobiography, 265-66. Had the original Republican nomination of Nathaniel Gilman prevailed, or the intrigue to support Nicholas Gilman succeeded, New Hampshire would have witnessed the interesting phenomenon of brothers opposing each other as nominees of different parties.

9. Levi Bartlett to Josiah Bartlett, Jan. 1812, Bartlett Papers, Lib. Cong.

treason.[10] The Federalists, for their part, accused their opponents of rushing headlong toward a senseless war with England, which would result in misery, defeat, and bankruptcy. Gallatin chose this unpropitious moment to recommend that the federal government levy direct taxes in preparation for war. The *Patriot* hastened to assure its readers that a war could be won without taxes and that Gallatin was evidently turning Federalist. Nevertheless, the Secretary had touched a sensitive nerve in New Hampshire agrarianism, and the younger Plumer estimated the cost of Gallatin's announcement at a thousand votes gone over to the Federalists.[11]

In the face of these handicaps, it is surprising that Plumer was not badly beaten. Newspaper reports, however, showed the voting to be so close that no one knew the result until after the legislature's official count in June. Contrary to Republican hopes, the Federalists did not divide between their candidates but supported Gilman with disciplined vigor. Plumer ran well, but against a strong ebb tide. His son Samuel, who was a merchant's clerk in Portsmouth at the time of the election, reported that even in this stronghold of Republicanism, his "Paa" received only 525 votes to Gilman's 514, and that Daniel Webster, who was moderator of the town meeting, had come within a hair's breadth of being elected one of Portsmouth's five representatives in place of a prominent deist on the Republican ticket. Such religious prejudice could explain why Plumer received 2,000 fewer votes from the Republicans throughout the state than had Langdon in 1811.[12]

When the legislature canvassed the votes in June, they learned that there had been no election. Gilman had 15,612 votes, just three more than the number that had elected Smith in 1809, while Plumer's total of 15,492 was considerably less than his party's previous two-year record. Neither candidate had a majority, since 877 scattered votes for various candidates had been cast by Republicans who disliked Plumer

---

10. For this purpose, they regretted deeply the fact that the Henry letters were not published in time to influence the election, supposing that they "would have made thousands of votes difference in this State." Plumer, Jr., to William Claggett, Mar. 24, 1812, Plumer Papers, N. H. State Lib.; Plumer to John Harper, Mar. 23, 1812, Plumer Papers, N.-Y. Hist. Soc.

11. *N. H. Patriot* (Concord), Feb. 11, 1812; William Plumer, Jr., to Obed Hall, Mar. 11, 1812, Plumer Papers, N. H. State Lib.

12. Samuel Plumer to William Plumer, Jr., Mar. 14, 1812, *ibid.*; Lyon, ed., *New Hampshire Register . . . 1860*, 41. On the other hand, this prejudice might have been offset by Plumer's reputation among the dissenters as a legal champion of their liberties. Plumer received letters of congratulation after the election from prominent Quakers. Richard Dame to Plumer, June 8, 1812, Letter Book, VI, Lib. Cong.

and Federalists who were still loyal to Jeremiah Smith. Although the Federalists came close to winning control of the senate, by some peculiar chance they lost seats in the lower house, where the Republicans had a clear majority of twenty. Because the constitution provided that elections in which no candidate obtained a majority were to be thrown into the legislature, the Republican victory in the lower house was decisive. The two houses, meeting in convention, elected Plumer to the governorship and chose Republicans in each of the two undetermined senatorial districts, thus giving the party a seven to five majority in the upper house. The Republicans also retained control of the council, three to two. Although Plumer had been elected as a minority governor, he was thus given working majorities in every branch of the government.

The Plumers learned all of this at one o'clock in the morning of June 5, 1812, when they were aroused by a neighbor who had news of the election. Five hours later a committee of legislators appeared in Epping with the official notice of Plumer's elevation to the office of governor.[13] After taking breakfast with the committee, the new chief magistrate set out on horseback for Concord with his legislative escort, gathering new troops of a dozen or more horsemen at every town line until he reached Epsom, where he encountered John Langdon, already fleeing from the burdens of office. "When he took leave of me he was much affected," wrote Plumer. Having dined, the new governor mounted again, ready to participate in the pageantry which was still so much a part of republican government.

Two miles from thence I was met by an escort of about eighty gentlemen on horseback. The six first were mounted on grey horses, followed by the marshals of the day, the sheriffs of Strafford & Grafton, myself & two captains of the army of the United States, & after me the remainder of the escort. The last six miles of the road was dusty, & I was literally covered with it. As soon as we passed Concord bridge we were met by an additional escort of forty or fifty gentlemen—the procession proceeded to Barker's tavern, where we arrived at four O'clock in the afternoon. I ordered refreshment for all who attended. The day was favorable to the journey, & tho I had not for many years rode so far on horseback in one day, I was less fatigued than I expected.[14]

13. Entry for June 5, 1812, Plumer, Jr., Memoirs, I, N. H. State Lib.
14. Plumer, Autobiography, 268. On his return from Concord, Plumer had an even more imposing escort, which filled his house, and consumed large quantities of punch, rum, wine, brandy, cider, bacon, veal, fish, biscuit, and bread. William, Jr., in his Journal, I, N. H. State Lib., candidly admitted that the Plumers were trying to outdo, not the Joneses, but the *Smiths*.

With his customary prudence and foresight, Plumer had carefully drafted, rewritten, and copied his inaugural address, long before he knew whether he should ever have occasion to deliver it. In this task he had been embarrassed by uncertainty as to the probable state of affairs when he should take office. The country was suspended in a fog of indecision between war and more embargo. John Harper, a New Hampshire War Hawk in the Twelfth Congress, had assured Plumer as early as December 2 that "the present Session will not be closed, without an *arrangement,* or an actual *war* with Great Britain." [15] The newspapers were full of martial anticipations, but when Plumer wrote his speech, most of the congressmen were home on leave, and nothing really decisive had been done. His own conviction, however, was that the "present state of things cannot long continue . . . our suit with Britain must be settled in the tented field, & not by wager of law but *trial by battle.*" [16]

On the morning of June 6, when Plumer arose before the legislature and a throng of visitors, Congress was still debating in secret session a resolution to declare war against Great Britain. The burden imposed upon him, of anticipating and defending the momentous decision he believed his party was about to make, suddenly weighed so heavily upon Plumer that his confidence almost failed. "I was agitated," he confessed, "my hands trembled, & before I had read thro the second paragraph I was apprehensive I should be obliged to stop; but my confidence increased, & I pronounced the remainder with ease & propriety." Sympathetic spectators declared that Plumer not only recovered from his embarrassment, but injected a dynamic virility into his words "which lifted men, at times, from their seats." [17] This speech did more than any act of Plumer's life to establish his claim to the laurels of statesmanship.

On a question that had been debated for two decades, Plumer could hardly have been expected to contribute any new ideas. Nor is it to be supposed that he produced an objective treatise on foreign relations. Plumer's speech was weakest in the earlier paragraphs, which dealt with the causes of the coming war. He blamed England and France equally for the wrongs Americans had suffered on the high seas; but

15. John Harper to Plumer, Dec. 2, 1811, Letter Book, VI, Lib. Cong.
16. Plumer to John Harper, Apr. 13, 1812, *ibid.*
17. Plumer, Autobiography, 268; Plumer, Jr., *Life of Plumer,* 391.

England, he said, had persisted in "a spirit of obstinate perseverance in measures hostile to our ... most essential rights." He pictured the American government as having patiently negotiated and even begged for justice until it had "approached a state of humiliation incompatible with national dignity." To Plumer, the only remaining alternative was war. "Though war is a great calamity, the sacrifice of our essential rights is greater." [18]

Plumer found his *casus belli,* not in any new outrage nor in a diplomatic rupture, but in a profound psychological principle. "If we cherish a spirit of submission to a foreign power, and tamely acquiesce in the loss of one right after another," he insisted, "we shall thereby prepare the public mind for a state of degradation and servitude, more dreadful in its consequences than that of war; for a nation cannot long survive the loss of its spirit." Territorial ambitions, defense of the carrying trade, and sailors' rights may have concerned him, but Plumer had a deeper conviction that the nation must fight for its integrity and its own spirit.[19] Such a struggle would be hopeless, however, unless national policy could be founded upon a union of parties and interests. Former governors of New Hampshire had done more to destroy than to encourage such unity by their indiscriminate attacks upon the opposite party. In avoiding the recriminations of the past and placing patriotism superior to party, Plumer rose to new heights of statesmanship.

It is one of the first principles of government that the will of the constituted authorities, expressed by the acts of the majority, demand the obedience of every citizen. Nor is it less the peculiar province of the General Government to direct and manage our national affairs, than it is our indispensable duty and highest interest, to afford them our prompt and effective aid, in carrying into operation all their constitutional measures.... It is from a spirit of jealousy and division, that we have more to apprehend, than from the boasted power of both the belligerents of Europe. But as the danger to which we are exposed from abroad increases, may we not reasonably hope that our union

18. *Speech of His Excellency, William Plumer, to the Legislature, June, 1812* (n.p., 1812); also *Journal of the House of Representatives, June Session, 1812* (Concord, 1812), 23-30.

19. After much emphasis on expansionism, land hunger, and manifest destiny as the real causes of the War of 1812, historians are moving toward a greater appreciation of Plumer's point of view. See Warren Goodman, "The Origins of the War of 1812: A Survey of Changing Interpretations," *Miss. Valley Hist. Rev.,* 28 (1941), 171-86.

among ourselves will also increase. . . . Our union is our safety—*a house divided against itself cannot stand.* An indissoluble union of the States is essential, not only to our prosperity, but even to our existence as a nation.

If there had been no previous evidence of the fact, these paragraphs would have established Governor Plumer as something more than a politician and a newspaper controversialist. The remainder of his speech proved that he had the qualifications of an administrator as well. Harper later assured the Governor that in Washington his speech was "pronounced not only as highly honorable to the *person,* but to the *State,* which boasts of so distinguished a Statesman." [20]

Even the savage *Portsmouth Oracle* paid grudging tribute to the "many things to admire in this communication." [21] Admiration, however, did not dispel politics. The Federalist legislators presented a resolution stating that a war with Great Britain "under existing circumstances would be highly inconvenient, destructive of the prosperity and happiness of our country, burdensome to the people, and eminently hazardous to the existence of our republican form of government," and directing their congressmen to vote against it. [22] The unbroken ranks of the Republican majority, however, disposed of this resolution by postponement and promised strong support for the war policy of the administration.

This brief session of the legislature revealed Plumer as a forceful leader and a skillful party manager. He exercised his veto power only once, on another bill to incorporate John Sullivan's boating monopoly, and the House of Representatives sustained him unanimously. [23] The lawmakers also followed his advice by inserting in most of their acts of incorporation a clause allowing repeal in the public interest, although the Senate defeated a resolution to make such a provision mandatory in all charters. They also revised the criminal code, ordered a new

---

20. John Harper to Plumer, June 14, 1812, Letter Book, VI, Lib. Cong.
21. *Portsmouth Oracle,* June 13, 1812.
22. *House Journal, June Sess., 1812,* 117.
23. *Ibid.,* 87-91. Plumer objected, not to the charter itself, but to its indefinite terms. The bill was written in such language as to convey unlimited use of the Merrimack River for unidentified purposes. "Considering the extent & importance to which this institution may be carried, & the great uncertainty respecting its operation & effects upon the rights & interest of a large & increasing portion of our citizens, the governor had considered it his duty to state these objections to this bill," wrote Plumer. The company was subsequently incorporated under a more carefully limited charter. See Plumer, Essays, I, 96, Lib. Cong.

valuation in preparation for a reapportionment of taxes, and subjected sheriffs and town clerks to penalties for delinquency in returning votes. All these Plumer had recommended as specific objects of legislative action.[24] As the Governor prepared to leave Concord on June 19, after adjourning the General Court, he had reason to feel well satisfied with the performance of a difficult part of his task.

At nine o'clock on the evening of June 23, a uniformed horseman galloped through the dusk deepening over Epping village and pulled up sharply at Plumer's gate. He carried dispatches from an old Epping resident, Major General Henry Dearborn, now commander of the northern division of the United States Army, stating that war had been declared against Great Britain and requesting the Governor to order out two companies of the detached militia for the defense of Portsmouth harbor. A few minutes later, Colonel Daniel Plumer, aide to the Governor, was riding swiftly northward toward Epsom with orders for the adjutant general of the state militia, Michael McClary, to attend the captain general at his headquarters in Epping. McClary appeared at noon the next day, with a woeful tale of military unpreparedness. So far as he knew, not a single militiaman had been detached for special service, and no provision had been made for officers, even if the soldiers were available. Under Plumer's direction, however, he immediately ordered the two companies to be taken from the First Brigade of the New Hampshire militia and placed under the command of Major Upham of the United States Army, stationed at Portsmouth.[25] Two days after this flurry of activity Plumer received official notice from James Monroe, the Secretary of State, that war had been declared. "You may with confidence assure the president of the United States, that I will promptly afford my aid and assistance to the full extent of my power, to mitigate the evils of war to our citizens, & render it effectual against the enemies of our beloved country," he answered.[26] In his journal that same evening, he sought consolation in philosophy: "I have been elevated to office in a time of difficulty, when the multitude will judge of my conduct, not by the wisdom & fitness of my measures . . . but by their success, which cannot depend on me. My object will be to merit, if I do not obtain, their approbation. The greater the difficulty

24. *Journal of the Senate, June Session, 1812* (Concord, 1812), 53; Plumer, Autobiography, 270.

25. Henry Dearborn to Plumer, June 22, 1812, Plumer to Henry Dearborn, June 24, 1812, Letter Book, III, Lib. Cong.; General Orders to Brigadier-General Clement Storer, June 24, 1812, in Plumer, Essays, I, 97-98, Lib. Cong.

26. Plumer to James Monroe, June 27, 1812, Letter Book, III, Lib. Cong.

I have to encounter, the greater will be the honor if I perform my duty with propriety." [27]

William Plumer was the first war governor in the history of the state of New Hampshire.[28] He was called upon to assume responsibilities and to decide questions of constitutionality and legality that none of his predecessors under the state constitution had faced. Hampered on the one hand by the exasperating inefficiency and red tape of the national government's war effort and beset on the other by disheartening apathy or antipathy in his own state, Plumer controlled his temper and proved even to his enemies that he was more than a fleshpot-seeking politician. Since New Hampshire was not a theater of war, he was not called upon for such exertions as were the governors of New York or Ohio. Nevertheless, even for the single year during which he was captain general of the state's armed forces, his military correspondence, orders, accounts, and messages comprise a sizable sheaf of documents.[29] As an important part of the burden which Plumer carried until June 1813, certain aspects of New Hampshire's military posture must be considered.

Plumer's military duty was simple in essence, but it was complicated by unnecessary and sometimes malevolent interference. The defense of New Hampshire resolved itself into two problems: the prevention of an assault upon Portsmouth harbor by the British fleet, and the protection of the northern frontier against raids from Canada. When the war began, the United States had no forces whatever on the northern frontier and only a single company of garrison troops stationed in two dilapidated forts on either side of the entrance to Portsmouth harbor. No one believed that these forces could save the city from a spirited attack.

Nor was the state militia a force of absolute dependability. It was supposed to have been in an especially "flourishing" [30] condition under John Langdon, who loved pomp and display, but Langdon in 1812 was a very different man from the dashing young cavalry captain of

---

27. Plumer, Autobiography, 271.

28. New Hampshire had no governor during the War of Independence.

29. The following narrative is based on material which is preserved chiefly in three sets of manuscripts: Plumer's Letter Books, III and VI, and his Essays, I, all in the Library of Congress. References will be given only for quotations.

30. This adjective is used both by Emma Watts, "New Hampshire in the War of 1812," *Granite Monthly*, 30(1898), 357-66, and the editor of the *New Hampshire Manual for the General Court* (Concord, 1889), 122. Neither of these sources is very reliable.

Revolutionary days, and his militia companies were better equipped with bright uniforms than with bullets. On paper, New Hampshire had an imposing citizen's army of three divisions, made up of six brigades and thirty-seven regiments, but few of these units were ready or even willing to fight.[31] Plumer had little faith in the cardinal Republican principle of dependence upon the armed citizens of the nation, but he agreed, at least, that they should be armed. Consequently he had been very critical in private of Langdon's feeble preparations and the state's inadequate militia laws.[32]

By a law of April 10, 1812, Congress had ordered the state executives to detach their respective proportions of a body of 100,000 men from the regular militia, to be ready to march "at a moment's warning" under the command of the War Department.[33] This was not a new or revolutionary device. It had first been written into the laws of the United States by the Federalists as early as 1792, at which time no one but a few Jacobins considered it arbitrary or unconstitutional. The principle went back still further to the minutemen of the Revolutionary War and to the trainbands of Elizabethan England.

New Hampshire's proportion of the 100,000 men to be detached in 1812 amounted to 3,500 soldiers and officers.[34] Langdon was still in office when the order to constitute this force arrived, and he had promptly issued his own orders of compliance to his militia officers. The orders were unpopular,[35] however, and not a single officer had made his returns by June 23. After a month of prodding his officers, the adjutant general, and the War Department, Plumer finally finished the job that should have been done in April and had the New Hampshire detached militia properly organized into a division, officered, and ready to function as a whole or by companies, if necessary. Whether it would actually fight remained to be seen, but Plumer tried to infuse some of his own spirit into the citizen soldiery by his general orders. "The captain general has entire confidence in the zeal & patriotism of the officers & privates composing this detachment, that they will, when required, promptly rally round the standard of their country, & by their

31. Chandler Potter, *Military History of New Hampshire, Adjutant-General's Report for 1866* (Concord, 1866), II, 394.
32. Plumer, Diary, 5-6, Lib. Cong.
33. *Annals of Congress,* 12th Cong., 1st Sess., II, 2267.
34. William Eustis to Plumer, June 22, 1812, Plumer Papers, N.-Y. Hist. Soc.
35. Roughly comparable now to calling the National Guard into active service during peace.

effective & heroic conduct evince to the world their unshaken resolution to maintain its independence, & vindicate its injured rights." [36]

Although General Dearborn's first concern had been for the defense of Portsmouth, the New Hampshire frontier felt the earliest apprehensions of attack. Two weeks before the declaration of war, a petition had come to Plumer from many of the towns in Coös County, urgently begging for armed forces to protect them from Indians and Tory neighbors. Having no constitutional authority to act except in case of invasion, Plumer had sent the petition to the legislature, which had ignored it. Alarming letters continued to pour in, describing the potential danger in Canada with a note of panic.[37] Plumer consequently suggested to General Dearborn that a company of detached militia be sent to guard the United States frontier in the region of the upper Connecticut. Dearborn gave the requisite orders, and Plumer hastened to carry them out by detaching a company from the northernmost brigade under a militia officer, Captain Ephraim Mahurin, and stationing the major part of it at Stewartstown. A small scouting party was also established on the shores of Lake Umbagog to the eastward. By the latter part of August, the band of fifty soldiers had reached Stewartstown and built a blockhouse which they called Fort Plumer.

In spite of the delays and vexations involved in getting this small body of men to the point of possible invasion, Plumer had executed an admirable stroke of policy. Whether the danger had been real or imaginary, there was no invasion of New Hampshire during the war, and Plumer's little company apparently quieted the fears of the inhabitants. The plan of committing defense to the detached militia shifted the burden from the townspeople and the state to the national treasury. It also provided escape for Plumer and the Republican party from the odium of abandoning the frontier. Since the legislature had appropriated no money for munitions nor authorized the governor to furnish any to towns, Plumer would have been helpless if Dearborn had not come to his aid.[38]

Local historians declare that the troops were placed on the frontier, not to defend the inhabitants, but to prevent trading with Canada.[39] Whether Dearborn's original alacrity was influenced by that considera-

---

36. General Orders by Captain-General, June 23, 1812, Plumer, Essays, I, 100-1, Lib. Cong.
37. Joseph Whipple to Plumer, June 1812, Letter Book, VI, *ibid.*
38. Plumer, Autobiography, 274-75.
39. See Georgia Merrill, ed., *History of Coös County* (Syracuse, N. Y., 1888), 95 ff.

tion, or whether Plumer had found a way to avoid arming local militia-men who were potential smugglers, the fact is that the actual presence of the soldiers discouraged illegal activities. Captain Mahurin wrote, "The check which has been put to smuggling by the men Stationed at this place has excited much warmth & irritation among the friends of Great Britain in this part of the State." [40] By December, the inhabitants who had begged so piteously for help in June were doing all that they could to embarrass the people who had responded to their call. False rumors were spread, causing serious disputes among the militia officers, and the soldiers were made mutinous by carefully sown propaganda. These difficulties Plumer patiently straightened out by constant corre-spondence.

Some time before the six-month term of Captain Mahurin's company expired in January, Governor Plumer issued orders for the dispatch of replacements. Three months elapsed before these commands were carried out. Plumer learned that the officers ordered to relieve Captain Mahurin had taken advantage of various technicalities to decline the service, and the privates had been infected by the disobedience of their officers. Had it not been for a Maine company that marched to Stewarts-town, the refusal of New Hampshire men to obey orders would have left their own homes unprotected during a favorite raiding season of the Indians. The difficulty had been largely political. In apologizing for the delay, Brigadier General John Montgomery had written, "I sincerely regret that so much division and party spirit prevails in our country as to render it almost impossible for an Officer in my situation to do his duty to acceptance." [41]

Political opposition within the state would have been easier to bear if Plumer and his followers had received steady and efficient support from their own party. Unfortunately, the paralysis of Washington bureaucracy affected the simple defense of the small state as much as the general conduct of the war. A single incident will illustrate a chronic condition. Dearborn had given his order to call the detached company of Coös militia into the service of the United States with handsome largesse, but had neglected to inform the army officers of his arrange-ments. When accordingly, Captain Mahurin sent his muster-roll and expense account to Captain Walbach at Fort Constitution—two hun-dred miles by forest trail, country road, and turnpike from one end of New Hampshire to the other—Captain Walbach regretted that he was

40. Ephraim Mahurin to Plumer, Dec. 14, 1812, Letter Book, VI, Lib. Cong.
41. John Montgomery to Plumer, May 19, 1813, *ibid.*

not the proper authority and routed them to the district paymaster in Boston. This functionary returned them to Captain Mahurin, saying that it was not his province to allow expense accounts. Two "pressing letters" from Mahurin obtained no result, and the doughty captain was forced to lend his own money to his soldiers to keep them decently clothed.[42]

Plumer received news of this dilemma on November 10, when the men had already completed half their service. He promptly dispatched letters to the secretary of war and to Brigadier General Montgomery, which brought results in the form of pay to the soldiers, but Plumer could only tell Mahurin to write to General Dearborn, now at Albany, in regard to his expense account. A letter from Dearborn to Plumer in December indicated that Mahurin had made the application and the proper orders had been issued for his reimbursement. Thus, after letters had passed at least eight times from Fort Plumer to Portsmouth, Boston, Epping, and Albany, the simple matter of providing for a company of fifty men was finally settled. Even this was not the end, for the same round of irresponsibility had to be followed for the company that relieved Mahurin's. In the process of grappling with this problem of logistics, Plumer stands out as the figure endowed with the least authority but the most energy. Captain Mahurin, at the end of his six-month service, wrote a letter to the Governor which contained a sincere and voluntary tribute: "Permit me, at this time, to express the high sense I entertain of your Excellency's unwearied attention to the safety and interest of this State and the Union, and in particular, accept my grateful acknowledgments for the civilities and attention you have been pleased to shew to myself and the officers and soldiers under my command." [43]

It was fortunate for New Hampshire that she was not invaded, for she was woefully unprepared. Governor Plumer labored diligently to replenish the miserable supply of arms that he found in the state arsenals, but his efforts were often balked by the accumulated carelessness of years or by partisan non-co-operation. He was able to wheedle from the United States authorities a quantity of bullets for the frontier guard and a stand of 1,000 arms for the state militia. In November, he advised the legislature to reorganize the militia, to authorize the distribution of the arms he had received from the War Department, to provide additional compensation for the detached militia in actual service, and

42. Ephraim Mahurin to Plumer, Oct. 27, 1812, Letter Book, III, *ibid.*
43. Ephraim Mahurin to Plumer, Feb. 9, 1813, *ibid.*

finally, to purchase a supply of armament for the state.[44] The first of these, the legislature refused to do; the second it bungled so that Plumer had to return the resolution for the inclusion of proper safeguards; and the third it did reluctantly, after instructing the state's congressmen to see that the United States eventually assumed the additional burden.[45] But on the last and most important matter, the legislature procrastinated until Plumer feared that nothing would be done. Finally, he called in the key men of both parties and expostulated with them, pointing out that no matter how great or how honest was the difference of opinion on the justice of the war, war actually existed—that the state might be invaded before the next session of the legislature—and that the law of self-preservation ought to deter even the Federalists from sending out their militia to fight barehanded. Plumer's personal work was effective in securing an appropriation to purchase 2,000 rounds of powder, 5,000 pounds of lead, and 12,000 flints.[46] This was virtually the extent of New Hampshire's military preparation during the War of 1812.

William Plumer, who ordinarily expected the worst of public opinion, cherished throughout his year as governor the illusion that war would compel a cessation of political hostilities in the United States. No expectation could have been more cruelly deceptive. Even before the fighting began, Plumer had to concede that the loan from which Congress had expected to realize $11,000,000 would "not be full" in New England. "Every means has been taken by the federalists to defeat it," he complained, "not content by withholding their own money they have done everything in their power to prevent others." [47] Plumer himself was offered several excellent investment opportunities in order to seduce him from the poor yield of the new 6 per cents, but he loyally subscribed to the amount of $4,000.[48] There were not enough like him, however, to produce a single million in New England, nor more than six million in the entire country.

The war had not been many weeks in progress before Plumer found the Federalists "doing everything they can to embarrass & perplex the measures of the general government; they not only discourage inlistments into the army, but do all they dare to prevent the detached officers

44. *Speech of His Excellency, William Plumer, to the Legislature, November, 1812* (Concord, 1812), 7-8.
45. *Journal of the House of Representatives, November Session, 1812* (Concord, 1813), 46-47, 122, 136, 171.
46. Plumer, Autobiography, 286; *House Journal, Nov. Sess., 1812,* 148.
47. Plumer to John Harper, May 11, 1812, Letter Book, VI, Lib. Cong.
48. Plumer, Autobiography, 266.

& privates performing their duty." [49] Throughout the summer of 1812, war party and peace party faced each other with increasing antagonism. At a Republican Fourth of July celebration in Portsmouth, Governor Plumer gave the toast: "The United States—The *spirit* which produced will *support* the independence of our country, & vindicate its injured rights. *God nerves the patriot's arm.*" [50] At another Independence Day celebration in the same city, however, Daniel Webster proclaimed to the Washington Benevolent Society that the war was "premature and inexpedient." [51] Opposition to the war not only brought Webster to prominence among the Federalists but led also to the defection of such prominent Republicans as John Goddard, Josiah Bartlett, and the two younger Gilmans. Taking advantage of this dissatisfaction, the Federalists devised a "Peace Ticket," ostensibly bipartisan but heavily Federalist in composition, which proposed to elect DeWitt Clinton to the presidency. [52] Their effective machine not only sent Webster and a complete Federalist delegation to Congress in August but also captured the state's eight electoral votes in November.

The indignant Governor of New Hampshire, believing that the November elections were of critical importance, had taken time from his manifold tasks to write two mediocre campaign squibs for the *Patriot,* reciting the old arguments in favor of the war, and exposing the inconsistency and folly of the peace party. To readers who could penetrate the classical signature and the anonymous allusions, these articles presented the diverting spectacle of New Hampshire's governor calling the state treasurer a "wolf in sheep's clothing," a "secret foe," and a "sunshine patriot." [53] Many of Plumer's colleagues were discouraged by their failures in the fall elections, but the Governor refused to lose heart. "Notwithstanding the shock the war has given to our Republicans & the unfavorable result of the recent elections, I still believe N. H. is a republican State," he wrote to Harper. [54]

Governor Plumer had not expected to deal with war-shocked fol-

49. Plumer to Henry Dearborn, July 29, 1812, Letter Book, III, Lib. Cong.

50. Plumer, Autobiography, 274.

51. Daniel Webster, *Writings and Speeches,* ed. J. W. McIntyre (Boston, 1903), XV, 595.

52. Plumer, Autobiography, 280.

53. [William Plumer], "Demosthenes," "To the Republicans of New Hampshire," No. 2, Plumer, Essays, I, 105-7, Lib. Cong., publ. in *N. H. Patriot* (Concord), Oct. 27, 1812.

54. Plumer to John Harper, Nov. 9, 1812, Letter Book, VI, Lib. Cong.

lowers, but he had anticipated trouble with appointments. His one opportunity to improve the judiciary inherited from his predecessor was lost by political dissension in his council. When Judge Steele resigned from the Superior Court,[55] Plumer called his council together and brought forward the name of Samuel Bell, a man of strict integrity and great ability, but handicapped by his connection with the Hillsborough Bank failure in 1808. The three Republican members of the council, however, refused to support Plumer's proposal, and he was forced to abandon Bell. After rejecting two nominations by the Federalist councilors, Plumer's party colleagues suggested Clifton Claggett, who was distinguished primarily for his faithful services to the party. "I thot him honest, but his talents & legal information were not above mediocrity," Plumer commented. Nevertheless, he reluctantly agreed to Claggett's appointment. It was the one act of his year in office that he subsequently had real cause to regret.[56]

Plumer's Superior Court thereafter consisted of Arthur Livermore, a judicial despot, Richard Evans, a chronic invalid, and Claggett, a mediocrity, while the attorney general who argued the state's cases before this bench was a drunkard. The Governor was unable to remedy this deplorable situation. Judge Evans, dying of tuberculosis, called upon Plumer for his quarter's salary in August, after illness had prevented him for eighteen months from attending court. "Your sickness is a misfortune both to you and the state," Plumer remarked pointedly. Yet Evans stubbornly refused to resign. "If a federal administration removes him they cannot with propriety be blamed," wrote the disgusted Governor.[57]

It was only by sheer intuition that Governor Plumer escaped the intrigues of his own councilors and prevented the kind of office-jobbing that had stained Langdon's administration.[58] He was not so fortunate in preventing political dereliction in his legislature, which sat for a whole month in November without being able to elect a United States senator. By voting with the Federalists for John Goddard, one peace-

55. Plumer, "Jonathan Steele," Biographies, V, 327 ff., N. H. Hist. Soc. Through a clerk's error, Steele had collected money in excess of his salary, refused to return it, and resigned when Plumer placed the matter before the legislature.

56. Plumer, Autobiography, 276, 277, 294; Plumer, "Clifton Clagett," Biographies, V, 459, N. H. Hist. Soc.

57. Plumer, Autobiography, 279; Plumer, Biographies, V, 102-5; entry for May 19, 1813, Plumer's Diary, Lib. Cong.

58. Plumer, Autobiography, 291-93.

party Republican created a stalemate in the upper house, which could not be broken even by the proposal of Plumer's name as a compromise.[59] The consequence of this impasse was the election of Jeremiah Mason to the vacant seat by the Federalist legislature of 1813. Henceforth, throughout the war, New Hampshire was represented in both houses of Congress by a solid block of oppositionist votes.

Republicans were agreed upon one thing, however; during the winter session of 1812, the Republican caucus unanimously renominated Plumer for the governorship.[60] If doubts had previously existed in party circles, they had given way to genuine admiration for Plumer's effective administration. "Politics out of the question, never have we had a Governor so capable ... never one that gave more universal satisfaction," declared the *New Hampshire Patriot*.[61] His promptness in calling out the militia was loudly praised and his state papers were said to equal the best in the Union. The *New Hampshire Gazette* was not behind the *Patriot* in its adulation: "With a vigorous and well cultivated mind richly stored in knowledge of history and jurisprudence; endowed with the various qualities that constitute the acute statesman and profound civilian; with an indefatigable industry and application to business; with a ken and penetration peculiarly his own: he has discharged the high duty of Governor of New-Hampshire to entire satisfaction." [62]

Plumer himself helped to focus the campaign for his re-election upon the single great issue of the war by writing six newspaper articles, published under the pseudonym of "Columbus." Although they were composed during the busy months of January and February, they were among the best productions from Plumer's pen. He stated once again, with perspicuity, his conception of the justice of the war, the duty of every citizen to obey the laws and support his country in her hour of crisis, the criminal folly of resistance and nullification, and the dangers of the course taken by the Federalists.[63] Although the essays were published during the campaigning season, Plumer did not even mention

59. Plumer to Plumer, Jr., Dec. 5, 1812, Letter Book, VI, Lib. Cong.; *Journal of the Senate, November Session, 1812* (Concord, 1813), 110. William Jr., thought that his father would probably have accepted this opportunity to return to Washington. Plumer, Jr., Journal, I, 392, N. H. State Lib.

60. Plumer, Autobiography, 287.

61. *N. H. Patriot* (Concord), Dec. 29, 1812, Feb. 23, 1813.

62. *Ibid.*, Feb. 9, 1813, copied from the *N. H. Gazette* (Portsmouth).

63. These articles, entitled "Plain Truth" and signed "Columbus," were published in the *N. H. Patriot* (Concord), Jan. 19-Feb. 2, Feb. 16-Mar. 2, 1813. Plumer preserved manuscript copies in his Essays, II (1813-23), 1-29, Plumer Papers, Lib. Cong.

the state elections. In these articles Plumer appears as an unselfish patriot, willing to stand or fall on the issue of the war alone. At the same time, discovering that John Taylor Gilman was again to be his opponent, Plumer composed and published anonymously several letters, supposed to have been exchanged between Federalists, deprecating the shortcomings of the candidate whom they were forced to support.[64] The tawdry and the sublime in Plumer appeared nowhere so clearly as in the columns of the *New Hampshire Patriot.*

The act of Plumer's administration that the Federalists most bitterly condemned was the one of which he was most proud—his prompt compliance with national requests for the service of the detached militia. During his twelve months in office, Plumer received four such requisitions, each of which he fulfilled unhesitatingly. His obedience gave him a certain claim to distinction, for the Federalist governors of Massachusetts, Connecticut, and Rhode Island refused to recognize the authority of the United States in this matter.[65] Although Plumer would undoubtedly have done so, if required, he was not asked to send militia out of the state; all the requisitions were for internal defense, paid for by the national government. This made no difference to the Federalists; his guilt was that he obeyed a law passed by a Republican Congress. Yet by a curious inversion of logic the Federalists of Portsmouth cursed Madison's administration for leaving them exposed to the enemy.[66]

The most reasoned version of the Federalist viewpoint on this question appeared in a minority protest against the reply to the Governor's address at the November session of the legislature. Founding their argument upon the assertion that New Hampshire was a *"free, sovereign and independent* State," the seventy protestants insisted that she could not surrender control of her armed forces to an outside authority except under the exigencies mentioned in the Federal Constitution, and that it was the duty of the governor to determine whether these conditions actually existed.[67]

64. *Ibid.,* 17-18.
65. James T. Adams, *New England in the Republic, 1776-1850* (Boston, 1926), 270.
66. Some historians have defended the Federalist contention on this point by declaring that the withdrawal of the regular army for the invasion of Canada left the New England coast defenseless and justified the governors in keeping their militia at home. The fact is, however, that General Dearborn's first requisition was for precisely the purpose of defending the ports of New England, and it was the governors' defiance of federal law and the War Department's plans which left their own coasts defenseless. See Morison, *Otis,* II, 52-64.
67. *House Journal, Nov. Sess., 1812,* 160 ff.

The address that Governor Plumer had already made to the legislature, however, contained so forceful a defense of his action that the Federalist argument was refuted before it was made. If each of eighteen local sovereigns was to decide when the militia ought to be turned out, he said, the British could conquer all of North America piecemeal while New Hampshire was waiting to be invaded. Plumer based his defense on precedent as well as reason. The earliest laws placing the militia under control of the President had been passed during Washington's administration by a Federalist Congress. Governor Gilman had not only failed to find the act of 1794 unconstitutional, but he had persuaded his legislature to sanction marching the militia out of the state if President Washington found it convenient so to order.[68] The resolution of 1794 had never been repealed, and by its provisions Plumer could legally have sent New Hampshire militiamen as far as Louisiana. Even according to Federalist arguments, Plumer had the discretionary authority to comply or not to comply.

Plumer was eventually vindicated by compelling circumstances, as well as by logic and law. As to the law, Justice Joseph Story told Plumer himself in 1815 that the Supreme Court judges had informally but unanimously decided that governors were constitutionally bound to obey requisitions by the federal government upon their militia and that Plumer's reasoning upon this question was conclusive.[69] The circumstances were British control of the sea and the existence of a navy yard on Great Island, which subjected Portsmouth to constant danger of attack and her citizens to frequent alarms. Even the Federalists realized that a British army of invasion would pay little attention to fine constitutional distinctions and that Portsmouth had to be defended.[70]

---

68. Plumer, *Speech to the Legislature, November, 1812*, 4-6; *Journal of the House of Representatives, June Session, 1794* (Portsmouth, 1794), 49.

69. Plumer, Autobiography, 311. This became the official opinion of the court in the case of *Martin v. Mott*, decided in 1827. See Henry Wheaton, comp., *Reports of Cases Argued and Adjudged in the Supreme Court, 1816-1827* (Phila., 1816-27), XII, 19-39.

70. At the same time that Plumer was hounded for prosecuting the war too well, he was also the victim of a whispering campaign, designed to cripple his credit with the war party. The Exeter *Constitutionalist* printed a wholly fictitious statement that Governor Plumer had pronounced the war "premature and impolitic." Plumer immediately sent a letter of denial to the *Patriot*, but the damage was done; the false statement was copied everywhere by the Federalist papers and it shook the convictions even of Plumer's councilors. See Plumer to editor of the *Constitutionalist*, Mar. 11, 1813, Letter Book, III, Lib. Cong.; J. G. Folsom (the editor) to Plumer, Mar. 16, 1813, Letter Book, VI, *ibid.;* Plumer, Autobiography, 278-79. Seventeen years later, the story appeared, much to Plumer's disgust, in Bradford's *History of Massachusetts;*

Moral and constitutional rectitude, however, were no match for military disasters and direct taxes in the minds of the voters, and Governor Plumer foresaw disaster as the March elections approached. "The *hobgoblin* that the republican party raised against the necessary system of taxes in 1798 and 1799, & the violent prejudices they then unjustly excited, will now give them, & our country, much trouble," wrote Plumer to the patriarch, John Adams.[71] Trading on these issues, the Federalists rallied strongly behind John Taylor Gilman and swept the state election, recovering by considerable majorities both houses of the General Assembly and the executive council. Plumer, however, received 1,918 more votes than in 1812, and only 697 fewer than Gilman. A little more than two additional votes from each town for Plumer would have reversed the verdict of the people. This being so, it is possible that Plumer was right when he attributed his defeat to the absence of Republican voters serving in the army and on privateers.[72] In 1812 Plumer had run behind his party's ticket; in 1813 he ran far ahead of it.

Defeat in this instance did not plunge Plumer into a black pit of pessimism. He notified President Madison of the misfortune but added firmly, "I still consider New Hampshire as a republican state; & I trust that our failure in the election will not in the least influence the administration to relax in their efforts to prosecute the war, or to conclude a peace on terms unfavorable to the real security & future prosperity of the nation." [73] Plumer pointed out that the Republicans had cast very nearly half the votes in the election. "This circumstance distances the project of dismemberment of the Union, & greatly embarrasses & perplexes our opposers of the General Government, the friends of Britain," he wrote. The Republican organizations in other parts of New England, even in radical Vermont, tended to collapse under the weight of pro-British sentiment and to abandon the task of opposing Federalist sectionalism.[74] But in New Hampshire, the Federalists were never sufficiently secure in office to embark upon schemes of secession.

Although Plumer's single term as governor of New Hampshire had been in many ways a disappointing one, there were also some pleasant

---

Plumer, Jr., *Life of Plumer,* 394-95. When Plumer wrote Bradford a letter of protest, he apologized and said that he had obtained the statement from the Boston *Centinel;* A. Bradford to Plumer, Dec. 25, 1829, Plumer Papers, N. H. Hist. Soc.

71. Plumer to John Adams, Mar. 19, 1813, Letter Book, III, Lib. Cong.

72. Lyon, ed., *New Hampshire Register . . . 1860,* 41. Plumer to James Madison, Mar. 27, 1813, Madison Papers, LI, Lib. Cong.

73. *Ibid.*

74. Robinson, *Jeffersonian Democracy in New England,* chap. 4.

memories. His name had become public property—a fort, a ship, and at least one baby had been named after him.[75] The Federalists may have interfered with recruiting, but at the same time a group of Revolutionary War veterans, too old for militia service, had organized in Westmoreland to volunteer their services in case of invasion or insurrection.[76] Goddard and Bartlett proved to be broken reeds, but sturdy old John Adams sent a simple message of encouragement: "The taxes must be laid and the War supported." [77] The abuse in the Federalist papers was abrasive but it could be forgotten in the light of such commendation as appeared, even after Plumer's defeat, in the *New Hampshire Patriot:* "Not only has Governor Plumer discharged every other duty of his responsible office with the ability and integrity which in that respect have silenced the cavelling [*sic*] of his most inveterate enemies, and even extorted from them tacit approbation—but when called on by the President and Congress he promptly ordered into the field that portion of the militia required for our country's defence." [78]

On June 1, 1813, Governor Plumer went to Concord for the last time in his official capacity. With the council and a judge of the Superior Court, he visited and inspected the new state prison, which had just been completed. On the morning of the second, he administered the oath of office to the members of the legislature, and unhappily witnessed the political housecleaning that the Federalists gleefully performed. That afternoon he transmitted to the legislature a necessarily long report of the expenditures and military orders he had made since December. Then he wrote in his journal:

This was my last official act; & I leave the office without disgust or regret. I exchange its cares, its burthen & high responsibilities, for the more tranquil scenes of private life. I am conscious I have discharged the duties of office faithfully & impartially, neither doing or omitting a single official act with reference to a re-election, or from the influence of improper motives. I performed my duty on the same principles, with

75. For the fort, see above, p. 212. The privateer, *Gov. Plumer,* was a schooner, Captain Mudge, George Long of Portsmouth, owner. The *Gov. Plumer* enjoyed a short but highly successful career before being taken by a British brig; *War Journal* (Portsmouth), June 4, 1813. The Governor's namesake, William Plumer Wheeler, was born in Croyden, July 31, 1812, and later became a noted lawyer; Bell, *Bench and Bar,* 734.

76. Ephraim Brown to Plumer, Aug. 25, 1812, Plumer Papers, N.-Y. Hist. Soc.

77. John Adams to Plumer, Mar. 28, 1813, photostat copy in Lib. Cong. This is the famous letter in which Adams reminisces for Plumer's benefit about the adoption of the resolution for independence.

78. *N. H. Patriot* (Concord), Apr. 20, 1813.

the same care, punctuality, economy, & dispatch as I usually did my own business, considering the interest of the State my own.[79]

After listening to the election sermon and paying his farewells, Plumer spent his last night in Concord and left the inn at five o'clock in the morning, refusing the escort of honor that had planned to accompany him to his home. He left behind him, in possession of the capital and of the government, a gloating group of Federalists. "At this moment the bells are ringing & cannon firing, in demonstration of the people's joy," wrote Ezekiel Webster to his brother in Congress.[80] Plumer took what consolation he could from a unanimous renomination by the Republican caucus on June 23. Two days later, as Plumer celebrated his fifty-fourth birthday quietly at home, Governor Gilman rode through Epping Center on his way to Exeter from Concord, escorted by a cavalcade of triumphant Federalists. "How uncertain is public office—how unstable public opinion!" thought Plumer. But his puritan sense of self-righteousness was proof against despondency. "The reflection costs me no pain, or the change any uneasiness. I never wanted the office, But I thot it wanted my aid, & I yielded to it as a duty. I have done as much to honor the station as I received from it." [81]

79. Plumer, Autobiography, 294.
80. Ezekiel to Daniel Webster, June 4, 1813, Dartmouth MSS., 813354.1, Dartmouth College.
81. Plumer, Autobiography, 297.

CHAPTER XII

A Waiting Period

> "When passion and prejudice shall have sub-
> sided—when ignorance and imbecility shall have
> punished itself and those who have placed their
> trust in it—when Haman shall be suspended on his
> own gallows—WILLIAM PLUMER shall be the
> Mordecai whom the people will delight to honor."[1]

IN June 1813, for the fifth time in his active career, Plumer retired
from the bustle of politics. But this retirement was different; neither
Plumer nor anyone else expected it to be permanent. The Republican
party would not let him go; with little dissent they continued to make
him their candidate for governor each year until victory returned to their
standard. He made no effort to return to the legislature, as Gilman had
done, nor to the courts, as had Jeremiah Smith, but he continued to
write for the newspapers and to take an active interest in politics. There
is not much doubt that he confidently expected to be governor of New
Hampshire again at no distant period.

Plumer denied this, of course. "You will perhaps scarsely credit the
declaration, when I assure you that I feel a deeper interest in past than
in passing events," he wrote a skeptical Federalist congressman, but
hastened to add, "tho in the peculiar state of the nation I cannot & ought
not to be indifferent."[2] Isaac Hill assured his readers that public life,
indeed, had few charms for the happy scholar, immured in a private
library without "parallel probably in this country" and engaged in a
work that would "live to future ages as a memento of what the industry
of one man is capable of producing." Hill then drew the inevitable political conclusion: the people "must appreciate his talents and his integrity
—they never will permit this bright flower of our State, whose singular

1. *N. H. Patriot* (Concord), Aug. 20, 1813.
2. Plumer to Roger Vose, Dec. 20, 1814, Letter Book, VI, Lib. Cong.

good qualities have *once* delighted us, to 'waste its fragrance on the desart [*sic*] air.' " [3] It was a long time before the Epping "flower" heard the last of this unfortunate metaphor.

Although Plumer was not as indifferent to his political fortunes as Hill represented him to be, he certainly did not spend his three years of retirement sulking in his tent.[4] In June 1815, he was elected to membership in the American Antiquarian Society, second oldest historical organization in New England.[5] At the moment, Plumer deserved the honor, for he had made considerable progress with his writing. During the following September he finished the sixth chapter of his "History of North America," but with something less than mounting enthusiasm. "It takes more time and labor than I expected," he confessed,[6] and began to turn his attention to the more congenial task of composing biographical sketches of historical personages.

Plumer's concern with politics during these years of retirement was kept alive by two very vigorous anxieties: the uncertain course of the war, and the very pronounced course followed by the New England Federalists. The New Hampshire branch of that resurgent group was in much the same position as was Jefferson at his inauguration in 1801. Their triumph at the polls had put them in command of executive and legislative bastions but had left the judiciary in the hands of the defeated faction. Jefferson had regarded this situation as undemocratic in 1801, and the Federalists had raged at his subsequent assaults on their judiciary. In 1813, the Federalists of New Hampshire found history repeating itself on a lesser scale, except that they were now the party aggrieved by an entrenched body of partisan judges. Feeling against the judges had mounted to the point where Plumer expected them to be removed by address as soon as the Federalist legislature convened.[7]

Instead, the Federalists surprised him by resorting to the device for which they had condemned Jefferson's party in 1801—removal of the office from the judge. This they accomplished by a Judiciary Act, which abolished the existing judicial system and replaced it with an entirely new set of courts.[8] These were modeled to some extent after the judiciary of Massachusetts and incorporated some of the changes which the Fed-

3. *N. H. Patriot* (Concord), Aug. 20, 1813.
4. He maintained a lively correspondence with former Presidents John Adams and Thomas Jefferson and numerous cabinet officials and congressmen.
5. Oliver Fiske, Secy., to Plumer, July 15, 1815, Letter Book, VI, Lib. Cong.
6. Plumer, Autobiography, 310, 306.
7. Plumer, "Richard Evans," Biographies, V, 104, N. H. Hist. Soc.
8. *Laws of New Hampshire,* VIII, 1813, chap. 36.

cralist lawyers had been demanding since the days when William Plumer and Jeremiah Smith had collaborated on the judiciary sections of the state constitution. Smith, in fact, was so deeply committed to the reforms written into the new system that he accepted appointment as chief justice of the new Supreme Court, although it exposed to merciless attacks his self-proclaimed principles of judicial integrity and consistency.[9] The Republican writers had not forgotten that Smith was one of John Adams's circuit judges in 1801 and that he had denied the constitutionality of the act which abolished his office.[10] It would have been difficult for the Federalists to have emphasized more strongly the inconsistency, constitutional weakness, and partisan purpose of their judicial purge than by elevating Smith to the head of the New Hampshire bench.

From the moment of its introduction the Judiciary Act was attacked from every angle, but the heaviest offensive was directed at its alleged unconstitutionality.[11] The debate on this question ranged far and wide, but the issue was very simple: if Jefferson's Judiciary Act of 1802 was unconstitutional, Gilman's Judiciary Act of 1813 was unconstitutional and vice versa. Neither party could defend the consistency of its record on this point. William Plumer, however, having changed parties, could and did take the same position on this issue in 1813 that he had held in 1802.

Public opinion at first was shocked by the Federalist purge, but began to change as Evans and Claggett protested shrilly against being discarded.[12] With the complicity of two Republican sheriffs, they turned two terms of the new Supreme Court into travesties and forced Gilman to call a special session of the legislature to deal with the situation.[13] Annoyed by the virulence with which Isaac Hill and the *New Hamp-*

9. So Smith himself insisted. See Morison, *Jeremiah Smith*, 268-72.

10. *Speech of William Claggett, Esq.: on the Repeal of the Judiciary Act of 1813* (n.p., 1814).

11. [William Plumer, Jr.], "Phocian," "The Federalism of New Hampshire for 1813," No. 7, MS. in N. H. State Lib.

12. The two judges took the line that the legislature had the authority to erect as many new courts as it wished, so long as they did not interfere with the jurisdictions established by the state constitution, nor with the tenure of existing judges. Under this reasoning, new courts and old courts might have functioned side by side had both parties been willing. *Opinions of Claggett and Evans on an Act of the Legislature of 1813* (Concord, 1813).

13. The prospect of a violent clash between old and new courts attracted a mob of spectators to Exeter. William Plumer, Jr., who came down from Epping to witness the fun, left a very interesting account of the proceedings in his Journal, I, 449 ff., N. H. State Lib. See also an entertaining but highly prejudiced account in the *Constitutionalist* (Exeter), reprinted in the *Portsmouth Oracle*, Oct. 9, 1813.

shire Patriot attacked their new courts, the Federalist newspapers raged at Plumer as a diabolical figure "managing the wires behind the scene," and at the *Patriot* as "Gov. Plumer's paper." [14] Neither charge was true. Plumer agreed fully with the ousted judges on the unconstitutionality of the Federalist Judiciary Act, but held himself entirely aloof from the controversy until a more practical means of settling it could be employed. No doubt, however, he thoroughly enjoyed the discomfiture of Smith and Gilman.

William Plumer had observed the autocratic action of the Federalists in his state with keen interest, but he was more concerned with the peril created by Federalist opposition to the national government. After a year and a half of vain expectation that a common crisis would unite Americans against a foreign enemy, Plumer's optimism had given way to concern. He sought a fundamental explanation for Federalist disaffection and found it, not in economic, social, or sectional antagonisms, but in the influence of the Congregationalist clergy. It was notorious that with few exceptions Congregationalist ministers were solidly and vocally opposed to the war. After 1813, the Election Day sermons were used in all the New England states as opportunities for bristling denunciations of "Mr. Madison's War." The ministers even turned Republican guns against the administration by preaching peace sermons on officially proclaimed Fast Days. Although no longer an admirer of the Reverend Peter Holt, Plumer attended public meeting on one such occasion, hoping to hear a plea for unity in the midst of war, but only words of condemnation fell from the preacher's lips. "Formerly the clergy used to excuse men from both good & evil," wrote the disgusted auditor, "by ascribing one to God & the other to the Devil; but they now substitute our government in the place of his satanic majesty." [15]

Ever suspicious of the clergy, William Plumer found a ready explanation for the contrast between their ardent support of the Revolution and their treason in the second war against Britain. In 1775, they had been worried by the threat of an Episcopal establishment and had taken up arms against it. The removal of this threat had been accompanied by an alarming growth of the new sects, and the Puritan clerics now longed for an establishment of their own. Finding many Federalists willing to support such pretensions, but Republicans firmly opposed to them, the clergymen became political partisans of their government's opponents.

14. *Portsmouth Oracle,* Oct. 16, Nov. 13, 1816.
15. Plumer, Autobiography, 308.

By such ex post facto reasoning, Plumer arrived at a firm conviction that religion had determined politics in New England.[16]

With plenty of leisure time, the former Governor decided to propagate his new thesis and, during the month of December 1813, published in the *Patriot* a series of five articles, entitled "An Address to the Clergy of New England on Their Opposition to the Government," and signed by "A Layman." Much of Plumer's space was given over to quotations of the more lurid passages from printed sermons—statements in which the war was denounced and the officials of the Republican administration were labeled "Devils" to whom "Satan, blushing owns himself outdone in the work of deception." By contrast, Great Britain was called "a nation of . . . religion, virtue, good faith, generosity and beneficence" whose destruction would bring the loss of "ALL our privileges and happiness." In one discourse, Plumer found the statement, "Though our government . . . rush forward with the torch of war blazing in their hands, the *English* are determined to give the contest every feature of *mildness and humanity* which the nature of the case will admit." [17]

Plumer's familiarity with the Bible enabled him to turn the powerful weapon of scriptural quotation against his clerical foes. Jesus Christ, he argued, had been interested solely in spiritual, not in temporal, affairs. "My kingdom is *not of this world*," Jesus told his followers, and enjoined them, while concentrating on their mission of spiritual deliverance, to render unto Caesar the things that were Caesar's. "Let every soul be subject unto the higher power," St. Paul had admonished the Romans, *"for there is no power but of God; the powers that be are ordained of God. Whosoever therefore resisteth the power resisteth the ordinance of God, and they that resist shall receive to themselves damnation."* If this was strange doctrine for a Republican and a citizen of a country that owed its birth to a successful rebellion, Plumer seemed to imply that the Scriptures might be ignored by ordinary people but hardly by the clergy. "If Paul was in duty bound," he wrote, "to exhort his fellow Christians to obey even a NERO, because he was a *magistrate,* how can you answer to your God, to your conscience, or to your country, to spend your time and talents in exciting your people, not only to distrust, but to acts of insurrection and rebellion against a free elective government?" [18]

16. [William Plumer], "A Layman," *Address to the Clergy of New England on Their Opposition to the Government* (Concord, 1814), No. 1.

17. *Ibid.,* Nos. 2 and 3.

18. *Ibid.,* No. 4.

The Congregational clergy had lost influence, Plumer said, not because their parishioners loved vice and irreligion but because of their own narrow training, their preoccupation with Hebrew syntax rather than with history and civil polity, their ignorance of the realities that composed the outside world. In deviating from the proper duties of the clerical office, in mixing partisanship with religion and discarding spiritual for carnal weapons, the clergy betrayed only too clearly their anxiety for a reunion of church and state, and their thirst for riches and power rather than for the salvation of souls. These were the aberrations, concluded the "Layman," which were "alike fatal to genuine religion and the political rights" of our country. *"Our teachers have caused us to err from the right way."* [19]

For a while Plumer was apprehensive that his challenge would go unanswered and therefore be forgotten. The Reverend Asa McFarland, minister of the Congregational Church at Concord, came to his rescue by publishing in the *Concord Gazette* a series of nine articles, answering Plumer's five.[20] McFarland made a gesture toward anonymity by signing his own articles "W," but he had no difficulty in penetrating "Layman's" disguise. "Whether you are an apostate and treacherous clergyman, or have been a Laypreacher, violently engaged to prostrate all religious and social order, we are left to conjecture," he wrote. "We have evidence, however, that you are not remarkable for a devotional and correct manner of thinking." [21] Whether McFarland's philosophical discipline was any superior is at least doubtful. Much of his argument was a cogent but irrelevant denunciation of war in the abstract, although he weakened his case by defending the clergy's belligerence during the War for Independence. He pointed out the fallacy in Plumer's identifying criticism of rulers with opposition to laws, and he denied any plan to set up a Congregationalist priesthood; but he attempted no defense

19. *Ibid.*, No. 5. Plumer made no effort in these pieces to distinguish between clerico-political hypocrisy and a possibly sincere pacifism based upon the ancient traditions of the Christian faith. The latter motivation, however, was certainly evident in the career of Noah Worcester, the Congregational pastor of Thornton and Salisbury, whose specific opposition to the War of 1812 blossomed into general condemnation of war as an instrument of national policy. In 1815, Worcester became secretary of the Massachusetts Peace Society. See Harris Elwood Starr in *DAB* s.v. "Worcester, Noah."

20. [Asa McFarland], "W," "Defence of the Clergy of New England," nine articles in the *Concord Gazette*, Dec. 28, 1813-Feb. 22, 1814.

21. [Asa McFarland], "A Clergyman," letter in *Concord Gazette*, Aug. 16, 1814. McFarland wrote a series of these letters after Plumer sent him a copy of his *Address to the Clergy* in pamphlet form, postage *not prepaid*. The tone of these letters indicates that the clergyman was a little nettled.

of the open encouragement to resistance and secession that Plumer had condemned. He made it crystal clear, however, that in the eyes of the clergy the war was a religious issue—a war in which the Republicans were the allies of degenerate, atheistic France against a "people, who, with all their faults, do more than all the rest of the world beside to extend the knowledge of revealed religion." [22]

Plumer was so elated by McFarland's sensitive reaction that he dashed off a reply, then had 3,000 copies of his six addresses printed in pamphlet form.[23] Copies were mailed to each of the principal Congregationalist ministers in New Hampshire and to a host of Plumer's friends, including John Adams and Thomas Jefferson. The latter expressed gratitude for the gift but skepticism about its effectiveness. "With those to whom it is addressed," he declared, "Moses and the prophets have no authority but when administering to their worldly gain." [24]

There was an element of personal conviction, certainly, in Plumer's battle with the Federalist clergymen, but he reverted to pure politician in a subsequent attack upon Governor Gilman.[25] It was not then accepted practice in New England for candidates to vilify each other in public, but there were no recognized limits to what could be said in print, provided that it was said under a classical pen-name. William, Jr., whose politics had changed with his father's, contributed to the *Patriot,* under the alias of "Phocian," an excellent series of articles on the arbitrary conduct of the Federalist administration, especially in regard to the judiciary. With such an auxiliary in the family, the senior Plumer's compulsion to write his own campaign literature might well have been suppressed. He did not forbear, although a twinge of shame or at least a doubt as to the merits of these latest articles is suggested by the fact that he took elaborate precautions to prevent his authorship being suspected. He might have saved himself the trouble. His vigorous, jagged style, his persistent use of peculiar grammatical constructions, and his fondness for certain overworked epigrams betrayed him to every discerning reader. "Certain electioneering articles in the democratic Newspapers have so much of the fragrance of the Epping 'flower,'" jeered the *Concord Gazette,* "that we are at no loss to determine their

22. *Concord Gazette,* Feb. 15, 1814.

23. Plumer, Autobiography, 300; Plumer, Jr., *Life of Plumer,* 417; Plumer to Isaac Hill, Mar. 31, 1814, Letter Book, III, Lib. Cong.

24. Jefferson to Plumer, Jan. 31, 1815, Jefferson Papers, CCIII, Lib. Cong.

25. Plumer, Autobiography, 299; [William Plumer], "Cato," "The Examiner," Nos. 1-7, Plumer, Essays, II, 58-108, Lib. Cong., publ. in *N. H. Patriot* (Concord), Jan. 7 to Feb. 17, 1814.

origin or their object. But it is all right—If a man will not help himself, can he expect others to help him?"

For the most part, the Federalist objections to Plumer's candidacy were of such a nature that he could take honest pride in being the target of their criticisms. Appeals were made to religious prejudice by listing him as an unbeliever in revelation, the divinity of Christ, and a state of future punishment. Scorn was poured upon his "pretended" aversion to high salaries, and all the charges were rung again upon his "apostacy" —"he was always too crooked a stick to lay easy." The most persistent clamor arose over his having called out the militia for national service. He had sacrificed the rights of his constituents and perverted the state constitution to curry favor with Washington; he had degraded the independent yeomanry of New Hampshire to a condition of military slavery; he had aped his French master by attempting to introduce the system of conscription natural to European tyrants. Farmers who wanted to lose their sons, mechanics who wished to see their apprentices drafted, young men who hoped to die on a foreign battlefield should cast their votes for Plumer.[26]

Plumer's efforts on his own behalf were fruitless, but the Republicans did succeed in winning a majority in the Executive Council in 1814.[27] This fact was decisive in preventing New Hampshire's participation in the Hartford Convention in December.[28] No one at the time knew what went on behind the closed doors of the Connecticut State House but Plumer felt that he had the foundation for guessing more accurately than other outsiders. "I think their prime object is to effect a revolution —a dismemberment of the Union," he wrote to Jeremiah Mason. "Some of its members, for more than ten years have considered such a measure necessary. Of this fact I have conclusive evidence." Plumer's own attitude toward this measure had certainly changed. Secession could "be effected only at the point of the bayonet," he warned the Federalist Senator. "Should it succeed it will be the ruin of New England, & the grave of its commerce." [29]

The late summer of 1814 had brought tribulations of another sort

26. *Concord Gazette,* Jan. 25, Feb. 8, 22, Mar. 5, 1814.
27. Lyon, ed., *New Hampshire Register . . . 1860,* 41; *Journal of the Senate, June Session, 1814* (Concord, 1814), 9.
28. Morison, *Otis,* II, 181-82. Gilman would have had to call a special session of the legislature to elect delegates to the convention, but the three Republican councilors, of course, would not have consented to this call; therefore, Gilman did not even attempt it.
29. Plumer to Jeremiah Mason, Dec. 29, 1814, Letter Book, III, Lib. Cong.

to Governor Gilman and vindication of an especially satisfactory nature to Plumer. The threat of a British attack upon Portsmouth became so ominous that even the Federalists insisted that Gilman provide for its defense.[30] Since he had no other means, the Governor was forced to comply with an authorization from President Madison to call out the detached militia—exactly as Plumer had done in 1812. The soldiers, Plumer noted, were "more prompt in obeying the orders than the governor was in issuing them." [31]

That the infant American republic emerged from its first deliberate plunge into international warfare with relatively little damage was due to a rising national spirit that Plumer exemplified. To his friends, re-establishing themselves in a national capital recently gutted and burned by an invading army, he staunchly wrote: "I am sorry that any republicans despair of the Republic. Tho our prospects are gloomy, yet instead of desponding, our courage & fortitude ought to rise in proportion as our difficulties increase. At the commencement of the war, I expected it would involve us in serious trials. I then thot, & still beleive, it, a just & necessary war; & I have no doubts but that we shall eventually succeed." [32] This determination Plumer maintained in spite of many personal sacrifices. His northern lands had became unsalable, yet were more heavily taxed than ever before. His investments in bank stock and insurance companies virtually ceased to yield dividends, yet he had loyally purchased depressed national securities to the limit of his ability. Finally, the war had undoubtedly deprived him of three years in the governor's office.[33] There was certainly no economic motivation in Plumer's politics. Despite his unwavering support of the war, he had nothing to gain from it, and never thought of it as anything other than a necessary evil.

When the terms of the Treaty of Ghent were published in New Hampshire, Plumer was happy to settle for the *status quo ante bellum.* "It leaves all our territory entire," he wrote thankfully, "& has secured us the respect of the civilized world." [34] It had also "given a quietus to the Hartford convention," and Plumer hoped that it would terminate "for a long period" at least, "the fatal project of dismembering the

---

30. Watts, "New Hampshire in the War of 1812," *Granite Monthly,* 30 (1898), 360.
31. Plumer, Autobiography, 305.
32. Plumer to Charles Cutts, Nov. 21, 1814, Letter Book, III, Lib. Cong.
33. Plumer, Autobiography, 300. Plumer's Property Book, N. H. State Lib., entries for Apr. 1, 1812 and Apr. 1, 1816, show that his holdings of "Public Stocks U. States" increased from $12,392.25 to $27,750.37 during the war.
34. Plumer, Autobiography, 307.

Union." But he was too realistic, and too familiar with separatist sentiment, to believe that it had been permanently destroyed. "I fear that question will eventually tho at a distant period, remain to be settled by the bayonet," he prophesied with remarkable clarity.[35]

The end of the war and the collapse of the Hartford Convention program virtually guaranteed the ultimate defeat of Federalism in New Hampshire, but it took a little time for these things to make their impact. William Plumer approached the 1815 elections with indifference, and although he was nominated again by his party, as was Gilman after much hesitation by the Federalists, he made not the slightest effort to influence the voters.[36] Increasingly, he regarded his political friends as "troublesome companions, [who] waste my time, drink my wine & ardent spirits, & often remind me of the great services they have done and intend to do me." Plumer, therefore, professed to be not a whit disappointed when the electorate preferred Gilman again by a majority of only 259 votes. There were rumors that the national administration would reward his party services by sending him as minister to Russia, but Plumer had the wit to laugh at this fantasy.

Instead of going to St. Petersburg, Plumer spent much of the year 1815 in modest but profitable travel to nearby towns in New England. In September, when the glorious colors of a New Hampshire autumn were beginning to appear, Plumer and his wife drove their chaise down the Newbury Turnpike for a visit to his ancestral home and with friends as far south as Salem. Evenings with Justice Story, Secretary of the Navy Crowninshield, and the Reverend William Bentley yielded interesting information and encouragement for Plumer's historical ventures.[37] Thus passed a quiet and peaceful summer—the last that Plumer was to enjoy for some time.

One development Plumer had been watching closely was a nasty quarrel between the president and the trustees of Dartmouth College.[38] It had

35. Plumer to Charles Cutts, Feb. 28, 1815, Letter Book, III, Lib. Cong.

36. Plumer, Autobiography, 307. Many of the Federalist lawyers were opposed to Gilman's candidacy and there were efforts to persuade Mason or Farrar or even old Benjamin West to accept the nomination. When Daniel Webster learned that "Gov. G. is to run again," he wrote to his brother, "I do not at all like this ... I think it a very foolish affair...." Daniel to Ezekiel Webster, Jan. 30, 1815, Dartmouth MSS., 815130, Dartmouth College. Other letters in this collection which reveal these intrigues are: John Wheelock to T. W. Thompson, May 7, 1814; Daniel to Ezekiel Webster, Nov. 29, 1814; H. Chase to P. M. Olcott, Jan. 10, 1815; 814307, 814629, 815110, *ibid.*

37. Plumer, Autobiography, 307, 310-13.

38. A good account of this affair may be found in Leon Richardson, *History of Dartmouth College* (Hanover, 1933), I, 300 ff.

actually been brewing for many years, but had erupted into open vio-lence in the spring when President Wheelock published a bitter denun-ciation of the trustees [39] and asked for a legislative investigation of the college's affairs.[40] Following the visit of a legislative committee to Han-over, the trustees had struck back by dismissing Wheelock and electing a young Dartmouth alumnus, the Reverend Francis Brown, as his suc-cessor.[41] Thus was precipitated a feud that was to become a major issue in New Hampshire politics and reach to the Supreme Court of the United States.

Toward the Dartmouth imbroglio itself, Plumer's original attitude was one of mild skepticism. He had no sympathy whatever with the eight trustees who were at odds with Wheelock—with one exception they were Federalists of the sort he had long since come to distrust [42] —but his feeling toward Wheelock was not much warmer. He remem-bered the dismissed president, during the late war, as a carping critic of the national administration and as a recognized leader of the party attempting to interfere with its conduct.[43] The fact that the president had now become a victim of the intolerances inherent in Federalism did not necessarily purge him of his past sins. Plumer's main reaction to the personal quarrel between Wheelock and "the Octagon" was "a plague on both your houses" sort of irritation.

Plumer could not ignore, however, the obvious political advantages which the Republicans might reap from this scandal. Isaac Hill seized the opportunity at once, portraying the "venerable" president as the victim of a fearful plot for the establishment of a "law-religion" by the confederated "priests," lawyers, college trustees, and Federalists of New England. The Federalists, reasoned Hill, foreseeing their inevit-able political extinction, even in New England, were conspiring to per-petuate their aristocracy in the religious and educational institutions of the country. The clergy clamored for a state establishment with a hier-

39. [John Wheelock], *Sketches of the History of Dartmouth College* (Newburyport, 1813). Strangely enough, this attack on clerical influence was prepared with the aid and enthusiastic support of the Reverend Elijah Parish, whom Plumer had charged with seeking to create a priestly hierarchy.

40. *Documents Relative to Dartmouth College,* published by order of the General Court (Concord, 1816).

41. John Shirley, *The Dartmouth College Causes and the Supreme Court of the United States* (Chicago, 1895), 96.

42. *Ibid.,* 100; Plumer, Autobiography, 313.

43. Wheelock voiced the common Federalist opinion of hostility to "an unjust war, conducted in weakness and folly." Wheelock to Nicholas Gilman, Feb. 15, 1814, Dartmouth MSS., 814155, Dartmouth College.

archy headed by a "Pope of New Hampshire." There had been evidence enough of this intrigue when the clergy had opposed the late war and encouraged sedition in New England—as Governor Plumer had courageously revealed. Now multiplying signs indicated that the plot was reaching the point of fruition in the seizure of the colleges by the Hopkinsian Calvinists.[44]

William Plumer was a candidate who could stand sturdily on a platform of opposition to these machinations. Isaac Hill reminded the voters that even in his Federalist days, Plumer had been "the undeviating advocate for religious freedom," offering his services freely to the poor dissenter who sought escape in the courts from taxation contrary to his conscience. It was when he became convinced that the Federalist leaders had combined with the clergy in favor of an established church that he left the party, according to Hill's editorial opinion. Was it not Plumer, too, who had exposed the clergy's treason during the recent war? Whose name, indeed, could better grace the leading place on a ticket of "Religious Freedom the Rights of the Baptist, Quaker, Methodist, and of all denominations—in room of a Law Religion, imposed by an intolerant sect, who boast that they 'will manage the Civil Government as they please' "?[45]

The extent to which the Dartmouth controversy had become political was demonstrated on Christmas Day 1815. Early that morning, Plumer was surprised to see at his door two well-known Federalist citizens of Hanover, Colonel Amos Brewster and Dr. Cyrus Perkins, professor of medicine at Dartmouth College. These men, neither of them well acquainted with Plumer but both staunch friends of John Wheelock, proposed to the Epping statesman that he withdraw his candidacy for a year in order to allow Wheelock to be elected governor on the Republican ticket. The ex-president, they explained, would not only thereby be vindicated but would control the political power through which his beloved college could be properly reformed and the intrigues of the trustees confounded. After one year as governor, Wheelock would gladly retire and hand the scepter to Plumer.

The Republican leader handled this absurd and tactless proposal skillfully. He had often, he said, been placed in situations where he was not free to consult his own inclinations but forced to submit to public

44. *N. H. Patriot* (Concord), Feb. 13, 20, 27, 1816. The same idea is expressed in a letter from Samuel Allen to John Wheelock, July 1, 1815, Dartmouth MSS., 815401.1, Dartmouth College.
45. *N. H. Patriot* (Concord), Feb. 13, 1816, Mar. 5, 1816.

opinion. He had emerged from retirement in 1810 and accepted the office of governor in 1812, not from any wish to re-enter public life, but at the importunity of his friends. He had been as willing to face defeat in 1813 as victory in 1812, and during the following three years, when the Republicans had honored him with three successive nominations, he had felt no liberty to withdraw his name, although the prospects of success had been negligible. Now, on the eve of another election, he could not disappoint those who had nominated him unless "imperious necessity" required it.[46]

Although Plumer recorded no subsequent bargain in his journal, it is highly probable that he indicated sympathy with Wheelock's claims to restitution, and that the two Federalists promised Plumer the support of Wheelock's adherents in the coming campaign.[47] The Republican leader, however, had more in mind than the mere restoration of the deposed president. "Will it not be requisite that his friends in your vicinity should before June devise a system not only to restore him to his rights, but to prevent the college being again exposed to similar evils?" he asked Brewster.[48]

The Dartmouth difficulties nearly stalled the Federalist political machine in 1816. The Federalist caucus had, in June 1815, promoted Gilman, with whom they had long been dissatisfied, to an emeritus status and thrown the mantle of succession around Timothy Farrar, completely overlooking the fact that their new candidate was deeply involved in the Dartmouth quarrel as one of the eight anti-Wheelock trustees.[49] When Isaac Hill gave this fact embarrassing publicity, the desperate caucus offered the party's leadership to six different men, even turning back to Gilman, who contemptuously spurned their advances.[50] The man who finally accepted the unwanted job was James Sheafe.[51]

46. Plumer, Autobiography, 314. It is an interesting fact that William Plumer, Jr., does not relate this incident in his biography of his father.

47. The understanding is implied in later correspondence. See Plumer's draft reply to Perkins's letter of Feb. 11; Plumer to Cyrus Perkins, Feb. 15, 1816, Plumer Papers, N. H. State Lib.

48. Plumer to Amos Brewster, Mar. 22, 1816, *ibid.*, draft copy on letter from Brewster to Plumer, Mar. 13, 1816.

49. *N. H. Patriot* (Concord), Jan. 2, 1816.

50. Jeremiah Mason to Mrs. Mason, Jan. 24, 27, 1816, quoted in Hillard, *Mason,* 130, 131. Mason worried about these developments but was not sorry that he himself had declined the nomination.

51. *N. H. Patriot* (Concord), Jan. 23, Feb. 6, 1816. That Isaac Hill's news sources were very good is confirmed in a letter from Peyton to Jonathan Freeman, Feb. 17,

Sheafe had the advantage of being unconcerned with the Dartmouth quarrel and of having few political enemies, but in every other respect, he was a choice of desperation. As the richest merchant in New Hampshire, he was vulnerable to Hill's evocation of class prejudices.[52] His earlier political career had consisted of a term in the notorious Sixth Congress, where he had voted thirty-six times to put Aaron Burr into the presidency, and a subsequent election to the Senate, from which he had resigned after attending only one session. His most serious liability as a vote-getter lay in his lifelong Toryism, from the time of his arrest and confinement by the patriot party during the Revolution to the late war with Britain, in which he had condemned the Washington government and refused to subscribe to its loans. "I know of no man in the state more strongly attached to Great Britain," wrote Plumer of the man he had succeeded in the Senate.[53]

Writing political "slang" for the newspapers had by now become an unbreakable habit with Plumer. In spite of his long friendship with Sheafe and his earlier admiration for him as a levelheaded business man, Plumer decided to "exhibit the leading traits of his character" in an anonymous contribution to the *New Hampshire Patriot*.[54] His piece was an unprincipled attack, in the worst traditions of contemporary journalism, even hinting broadly at sexual misdemeanors on Sheafe's part.[55] William Plumer, Jr., entered the lists again for his father with a pamphlet written in the same vein. Pointing out that Upper Canada's governor bore the name of Sheafe, "a name justly odious during the revolution," he urged the Federalists to desert their sinking ship and "Come Over To The Republicans In A Body." [56]

Having dipped his hand in the common tar barrel, Plumer could hardly object to being smeared with the same brush. The usual indictments of apostasy, atheism, usury, blasphemy, and treason were elabo-

---

1816, Dartmouth MSS., 816167, Dartmouth College, which contains an illuminating discussion of the political situation between two embarrassed Federalists who supported Wheelock.

52. *N. H. Patriot* (Concord), Feb. 6, 1816.

53. Plumer, Autobiography, 315.

54. *Ibid.* Plumer had one of his sons transcribe the article so that his handwriting would not betray him.

55. [William Plumer], "An Observer," "Facts are Stubborn Things," Plumer, Essays, I, 133-34, Lib. Cong., publ. in *N. H. Patriot* (Concord), Feb. 13, 1816.

56. [William Plumer, Jr.], *General Address to the Freemen of New Hampshire* (Concord, 1816), 32, 34-35.

rated in the Federalist press,[57] but the one charge that stung Plumer into a rebuttal reached back to the days of his Baptist itinerary. A contributor to the *Portsmouth Oracle* accused him of having preached the divine right of King George III as well as of the King of Kings during those times.[58] "On one occasion," it was stated, "while holding forth, on his usual themes in favor of . . . *passive obedience* and *non-resistance,* he was arrested in the County of Grafton for his political heresy, and threatened with summary punishment . . . . Whether he afterwards became a Whig, when the cause of the Revolution became more successful, is not distinctly known; but if he did not, he must have acted contrary to his usual practice of always keeping in the sunshine of power." [59] There was enough truth in this slander to make it sting, and the author, Plumer had reason to believe, was John Samuel Sherburne, who, of all men, had always been most able to irritate him. The would-be governor could not refrain from rushing into print again, incognito, with a vigorous denial of the calumny and a scarcely novel assertion that it proceeded from political motives.[60] On the whole Plumer suffered more blows than he inflicted in the epistolary battle of 1816.

Perhaps the very virulence of the attack on Plumer was a measure of his approaching success. The gradual accretion of votes in his favor —from 48.44 per cent of the total in 1812, to 49.12 per cent in 1815— would probably have brought success in 1816 without help from any unusual quarter. The Dartmouth issue, however, turned what might have been a moderate conquest into a rout. Plumer received 52.95 per cent of the second largest total ever cast in a New Hampshire election, and defeated Sheafe by more than 2,300 votes.[61] The Federalist majority of eighteen in the lower house of the assembly turned into a deficit of twelve. In spite of an 1813 gerrymander, three Federalist senators lost their seats outright to Republican rivals and two others failed to win more than a plurality in their districts. The Republicans also main-

57. *Concord Gazette,* Mar. 9, 1816. To a modern observer, the most effective trick of Federalist propaganda would seem to have been the reprinting in full of "Impartialis" by the newspaper which had originally published it in 1804, this time with the name of the author. *Portsmouth Oracle,* Feb. 10, 17, 24, 1816. But this was probably too subtle for the times. See above, pp. 144-47.

58. See above, p. 7.

59. "Seventy-five," "Who is William Plumer?" *Portsmouth Oracle,* Feb. 17, 1816; quotations from clipping of the article in Plumer's Scrapbook, Plumer Papers, N. H. State Lib.

60. [William Plumer], "Calumny Exposed," Plumer, Essays, II, 134-36, Lib. Cong., publ. in *N. H. Patriot* (Concord), Feb. 27, 1816.

61. Lyon, ed., *New Hampshire Register . . . 1860,* 41, 42.

tained their advantage of three to two in the governor's council. Every branch of the government except the judiciary was lost by the Federalists, and it was taken for granted that the judiciary would not long remain in status quo.

Such an unmitigated defeat demanded explanations and the Federalist press was quick to supply them. The Republicans, declared the *Concord Gazette,* had won the election by the aid of two thousand Federalist friends of Wheelock who would now be bitterly disappointed in their expectation of seeing him reinstated.[62] Election statistics, however, do not bear out this claim of Federalist defection. Sheafe lost only 363 votes from the total which Gilman had obtained in 1815, but Plumer gained more than 2,500 over his total of the previous year. It seems obvious that something nearer 400 to 500 than 2,000 Federalists changed party in 1816.[63] It also becomes clear, through the election results, that Sheafe lost 500 votes in the Connecticut Valley, where Wheelock's friends would naturally have defected, while Plumer gained almost the same number there over his 1815 record. The Dartmouth excitement animated Republicans more than it converted Federalists. Plumer's victory did not "revolutionize" the state, but returned it to a condition of normalcy that the war had, for four years, disturbed.

62. *Concord Gazette,* Apr. 30, 1816; *Portsmouth Oracle,* Mar. 16; *New Hampshire Sentinel* (Keene), Mar. 16, 1816.
63. See Appendix B for election statistics.

CHAPTER XIII

Dartmouth College and the Courts

"Yet our lawyers and priests generally ... suppose that preceding generations held the earth more freely than we do; had a right to impose laws on us, unalterable by ourselves, and that we, in like manner, can make laws and impose burthens on future generations, which they will have no right to alter; in fine, that the earth belongs to the dead, & not the living." [1]

WILLIAM PLUMER was approaching his fifty-eighth year in 1816 when he was elected for the second time to the highest post in the state government of New Hampshire. The attentions that were automatically paid a governor began to be heaped upon him before his election was even certain, and Plumer devoted much of his time to correspondence with high government officials in Washington, soliciting offices in behalf of friends and political supporters. The network of influence and patronage extended even to faraway Indiana Territory, where an old soldier from New Hampshire, settled in the frontier village of Charlestown, begged Plumer's help in obtaining a federal post.[2] Nor was the new governor unwilling to use his influence in behalf of his family. Having "received confidential word" that the federal loan officer in Portsmouth was about to resign, he immediately wrote to the President and the Secretary of the Treasury recommending his oldest son for the vacancy. Within a month, the appointment had been made. Without mentioning his own agency in the matter, Plumer noted the

---

1. Thomas Jefferson to Plumer, July 21, 1816, Jefferson Papers, CCVII, Lib. Cong. Thus did Jefferson express his approval of Plumer's proposal to amend the charter of Dartmouth College.

2. Timothy Upham to Plumer, Mar. 29; Plumer to Upham, Mar. 30, 1816; Stephen Rannay to Plumer, Feb. 3, to Plumer, Jr., Apr. 11, 1816; Plumer, Jr., to Rannay, Feb. 5, 1816, all in Plumer Papers, N. H. State Lib. Colonel Rannay's letter of Apr. 11 is published in the *Indiana Magazine of History,* 35 (1938), 182.

event in his journal and smugly added, "A handsome office for a young man." [3] He then succeeded in having his son George appointed to follow William, Jr., in the Epping postmastership, which William had inherited when his father became a state senator.[4] These arrangements naturally laid Plumer open to charges of nepotism, and were to prove acutely embarrassing to the whole family before the year was out.[5]

For the moment, young William's appointment seemed peculiarly fortunate, because it enabled him to take up his residence in the Portsmouth home of his sister Sarah, to whom he had always been especially attached. This unlucky girl, already rejected by one suitor, had subsequently been married to William Claggett, who combined the mediocrity of his father Clifton with the truculence of his grandfather Wyseman. In spite of young Claggett's assiduous attentions to the entire family, neither of the William Plumers had attended the wedding in May 1815 with much enthusiasm. "Her choice was different from the one I wished," Plumer wrote resignedly, "but as it was hers I consented." [6] The Claggetts, however, were ardent Republicans, and in the early, halcyon days of their party's return to power, all was harmony and satisfaction.

With full realization of the extraordinary problems that would face his government, Plumer made serious preparation for the momentous session of the legislature in June. Long before he was even certain that he had been elected, he was writing to the governors of nearby states and to friends and officials in Washington, seeking information on matters he wished to bring before the lawmakers at Concord.[7] And in order to avoid the sins of hasty preparation and poor composition of which he had so frequently accused Gilman, he began to write his inaugural address in mid-May, as soon as his election was "reduced to nearly a moral certainty." [8] Then, remembering the dust, and possibly the expense, of his triumphal entry into Concord in 1812, he packed the fin-

3. Plumer to Plumer, Jr., June 23, 1816, Plumer Papers, N. H. State Lib.; entry for June 28, Plumer, Jr., Memoirs, I, *ibid.;* Plumer, Autobiography, 330.

4. Plumer to Samuel Plumer, Aug. 5, 1816, Plumer Papers, N. H. State Lib.

5. *Concord Gazette,* Dec. 31, 1816.

6. Entry for Oct. 20, 1815, Plumer, Jr., Memoirs, I, N. H. State Lib.; Plumer, Autobiography, 317.

7. For example: Plumer to Timothy Pitkin, Jan. 31, 1816, Letter Book, III, Lib. Cong., inquiries about salaries of state officials; J. C. Smith, Sharon, Connecticut, to Plumer, Apr. 17, 1816, Plumer Papers, N. H. State Lib., answers questions about Connecticut's judiciary; Plumer to Alexander Dallas, May 7, 1816, Letter Book, III, Lib. Cong., asks if his state may still assume collection of federal direct taxes.

8. Plumer, Autobiography, 317.

ished speech into his saddlebags and rode quietly into the capital on the day before the legislature convened, occupying bachelor's quarters in Isaac Hill's house. Although this flouting of protocol saved the militia officers in towns between Epping and Concord a day's ride, it aroused dire suspicions in the Federalist press. The Governor was losing no time in advancing to the work of destruction, observed the *Portsmouth Oracle*.[9] The *Concord Gazette* shifted its attack from Hill's printshop to his parlor and agreed that "the will of the Governor will be the law of the State, and everything recommended by him crammed down our throats." [10]

If this prophecy were to be fulfilled, the New Hampshire legislature would require a hearty appetite, for Plumer had prepared an extensive menu of proposals. At noon, June 6, the Governor stepped before an overflowing audience in the representatives' hall and delivered his second inaugural address. "I was some embarrassed, but less than I was in 1812," he recalled. "There were several gentlemen present from other States, which excited my animation." [11]

Plumer began his address to the legislature with a panegyric upon the peaceful and prosperous condition of the country. He pointed out how this contrasted with the anxiety of the moment when he last addressed the lawmakers in 1812, then linked cause and effect in a blaze of involved oratory and political propaganda. "The brilliant achievments of our fellow-citizens, both by sea and land," he asserted, "have nobly sustained and increased our former reputation for enterprize and valor; and by the signal proofs which we gave, of a firm and resolute determination to defend, at all hazards, our violated rights, we have, with the blessing of Heaven, raised our public character in the estimation of other nations, and obtained an honorable peace." [12] This flight of enthusiasm was followed by specific recommendations: that New Hampshire's militia laws be altered to conform to those of the United States, that her rising manufactures be encouraged by exemption from taxes for a period of years, and that his party fulfill an old campaign promise by districting the state for the election of congressmen and

9. *Portsmouth Oracle,* June 8, 1816.

10. *Concord Gazette,* June 4, 18, 1816. This idea was also expressed by the correspondent of the *Daily Advertiser* (Boston), June 10, 1816.

11. Plumer, Autobiography, 318.

12. *Speech of His Excellency, William Plumer, Governor of New Hampshire, Before the Legislature* (Concord, 1816). Also *Journal of the Senate, June Session, 1816* (Concord, 1816), 13.

presidential electors.[13] He then reminded the legislators of the unpleasant fact that a new proportion act for the assessment of taxes was due and that a hard look at the state of the treasury was requisite. For the relief of the taxpayer, the new governor made a proposal that must have caused his auditors to doubt the evidence of their senses—he recommended to them "the propriety of reducing the salaries of the governor, the justices of the supreme court, and the treasurer." [14]

This revival of a virtually extinct tenet of pure republicanism, trifling as its practical effect on the public purse might be, aroused almost as much excitement as any act of Plumer's administration. Thomas Jefferson, who had been one of the earliest American politicians to exploit the popularity of governmental economy, gave Plumer a warm word of approval. "I remark . . . the phaenomenon of a chief magistrate recommending the reduction of his own compensation," he wrote. "This is a solecism of which the wisdom of our late Congress cannot be accused. I, however, place economy among the first and most important of republican virtues." [15] Plumer had also placed it upon this lofty eminence: "Our public officers were made," he said, in phraseology that became a cliché with him, "not for the emolument of the officer, but to promote the public interest." He pointed out that the mass of taxpayers were farmers and mechanics with small incomes, that few offices required the full-time services of the incumbents, and that the salaries of nearly all state officials had more than doubled within the past several years. From this combination of circumstances he deduced that "whenever the salaries in a republic are raised so high as to excite a spirit of avarice, and induce men to seek office from sordid motives, it has a direct tendency to extinguish public spirit, and to destroy the laudable ambition of holding office for the noble purpose of promoting the public good. . . . This is an evil pregnant with danger to a free government." [16]

It is difficult to believe that even in the Arcadian simplicity of New Hampshire in 1816 a salary of $1,200 would excite a very active spirit

13. The legislature passed a bill to encourage manufactures, *ibid.*, 128, but postponed action on the districting proposal. The militia bill of 1816 corresponded only in part with Plumer's recommendations. See *Laws of New Hampshire*, VIII, 514-15.

14. *Senate Journal, June Sess., 1816*, 24.

15. Jefferson to Plumer, July 21, 1816, Jefferson Papers, CCVII, Lib. Cong. John Quincy Adams, who was later to be accused of extravagance in the White House, also approved of Plumer's principles, remarking that "the appetite of ambition for place is sufficiently sharp-set, without needing the stimulant dram of avarice to make it keener." Plumer, Jr., *Life of Plumer*, 436.

16. *Senate Journal, June Sess., 1816*, 23-24.

of avarice or constitute a serious danger to free government. The legislature, however, took the Governor at his word, lopped $200 off his stipend, and reduced other salaries (but not their own) accordingly.[17] Federalist newspapers all over the country regarded this business as sheer demagoguery. They scoffed at the "half-price Governor" and ridiculed the idea that the paltry savings in salary payments would make a noticeable difference in the tax schedules.[18] "A more Jesuitical, time-serving, popularity-hunting Speech never was delivered from the Executive Chair," declared the usually mild *New Hampshire Sentinel*.[19] Plumer's record, to be sure, gave some relevancy to their charges. He had been a principal actor, however reluctantly, in raising the gubernatorial stipend from its original modest sum of $800 in 1792 to $1,200 in 1797. He had also been, during his Federalist days, one of the strongest advocates of higher judicial salaries. If he had changed his opinions with his politics on this score, it could be said that, as a rich man, he could easily afford the gesture. Those who were involuntarily associated with him in this act of renunciation—particularly the judges, who were precluded by their office from other occupations—might not be so fortunate. Plumer was undoubtedly sincere in his demand for public economy; that he was not unaware of the popularity procurable at this small monetary sacrifice is equally evident.[20]

In Plumer's view, the most important task for the legislature of 1816 was the overthrow of the Federalist Judiciary Acts of 1813. In destroying the tenure of judges by abolishing their courts, he declared, they had been unconstitutional; for that reason alone such laws were deserving of the death sentence. "To repeal these laws," he reassured the legislators, "will not be innovating, but restoring a system of administering justice, that has, in substance, been coeval with the early settlement of the country." [21] The Governor thus pleaded for the restoration of a judicial system which he had spent a lifetime in criticizing and asked for the overthrow of reforms that he himself had advocated.

This was more, however, than just another evidence of Plumer's capacity for "wheeling about,"—or a surrender to political expediency.

---

17. *Ibid.*, 161.

18. *Portsmouth Oracle,* June 15, 1816.

19. *N. H. Sentinel* (Keene), June 15, 1816. See also the *Daily Advertiser* (Boston), June 10, 1816.

20. Plumer's example of Spartan virtue aroused so much interest that his speech was printed in the *Morning Chronicle* (London), Sept. 20. See *Daily Advertiser* (Boston), Nov. 2, 1816.

21. *Senate Journal, June Sess., 1816,* 21.

In some respects the judicial system of 1813 contained more of dangerous innovation than of genuine reform. It entrusted too much power to a single judge, placed the prudential affairs of the counties in the hands of irresponsible tribunals, and encouraged the practice of setting aside the verdicts of juries.[22] Reverting again to the reliable propaganda line of his party, Plumer declared that these practices, like the provisions of the Dartmouth College charter, were "better suited to the nature of a monarchical than to a republican government." [23] This was always the crushing blow!

Unquestionably the most urgent, but at the same time the most difficult, issue upon which he had to recommend a policy was the future of Dartmouth College. Prior to the meeting of the legislature, Plumer had discussed this subject with agents of the trustees, and had also taken heed of Isaac Hill's observation that "the future governance of D. College... judiciously managed, will be a mean of perpetuating the republican majority in the State." [24] The effect of such advice upon a self-educated man who scorned the dead languages but had sent his son to Harvard was the key to the coming struggle. Plumer was committed politically to the restoration of John Wheelock to the presidency and to amending the college charter, but there remained the further question of the extent and character of the changes to be made at Dartmouth, and Plumer's recommendations were certain to carry a great deal of weight.

Exciting currents of educational experimentalism were flowing through the Western world in the early nineteenth century and finding outlet in newspaper columns as well as in books and pamphlets. There is some evidence that Plumer was sensitive to these impulses. His reading of Rousseau and Bentham is a matter of record, and his own writings reflect some of the educational theories of his countrymen— Thomas Jefferson, Noah Webster, Benjamin Rush, James Sullivan, and Du Pont de Nemours.[25] He was aware of the disposition to found state universities which had already been incorporated into some of the earliest state constitutions and had resulted in eight new educational

22. *Ibid.,* 20. Plumer had himself suffered what he thought to be an injustice at the hands of Judge Parker in an assessment for road taxes in the northern towns where he held so much property.

23. *Ibid.,* 20-21.

24. Isaac Hill to Plumer, Jr., Apr. 22, 1816, Plumer Papers, N. H. State Lib.

25. Charles Arrowood, *Thomas Jefferson and Education in a Republic* (N. Y., 1930), 31-37.

institutions, one of which was in neighboring Vermont.[26] Even more reflective of current trends in education were the briefly successful attempts of Pennsylvania and New York to turn their old colonial colleges into state institutions, as well as the administrative changes which Harvard and Yale had accepted at the will of their state legislatures.[27] It may be assumed that Plumer was familiar with the thorough discussion of these subjects in the newspapers.

Consequently, the section of his inaugural address dealing with the Dartmouth College issue probably engaged the interest of Plumer's auditors more than all the remainder of his speech. The Governor centered his attention almost entirely upon a consideration of the charter itself. Ignoring completely the quarrel between Wheelock and the trustees, Plumer treated the "state and condition of Dartmouth College" as a legitimate and normal concern of the legislature, particularly since the state had "contributed liberally to the establishment of its funds." Certain provisions of the royal charter were "hostile to the spirit and genius of a free government," and should be changed. Specifically, Plumer recommended that the trustees should, in the future, be elected by some body of men other than themselves, that their number should be increased, and that the president of the college should be required to submit an annual report to the state government. Plumer's defense of the legislature's right to make such alterations was equally uncomplicated. "The college was formed for the public good," he asserted, "not for the benefit or emolument of its trustees; and the right to amend and improve acts of incorporation of this nature, has been exercised by all governments, both monarchical and republican." He therefore called upon the legislature to "make such further provisions as will render this important institution more useful to mankind." [28]

It is apparent from these remarks that Plumer already considered Dartmouth College a public institution. In the days before rigid separation of civil and private corporations, colonial and early state governments had patronized, subsidized, supervised, and interfered with all of the colleges in the country, from Harvard to Transylvania. Plumer could easily have cited chapter and verse from his own experience in the legislature to prove that, even if Dartmouth were a purely eleemosynary institution, the state of New Hampshire had been her principal

26. Donald Tewksbury, *The Founding of American Colleges and Universities before the Civil War* (N. Y., 1932), 167, particularly Table XXII.
27. Elmer Brown, *The Origin of State Universities* (Berkeley, Cal., 1903), 31-36.
28. *Senate Journal, June Sess., 1816,* 25-28.

benefactor.[29] Not only had the government given financial support to Dartmouth College, but it had, on several occasions, legislated in regard to her government.[30] With these precedents in mind, Plumer was not entirely unjustified in supposing that he was asking the legislature merely to alter the charter of a public institution.

Plumer laid no claim to magical powers of oratory, but he believed strongly in the importance of well-constructed state papers and in the leadership that a governor could exercise by the persuasive presentation of a legislative program. His speech had encompassed proposals that nearly half of his audience regarded as revolutionary and the remainder recognized as a severe challenge. He closed his address with memorable words.

We are the representatives of an important member of the only great Republic that now exists. The principles of our policy should therefore be just and liberal, and our views extended beyond the interest and feelings of the present moment. As we are legislating for future times, we cannot too often reflect, what judgment posterity will pass on our public character, when the spirit of party shall subside, and the passions and petty interests of the present times are forgotten. . . . And let us never forget, that office however exalted, titles however splendid, and emoluments however great, can confer no honor on the officer, unless he faithfully discharges the duty of his trust; and that a faithless man raised to office, is but the herald of his own disgrace, and the scourge of those who clothed him with power. If the people have placed us in authority, it is to promote their interest, not our own, that we are bound to act.[31]

Governor Plumer followed his address by conferring frequently with legislative leaders, seeking, as he told his son, rather to "impart than receive the tone." Constructive statesmanship, however, often had to

29. The colony and state of New Hampshire had given three townships of land to Dartmouth College, had made a donation of $900 in 1805 to clear up a deficit, and had granted $3,450 in 1809 for the erection of a medical school building. These and other donations are partially summarized in Shirley, *Dartmouth College Causes*, 7-9, 44-52. In their frequent petitions to the legislature for further donations, the trustees invariably stressed the constitutional mandate to "cherish the interest of . . . seminaries" and declared that it was "only under the patronage and by the aids of the public" that the college could perform its function. See "Memorial of the Trustees of Dartmouth College to the Legislature of New-Hampshire, December, 1795," N. Y. Pub. Lib.; "Memorial of the Trustees," etc., Dec. 14, 1803, Dartmouth MSS., Dartmouth College.

30. See draft of an "Act more effectually to define and improve . . . Moor's charity school," Dartmouth MSS., 807360.11, Dartmouth College. The act was passed in different form on June 10, 1807.

31. *Senate Journal, June Sess., 1816*, 29-30.

give way to what Plumer called the "prevailing extensive inordinate thirst for office which pervades all ranks in both political parties." A continuous parade of plotters and petitioners streamed through his office, begging for undeserved favors or hatching corrupt conspiracies.[32] Among the most persistent, if not the most selfish, of the visitors who besieged Governor Plumer were the lobbyists on either side of the Dartmouth College fight.[33]

The friends of John Wheelock were an interesting group. Besides Brewster and Perkins, whom Plumer had already met, there was William H. Woodward, Wheelock's nephew and the treasurer of Dartmouth College; William Allen, Wheelock's son-in-law, a Dartmouth alumnus; and the Reverend Elijah Parish of Byfield, Massachusetts, who had been one of Plumer's principal targets in his *Address to the Clergy* but who had helped Wheelock prepare his case against the trustees and was his devoted partisan.[34] The most colorful lobbyist was undoubtedly General Eleazer Wheelock Ripley, lawyer, army officer, alumnus of Dartmouth College, grandson of its founder, son of its first theology professor, and nephew of its deposed president.[35] As one of New England's few military heroes in the War of 1812, General Ripley enjoyed a considerable popularity, even in Federalist Concord, which honored him with a public dinner.[36] His interest in the Dartmouth business was a curious blend of avuncular loyalty and political intrigue. He painted grandiose pictures to Plumer of a reformed Dartmouth as the center from which Republicanism would spread irresistibly throughout the country,[37] and before Dartmouth University had even been created by the legislature, he had it subdivided into colleges of medicine, law, arts, politics, and two kinds of theology (Baptist and Methodist)—each with a complete set of proposed teachers and officers.[38] The value of such a device for bargaining purposes was

32. Plumer to Plumer, Jr., June 10, 1816, Plumer Papers, N. H. State Lib.; Plumer, Autobiography, 317-18. Plumer's journal narrates these intrigues in wearisome detail.
33. Daniel French to Francis Brown, May 23, 1816, Dartmouth MSS., 816323.1, Dartmouth College.
34. Plumer, Autobiography, 318.
35. See Thomas Spaulding in *DAB* s.v. "Ripley, Eleazer Wheelock."
36. Plumer, Autobiography, 321. The diners numbered 130, of both parties. Governor Plumer's toast was "The military establishment of the United States—their prowess commanded respect from the enemy—their valor defended the rights of our country."
37. Plumer, Jr., Journal, II (1814-16), 314, N. H. State Lib.
38. Plumer, Repository, IV, 667, *ibid*. Plumer preserved this curious plan, no doubt as a reminder of the kind of thinking with which he had to deal during the Dartmouth controversy.

transparent—even young William Plumer recognized the snare when Ripley proposed that he should be the professor of civil history in the new institution [39]—but its educational usefulness was questionable.

Ripley's ideas, however, had the merit of being tangible, and he brought them to Concord in the form of a legislative proposal.[40] After Plumer had added several amendments, this bill was presented to the grand Committee of Eighteen, which had been named by the legislature to consider the Dartmouth problem.[41] The Ripley-Plumer bill would have made sweeping changes in Dartmouth. The existing board of trustees was to be removed and the name of the institution changed to Dartmouth University. Two new boards, one of fifteen trustees, and another of thirty to fifty overseers, were to be created, the original members of each to be named in the act itself.[42] Vacancies on the board of overseers were to be filled by the governor and council; those on the board of trustees by the overseers and the state executive. The new board of trustees was to elect a new president at its first meeting, and the governor and council of the state were to make a supervisory visit to the university at least once in every five years.[43]

Governor Plumer surmised that the trustees would employ delaying and diversionary tactics against this bill.[44] He had in his own hands a document upon which they relied heavily—the factual and dispassionate report of the investigating committee that the Federalist legislature of 1815 had sent to the Dartmouth campus. Although this report tended to throw cold water on Wheelock's extravagant charges, the Republicans made no attempt to suppress it. Plumer transmitted it immediately to the legislature, and it was given wide publicity.[45] The college

39. Entry for June 15, 1816, Plumer, Jr., Memoirs, I, *ibid.*
40. Eleazer Ripley to John Wheelock, Dec. 6, 1815, Dartmouth MSS., 815656, Dartmouth College.
41. *Journal of the House of Representatives, June Session, 1816* (Concord, 1816), 30, 45, 46; *Senate Journal, June Sess., 1816,* 45, 47.
42. Both Plumer and his oldest son were named as trustees in this first version of the bill. Plumer struck his own name off the list.
43. These details were reported in a letter from Plumer to Plumer, Jr., June 10, 1816, Plumer Papers, N. H. State Lib.
44. This is what Daniel Webster was advising from Portsmouth and T. W. Thompson was trying to achieve in Concord. Daniel Webster to William Handerson, June 1816; T. W. Thompson to Francis Brown, June 10, 1816, Dartmouth MSS., 816390.1, 816360, Dartmouth College.
45. The House of Representatives passed a resolution to print 300 copies of the report and of Wheelock's original memorial to the legislature. *House Journal, June Sess., 1816,* 51, 60. Richardson's statement, *Dartmouth College,* I, 318, that the "party devoted to the president now endeavored to suppress this document" is contradicted by this evidence. For the printed report, see *n.* 40 of the preceding chapter.

party was permitted to move for a special committee to consider the report—a committee that was, of course, appointed by their opponents. This special committee pointed out that the constant friction between the governing bodies at Dartmouth demonstrated convincingly the need of reform, and that it was not the legislature's business to arbitrate between factions which ought not to exist, but to remove the source of factionalism by excising the defects in Dartmouth's charter.[46] In spite of desperate efforts by the Federalists to block this report, it was accepted. Plumer's cohorts had turned the enemy's own guns against them.

On June 18 the Committee of Eighteen reported a version of the bill to amend the charter of Dartmouth College that corresponded much more closely to Governor Plumer's views on the subject than had the original measure. The bill now proposed, not to remove the incumbent college trustees, but to enlarge the board by the appointment of as many as nine additional members. However, a further provision that trustees must be citizens of New Hampshire would automatically remove the four Vermont incumbents and thus allow the executive to appoint thirteen new men in a possible board of twenty-one. The board of overseers remained, and vacancies in both boards were to be filled by the governor and council. No stipulation was made that the university board of trustees elect a new president, but they were given the significant power "to revise, correct, confirm or annul any act of the Trustees of the College." [47]

Plumer's thinking was clearly evident in this version of the Dartmouth University bill. "My object," he wrote later, "was ... to establish not a nominal, but real authority in the civil government over the college, in such a manner that the rights of the legislature to superintend it so as to promote the public good should not hereafter be drawn in question." [48] Unfortunately for Plumer's object, he encountered opposition on his own side. Although the partisans of Wheelock had been among the foremost in their original demands for material changes in the college charter, they had no real sympathy for the principle of state control. Once the board of trustees had been properly reconstituted,

46. *Senate Journal, June Sess., 1816,* 104; *House Journal, June Sess., 1816,* 124-29.
47. *Ibid.,* 90. Copies of this version of the bill were printed and distributed. See an *Act to Amend, Enlarge and Improve the Corporation of Dartmouth College* (Concord, 1816), Moore's Pamphlets, Lib. Cong.
48. Plumer, Autobiography, 319.

Ripley and Allen preferred that it remain a self-perpetuating body. They tried to indoctrinate Plumer with the idea. At the same time, party lines were drawing closer and the Dartmouth question, much to Plumer's professed regret, had become definitely a partisan issue. The former Federalists whose loyalty to Wheelock was greater than their Federalism—Brewster, Perkins, and Woodward—changed parties and were accepted into the Republican caucus.[49] Other pro-Wheelock Federalists, such as John Taylor Gilman, now abandoned the president and either rallied to the support of the trustees or withdrew from the struggle. As an organization, the Federalist party adopted the cause of the Octagon and submitted to its leadership.

This combination of circumstances was too much for General Ripley, who became convinced that the Republicans intended to abandon his uncle's cause. In a stormy interview with the Governor, Ripley plainly intimated that he had violated his promises and that "the Republicans had acted like *hell*." Rushing out of Plumer's chambers, the General belabored every Republican within earshot, "raved like a madman," behaved rudely at table, and finally drove away from town declaring that the college meant nothing to him and that he was returning to Massachusetts. On Sunday evening, however, he was back again, apologizing for his behavior and "imprudently active," as before, in visiting legislators.[50]

The Dartmouth College trustees, on the other hand, with a strong minority in the legislature firmly behind them, were trying the seductive effects of a compromise. On June 19, they addressed to the General Court a lengthy remonstrance against the proposed legislation but offered to accept "a law connecting the Government of the State with that of the College, and creating every salutary check and restraint . . . that can be reasonably required." [51] Their conception of a reasonable check was a board of eighteen overseers consisting exclusively of state officeholders with full veto power over the acts of the trustees. A willingness to concede so much in order to save the rest certainly vitiated later protests by the trustees against political control. Fortunately for them, the Republican majority rejected their compromise bait.[52]

49. *Portsmouth Oracle,* June 29, 1816.
50. Plumer, Autobiography, 322-23.
51. Shirley, *Dartmouth College Causes,* 9-10.
52. *House Journal, June Sess., 1816,* 119, 121. Had a bill incorporating these changes been passed, the trustees could not have claimed violation of contract, since they had themselves proposed the changes.

T. W. Thompson, a trustee and minority leader in the House, then submitted a petition that the trustees be given an open hearing before the Dartmouth bill passed to second reading. This request, as expected, was buried in a hostile committee. The Federalists moved to delay further consideration of the Dartmouth bill until its report was submitted, but their maneuver was defeated, eighty-four to ninety-seven.[53]

This parliamentary battle had been proceeding simultaneously with an equally severe struggle over a judiciary bill and with debates upon other bitterly contested issues. By persistent filibustering, the college party had already forced five roll calls in the House of Representatives and had thoroughly exhausted both themselves and the patience of their opponents. "We are all well but almost worn out by College business," wrote Thompson to his friends in Hanover.[54] Among those wearied of the fray was Governor Plumer, who was finding Thompson's labors only too effective. The "leaders of both parties . . . have conducted in a very improper manner," he complained to his son. "Each have offended & disquieted their friends & enflamed their opponents." [55] By a stern exercise of discipline, he and Morrill, the speaker, finally closed the Republican ranks and brought the College and the judiciary bills to second reading. "Such is now the state of the battle—the Trustees failed & oscillating—their next movement doubtful," exulted Levi Woodbury, the young Senate clerk, and he added that the Republicans would stay in session until October, if necessary, in order to pass the Dartmouth and the judiciary bills.[56]

The trustees had by no means failed, however, for at this point Governor Plumer had to surrender his own plans for the college, probably in order to save the rest of his legislative program. On second reading, seven of the ten sections of the college bill were recommitted, while the judiciary repeal act moved on without modification. Since these motions were passed without roll call, it is impossible to analyze them accurately, but it would appear highly probable that the Wheelock faction voted with the Federalist minority in order to carry the recommitment against Plumer's followers. The committee was instructed to allow the new trustees to fill up their own vacancies on the board. This had been the chief point of contention between the faction interested only in restor-

53. *Ibid.*, 124, 132.
54. T. W. Thompson to Mills Olcott, June 21, 1816, Dartmouth MSS., 816371, Dartmouth College.
55. Plumer to Plumer, Jr., June 24, 1816, Plumer Papers, N. H. State Lib.
56. Levi Woodbury to Plumer, Jr., June 21, 1816, *ibid.*

ing John Wheelock and the Republicans who really wanted a state university.[57]

In the hands of the Committee of Eighteen again, the Dartmouth bill underwent important changes. The board of overseers remained, but with membership limited to twenty-five, all to be appointed by the governor and council, "now and evermore." [58] The number of trustees was fixed at twenty-one, but the existing members of the board were not to be removed and the limitation of membership to citizens of the state was dropped. This left the Octagon intact but supposedly outnumbered and neutralized by the nine new members appointed by the state executive. The most significant change, however, was that, after the governor and council had once filled the board to the required number, it was to become self-perpetuating as it had always been. In this respect, the Dartmouth bill was a severe defeat for Plumer at the hands of his own party, and it exposed him to newspaper jibes at the inconsistency between the statements in his inaugural address and his signature on the statute.[59] Sorely disappointed, he threatened to veto the bill unless it was amended in this particular, yet in the end he allowed the objectionable provision to stand.[60] His excuse was the one employed throughout American history by frustrated executives—"as it may hereafter be amended, I did not feel myself at liberty to place my veto upon it." [61]

The Governor's willingness to accept an unsatisfactory bill was undoubtedly produced by the realization that he was fortunate to obtain any kind of bill at all. The amended measure finally passed the House on June 26 by the narrow margin of ten votes, and the Senate two days later, eight to four.[62] The Federalists, inspired perhaps by the arrival in Concord of Daniel Webster, fought shrewdly and desperately to the end, using every conceivable parliamentary device to divide and confuse

57. *House Journal, June Sess., 1816,* 133, 165; Thompson to Olcott, June 21, 1816, Dartmouth MSS., 816371, Dartmouth College. It is significant that Thompson reported essentially all the amendments made by the committee on the day after the bill was recommitted.

58. *Ibid.*

59. *Concord Gazette,* Aug. 6, 1816.

60. Plumer to Plumer, Jr., June 24, 1816, Plumer Papers, N. H. State Lib.

61. Plumer, Autobiography, 323. Plumer later described his plans for the future of Dartmouth University in an interesting letter to his old friend, John Quincy Adams, in London. Plumer to Adams, July 30, 1816, Letter Book, III, Lib. Cong.

62. *House Journal, June Sess., 1816,* 194-99; *Senate Journal, June Sess., 1816,* 142-43. It was a party vote, with all the Federalists and two Republicans making up the minority. Squires, *Granite State,* I, 190.

their enemies, but none of these maneuvers shook the small Republican majorities.[63] Ignoring all protests, leaving the trustees' requests for a hearing buried in committee, responding with disciplined solidarity to every demand for a roll call, the Republicans carried the bill through, making it a test of party loyalty. For their part, the Federalists were equally unanimous in their defense of the Octagon. If Dartmouth College had not been a party issue before the legislature met, it certainly emerged from this session as simon-pure politics.[64]

While the Dartmouth College bill had been struggling for survival, the legislature had also been deeply involved in dealing with Governor Plumer's recommendations on the state judiciary. The Republicans had made it clear from the beginning that they would repeal the Federalist Judiciary Act of 1813 as soon as they obtained the power to do so. Governor Plumer had endorsed this political gesture but he had also recommended reforms in the protection of jury verdicts. The Republican caucus cut itself an easier pattern, however, by eschewing reform and confining itself to the single issue of repeal.[65]

It required a fortnight for a joint committee to report a repeal bill, but the time had been spent, not in deciding upon a course of action, but in composing a lengthy apology for it. Plumer reported, three days later, that there had been little discussion of the bill, but that Webster was in town to lobby against it.[66] Webster's sounding of public opinion in Portsmouth had led him to hope that there was Republican sentiment in favor of keeping the new courts, but Plumer thought differently.[67] "If the bill does not pass," he commented positively, "it will disgrace the Republicans." [68] Mason had also appeared in Concord, not with Webster's false optimism, but with some idea of persuading Plumer to reappoint the existing judges after the old courts had been reorganized.[69] Even the Republican lobbyists were more concerned about prospective appointments than with the bill in the legislative hopper. After all, there could not be much room for maneuver in a repeal bill; it was an either/or proposition.

63. Plumer to Plumer, Jr., June 24, 1816, Plumer Papers, N. H. State Lib. "D. Webster is here active & overbearing."
64. The Dartmouth Bill as finally passed may be found in *Laws of New Hampshire,* VIII, 505-8.
65. Plumer, Jr., Journal, II, 318, N. H. State Lib.
66. *Senate Journal, June Sess., 1816,* 90-98; *House Journal, June Sess., 1816,* 95.
67. Webster to Handerson, June 1816, Dartmouth MSS., 816390.1, Dartmouth College.
68. Plumer to Plumer, Jr., June 24, 1816, Plumer Papers, N. H. State Lib.
69. Plumer, Autobiography, 319-21.

Since there was little to debate, the Federalists were reduced almost entirely to delaying tactics, but they pursued these relentlessly. Six roll calls on motions for amendment or postponement were demanded before the repeal bill, unharmed by the sniping, passed to third reading. On the next day, the weary Republicans added a house rule that the names of members who demanded roll calls should be recorded. Aided by this anti-filibustering device, the judiciary bill passed the House on the following day by a strict party vote, ninety-seven to eighty-three, and reached the desk of Governor Plumer on June 27, shortly before the Dartmouth College measure. Although he felt that "the bill was susceptible of amendments," Plumer believed it to be "substantially correct" and approved it, thus bringing the two great objectives of his party to a successful consummation on the same day.[70]

What remained was a somewhat messy but necessary and, in Plumer's opinion, legitimate mopping-up operation. Both houses passed resolutions addressing the executive for the removal of the seven judges who occupied the Supreme and Appellate Court benches under the law just repealed.[71] This maintained the orthodoxy of the Republican doctrine that a judge could not be dismissed by the abolition of his court, but it raised the question of whether the party was not employing the provision for removal by address in an unconstitutional and purely partisan manner. Many discussions of this subject have maintained that there was no essential difference between the Federalist purge of 1813 and this Republican grand sweep of 1816.[72] The Republicans, however, were at least consistent; and Governor Plumer, who was more consistent on this subject than either Republicans or Federalists, argued ingeniously in defense of these removals. The purpose of the impeachment and address clauses in the state constitution, he declared, was to provide for the removal of judges who had lost their ability to judge properly, either through criminal behavior or physical incapacity. Willingness to hold a judicial office under a law that violated the constitution he had sworn to uphold indicated indifference to the sanctity of an oath,

70. *House Journal, June Sess., 1816*, 151-70, 185; Plumer, *Autobiography*, 323. The repeal bill is printed in *Laws of New Hampshire*, VIII, 501-5.

71. *House Journal, June Sess., 1816*, 148. There were two vacancies at the time.

72. Albert S. Batchellor, "The Tenure of Office of the Judges of the Supreme Court of the State under the Constitution," N. H. Bar Assoc., *Proceedings*, 6 (1902), 527. After 1816 there was not another judicial purge in New Hampshire until 1855, then two more in 1874 and 1876. Batchellor noted that although Massachusetts had the same constitutional provisions for removal as New Hampshire, no judge had ever been removed by address, and no court ever destroyed.

which rendered a man unfit to be a judge.[73] If this was somewhat strange reasoning for a lawyer who himself refused to take oaths, it was at least logical, and contrasted forcefully with the weak rationalizations by which Jeremiah Smith persuaded himself to accept his appointment to the chief justiceship in 1813.

But the legislature was not yet finished with the state judiciary. The preposterous claims of Claggett and Evans to a resumption of their old places on the bench and to their full salaries with interest for the three years since they had been ousted by the Federalists forced the legislature to address the Governor again, this time for the removal of all surviving judges "whose offices have not been otherwise legally vacated." [74] This precipitate action could not be supported by arguments either logical or constitutional, but it had at least the merit of clearing away all the debris of claims and counterclaims.[75] It made a clean sweep of the judiciary in the only possible manner, leaving the executive free to rebuild the courts from foundation to superstructure.

When this unusually long session of twenty-five days had ended, the General Court had added ninety-six laws to the statute books, elected David Morrill to the United States Senate, decided to build a new State House, and transferred the state's printing contract to Isaac Hill. It had followed the recommendations of Governor Plumer in the incorporation of sixteen religious societies, half of them sectarian; in the passage of a new militia act; and in a law for the relief of imprisoned debtors. It had reposed unusual confidence in the Governor by allowing him and the council to let the contract and choose the site for a new State House and to take whatever measures he thought necessary to adjust the state's claims for military compensation against the federal treasury. It had refused, however, to adopt the more liberal of Plumer's recommendations, such as the one by which the Republican majority

73. Plumer vitiated his own reasoning, however, by reappointing William Woodward to the western Circuit Court after he had been removed by the first address. Plumer's council insisted on this reward to the man who had left the Federalist party and joined theirs.

74. *Senate Journal, June Sess., 1816,* 162-63. A comic result of this action was that Arthur Livermore was removed twice, once by each address.

75. The tenure of judges is one subject on which Plumer maintained an unswervingly consistent record throughout his long life and experience. In his "Cincinnatus" essays, written in 1825, he denounced both the Jeffersonian Repeal Act of 1802 and the Federalist Judiciary Act of 1813 for violating the principle of life tenure. "Cincinnatus," No. 130, *Portsmouth Journal,* May 5, 1826, says, "It ... appears to me ... that the removal of judges from office by a law abolishing courts, or by a law repealing the statute under which the judges were appointed, is a direct & palpable violation of the constitution."

would surrender its chance to elect a solid slate of congressmen and presidential electors. Most remarkable of all in the relations between executive and legislature was the calm acceptance of Plumer's vetoes, which ranged from his objections to a loosely-drawn "act for the suppression of vice and immorality" to the return of a Walpole bank charter and the rejection of an act to relieve Daniel Webster from one of his financial indiscretions.[76]

When the state lawmakers finally packed their bags and rode out of Concord on the afternoon of June 29, they had every reason to feel pleased with themselves and their new governor. Behind them, Plumer and his council were still at work, for the executive duties of this extraordinary year had only begun.

76. *House Journal, June Sess., 1816,* 179-82, 223-30.

CHAPTER XIV

Trials and Errors

"The consciousness that my posthumous fame will exceed my present, is a consoling reflection; for I know that those who now censure, if they survive me, will be my encomiasts." [1]

FEW executives have ever had such an opportunity to exert influence through exercise of the appointive power as that which lay before Governor Plumer and his council on Saturday, June 29, 1816. The departing legislators had removed virtually every judge in the state courts and created a new government for Dartmouth University, leaving the executive authorities with the responsibility for appointing seventeen judges, nine trustees, and twenty-one overseers. Remembering the length of time it had sometimes taken to make one appointment in a sharply divided council, Plumer might well have looked forward to spending the remainder of the summer in Concord. Wasting no time, therefore, the Governor called his councilors together and preached a sermon on the uses and abuses of the appointive power. He urged them particularly to appoint "men of talents, legal information, & of strict integrity to be judges." Furthermore he insisted that some of these judges be Federalists, not only because "the minority had rights we were bound to protect" but because the replacement of judges deprived of their office by a political act with members of the party that sponsored the act would rightly be regarded as a species of ruthlessness deserving of retaliation. It would have a wonderful effect, he said, if their appointments could be unanimous, and he ended by pleading for a "spirit of mutual concession." [2]

None of the five members of Plumer's council was a man hitherto

1. Plumer to Plumer, Jr., Oct. 21, 1816, Plumer Papers, N. H. State Lib.
2. This is taken from the notes on his remarks which Plumer inserted in his Autobiography, 324-25.

distinguished for cherishing a spirit of mutual concession. General Benjamin Pierce, the Republican councilor from Hillsborough who later served two terms as governor of New Hampshire and became the father of a President, had been addressed out of his job as sheriff by the Federalist administration in 1813, and he was not the man to forget such an injury easily. Elijah Hall, the councilor from Rockingham County, was a faithful but uninspired Republican, while Samuel Quarles, elected by the Republicans of Strafford County, was "ignorant, obstinate, & unqualified"—an animated illustration of his name. Plumer's lecture, therefore, fell on deaf Republican ears. The two Federalists were delighted but skeptical. At the Governor's insistence, however, a list of forty names, including some of the best men in the state, was drawn up as a catalogue of potential judges.[3]

If Plumer had been able to exercise unhampered authority, his Superior Court would have consisted of Jeremiah Mason, William Richardson, and Samuel Bell—excellent appointments, but each full of political peril. Particularly daring was his plan to offer the chief justiceship to Mason—as confirmed a Federalist as one could have found in all New England. Plumer had broached the subject to him during the early days of the legislative session, but the Federalist Senator had refused to consider it seriously, insisting that Plumer was too liberal for his party or his council, neither of which would support his nomination.[4] Nevertheless, Mason's name was the first one Plumer suggested to his council on June 29.

The Governor's subsequent maneuvering in this lengthy session of the council displayed an adroitness and persistence that ultimately achieved a marked degree of success in the face of obstinacy, ineptitude, and deceit. Much to Plumer's delight, the councilors were unanimously willing to nominate Richardson. The vote for Bell stood three to two, the Federalists arguing with some pertinence that his connection with the bank failure would deprive him of the people's confidence. Plumer could not override the Republican majority against Mason, but he ultimately persuaded one Republican councilor to join with him and the Federalists in appointing George B. Upham, "a federalist, a good

---

3. Plumer, *Autobiography*, 325, 350.
4. *Ibid.*, 317, 319. Bell had not yet escaped from the ominous shadow of the Hillsborough Bank failure. Richardson had only two years previously returned to New Hampshire after a long residence in Massachusetts, and his rapid rise was regarded with jealous mistrust by many of his fellow Republicans; Charles Bell, *Life of William M. Richardson* (Concord, 1839), 33 (mislabeled 31) ; see C. S. Lobinger in *DAB* s.v. "Richardson, William Merchant."

lawyer, & a man of a fair irreproachable character." [5] William H. Woodward was also unanimously returned to the chief justiceship of the western circuit court. When the council finished, six of the seventeen new appointments had gone to Federalists, and Plumer was convinced that his new policy would work well. Had he not been hampered by a divided council, the proportions would have been more nearly balanced.

Plumer and his councilors celebrated the nation's birthday by choosing the site for New Hampshire's first—and only—State House. A committee was chosen to superintend the actual construction of the building, and Plumer had the satisfaction of knowing that the work would progress during the summer building season. The council then finally adjourned, and after breakfast on the fifth of July, Plumer rode out of Concord on his way home with "2 clean shirts, a silk handkerchief, a piller case" and his man Henry, hoping to avoid an excessive display of pomp and ceremony. At the Deerfield line, however, he was met by a mounted escort that grew hourly until more than five hundred gentlemen on horseback rode with him into his own yard. Another thousand on foot had gathered to welcome the Governor home. Refreshments were provided, sobriety prevailed, and by eight o'clock the weary executive was left alone with his family. Although the Federalist papers commented sourly that windows and crockery were broken and that the Rockingham grand jury might well look into the dispensing of spiritous liquors so soon after an election, it is evident that Plumer had been paid a notable tribute of admiration by his fellow citizens.[6]

For a few days in the early summer, it appeared that Plumer's bold effort to heal the breach between parties might succeed with New Hampshire's moderates.[7] But his appointments proved unacceptable to two determined groups—the die-hard Federalists who would not forgive him for deserting their ranks and the undeserving Republicans who could not forget their own exaggerated claims to preferment. "My candor & liberality gains no credit with either party," Plumer lamented. "It offends one . . . without conciliating the other." Ugly rumors reached Plumer's ears that such leaders as Webster and Thompson were actively dissuading his appointees from accepting office, and a correspondent

5. Plumer, Autobiography, 325, 326.
6. Plumer to Plumer, Jr., July 1, 1816, Plumer Papers, N. H. State Lib.; Plumer, Autobiography, 326; *N. H. Sentinel* (Keene), July 27, 1816.
7. See *ibid.*, July 13, 1816, and *N. H. Patriot* (Concord), July 9, 1816, for examples of favorable press comment.

reported that Judge Farrar, inflamed by the controversy over the Dartmouth charter, had insulted the executive by posting his commission in a grogshop.[8] This was a cruel blow to Plumer, who had been on friendly terms with Farrar for more than twenty years. Such conduct made the Governor's dream of a nonpartisan judiciary almost impossible of realization.

The Federalist newspapers added to Plumer's discomfiture by changing their tone from the original note of faint approval to shrill vituperation. Far from crediting Plumer with any genuine desire for reconciliation, they attributed his moderation to expediency and cowardice. Richardson was berated as a foreigner who had hardly resided in the state long enough to know its laws. As for Bell, his unfortunate venture into the banking world provided material for choice sarcasm. Noting that suits against Bell's defaulting bank were likely to be tried in his own court, the *Concord Gazette* resorted to literary analogy by quoting from *King Lear:* "Change places; handy-dandy; which is the justice, which is the thief?" [9]

This kind of pressure was too much for Plumer's seven Federalist appointees; led by Upham they unanimously declined their commissions, except for Woodward, who was no longer in a state of grace. Unwilling to accept total defeat, Plumer again urged Mason to accept an appointment which he felt could ultimately be extracted from his council.[10] "It is an office worthy of your ambition," Plumer argued, "and one which I hope you will hold till you are removed to the bench of the Supreme Court of the United States." During the eleven days that elapsed before Mason's answer was received, Plumer had plenty of gratuitous advice from other quarters. His son warned him from Portsmouth that "nobody" liked his plan of putting Federalists on the bench, and that Clifton Claggett expected to receive the appointment that Upham had declined. "Must the demon of party exist forever, & embitter the blessing of society & arm good men against each other!" exclaimed the exasperated Governor. Then came Mason's final refusal to consider an appointment. "Political considerations," he assured Plumer, "which in these times are often supposed to determine almost everything, have with me on this subject no influence." This was small consolation to the Governor,

8. Plumer, Autobiography, 327, 331; H. W. Gordon to Plumer, July 24, Plumer to Gordon, July 27, 1816, Plumer Papers, N. H. State Lib.

9. *Concord Gazette,* July 23, Aug. 13, 1816; *Portsmouth Oracle,* July 13, 1816.

10. Plumer, Autobiography, 327-28. Richardson magnanimously offered to step down to an associate justiceship, if Plumer could secure Mason's nomination as Chief Justice.

whose son informed him that he now had no alternative but to reappoint Clifton Claggett.[11]

"Claggetting" had become an accepted word in colonial New Hampshire in the days when Clifton's father had dealt heavy blows to culprits in the King's courts.[12] Plumer probably felt like reviving the term in 1816, for not even the Federalist newspapers bedeviled him as unceasingly as did the son and grandson of Wyseman Claggett. Long before the Judiciary Act of 1813 had been repealed, Clifton Claggett informed the Governor that he expected to be restored to the Superior Court bench. Having early repented of his agency in making Claggett's original appointment, Plumer did not intend to repeat his mistake. Claggett's demands, however, were not easily resisted. As a victim of the Federalist judicial purge in 1813, he was a Republican martyr with a claim upon the sympathies of his fellows, which they were bound to recognize, little as they may have esteemed his conduct or ability.[13]

The situation was greatly complicated by the fact that William Claggett, who passionately championed his father's cause, was Plumer's son-in-law. The temptation to preserve domestic harmony and to please both of his children who lived in William Claggett's house placed a severe strain upon the Governor's sense of duty. By refusing to yield, Plumer not only made things uncomfortable for himself but brought suffering upon his family. Instead of telling Clifton Claggett plainly that he did not intend to reappoint him, Plumer merely said that his claims would be impartially considered—a statement that was too scrupulously exact.[14]

When the judicial appointments were first announced, the Claggetts were furious, and Sally wrote a piteous letter to her brother describing her distress at the situation. William, Jr., undertook to soothe the ruffled feelings of his brother-in-law by assuring him that the insult to his

11. Plumer to Mason, Aug. 7, 1816, Letter Book, III, Lib. Cong.; Plumer, Jr., to Plumer, Aug. 14, 1816, Mason to Plumer, Aug. 18, 1816, Plumer, Jr., to Plumer, Aug. 30, 1816, Plumer Papers, N. H. State Lib.; Plumer, Autobiography, 331.

12. See H. W. Howard Knott in *DAB* s.v. "Clagett, Wyseman." The name was spelled with varying numbers of *g*'s and *t*'s.

13. Fortunately for Plumer, Richard Evans, who, although in the last stages of "a consumption," made the same claims as Claggett for restitution, died on July 18. See Plumer, Biographies, V, 105, 459, N. H. Hist Soc. At the same time that Claggett insisted on being reappointed to the Superior Court, he was a candidate for both houses of Congress. After being elected to the House of Representatives, he insisted on being made clerk of both courts in Hillsborough County, and Judge of Probate. William Richardson to Plumer, Oct. 6, 1816, Plumer Papers, N. H. State Lib.; Plumer, Autobiography, 320.

14. Plumer, Autobiography, 320.

father was the result of intrigue and disloyalty against which the Governor had struggled in vain.[15] Since Plumer had noted in his journal that he had carefully refrained from mentioning Claggett in the council meeting, his son's story is an obvious fabrication, probably representing a personal effort to keep peace in the family, even at the sacrifice of truth.[16] It was scornfully rejected by William Claggett, who wrote, "I look to the *secret* motives of the mind & far be it from me to let my indignation kindle against such weak men as Quarles." [17]

Governor Plumer probably turned with relief from these family quarrels to his plans for reorganizing Dartmouth University. On July 17 he exercised the authority conferred upon him by the statute to call the first meeting of the newly constituted boards.[18] The politely noncommittal acknowledgments of their notices that the members of the Octagon returned to Plumer would alone have aroused his suspicions, but rumors of their plans of open opposition leaked out and caused a flurry of exhortative letter-writing among members of the university party.[19] The Governor could have felt no great sense of confidence when he alighted from the Concord stage in Hanover on the evening of August 20 and walked into the Dartmouth Hotel.[20] He carried in his pocket an invitation from President Brown to attend a meeting of the *college* trustees that had been called for the twenty-third.

On the morning of August 26, when Plumer and his friends walked to the college library, the designated meeting place of the University

15. Sarah Claggett to Plumer, Jr., July 13, 1816, Plumer Papers, N. H. State Lib.; Plumer, Jr., to William Claggett, July 9, 1816, William Plumer, Jr., Letter Book, III (1803-19), N. H. State Lib. (hereafter cited as Plumer, Jr., Letter Book, III).

16. The senior Plumer's version could, of course, be the falsified one, but the weight of circumstantial evidence is against this interpretation. William Plumer was made of sterner stuff than his son, was less likely to invent fiction in order to keep the peace.

17. William Claggett to Plumer, Jr., July 30, 1816, Plumer Papers, N. H. State Lib. Claggett was a foolish man, but not easily fooled.

18. Copy of notice sent to Nathaniel Niles *et al.*, of meeting to be held in Hanover, Aug. 26, 1816, Dartmouth MSS., 816417, Dartmouth College. On the same day, Charles Marsh had written to President Brown, advising him to withhold all active co-operation with the new boards until the old trustees had met to consider their future course. Marsh to Brown, July 17, 29, 1816, *ibid.*, 816417.2, 816427.1.

19. Plumer received acknowledgments from Paine, Farrar, Thompson, Smith, McFarland, Brown, and Payson, all preserved among Dartmouth MSS., 816429.1, 816429.2, 816429.3, 816455, 816459, 816462, and 816470, Dartmouth College. Most of these managed to convey in subtle terms their intention of resisting the new regime. For the panic in the university party, see Levi Woodbury to Plumer, Jr., Aug. 7, 1816, Plumer Papers, N. H. State Lib.; Josiah Bartlett to Clement Storer, Aug. 13, 1816, Joshua Darling to Josiah Bartlett, Aug. 20, 1816, Bartlett Papers, Lib. Cong.

20. Plumer, Autobiography, 331.

Board of Trustees, they discovered that the door was fast locked. Returning to his writing desk, Plumer penned a brisk note to Francis Brown, asking whether he, as president, had provided a place for the trustees' meeting. Brown replied that, since the act of June 27 had not authorized him to call the trustees together, he did not consider it his duty either to provide a room for the meeting or to attend it. Plumer then wrote to Professor Shurtleff, who, among his many other duties, acted as the college librarian, asking for the key to the library room. Shurtleff answered that President Brown had the key, but Brown declared that Shurtleff was mistaken. Plumer then gave up his search for the elusive key and sent out notices that the university trustees would meet in the treasurer's office—at an hour somewhat later than the one originally announced.[21]

Only eight men responded to the Governor's call. Although most of them were in Hanover, none of the old college board attended except Judge Jacobs of Vermont, who came out of friendship for John Wheelock. The absence of two of Plumer's own appointees made it impossible to achieve the attendance of the eleven necessary for a quorum. With the Octagon meeting in the college library and governing the institution in defiance of the June law, it was necessary that something be done, even if it were only to write letters.

On the next day, a tenth trustee appeared in response to urgent summons, but the Octagon remained aloof and the university board still lacked one of making a quorum. Someone suggested that the Governor send for the Grafton County sheriff, take possession of the stage, and hold commencement, if necessary without faculty, graduates, or spectators. Plumer refused; he was not a man of violence. Instead, he wrote another letter to President Brown, requesting his "attendance as required by statute to preside over their meeting." Brown replied that he did not suppose himself bound by the new law to act as a trustee of the university against his will and that he would not decide upon his course of action until the trustees under the old law had determined theirs.[22] A complete stalemate had been reached.

Commencement Day, on August 28, brought a climax of frustration to Plumer and his nine colleagues. Professors Adams and Shurtleff refused to attend their meeting with a list of the candidates for degrees,

21. These notes are all preserved among the Dartmouth MSS., Nos. 816475 through 816476.10, Dartmouth College.
22. Plumer, Autobiography, 333; Plumer to Brown, Aug. 27, 1816, Brown to Plumer, Aug. 27, 1816, Dartmouth MSS., 816477, 816477.1, Dartmouth College.

but they and President Brown held commencement in the college chapel without the benefit of the Governor's presence. In the meantime, the college trustees formally resolved not to accept the act of June 27 and expressly refused to act under its provisions. Plumer and his colleagues answered this act of defiance by drawing up a remonstrance against any act of government that the old trustees might attempt in the future and warned that their actions subsequent to June 27 were null and void.[23] This was equally true of those taken by Plumer's board, in the absence of a quorum. The final hours of its session on August 28, therefore, were devoted to recommending measures which a future legal meeting might ratify.[24] Though yet unborn, Dartmouth University was furnished with six administrative officers, six professors, a curriculum for a "general course of instruction," and professional schools of theology, law, and medicine.

What Plumer may have contributed, beyond his vote of approval, to this plan for a genuine university is not recorded, but its emphases were consonant with his educational theories. If this paper university could have come into immediate corporeal existence, New Hampshire would have possessed an institution of higher learning far superior to the jumbled structure of Dartmouth College. The college supporters answered, of course, that while the "Decagon" built universities in the ethereal realms of the imagination, *they* were faced with the hard problems of physical reality, and that their task was not made easier by the interference of the state. "It was a dispensation of Providence which prevented the Trustees of Dartmouth University from making a quorum," they concluded.[25]

Whether Providence or something considerably less exalted had been responsible for his dilemma, Plumer went home from Hanover with a sense of peculiar exasperation. He had been checkmated, not through the obduracy of the Octagon, which he had expected, but by the delinquency of a fellow Republican, whose reported illness Plumer suspected "was strongly tinctured with hypocondriac affections." [26] Before many

23. These documents are printed in full in the *American* (Hanover), Sept. 11, 1816.
24. The minutes of this meeting were printed in full in *ibid*. Plumer kept two MS. copies, one of which was purchased by Dartmouth College at the sale of his library in 1910 and is now preserved in Dartmouth MSS., 816900, Dartmouth College. The other is in Plumer's Repository, IV, 671-90, N. H. State Lib.
25. *Concord Gazette,* Nov. 26, 1816.
26. Plumer to Brown, Aug. 29, 1816, Dartmouth MSS., 816479.2, Dartmouth College; Plumer to Plumer, Jr., Sept. 2, 1816, Plumer Papers, N. H. State Lib. The delinquent trustee was Jonathan Harvey, a state senator.

days, his problems were greatly increased by the resignation of this same trustee and the death of Stephen Jacobs. The only balm to his humiliation was a flattering article in the Hanover *American,* which praised the "combined mildness and decision of the Chief Magistrate on this unpleasant occasion," and "the tenderness he manifested towards the young men about to be graduated." [27]

Either the mildness or the decision of the chief magistrate led him, after reflection, to doubt the legality of the action taken by the rump university board at Hanover and to cancel their proposed meeting in September.[28] More than ever now, Plumer had reason to be dissatisfied with the law that he had found imperfect in June. Nothing could be done until it was modified, but, fortunately, Plumer did not have to call a special session of the legislature. It was an assessment year, and the General Court had itself scheduled a second meeting in November.

Plumer decided, however, that before the legislature met again, it would be well to ask the Superior Court for an opinion on the constitutionality of the Dartmouth Act. He argued that the constitution gave either branch of the government the right to ask for an opinion from the judiciary, which was true. He then reasoned, somewhat speciously, that the court's opinion, given now, would forestall the inconvenience and expense of a lawsuit.[29] Presumably, the old trustees would be grateful to him for saving them so much trouble.

This was a serious error in judgment, and William, Jr., undertook to educate his father in delicacy and prudence. He recalled that, when the act was before the legislature, the trustees were denied a hearing on the ground that they would have recourse to courts of law for any injuries done them. "But now," he said plainly to his father, "without giving them time to do this, you apply to the court—a court too of your own appointing, & would get an opinion, which, without hearing the other side, must settle the question against them. With so plausible a ground of complaint, they would be able, at once, to gain friends to themselves & degrade the Court by representing them as the mere tools

27. The *American* (Hanover), Aug. 28, 1816.
28. Plumer to Josiah Bartlett, Sept. 10, 1816, Bartlett Papers, Lib. Cong.; Plumer to Levi Woodbury, Sept. 9, 1816, Woodbury Papers, IV, Lib. Cong. In this action, Plumer was advised by the new Chief Justice, Judge Richardson, who doubted whether the June law permitted these actions. Plumer, Jr., to Plumer, Sept. 3, 1816, Plumer Papers, N. H. State Lib.
29. Questions proposed by Governor and Council to Superior Court, Sept. 1816 (extract from council minutes), Dartmouth MSS., 816450.1, Dartmouth College; Plumer to William Richardson, Sept. 28, 1816, Letter Book, III, Lib. Cong.

of party." [30] The only advantage in Plumer's policy accrued to the Federalists, who shrewdly used the incident as proof that Plumer himself doubted the validity of the Dartmouth Act.[31] His two Federalist councilors refused to sign the official request, one stating that he thought the legislature ought to make it, and the other that he himself had no doubts about the law, or he would never have made appointments under it. The Federalist papers hailed these statements as criticism of Plumer's policy and evidence of the law's unconstitutionality.[32]

Fortunately, perhaps, for everyone concerned, Richardson and Bell excused themselves from "forming an opinion upon a question supposed to affect private rights alone, till those who may think themselves interested in the question, have had an opportunity to be heard." This left the future of Dartmouth University squarely in the hands of the legislators, who, Plumer confidently asserted, would "amend the act, &, if necessary, provide for inflicting penalties on those who hereafter may have the hardihood of setting the constituted authorities & laws of the state at defiance." [33]

A constitutional opinion by a court of only two justices reminded Plumer that important vacancies were yet to be filled in the judiciary. William, Jr., in touch with all the important Republicans in Portsmouth, was plainly frightened by the rising tide of opposition to his father's bipartisan policy and begged him to appoint no more Federalists. "It was an act of justice & magnanimity which neither party knew how duly to appreciate," he said consolingly, and urged that Claggett be sent back to the Superior Court. "There will be no peace in *this quarter* if he is not appointed," he warned.[34] If Plumer had been inclined by his son's pleading toward compromising with his conscience, another letter which he found waiting upon his return from Hanover

30. Plumer, Jr., to Plumer, Oct. 26, 1816, Plumer, Jr., Letter Book, III, N. H. State Lib.

31. In refusing later to comply with the summons to show cause why they should not be removed from office, Brown, Adams, and Shurtleff declared that their opinion of the unconstitutionality of the act of 1816 had "received no small degree of confirmation ... from the doubts entertained on this subject by his Excellency ... and the honorable Council, as implied in their application to the judges of the Superior Court for their opinion; and from the answer of the said judges, in which they expressly state that they had not formed any opinion on the question." Shirley, *Dartmouth College Causes,* 135.

32. Plumer, Autobiography, 335; *Concord Gazette,* Feb. 11, 1817.

33. *Journal of the House of Representatives, November Session, 1816* (Concord, 1817), 200 ff.; Plumer to William Woodward, Oct. 11, 1816, Letter Book, III, Lib. Cong.

34. Entry for Aug. 13, 1816, Plumer, Jr., Journal, II, N. H. State Lib.; Plumer, Jr., to Plumer, Aug. 30, 1816, Plumer Papers, N. H. State Lib.

made him more determined than ever to remain independent. It contained a set of resolutions adopted by a convention which purported to represent the Republicans of Portsmouth. They objected strenuously to the appointment of any more Federalists and threatened retribution at the polls if Plumer and his councilors did not mend their ways. The Governor was honestly indignant at this attempt to dictate in an area where he thought partisan considerations should have no weight. "I neither seek for nor avoid office," he bluntly informed his son, "but tho the many, directed by the few, may decline re-electing me, they shall never by threats, and I might add [for Junior's benefit] nor persuasion induce me to do a single official act that I deem improper, or that may justly reflect disgrace or weakness on my character." [35] He was human enough, however, to ask who was back of these resolves.

By this time, the supply of qualified and available Federalists was pretty well exhausted. However, John Harris, a Concord attorney who was widely respected by men of both parties, had indicated to Plumer, though rather ambiguously, that he would not decline an appointment. Forearmed with this assurance, Plumer placed his name before the council at their September meeting and finally obtained its approval, although the two Federalists voted against him. Four moderate Republicans were then unanimously chosen to fill the remaining vacancies, and with more relief than accuracy, Plumer wrote, "Our courts of law were never filled by men so well qualified as they now are." [36]

The appointment of Harris brought a predictably violent reaction from the Claggetts. Late in September the younger Claggett and a few other contentious Republicans in Portsmouth established a newspaper, sententiously called the *People's Advocate*.[37] The term "newspaper" is hardly appropriate; it was devoted solely to political invective. William Plumer, Jr., from his uncomfortable post in Claggett's very house, reported that his brother-in-law was ridiculed in Portsmouth for his pretentions, but that his misguided zeal for intrigue could bring injury to the Republican cause.[38] The situation became really alarming when

35. Plumer, Autobiography, 333; Plumer to Plumer, Jr., Sept. 2, 1816, Plumer Papers, N. H. State Lib.
36. Plumer, Autobiography, 334-36. Pierce tried hard again for Claggett, but Quarles blocked him.
37. *People's Advocate* (Portsmouth), 1816-17. Claggett announced that he expected to lose a thousand dollars on his newspaper but would have the satisfaction of effecting the removal of Governor Plumer. Plumer, Jr., Journal, II, Sept. 22, 1816, N. H. State Lib.
38. Plumer, Jr., to Plumer, Nov. 24, 1816, Plumer Papers, N. H. State Lib.

the second session of the legislature convened in November, and young Claggett came to Concord to fight his father's battles. "The young man ... boards a mile from me, which in all conscience is near enough," Plumer reassured his wife. "I have heard much of his imprudent scandalous abuse. . . . But enough of this—I wish you and Sarah was as much at ease upon this subject as I am. I am resolved that the conduct of those whom I cannot controul shall never render me unhappy." [39]

As if to emphasize the difference between Plumer's stubborn idealism and the hard realities of politics, Harris chose this moment to return his commission with a letter of feeble apology for the delay in his decision. For Plumer this was the last straw, and he decided to give up as profitless his quest for a bipartisan bench. "My object now is to obtain the best man," he wrote to his son. "I wish for one who will not only be an aid to the present judges, but agreeable to them." Claggett thought that he fit this description, but his importunities and his son's belligerence had so disgusted public opinion that Judge Richardson specifically asked the Governor not to appoint him. William, Jr., was equally explicit in warning his father against any further dealings with the Federalists. "[They] have so generally rejected all offers of a compromise that you seem almost precluded, by what is due to your own dignity, from making any further advances," he argued.[40] Since Plumer had reached the same conclusion he was glad to accept the advice, but the problem of finding an eligible Republican remained. "There is a dearth of talents, of legal science, and strict integrity at the New Hampshire bar," Plumer complained to Jeremiah Mason.[41] In his extremity, the Governor turned from his contemporaries and decided to gamble on the next generation; he offered the nomination to young Levi Woodbury.[42]

Although fourteen other candidates were presented, Plumer was able

39. Plumer to Mrs. Sarah Plumer, Nov. 24, 1816, *ibid.*

40. John Harris to Plumer, Nov. 25, 1816, Letter Book, III, Lib. Cong.; Plumer, Jr., to Plumer, Nov. 27, 1816; Plumer to Plumer, Jr., Nov. 28, 1816, Plumer Papers, N. H. State Lib.

41. Plumer to Jeremiah Mason, Nov. 25, 1816, Letter Book, III, Lib. Cong.

42. Plumer, Autobiography, 338. Judge Richardson had already mentioned Woodbury as probably the best man available except for his youth. Plumer, Jr., Nov. 27, 1816, Plumer Papers, N. H. State Lib. Woodbury's exuberant partisanship is well illustrated in a letter to Plumer, Jr., Aug. 7, 1816, in which he says, "I had considerable expectation that Federalism would bury the hatchet—and unite in the support of our common country—and leave you, and myself & others to study the science of government—meditate on the sublimities of philosophy—and bask in the Elysium of literature with those we love—But they appear inclined to throw away the scabbard; and if so, 'my voice is still for war.'"

to obtain confirmation of Woodbury's appointment by the Republican majority of his council. Having once determined upon this venture of faith, Plumer became enthusiastic about it. "I know he is young," he acknowledged, "but he is a gentleman of talents, science & legal requirements & of an irreproachable character. No other man in the State of half his worth would have accepted the office." Plumer dismissed the protests against Woodbury's tender years with one of his rare jokes, insisting that time would remove this handicap and prove Woodbury to be the best judge New Hampshire had seen for fifty years. Young Plumer heartily sustained his father's self-satisfaction. "More has been done by you this year," he wrote, "& I may say by you alone, towards bringing forward men of talents, whether young or old than was ever before done in New Hampshire." [43]

The appointment of Woodbury brought about a final break between Plumer and Clifton Claggett, who called upon the Governor immediately after the appointment was announced and declared that this ultimate insult would bring retribution at the polls. Plumer replied with equal bluntness. "To prevent my re-election, you & your son may injure yourselves," he declared, "but cannot affect my reputation or inflict new wounds on my feelings." [44]

Governor Plumer, however, had more important things than the belligerence of the Claggetts to occupy his thoughts at the November session of the legislature. Among these, the fiasco at Hanover was not the least, although Plumer spent little time upon it in his address. He simply informed the legislature of what had transpired at Hanover in August, emphasizing shrewdly the humiliation to the state of having summoned notable men to a meeting that proved impotent because of a defective law and the obduracy of a few private citizens. "It is an important question, and merits your serious consideration, whether a law, passed and approved by all the constituted authorities of the state, shall be carried into effect; or whether *a few individuals,* not vested with *any judicial authority,* shall be permitted to declare your statutes *dangerous and arbitrary, unconstitutional and void.*" [45]

A bill that embodied the Governor's proposals was introduced on the

43. Plumer, Autobiography, 338; Plumer to Plumer, Jr., Dec. 6, 8, 1816, Plumer, Jr., to Plumer, Dec. 8, 1816, Plumer Papers, N. H. State Lib. Other letters from William, Jr., to his father indicate that Richardson was very much pleased with the appointment and that it was well received in Portsmouth generally.

44. Plumer, Autobiography, 339-40.

45. *Journal of the Senate, November Session, 1816* (Concord, 1817), 13-14.

second day of the session and ultimately carried by the Republican majority in both houses. This measure partially restored Plumer's original concept of the university's proper government by authorizing the state executive, for an extended time, to fill vacancies in the boards, and by fixing their respective quorums at nine rather than eleven for the trustees, and twelve rather than fifteen for the overseers. In the latter part of the session, another statute was passed, subjecting to stiff penalties anyone who presumed to perform official duties for the purported institution, Dartmouth College.[46]

Opposition to these measures was perfunctory and mostly for the record.[47] In other matters, however, the autumn session revealed that some of the Republican leaders as well as the Federalists were becoming restive under Plumer's firm hand. The Governor's son analyzed this rebellious spirit as a natural reaction from the weak administrations of Langdon and Gilman, who had allowed themselves to become instruments for purely partisan designs. "Now that we have got a man who has an opinion of his own and who is determined, within his province to act for himself," mused William, Jr., "it is not strange that the dictators should at first complain & find fault." [48] Nor was it unnatural, since these "dictators" opposed Plumer's leadership of the party, that he should have questioned their motives and thrown doubt upon the purity of their characters, as they did his. But, aside from personalities, the tensions within the Republican party were the natural result of conflicting forces—Plumer's lifelong conception of a vigorous executive authority, and a growing maturity in the legislative branch as the society for which it made law became more complex.

Executive leadership appealed to Plumer's instincts and suited his capacities. He enjoyed power, especially when he could justify its exer-

46. The legislative history of the measure may be traced in *House Journal, Nov. Sess., 1816*, 33, 116-23, 237; *Senate Journal, Nov. Sess., 1816*, 101, 104, 153. The statute is in *Laws of New Hampshire*, VIII, 555-56, 584.

47. General Ripley was not present to confuse the Republicans; Levi Woodbury to Ripley, Sept. 28, 1816, Woodbury Papers, IV, Lib. Cong. Woodbury wrote, "We want you in the 'Third House' greatly; for the difficulties will be very formidable." The anticipated trouble did not develop, although Plumer's appeal to the judges and the court's ambiguous response were used to embarrass the university cause. Samuel Batchelder to Reuben Mussey, Dec. 6, 1816, Dartmouth MSS., 816656, Dartmouth College. Batchelder introduced a resolution to request a copy of the court's opinion from Governor Plumer. See also *N. H. Patriot* (Concord), Dec. 17, 1816.

48. Entry for Aug. 13, 1816, Plumer, Jr., Journal, II, N. H. State Lib. The "dictators" whom the younger Plumer had in mind were two members of his father's council, Pierce and Quarles; David Morrill, the speaker of the House and Senator-elect; Josiah Butler, ubiquitous politician from Nottingham; and the Claggetts, of course.

cise by championing a cause he considered especially righteous.[49] For this reason, his decisive and sometimes arbitrary actions were performed with an air of self-righteousness which must have been extremely irritating to those who by implication were classed as enemies of the public good because they opposed him. Their resentment at being told how to legislate found expression in petty insults; in a pointed ignoring of several recommendations for reform stressed in the Governor's speech, and most of all, in the failure of the lower house even to return an answer to that same speech. This was a major insult, unprecedented in New Hampshire's history, and it created extraordinary excitement in the newspapers. Isaac Hill explained it as an intentional abandonment of stale custom,[50] but Plumer knew it had been cleverly engineered "to induce the people to think unfavorably of the speech, & wound [his] feelings." [51] He insisted that in this design they had failed, but his very tone indicated that the affront rankled.

Two seemingly innocent references in Plumer's speech had given his vociferous opposition a chance to question both his judgment and his honesty. The first involved the location of the new State House. In referring to the council's choice of a site the previous July, Plumer spoke with pride of the progress made during the summer in actual construction, and of the need for continuing appropriations.[52] Many of the legislators, however, did not like the building's location. The townhouse, where the legislature had convened since 1788, was in the north end of Concord, but Plumer and his council had chosen a south-end site for the State House.[53] As soon as the legislature met again, the North-enders, with whom many of the lawmakers boarded, had begun to fill the ears of their roomers with outraged complaints.[54] William Claggett seized this opportunity to publish an article in the *Advocate,* accusing Plumer and his supporters on the council of having made an illegal, impractical, and virtually fraudulent choice of site and contract

---

49. "The first time I have power I will use it as I think duty directs," Plumer told his son. Plumer to Plumer, Jr., July 1, 1816, Plumer Papers, N. H. State Lib.

50. *N. H. Sentinel* (Keene), Jan. 11, 1817; *Portsmouth Oracle,* Jan. 4, 1817; *N. H. Patriot* (Concord), Jan. 7, 1817.

51. Plumer, Autobiography, 344.

52. *Senate Journal, Nov. Sess., 1816,* 8-9. Some accounts state that Plumer laid the cornerstone on Sept. 24, but he returned to his home from Hanover on the 20th, and makes no mention in his autobiography of another journey to Concord.

53. The old Concord Town House stood on the site of the present Merrimack County courthouse.

54. Plumer, Autobiography, 337-38; Fred Leighton, "Evolution of New Hampshire State House," *Granite Monthly,* 42 (1910), 323.

for building.[55] Although the editors retracted several of their charges in the next issue, the damage had already been done, and Plumer's enemies had a weapon to use against him.

On the third day of the session, the Governor transmitted to the legislature, with considerable satisfaction, a report from the building committee, which stated that all necessary legal steps had been taken, and construction had begun upon the heavy foundations, which exhibited "a specimen of workmanship, not deficient in beauty, and in strength not exceeded by any work of the kind ... in the United States." [56] A thousand tons of stone for this work had been quarried from Rattlesnake Hill north of the village and carried to the state prison, where convict labor had been employed to hammer and dress it. It was evident that changing the site of the building would be a highly impractical procedure.

Nevertheless, the Republican dissidents in the House of Representatives obtained the appointment of a committee to inquire whether their resolution on the building of the State House had been followed "agreeably to [its] true meaning and provisions." This committee questioned the Governor and councilors by letter, after obtaining expert advice from disgruntled politicians and Concordians in framing the questions. Although he considered the procedure indecorous, if not unconstitutional, Plumer decided to clear the atmosphere by returning a full and explicit answer to his questionnaire.[57] The notes that he was always careful to take on such occasions showed that councilor Quarles, on July 2, had obtained leave for the following day and had agreed to the council's proceeding in his absence with regular business. On July 3, the remaining five members of the executive committee had selected "the Green lot" by a vote of three to two, Hall, Plumer, and a Federalist councilor constituting the majority. Quarles had returned on July 4 and confirmed the previous day's action.

Quarles' reply to the committee did not dispute the facts stated by Plumer. He testified, however, that he had misunderstood the significance of the action taken during his absence and had wished to rescind his approval, but that the council, by a tie vote, had defeated reconsideration. Even if this were true, it indicated that Quarles was somewhat lacking in perception. The investigating committee made little

---

55. *People's Advocate* (Portsmouth), Nov. 19, 1816.
56. *Senate Journal, Nov. Sess., 1816,* 36-38.
57. *House Journal, Nov. Sess., 1816,* 119; Committee of the House to His Excellency William Plumer, Letter Book, III, Lib. Cong.; Plumer, Autobiography, 342.

effort to interpret these statements but decided that "the location of the lot . . . never was made agreeably to the true meaning and provisions of the resolve." [58]

In the subsequent debate, William Claggett and Josiah Butler enlarged upon the unfortunate precipitancy and indiscretion of the executive, but more sensible arguments finally prevailed with the legislature, which rejected its committee's report by a vote of seventy-three to eighty-four. A resolution to replace the construction committee appointed by the executive with a single agent responsible only to the legislature was also defeated. Instead, a report exonerating and commending Plumer's committee was adopted and another $4,000 was appropriated to speed the work.[59]

Before the lawmakers assembled again in the spring of 1817, so much progress had been made with the new building that all opposition was silenced. As the building grew and the town moved southward to surround it, the people of New Hampshire became fully satisfied with its location and inordinately proud of the "beautiful edifice" itself.[60] It was finished in 1819, just at the end of Plumer's administration, at a cash outlay of $67,372.44, certainly a modest sum for a building that still houses the legislative chambers.[61] Plumer was vindicated by events, and, as a dedication speaker said, "In the obloquy that was heaped upon him, he bore himself like the man he was in conscious rectitude." [62]

An even more vicious attack upon Plumer grew out of his efforts to relieve the state of its financial embarrassment. Gilman had left his

58. *House Journal, Nov. Sess., 1816,* 185-92.

59. *N. H. Patriot* (Concord), Dec. 24, 1816; *Senate Journal, Nov. Sess., 1816,* 143, 156.

60. John Farmer and Jacob Moore, *A Gazetteer of the State of New-Hampshire* (Concord, 1823), 41. Hosea Hildreth, *A Book for New Hampshire Children* (Exeter, 1823), 48, informed his juvenile readers that "I have seen many elegant buildings in the course of my life; but I never saw one so elegant as the State House." The *N. H. Patriot,* Sept. 2, 1817, carried an elaborate and commendatory description of the building at the time of completion of the outer walls.

61. The original State House forms the central part of the present building, which has been extensively remodeled and enlarged. The lower floor is devoted principally to a lobby and Hall of Flags. A copy of the Hoit portrait of Governor Plumer hangs in the Council Chamber, located in an addition built in 1909. Gov. Lane Dwinell to author, Aug. 10, 1956.

62. Albert Arnett, "The Builders: Address at Dedication of Remodeled State House," *Granite Monthly,* 43 (1911), 388. Visitors to Concord today would be surprised to learn that the beautiful civic center which has grown up around the Capitol and which seems to be ideally located just at the north end of the business section was ever considered to be too far south of the town's residences. The building erected during Plumer's administration is pictured in *ibid.,* 325.

successor less than one hundred dollars in the treasury, a number of unpaid bills, and a heavy indebtedness to the banks. Pending the assessment of taxes in November, the legislature authorized bank loans to meet current expenditures, but Plumer applied for such funds to every bank in Portsmouth without success. Fortunately, the adjustment of New Hampshire's claims against the federal government for the services of her detached militia during the recent war promised some relief. An urgent letter to the secretary of the treasury, explaining the financial predicament of the state and asking for an advance on the unadjusted accounts, produced a miracle. Within a month, Governor Plumer had received forty thousand dollars on account from the United States Treasury.[63]

The advance, however, came in the form of treasury notes, which presented a problem in redemption. The banks would not accept them at par, and Plumer saw no advantage in losing $1,200 for the state in order to put cash into the treasury. On the other hand, the notes carried interest at 5 2/5 per cent, but payable only when they were converted into U. S. stock. Since this could be done at the face value of the notes, and the stock earned 6 per cent, it was obviously an attractive investment. On the advice of Plumer's predecessor, Governor Gilman, the state treasurer had so funded more than $17,000 in treasury notes received during the year 1815 as earnings on national stock held by the state, and the transaction had been commended by the legislature in June. Under these circumstances, it did not occur to Plumer to dispose of the notes that came to his hand in any other way. On August 14, he sent the $40,000 by his son, Samuel, to the Portsmouth Federal Loan Office, with careful instructions to fund the notes and the accrued interest due in U. S. 6 per cents.[64]

In taking this action, Plumer committed two indiscretions that were to cause him serious trouble—he failed to consult the state treasurer, and he dealt with his own son, William, Jr., who had recently taken over the loan office. The whole operation, including the delivery of the notes, was a family transaction, conducted with suspicious dispatch and secrecy. It was perfectly legitimate, and of no financial advantage to any

63. Plumer, Autobiography, 330; *House Journal, June Sess., 1816,* 231; Plumer to William Crawford, July 11, 1816, Letter Book, III, Lib. Cong. See letters to Plumer from George Jackson, War Department, July 24; Peter Hagner, War Department, July 25; Thomas Tucker, Treasurer, July 31; Joseph Nourse, Register, Aug. 2, 1816, Plumer Papers, N. H. State Lib.

64. *Senate Journal, June Sess., 1816,* 64-66; Plumer to Plumer, Jr., Aug. 14, 1816, Plumer Papers, N. H. State Lib.

of the participants, yet it should have been easy enough to foresee the scandals that Federalists would purport to find in this unorthodox passage of state money through the hands of the reputedly tight-fisted Plumers.

It was not the Federalists who first opened the attack on this front, however, but Plumer's Republican opponents. A brief reference to the note transaction in the Governor's November speech gave Morrill the opportunity to appoint an unusual committee of four Federalists and a "feeble inefficient" Republican to consider it.[65] The Senate added to the House committee another Federalist, John Vose, an able man but a zealous opponent of the Governor.[66] Plumer was convinced that the entire business was arranged to discredit him, and William, Jr., declared that the plot was hatched in the *People's Advocate* office. That paper, indeed, was the first to publish an attack upon the Governor's funding operation, even before the Vose committee made its report to the legislature.[67]

Without consulting or questioning Plumer, this committee asked the state treasurer a few perfunctory questions, then turned over the writing of its report to John Vose. The legislature received the report on December 13, promptly accepted it, and ordered 250 copies printed.[68] This was a hard blow at Plumer, since the report was ingeniously malicious while seeming to be factual and objective. Had the treasury notes been retained, said Senator Vose, they might now be converted into cash at par, which, together with interest, would net the state $40,720. The stock in which Plumer had funded the treasury notes now sold at $96\frac{1}{4}$, so that if it were converted into cash, the income, even with accrued interest, would be $38,874.15. It was unnecessary for Vose to call attention specifically to the gap between these two figures. However, he proceeded to show that since the market price of treasury notes in August was 97 while that of U. S. stock was 88, the treasurer, "if it had been thought proper by His Excellency," might have sold the former and purchased $44,090 worth of the latter, rather than oblige the U. S. Treasury by exchanging them at face value. The committee carefully refrained from criticizing the Governor, but their report hinted that, if he had been a little sharper, New Hampshire could probably have gone without taxes for the current year.

65. Plumer, Autobiography, 341.

66. *Senate Journal, Nov. Sess., 1816,* 65. According to Isaac Hill, Vose himself was a speculator in state notes. See *N. H. Patriot* (Concord), Dec. 17, 1816.

67. Plumer, Jr., Journal, II, Jan. 12, 1817, N. H. State Lib.; *People's Advocate* (Portsmouth), Dec. 14, 1816.

68. *House Journal, Nov. Sess., 1816,* 125-26.

After two weeks of reflection, the legislature found reason to reconsider its hasty action and voted to recommit the Vose report.[69] By that time, however, the affair had become a serious scandal, industriously aired by the Federalist press.[70] "We refrain at present from saying much on the ... development of Gov. Plumer's financial talents," remarked a contributor to the *Exeter Watchman*. "It remains to be discovered whether his Excellency has enriched himself, or the national treasury by the four thousand dollars which is thus lost to the State by his officiousness." [71] In a series of progressively more libelous statements, the *Concord Gazette* extracted the last drop of implied scandal from the situation. Beginning with questions about secrecy and collusion, it finally ended with accusations of dishonesty. If the Governor had not gained by his speculation, it asserted cynically, he was guilty of "gross negligence"; if he had gained, he had *"defrauded* the public." The one was a weakness, the other a wickedness, and either was sufficient to disqualify him for the governorship.[72] Thompson's journal mockingly reassured its readers, however, that the losses suffered by the state would be restored within two decades by the two hundred dollars saved annually from the governor's salary.

Plumer and his friends were properly indignant at these gross calumnies perpetrated under cover of a legislative investigation. Even Jeremiah Mason deprecated the folly of his fellow partisans, while William Plumer, Jr., aghast at finding himself accused of corruption at the very beginning of his political career, rushed into print with a statement in his own defense.[73] Plumer felt the sting of censure sufficiently to publish his own statement. The specious reasoning that pronounced him guilty of losing a speculative profit to the state of $4,000 was refuted, almost impatiently, as a matter of juggling figures; it could as easily be argued, he said, that he had earned $1,200 by funding at 100 per cent notes worth only 97 per cent on the market. His critics had lamented the assessment of a state tax when the necessary funds could have been obtained by cashing the treasury notes. Plumer reminded them that any cash in the treasury would have to be used to discharge the state's debt to the banks, leaving the necessity for a tax no less pressing. It had been suggested that he should have deposited the treasury notes themselves

69. *Senate Journal, Nov. Sess., 1816,* 150.
70. *Daily Advertiser* (Boston), Dec. 23, 1816.
71. Quoted in *Concord Gazette,* Dec. 31, 1816.
72. *Ibid.,* Jan. 28, Feb. 25, 1817. See also *Farmer's Cabinet* (Amherst), Feb. 15, 1817.
73. Plumer, Autobiography, 349; entry for Jan. 12, 1817, Plumer, Jr., Journal, II, N. H. State Lib.

in the banks on the state's account. Then, "I should have been accused of sacrificing 3/5ths of one per cent, & acting counter to what the legislature on a similar occasion approved," said Plumer. He summarized his position by saying that he had disposed of the state's notes as he did his own,[74] and as he thought best for the public interest, that the funded stock was a sound investment, paying interest quarterly, and that it would soon sell above par.[75] This prediction was verified within a few months. Before the end of May, the state treasurer found it possible to sell the 6 per cent stock at one and a quarter above par and to apply the proceeds to the state debt.[76] Thus ended in vindication for Plumer and mortification for his opponents an unprincipled effort to destroy his popularity.

Plumer's liberal employment of the executive veto did not endear him to the champions of legislative supremacy within his own party, some of whom were interested in the Walpole Bank charter which the Governor had demolished in June. The charter reappeared in the November session, disguised as a proposed branch of the Cheshire Bank at Keene. The novelty of branch banking, added to the irresponsible character of the charter given to this institution by the legislature, caused Plumer to give it a second veto, but this time he was sustained by little more than the necessary two-thirds vote of the House, and was stubbornly opposed by Morrill and Butler.[77] In another political hassle, Plumer did not have to veto a project hatched by Josiah Butler and Benjamin Pierce, the two Republican sheriffs who had been "addressed off" in 1813, following their refusal to obey the orders of the new courts. They persuaded the Republican caucus in 1816 to place on the party agenda a resolution for the removal, by the same method, of their Federalist successors. Such treatment of officials against whom no misbehavior or disability was charged would have made a mockery of all the Republican protests against Federalist removals in 1813. Plumer felt that principle was superior to any party consideration, and he prepared a veto message in

74. This, of course, was one of the grounds of criticism against Plumer, and a strong one. His public and his private business were too closely associated. The same letter in which Plumer told his son to fund the treasury notes "not in my name but in that of the *State of New Hampshire*" carried instructions to credit the governor with $325 of the new stock, purchased with the interest earned on his extant holdings. Plumer to Plumer, Jr., Aug. 14, Oct. 4, 1816, Plumer Papers, N. H. State Lib.

75. [William Plumer], "Veritas," "Funding Treasury Notes." Plumer, Essays, II, 136-40, Lib. Cong., publ. in *N. H. Patriot* (Concord), Jan. 28, 1817.

76. Plumer, Autobiography, 348.

77. *House Journal, Nov. Sess., 1816,* 180.

case the resolution came to his desk.[78] William, Jr., who suspected his father's intentions, hoped fervently that they would not be put to the test. But when the resolution came before the House, enough Plumer Republicans joined with the Federalists to carry a motion for its indefinite postponement, and Plumer filed the unused veto message in his archives.[79]

These many evidences of friction within the Republican party led the Federalist papers, and even some of Plumer's friends, to anticipate his defeat for renomination.[80] An attempt to accomplish this end was made in the Republican caucus, where the chairman, General Pierce, urged that, because the divisions within the party might interfere with the legislative program if allowed to break out openly, the nomination of their candidate for governor be postponed. Although Claggett and Butler spoke in favor of the suggestion, it was defeated. The caucus then nominated Plumer, eighty-five to eight, with one vote for Morrill and seven for Levi Bartlett. Pierce, Morrill, Claggett, Butler, and Quarles had been supported in their attempted mutiny by only three rank-and-file Republicans.[81] Young William Plumer could hardly repress his astonishment "that these five men, who were properly next to my father, the leaders of the Republican party, should have been able to effect so little. In any manly & honest course, they would have carried the whole party with them. But the circumstance, fatal to all these men, was, that they were known to act from selfish motives in their opposition to my father, & that they had private interests which they sought to satisfy at the public expence; while, on the contrary, he laboured under no such suspicion." [82]

Since the caucus nomination had demonstrated beyond cavil that Plumer was still the leader of the party, the opposition to his control melted rapidly away. Quarles was dropped from the party ticket in Strafford County, while Butler and Bartlett hastened to deny any connection with the *Advocate* group and to declare renewed allegiance to

78. Plumer preserved this veto message in his Repository, IX, 327-30, N. H. State Lib.

79. Plumer to Plumer, Jr., Nov. 28, Dec. 14, 1816, Plumer, Jr., to Plumer, Dec. 14, 1816, Plumer Papers, N. H. State Lib.; Plumer, Autobiography, 340.

80. "It appears that the Woodenheads and those who belong to the Brickbat family in Portsmouth, all true blue Democrats, have just found out that each other were knaves," exulted the *Concord Gazette*, Oct. 22, 1816, "and pell-mell they are at it."

81. Plumer, Autobiography, 432-43. It is an interesting comment on William Claggett's character that he returned to Portsmouth from his caucus with the story that it had voted to support Levi Bartlett for governor, and that Plumer had received only eighteen votes. Plumer, Jr., to Plumer, Dec. 22, 1816, Plumer Papers, N. H. State Lib.

82. Entry for Jan. 2, 1817, Plumer, Jr., Journal, II, *ibid.*

the Governor. Plumer analyzed the *Advocate*'s future correctly when he wrote to his son, on January 21, that "seven weeks more will consign it, not to the tomb of the Capulets, but to that of the Scavengers." [83]

During that remaining interval the *Advocate* made a prodigious effort to defeat Plumer by nominating Josiah Bartlett in his place.[84] Dr. Bartlett, son of New Hampshire's first elected governor, enjoyed the advantage of a distinguished family name, with an undeviating record of republicanism extending back to the signing of the Declaration of Independence. In casting about for a suitable instrument of his vengeance, Claggett had discovered some pro-Bartlett sentiment, which he carefully nurtured through the columns of the *Advocate,* until, in January, he publicly announced the doctor's candidacy.[85] This step was to have been followed by endorsements in the county conventions, but the Bartlett bandwagon failed to roll. After the Strafford and Rockingham conventions enthusiastically endorsed Plumer's administration, Bartlett sent Claggett a letter of formal withdrawal from the gubernatorial race and insisted that it be printed in the *Advocate*.[86] This blow killed the *Advocate* party. Butler, who had been deeply involved in its schemes, hastened to make public denial of any connection with it and began obsequiously cultivating the Plumers.[87]

The *Patriot* proudly publicized the collapse of this intrigue and satirized the petty criticisms that constituted the sole argument against Plumer's re-election. "Let the voters weigh them," wrote one contributor, "against his splendid talents, his acknowledged experience in legislation, his high reputation abroad, as well as at home, and decide whether he has done anything to forfeit their confidence and whether the state can gain anything by a change." [88] The answer of the voters

83. Plumer to Plumer, Jr., Jan. 21, 1817, Plumer Papers, *ibid.*

84. Plumer realized that this intrigue was in progress but never learned the extent to which Claggett had pushed it.

85. Plumer, "Josiah Bartlett," Biographies, V, 608, N. H. Hist. Soc.; *People's Advocate* (Portsmouth), Jan. 18, 1817.

86. William Claggett to Josiah Bartlett, Feb. 10, 17, 1817, Bartlett Papers, Lib. Cong.; Josiah Bartlett to editors of *People's Advocate* (Portsmouth), Feb. 1816, printed in *N. H. Gazette* (Portsmouth), clipping in Plumer, Jr., Scrapbook, Plumer Papers, N. H. State Lib.

87. Plumer, Jr., to Plumer, Mar. 1, 1817, Plumer Papers, *ibid.;* entry for Apr. 21, 1817, Plumer, Jr., Journal, II, *ibid.*

88. *N. H. Patriot* (Concord), Feb. 25, 1817. The *American* (Hanover) sang Plumer's praise in the Connecticut Valley and the *New Hampshire Gazette* (Portsmouth), although suborned to some extent by Butler and Bartlett, ultimately took the proper line. William Plumer, Jr., assumed credit for the successes in Portmouth, where he wielded his pen vigorously and, as he viewed the scene in retrospect, successfully in defense of

was a hearty negative.[89] Plumer's share of the total vote in 1817 increased to nearly 54 per cent, while his majority over Sheafe, his nearest rival in the distracted Federalist party, was far greater than anything that had appeared in election statistics since the palmy days of Langdon. In spite of all the furor in the newspapers, the New Hampshire voters had not been very much excited by Plumer's reported derelictions; more than three thousand of those who had voted in 1816 stayed away from the polls the following spring, and at least two-thirds of these absentees were obviously Federalists. The sovereign people of New Hampshire made it very clear that Federalism was finally dead, that there was no genuine disunity in Republican ranks, and that William Plumer was the unquestioned leader of his party.

Plumer's triumphant vindication at the hands of the electorate knocked the last props from under the *Advocate*'s crazy structure. It suspended publication in May 1817, while everyone who had been connected with it, except Claggett, hastened to make his peace with Plumer.[90] The younger Plumer boasted with some justice that his father had "effected, singly & by his own weight, all his great objects in opposition to open enemies and pretended friends. On all party questions, his influence has been in favour of moderate measures. . . . There has been indeed an independence in his conduct which it is much easier to admire than to imitate." [91] Perhaps the greatest tribute to Plumer's administration came from an ally whom he had once condemned severely. In praise of the way Plumer had held the legislature to its duty in regard to Dartmouth University, the Reverend Elijah Parish wrote to congratulate him upon his re-election—and added that he considered it indicative that Plumer would be governor for life.[92] There were probably few men in New Hampshire in the spring of 1817, who, either in fear or in satisfaction, did not believe the same thing—except William Plumer himself.

---

his father and in castigation of waverers within the ranks. Entry for Feb. 11, 1817, Plumer, Jr., Memoirs, N. H. State Lib. Clippings of his articles signed "Advocate" and "An Elector of Rockingham" from the *N. H. Gazette* (Portsmouth) in January may be found in Plumer, Jr., Scrapbook, Plumer Papers, N. H. State Lib.

89. Lyon, ed., *New Hampshire Register . . . 1860*, 42. The election statistics were as follows: Whole number of votes cast, 35,375; necessary for a choice, 17,688; scattering, 112; Josiah Bartlett, 539; Jeremiah Mason, 3,607; James Sheafe, 12,029; William Plumer, 19,000.

90. Plumer, Jr., to Plumer, May 17, 1817, Plumer Papers, N. H. State Lib. An unsavory aftermath of the *Advocate*'s demise was a suit against Claggett by his publisher to force payment of subscribers' money which Claggett denied having received. William Weeks to Josiah Bartlett, July 24, 1817, Bartlett Papers, Lib. Cong.

91. Entry for Jan. 21, 1817, Plumer, Jr., Memoirs, N. H. State Lib.

92. Parish to Plumer, Apr. 8, 1817, Plumer Papers, *ibid.*

CHAPTER XV

The Era of Good Feelings

> *His Excellency William Plumer*—Let envy
> rankle and unprincipled ambition whet its enven-
> omed fangs; intent upon the public good, elevated
> upon the eminence of just and equal principles, and
> defended by the people's gratitude—the storm rolls
> harmless at his feet.[1]

WILLIAM PLUMER was a local beneficiary of that unique phenomenon in American history mislabeled by a Federalist editor the "Era of Good Feelings" and characterized by the extinction of a major political party. He was re-elected governor in 1818 by more than 59 per cent of the voters against a divided Federalist ticket and a token opposition of young Republicans in Portsmouth who had the backing of his old enemy, John Samuel Sherburne.[2] In 1819 the Federalists cast only 35 per cent of the total vote; in 1820 less than 3 per cent; after that, there was no semblance of an organized party effort at the polls. Republican majorities in the legislature increased in the same way; by 1818 there was not a single Federalist in the Senate, and soon thereafter, none in the House.[3]

Strangely enough, Plumer's equivocal attitude toward President Monroe and the national administration provided one of the few dis-cordant notes in the swelling political harmony of 1817. In his Feder-alist days, Plumer had seen little good in Monroe, but by 1816 he was ready to congratulate the Virginian on the prospect of his election to the presidency.[4] The appointment of Plumer's former colleague, John

1. Independence Day toast at Wentworth, N. H., reported in *N. H. Patriot* (Con-cord), July 22, 1817.
2. Plumer, Autobiography, 359-60.
3. Lyon, ed., *New Hampshire Register ... 1860*, 41; *Farmer's Cabinet* (Amherst), May 23, June 6, 1818.
4. Plumer to James Monroe, Mar. 7, 1816, Monroe Papers, New York Public Library.

Quincy Adams, to the "prime minister's" post in the cabinet got the new administration off, he believed, to a good start.[5] "I am sensible Mr Monroe's task is herculean," he admitted, "but if the public good is the motive that governs him, I think he has sufficient understanding to support himself in office." [6] This was a rather equivocal statement, and further evidence of Plumer's lukewarm attitude toward the national administration developed during an official visit of the President. In the summer of 1817 President Monroe made his celebrated tour of the New England states, leaving Washington on the last day of May and slowly making his way northward in time to celebrate the Fourth of July in Boston.[7] On July 2, two gentlemen from the Portsmouth reception committee came to Epping to discover what arrangements the Governor had made for entertaining the President in New Hampshire. They conveyed the seaport's opinion that several militia companies of cavalry should provide an escort of honor from the state boundary to Portsmouth, a distance of only fifteen miles. The Governor's visitors were dumbfounded to find that the man who had distinguished himself for his readiness to call out the militia in 1812 had now developed constitutional scruples against using the same authority in a peaceful and far more popular cause.

The state constitution, Plumer declared, gave him ample authority to order out the militia for the suppression of rebellion, the repulse of an invasion, or the improvement of discipline, but not for the escort of "dignified characters who might visit the state." The New Hampshire legislature had been in session almost until the time Monroe reached their borders, but they had authorized no escort nor appropriated funds for such services. "No governor ought to issue orders where he had no authority to inforce obediance," insisted Plumer, adding that a court-martial would not punish militiamen for failing to respond to an order for escort duty. Plumer told the committeemen that he intended himself to wait upon the President at Portsmouth, and that he would be gratified if a respectable group of volunteers should escort him from the state line, but that he would not take the responsibility for ordering

5. Plumer declared that Adams was actually the preference of New Hampshire for the presidency, but he was speaking primarily for himself. Plumer to John Quincy Adams, Mar. 6, 1816, Letter Book, III, Lib. Cong.

6. Plumer to Jeremiah Mason, Jan. 24, 1817, *ibid.*

7. The story of the President's pilgrimage is related in detail by Samuel Waldo, *The Tour of James Monroe, President of the United States, in the Year 1817* (Hartford, 1818).

it. Plumer had obviously devoted a good deal of thought and even some research to the problems presented by this unusual event.

Early the next morning, William, Jr., hastened from Portsmouth to urge that his father change his decision. Portsmouth's leading men, from Richardson to Mason, united in declaring the Governor's constitutional doubts groundless. His power in this case was incidental to his authority, they said, and there could be no doubt of the propriety of his orders. Young Plumer, however, could not shake the older man's convictions; he probably only hardened them. "The opinions & advise of men who are not responsible for the act ought not to be implicit [*sic*] received," Plumer sturdily maintained, and in this case they were explicitly rejected.[8] Portsmouth had to proceed with such pomp and ceremony as she could elicit from volunteer sources.

On the morning of July 9, Plumer was just stepping into his chaise for the journey to Portsmouth to greet the President, when a messenger arrived from his son with word that Monroe had postponed the date of his visit to New Hampshire. Two days later Plumer was stricken with "a typhus fever," which confined him to his bed for ten days and left him unable to attend to any business throughout the remainder of the summer. Consequently, when President Monroe did enter the state of New Hampshire on July 12, its governor was not on hand to greet him, nor were the militia officially assembled in his honor. William, Jr., explained the embarrassing situation in person to the President and later conveyed to his father Monroe's solicitous regrets at not having seen him.[9] When Monroe re-entered the state at Dover after a brief visit to Maine, Plumer had recovered sufficiently to leave his bed, and sent the President a handsome letter of apology for his personal absence and of explanation for the lack of formal civilities.

Part of Plumer's letter was perhaps a bit disingenuous:

A military escort having been called out by the Governours of some of the States, . . . I was desirous that the same tribute of respect should be paid you on your passage through New-Hampshire. The power to call out such an escort seemed, at first view, incident to the nature of my office as Commander in Chief of the militia; yet so accurately is this command defined, and so cautiously restricted, by the prudence, or the jealousy of our State constitution, that I have authority at no time to order out the militia, except for certain known objects particularly designated in the constitution and by the laws enacted under it. ****

8. Plumer, Autobiography, 353-55.
9. *Ibid.;* Plumer, Jr., to Plumer, July 14, 1817, Plumer Papers, N. H. State Lib.

I have thot proper to make this statement, both for its justice to myself, & to the State over which I preside,—[a State which yields to none in the Union; either in attachment to the general government, or in respect for the distinguished individual, who, with its full consent & approbation, has been raised to the first office in the gift of the nation].[10]

This was an argument that an old strict constructionist should have known how to appreciate, and Monroe did, in fact, send a courteous reply which displayed no umbrage.[11] Plumer's friends eventually dismissed the entire episode as another example of his eccentricity, but his political opponents could hardly find enough words to express their spurious indignation. New Hampshire readers were treated to the strange spectacle of Federalists shedding crocodile tears for the disrespect shown a Republican president. The *Portsmouth Oracle* found Plumer's reasoning on the constitutional question "frivolous and trifling" and asked what militia officer in the state "(the Captain General excepted) would have declined so reasonable a service." [12] The Exeter Federalists poured scorn upon Plumer's intensive study of the constitution "to determine how far a compliment would be LAWFUL. Other executives have . . . overwhelmed the President with *unconstitutional escorts*. Not so with Mr. Plumer." The distant *Albany Gazette* sagely concluded that Plumer's parsimony was responsible for his conduct—that "having generously relinquished a very considerable portion of his salary for the purchase of Popularity," he could not really afford to entertain the President.[13]

10. Plumer to Monroe, July 18, 1817, Letter Book, III, Lib. Cong. This is a rough copy of the letter actually sent to Monroe, which is printed in Waldo's *Tour,* 193-94. In his own quotation of this letter, William, Jr., inserted, at the point where the asterisks are placed in the text, this sentence: "Among these, there is none, which, by fair construction, can be extended to the present case." Plumer, Jr., *Life of Plumer,* 467. This is his own felicitous sentence, rather than his father's. He also omitted, without indicating that he had done so, the bombastic phrase which has been enclosed in brackets. This is an interesting example of the free hand with which the son edited the works of his father.

11. President Monroe to Plumer, July 21, 1817, Plumer Papers, N. H. State Lib.

12. *Portsmouth Oracle,* July 26, 1817. The Federalist attitude toward ordering out the militia contrasted so blatantly with their objections to such orders when they were really needed in 1812 that one Republican editor wrote, "Now look ye! gentlemen of *the martial spirit* . . . when you again wish to gratify your natural propensity for *grumbling,* in the name of consistency, choose some other subject than that of *calling out the militia." N. H. Gazette,* July 29, 1817.

13. *Exeter Watchman* and *Albany Gazette* quoted in *Portsmouth Oracle,* Aug. 2, 1817.

The illness which had prevented Plumer's meeting with President Monroe was only one of many such examples of a debility that robbed public office of its charms and rendered "its duties fatiguing." Plumer's physician diagnosed this disease as typhus fever. Plumer thought otherwise: "The error in the *name* has led physicians & patients into an improper & erroneous course of treatment," declared the sick man. Plumer baffled his doctor by following an exactly contrary course of treatment and ultimately recovering. His health, however, remained precarious. Twice again during the year, illness interfered with his official duties, preventing his attendance at a meeting of the Dartmouth University trustees and forcing him to absent himself from a council meeting.[14]

In September 1818, Governor Plumer suffered a severe personal loss in the death of his only daughter. Sarah's tragic life was ended by a painful and lingering malady which the doctors called rheumatism, but which her father decided was the "umbral abscess" (probably a spinal cancer). The young woman was confined to bed for eight months, suffering not only from the agonies of the disease but from the barbarous treatments employed by her physicians. The coolness between her husband's family and her own made the situation all the more difficult, although Plumer visited her frequently and remained, finally, at her bedside until death ended her sufferings. "Her dissolution was so easy that it was some time before it was certain she was dead," wrote the saddened father. "From the time I considered her disease incurable, I have not wished her life protracted, because it was to her an increase of suffering, & I am now reconciled to the event." [15]

Sarah's death was an even more severe blow to William, Jr., who had already suffered an abrupt termination of his civil service career by the liquidation of the federal loan office in 1817.[16] The young man returned to his father's house in Epping, very much at loose ends. His newspaper writing soon brought him into some prominence, and in 1818 he was elected to the state House of Representatives from Epping.[17] Following thus in his father's footsteps, he seemed well embarked upon an equally promising career. His younger brothers, Samuel and George, in the meantime, had opened a store in Epping and were prospering in

14. Plumer, Autobiography, 352, 355, 356, 366.
15. *Ibid.*, 360, 371.
16. Plumer, Jr., later paid a very tender tribute to his dead sister; Plumer, Jr., to Margaret Mead, Apr. 10, 1820, Plumer Papers, N.-Y. Hist. Soc.
17. Entry for Sept. 1817, Plumer, Jr., Memoirs, I, N. H. State Lib.; Plumer to Plumer, Jr., Oct. 7, 1817, Plumer Papers, *ibid.*

business. Jay, the youngest son, inherited his grandfather's love of the soil and showed no disposition to leave the parental homestead.

With the single exception of the prolonged Dartmouth controversy, the issues that faced Governor Plumer during his last two years in office were primarily local in character and significance. Such, for example, was Plumer's experience with the state prison, which had been finished at a cost of $37,000 in 1813 during his first term as governor, but which had not met the sanguine expectations of its proponents.[18] Not only did it fail to turn criminals into law-abiding citizens, but it fell far short of being the self-supporting institution that its champions had promised. By the end of the year 1816, the debt on the prison had nearly doubled and a legislative committee admitted ruefully that it could not be reduced.[19]

The New Hampshire prison was governed by a board of three directors, and was subject to annual inspections by the governor, council, and judges of the Superior Court. After performing this ritual in 1817, the Governor wrote in his journal, "I am convinced the accounts are not perfectly correct, & think it probable the State is defrauded of some of its property." The next year, he called upon the state legislature to find a solution for the problem. Noting that the prison had cost more than $61,000 since its founding, Plumer felt that too much money had been lavished upon the food and clothing of the prisoners; their diet, he said, should "satisfy nature but not provoke appetite." Other suggestions were made for improvement in prison management, "not to criminate the officers," Plumer declared, "but to suggest some of the defects of the present system." [20]

A committee appointed by the legislature to investigate possible economies admitted that it was unable to disentangle the hopelessly muddled accounts of the institution and frankly confessed its inability to prescribe anything more than temporary remedies.[21] This revelation of incompetence led to the resignation of the warden whom Governor Gilman had appointed, and a flood of applications from would-be suc-

18. Henry Robinson, "The New Hampshire State Prison," *Granite Monthly,* 22 (1890), 216-18.

19. *Senate Journal, Nov. Sess., 1816,* 136-40. During the first ten years of operation, the prison cost the state $5,676.67 more than it produced. Farmer and Moore, *Gazetteer,* 44.

20. Plumer, Autobiography, 349; *Journal of the House of Representatives, 1818* (Concord, 1818), 30-31.

21. *House Journal, 1818,* 166-94. Also published separately: *Report of the Committee to Investigate the State Prison* (Concord, 1818).

cessors, one of whom was supported by testimonials from more than seventy of New Hampshire's leading citizens. Governor Plumer had to consider this business during an illness that forced him to alternate short sessions of the council with periods of retirement to his bedroom—circumstances which might have excused poor judgment or a surrender to public pressures. Despite his weakened physical condition, he passed over the popular candidate and appointed Moses C. Pillsbury to the vacant position.[22] With the Governor's backing,[23] and the aid of subsequent legislation, Pillsbury turned the prison deficit into a surplus and made the institution a model of its kind in "management and progress" in the United States. "From my own knowledge of the effects of the penitentiary system in New Hampshire," Plumer wrote in 1820, "I am fully convinced, that it has more effectually suppressed crimes than any other mode of punishment previously established." [24]

Plumer devoted a large part of his message in 1818 to an eloquent condemnation of imprisonment for debt in New Hampshire. Reviewing the history of debt legislation, he pointed out that when his father had migrated to the northern colony, her laws for delinquent debtors were as harsh as those of England, permitting imprisonment until the debt was fully paid or death intervened. The creditor was compensated from the public treasury if a prisoner escaped. Much had been done since then to ameliorate the lot of the poor debtor,[25] but, as Plumer insisted, "the cause of humanity and of natural justice [required] further legislative aid. . . . The time appears to be approaching," he informed the legislature, "when imprisonment for debt will no longer exist in any case, but creditors will consider the industry, fidelity and property of their debt-

22. Plumer, Autobiography, 366.

23. Shortly after Pillsbury's appointment, Plumer wrote letters of inquiry about their penitentiaries and penal codes to the governors of Virginia, Pennsylvania, New York, Massachusetts, and Vermont. Copies of all these are preserved in his Letter Book, VIII, Lib. Cong. For a very interesting reply by the governor of Vermont, see Jonas Galusha to Plumer, July 25, 1818, William Plumer, Letters, IX (1817-21), Plumer Papers, Lib. Cong. (hereafter cited as Letter Book, IX).

24. Orlando Lewis, *The Development of American Prisons and Prison Customs, 1776-1845* (Albany, 1922), 149; Plumer to Cadwallader Colden, Sept. 21, 1820, Letter Book, I, Lib. Cong. This is a remarkable letter, showing a grasp of the problem which goes far to explain why New Hampshire had succeeded with her penitentiary system. Plumer developed a considerable interest in penology, stimulated in part by reading Jeremy Bentham's works and by corresponding with the great utilitarian. Jeremy Bentham to Plumer, n. d., Plumer Papers, N. H. State Lib.; Plumer to Bentham, Oct. 5, 1818, Letter Book, VIII, Lib. Cong.

25. The more important legislation on this subject is to be found in *Laws of New Hampshire*, III, 619, V, 704, VI, 321, VII, 583, 785, VIII, 50, 343, 499.

ors, and not the power of depriving them of liberty, as their only real and sufficient security." The Governor admitted, however, that society was not yet prepared for so clean a sweep. His recommendations, in contrast to his convictions on the subject, were relatively modest. "Let frauds in concealing property subject the offender to punishment," Plumer said in summarizing his position, "but preserve, as far as may be, the personal freedom of the citizen; for every unnecessary restraint on his natural liberty is a degree of tyranny, which no wise Legislature will inflict." [26]

The act "for the Relief of Poor Debtors," which was passed in response to this exhortation, did not completely please Plumer, but "because it was a point gained in favor of the liberty of the person," he signed the bill. After it was amended in 1819 in a way that satisfied his objections, the act left the institution of the debtor's jail in New Hampshire little more than a shadow of its former self.[27] So salutary was this reform in depopulating the county jails and thus inhibiting the production of professional criminals that the inmates in New Hampshire's state prison numbered only half as many as in Vermont's and a third of the number in Connecticut's during the decade of the thirties.[28] After reading Plumer's message to the legislature in 1818, an admirer in the far-away Genesee country wrote to compliment him "for being the file-leader, who first called the public mind to these subjects." [29] This was giving Plumer more credit than he deserved, but it is not improbable that, had he remained longer in public life, Plumer would have become an acknowledged leader among the reformers of criminal law.

During the last years of his political life, the long fight for religious

---

26. *House Journal, 1818,* 25.

27. Plumer, Autobiography, 367; *Laws of New Hampshire,* VIII, 870. In New Hampshire, as elsewhere in the nation, it had still been possible in Plumer's earlier days for such distinguished men as Nathaniel Peabody and Russell Freeman to end their lives in a debtor's prison, but it had also been true that the great majority of prisoners held in the filthy county jails were hapless small debtors whose incarceration certainly did society no good. See Tracy Carlton, "Abolition of Imprisonment for Debt in the United States," *Yale Review,* 18 (1909), 340. The Prison Discipline Society of Boston estimated in 1829 that seven-tenths of all imprisoned debtors owed less than $20. See Edwin Randall, "Imprisonment for Debt in America: Fact and Fiction," *Miss. Valley Hist. Rev.,* 39 (1952), 89-102, for a criticism of the figures given in Carlton and the Society's report, in the light of the many laws passed for the amelioration of debt imprisonment before 1830. However, Randall overlooks the fact that there were many loopholes in these laws; there are too many tragic cases of debt imprisonment on record to call it a fiction.

28. Lewis, *American Prisons,* 51.

29. Jesse Hawley to Plumer, June 16, 1818, Letter Book, IX, Lib. Cong.

freedom in New Hampshire, in which Plumer had played a prominent part, drew to a close. The final stages were marked by a series of comedies and paradoxes. Plumer himself, a deist presiding over a community of Calvinists and "enthusiasts," was the principal paradox. After struggling for some time to reconcile what he was expected to say in a proclamation for a public fast with what he really believed, the Governor on one occasion burst into a vigorous protest against the religious intolerance that prevented a man from communicating "his thots to the public if he differs from them, without rendering himself obnoxious." Yet, on the whole, he was satisfied with the results possible to attain in this art by the use of "general & liberal terms" and the total omission of "fanaticism" and "sectarianism." He also indulged his customary eccentricity by setting the date for New Hampshire's principal holiday, Thanksgiving, on December 25 in 1817, and December 31 in 1818. The "propriety in closing a healthy prosperous year in festivity & mirth" was the logic that excused his tampering with the calendar.[30] There was the usual grumbling among the Congregationalists at this arbitrary interference with what some regarded as an ordinance of God, but one Federalist newspaper thought there was "a peculiar propriety" in combining Christmas and Thanksgiving, while Isaac Hill loyally described Plumer's proclamation of 1818 as "an admirable specimen of chaste, forcible and comprehensive language."[31]

In the first message of his second administration, in June 1816, Governor Plumer had insisted that it was the duty of the legislature to grant acts of incorporation to any religious association that requested them. "The correctness of their tenets," he said, "is a subject that lies between God and their own consciences, and is one that no human tribunal has any right to decide. While therefore it becomes every man scrupulously to examine the foundations of his own belief, he cannot guard with too much jealousy against the encroachments of the civil power on his religious liberties." Plumer thus returned, after a few political wanderings, to the vigorous religious liberalism of his youth. The legislature not only accepted Plumer's reasoning on religious incorporations but it took a significant step toward the ultimate secularization of New Hampshire with the passage of a bill to tax the property of ministers of "every denomination" in the same manner as other people were taxed. Passed in the House, eighty-two to seventy-three,

30. Plumer, Autobiography, 358, 371.
31. *N. H. Sentinel* (Keene), quoted in *N. H. Patriot* (Concord), Nov. 11, 1817; *ibid.*, Nov. 10, 1818.

and signed without comment by Governor Plumer, this measure was condemned in Boston and applauded as far away as Rochester, New York.[32]

New Hampshire's famous Toleration Act, in which she finally joined all her sister states except Massachusetts in affirming the American principle of complete separation between church and state, was finally passed in June 1819, only a few days after Plumer had retired from political life. For strategic reasons, he had been content to remain in the background of this campaign. His sentiments, however, "as to the fitness and propriety of leaving every individual full and entire liberty of choosing his own religion, & to give or withhold his property, as he pleases, for its support," [33] had been given wide publicity at a time when the campaign against the established church was reaching its final stages. After the Toleration Act passed, Plumer wrote to Hill: "The law upon religious freedom meets my entire approbation; it reflects honor upon each branch of the legislature. It is a monument proclaiming the rights of man & the progress of liberal sentiments. I wish some gentleman of talents and information would write & publish a series of numbers, not simply vindicating that law, but stating & explaining the natural & unalienable rights of conscience & freedom of opinion." [34] He would do it himself, Plumer said, if he were not so engrossed "by other subjects & *other times,* that I cannot devote a single day to the consideration of it." He was spared the necessity. The Toleration Act proved to be so congenial to the people of New Hampshire that its vindication was not required.

Although Plumer's opposition to a state church included no particular sympathy for the sectarians, it was natural that many of his allies came from the ranks of extreme zealots. Among them were those strange communists, the Shakers, whose paradoxical behavior continued to fascinate Plumer as it had during his youth.[35] The Shakers paid their taxes cheerfully, supported their own poor, and stayed out of politics, but their conscientious objection to military service brought them into con-

32. *Senate Journal, June Sess., 1816,* 24-25; *Laws of New Hampshire,* VIII, 582; *House Journal, Nov. Sess., 1816,* 209.
33. Plumer to Daniel Coolidge, Jan. 27, 1818, Letter Book, IX, Lib. Cong.; *N. H. Patriot* (Concord), Feb. 3, 1818.
34. Plumer to Isaac Hill, Aug. 6, 1819, Letter Book, IX, Lib. Cong.
35. As late as the summer of 1816, Plumer visited Enfield, one of the three Shaker communities in New Hampshire, and was struck by their neatness, cleanliness, and hospitality, but noted also that "this sect has more despotism than there is in the army & navy. It's foundation is superstition; & the civil authority has not the means of correcting the evil." Plumer, Autobiography, 331.

flict with the civil authority. The militia laws of both state and nation had generally recognized the right of religious pacifists to exemption from military duty, but attempts were made in every legislature during Plumer's administration to tax them in lieu of military service. In the face of this threat, the Shakers appealed to the known liberalism of the Governor for assistance.[36] Plumer assured them that he opposed the principle of the equivalent tax and advised that they memorialize the legislature against the measure, which they did. It was finally abandoned, and Governor Plumer was spared the necessity of a veto which he would undoubtedly have placed upon the bill.

Another element of Shaker practice that eventually created a problem for Plumer was their method of recruiting. Since the Shaker religion prohibited normal family relationships, no one was ever born a Shaker. The sect would have died in its infancy had not a vigorous campaign of proselyting brought fresh blood, usually in the form of family groups, into the Shaker villages. If either partner of a Shaker marriage tired of the abnormal situation, as was bound frequently to be the case, the dissatisfied mate was inevitably expelled from the community while the children remained behind. Governor Plumer occasionally received complaints that children were being held in a Shaker community by one parent against the wishes of the other.[37]

This problem was brought forcibly to the attention of the New Hampshire legislature in 1817 by one Mary Dyer, a woman "not wanting in talents, whatever might have been the sincerity of her motives," whose case became a *cause célèbre* in New England's annals. With her husband Joseph and children, she had joined the Shaker community at Enfield; then, falling out with the elders, she had left community and family behind. Applying to the legislature for custody of her children, she appeared in person to support her cause with such ready wit and sharp rejoinder that she soon excited great public sympathy. After hearing Mary and her "sensible" but less spirited husband testify in person, the legislature passed an ambiguous bill, giving the Superior Court power to grant a divorce, settle alimony, and determine the custody of children in cases where one partner of a marriage joined a Shaker community and remained with it for six months.[38] On the evening before the last

36. *House Journal, Nov. Sess., 1816,* 172; *House Journal, 1818,* 82. See Daniel Coolidge to Plumer, Feb. 9, 1818, Letter Book, IX, Lib. Cong.

37. Jesse Hawley to Plumer, June 16, 1818, *ibid.*

38. *N. H. Gazette* (Portsmouth), July 8, 1817; Plumer, Autobiography, 352; *Journal of the House of Representatives, June Session, 1817* (Concord, 1817), 186.

day of the session, this measure was presented to Governor Plumer for his signature.

Plumer detested Shaker "despotism," and he could hardly help feeling a natural sympathy for Mrs. Dyer and others in her position. But he felt that the legislature had acted too hastily in allowing dissolution of the marriage bonds for a religious reason when it was permitted for very few others.[39] Harried by the rush of last minute business and convinced that the question required more study than he could then give it, Plumer allowed the bill to die by a pocket veto. Mary Dyer was back again in 1818, more determined and more persuasive than ever, as William Plumer, Jr., now a legislator exposed to her eloquence, could testify.[40] Plumer, Sr., meanwhile, had prepared himself for a possible divorce bill by studying similar legislation in other states, and had concluded to use his veto, if necessary.[41] The legislature agreed with him, however, that this singling out of the Shakers for invidious attention would do more harm than good. "The sect," Plumer wrote, "would consider all laws having a particular reference to them as a species of persecution ... [which] seldom fails to build up the sect agt. which it is directed. ... Nothing is more fatal to enthusiasm than toleration and neglect; it damps its ardor and cools its frantic spirit." [42]

The legislators of 1818, accustomed as they were to unorthodox views in their Governor, were nevertheless startled at one proposition that he laid before them. This was an offer from the world-renowned scholar and philosopher, Jeremy Bentham, to draw up "a code of statutory laws ... both civil and criminal to supercede the *unwritten law*" for any state or nation that wished to avail itself of his gratuitous services. This offer, which had already been declined by President Madison and Czar Alexander, was transmitted by John Quincy Adams to the governors of all the states; Governor Plumer was the only one who responded to it.[43] He immediately wrote Bentham a long letter in which he freely criticized the "numerous errors and gross absurdities" of the common

---

39. New Hampshire law, for example, did not allow divorce upon the grounds of drunkenness, conviction for crime, or incompatibility.

40. Plumer, Autobiography, 352-53; Plumer, Jr., *Life of Plumer,* 465.

41. Plumer asked the governor of New York for a copy of the objections made by his Council of Revision to a bill of divorcement granted to Mrs. Eunice Chapman, whose situation was virtually identical with that of Mrs. Dyer. Plumer to DeWitt Clinton, May 18, 1818, Letter Book, VIII, Lib. Cong.

42. Plumer to Jesse Hawley, July 11, 1818, Letter Book, IX, *ibid.*

43. John Quincy Adams to Plumer, Oct. 27, 1817, Plumer Papers, N. H. State Lib. Madison wrote, "Either I overrate or he underrates the task he wishes to undertake." Madison to Adams, Dec. 23, 1817, Madison Papers, LXV, Lib. Cong.

law and expressed hearty approval of Bentham's plan. It would encounter a "host of prejudices," he predicted, and the opposition "of a body of lawyers, many of whom here, as in all other countries, dread reform, fearing it would diminish their individual profits." Nevertheless, he promised to do everything in his power to insure a thorough investigation of the project.[44]

Plumer's intention received too good a press. Flattered by this solitary display of interest in his plan, Bentham injudiciously published the New Hampshire governor's letter in England, and it was soon copied in the American newspapers. The exacerbating effects of Plumer's comments upon the minds of professional patriots, New Hampshire lawyers, and self-styled "practical men" is easily imagined.[45] William, Jr., tried to counteract the unfavorable publicity by persuading Hill to re-publish some of Bentham's essays in the *Patriot,* but the soil for any favorable growth of consideration had become too acid.[46] Governor Plumer told his legislature that the "great importance of the object, and the peculiar talents of the author, render the subject worthy of your mature consideration," but they refused to give it. According to the younger Plumer, who worked hard to obtain a fair hearing for the project, his fellow committee members "united in declaring [it] visionary, injudicious, impracticable, & above all unworthy of attention, as proceeding from a foreigner, ignorant of our wants & unacquainted with our situation." Consideration of the subject was postponed by the House until the session of 1819 and never taken up again.[47]

On the whole, Plumer's last two years in office were pleasant and quiet. After the 1817 session of the legislature, he remarked upon the

44. Plumer to Jeremy Bentham, Oct. 2, 1817, Letter Book, IX, *ibid.*

45. *Concord Gazette,* June 16, 1818, copying item from the *Salem Gazette; N. H. Patriot* (Concord), commenting on article in *Daily Advertiser* (Boston), June 21, 1818. The tone in the Federalist press was uniformly sarcastic, but the best job of it was done by the *Salem Gazette,* under the title "New Hampshire Millenium," which mockingly saluted Governor Plumer for wishing to make his state "a Pattern Form for experiments in Legislation." Quoted in *Concord Gazette,* June 16, 1818.

46. *N. H. Patriot,* June 9, 21, 1818. Even so tolerant a man as Jeremiah Mason, facing the prospect of re-learning all his law, wrote that Bentham's "Utopian plans" might "suit metaphysicians, but would make sad work with everybody else." Jeremiah Mason to Rufus King, May 15, 1818, printed in Hillard, *Mason,* 205-6.

47. *House Journal, 1818,* 30; Plumer, Jr., to Jeremy Bentham, Oct. 2, 1818, Plumer, Jr., Letter Book, III, N. H. State Lib. The only result of this extraordinary international misadventure was an epistolary friendship between the English utilitarian and the New Hampshire Plumers which persisted for several years. Jeremy Bentham to William Plumer, Jr., n.d., 1819, Plumer to Plumer, Jr., Jan. 31, 1820, Plumer Papers, N. H. State Lib.; Plumer, Jr., *Life of Plumer,* 475-76.

good humor in which it had conducted business and dispersed: "there has been little of the bitterness of party, & but few occasions to excite its malignant spirit." [48] But one big exception remained to plague his entire administration and to leave the taste of defeat with him when he retired. This was the long battle over Dartmouth University.

At the end of the year 1816, it had seemed that the battle would soon be won. Armed with the new powers granted to him by the amended charter act, Governor Plumer had called a meeting of the university trustees for February 4 in Concord. This time, the necessary nine men appeared to make a quorum, and they proceeded immediately to business. Some members of the board wanted the summary dismissal of all college officers, but Plumer insisted that charges be specified and an opportunity for defense be granted. The board, accordingly, drew up letters requiring the college officers and six of the trustees to appear at a later meeting and show cause, if any, why they should not be removed from office for flagrant neglect of their duties. Encouraged by this decisive move against his enemies, John Wheelock presented the university with deeds to about $12,000 worth of property and a release of his financial claims against the college. It seemed, finally, that Dartmouth University was about to become something more than a disembodied, legislative apparition. [49]

It is improbable that Plumer expected to meet a penitent Octagon when he returned to Concord two weeks later, but nothing at all was heard from the trustees. The professors, however, had written a polite letter, declining their invitations to appear. [50] The university trustees, ten strong this time, waited until the afternoon and then voted unanimously to sever the unyielding officials from all connection with the university. [51] This action marked the final break between the university and the college parties; it was a declaration of war. [52]

The restoration of John Wheelock to the titular headship of the institution he had so long served was the next order of business. His triumph proved to be short-lived; within six weeks he was dead. In the

---

48. Plumer, Autobiography, 353.

49. Plumer to Francis Brown, Dec. 20, 1816, Dartmouth MSS., 816670, Dartmouth College; Plumer, Autobiography, 345-46. Plumer to Plumer, Jr., Feb. 11, 1817, Plumer Papers, N. H. State Lib. This last letter was written on the back of a printed report of the meeting.

50. Brown *et al.,* to Plumer, Repository, IX, 29-31, *ibid.*

51. Plumer acted on legal advice from Judge Richardson. Plumer, Jr., to Plumer, Jan. 18, 1817, Plumer Papers, *ibid.*

52. Plumer, Autobiography, 346-47.

meantime, the actual duties of the presidency had been conferred by the trustees upon his son-in-law, William Allen.[53] A professor of mathematics was also appointed, and committees were named to prepare a public address upon the state of the university, and to devise ways and means of raising funds for its support. Plumer was elected to both of these groups, but declined serving with the first. How much he may have contributed to the second is not altogether clear. It was to become an arduous assignment.[54]

From this point on, Governor Plumer's connection with the Dartmouth imbroglio was almost entirely at second hand. He attended board meetings held in Concord but no longer assumed any responsibility for leading their deliberations. Illness prevented his presence at some of the most important sessions, and, in fact, he never again made the long journey through the woods to Hanover.[55] Nevertheless, the problem of filling the two university boards with well-qualified men consumed much of Plumer's time and patience. During the brief life span of the institution, he made forty-six appointments, seventeen to the board of trustees and twenty-nine to the board of overseers. The Federalist councilors interposed no serious obstacles—the Governor's chief difficulties came from the appointees themselves.

Plumer's high hopes for a board of overseers with national prestige and democratic zeal were never to be realized; such men as Justice Story, Henry Gray, Benjamin Crowninshield, and Levi Lincoln were either too cautious or too indifferent to attend a meeting of the board. The overseers never made a quorum, and even the trustees had difficulty, after February 1817, in maintaining any stability of membership. In the end, Plumer found himself forced to fill this board with young men, able enough in their own right, but hardly known beyond the borders of New Hampshire. One of his best appointments was that of Salma Hale, a future historian but then a young Republican congressman from Keene, who hesitated to accept the trusteeship because he himself had no college degree. This was a qualification, however, that Plumer considered unnecessary. He assured Hale that, although neither

53. Minutes of the Trustees of Dartmouth University, Dartmouth MSS., 817854, Dartmouth College. Allen was a minister in Pittsfield, Mass. In a letter to Plumer, Jan. 13, 1817, Plumer Papers, N. H. State Lib., he had asked that his father-in-law be reinstated, and hinted politely at his own availability.

54. Plumer to William H. Woodward, Mar. 21, 1817, Letter Book, III, Lib. Cong.

55. Plumer to William Allen, Aug. 18, 1817, Gratz Coll., Pa. Hist. Soc.; Proceedings of the Trustees of Dartmouth University, June 6, 1818, Dartmouth MSS., 818356, Dartmouth College.

of them had been to college, they both had more sense than most "doctors of laws." [56] Hale accepted this reasoning and served the university cause faithfully, in Washington as well as in New Hampshire.

Whether he wished to be or not, Plumer was deeply involved in the legal struggle between Dartmouth College and Dartmouth University. A fairly complete history of the affair could be written from his correspondence alone, for everyone on the university side reported to him. On February 11, for example, only four days after the university trustees had finished their first legal meeting, William Woodward wrote in considerable agitation to Plumer that a writ of trover had been served upon him for the return of Dartmouth College properties to the value of $50,000. Although Judge Woodward suffered the peculiar embarrassment of having the suit begun in his own court, he had been notified that the trustees intended to carry it to the Superior Court immediately, and Woodward anxiously begged the Governor to inform his judicial appointees of the impending suit before it reached them.[57]

Governor Plumer exhorted Woodward to stand firm, trusting that "if we do our duty, we shall eventually succeed, & render the institution useful, respectable, & honorable to the State & to our country." [58] During the interval between February and May, Woodward became seriously ill, and besieged Plumer with urgent requests for advice and support. He particularly solicited the Governor's aid in the engagement of counsel, since the Federalist lawyers would rally to the college cause, and it would be difficult to match their cunning. Protesting that his long absence from the courts rendered him ill-suited to advise, Plumer proved his point by suggesting several poorly qualified persons, but he heartily endorsed Woodward's employment of George Sullivan and Ichabod Bartlett.[59] The latter, a relative newcomer to the New Hampshire courts and something of a protégé of Plumer's, gave the best

56. Salma Hale to Plumer, Jan. 3, 1817, Plumer to Hale, Jan. 8, 1817, Plumer Papers, N. H. State Lib.

57. William Woodward to Plumer, Feb. 11, 1817, *ibid.*

58. Plumer to Woodward, Mar. 21, 1817, Letter Book, III, Lib. Cong.

59. Plumer's son, William, Jr., then living in Portsmouth, was enlisted in the quest for able Republican lawyers but they were hard to find. The search extended into Massachusetts where Timothy Bigelow and Judge Dana were suggested and Nicholas Emery, Prentice Mellen, and John Holmes, all from Maine, were mentioned. Had the suit been non-political, Woodward might have realized his high hopes of engaging Jeremiah Mason for the defense, but Plumer realistically expected to find the Federalist giant on the other side, as the event proved. See Woodward to Plumer, Mar. 29, Apr. 5, 1817, Plumer to Woodward, Apr. 5, 1817, Plumer, Jr., to Plumer, Apr. 26, 1817, Plumer to Plumer, Jr., Apr. 28, 1817, Plumer Papers, N. H. State Lib.

argument for the university cause that it received anywhere, not exclud-ing Washington. Plumer had bound both men closely to the interests of the university by making Sullivan an overseer and Bartlett a trustee.[60]

Bartlett and Sullivan, however, were no match for the formidable team of college attorneys, Jeremiah Mason, Jeremiah Smith, and Daniel Webster.[61] These Federalist stalwarts did not expect to win their case in New Hampshire. "It would be a queer thing if Gov. P's Court should refuse to execute his Laws," wrote Webster.[62] This was a logical con-clusion, and Plumer's behavior did something to justify it. The Gov-ernor's political and personal intimacy with his own appointees enabled him to serve the cause of the university behind the scenes. Transmitting his questions through letters to his son in Portsmouth, he frequently sought legal advice from Judge Richardson on university questions and governed his conduct accordingly.[63] Such unconventional procedure hardly came within the prerogative granted to the executive branch of the government by the state constitution, but it seemed to be accepted practice; at any rate, the behavior of men on the other side such as Webster and Story was equally unconventional.[64] There is no evidence, however, that Plumer attempted to influence the opinions of the judges. Indeed, he would not have thought it necessary to do so.

Governor Plumer was not present in the Superior Court room when the Dartmouth College case was first argued and Webster favored the court with a rehearsal of the impassioned peroration he later used to such good effect at Washington.[65] The scene was reported to the Gov-ernor by young Judge Woodbury, who declared acidly, "We have

60. Timothy Farrar, *Report of the Dartmouth College Case* (Portsmouth, 1819), 116-206. Four of the eight men associated with the Dartmouth College Case as counsel or judges in the state courts were Dartmouth alumni. Only one of these, Webster, took the college side; Bell, Woodbury, and Bartlett favored the proposed reform of their alma mater.

61. Webster had accepted what might have been considered a retaining fee from Wheelock before he was engaged by the trustees. For details on this matter which is sidestepped by many Webster biographers, see Shirley, *Dartmouth College Causes,* 88-92. Webster's sentiment for his alma mater did not conflict with self-interest; his fee for arguing the case in Washington was $1,000. Webster to Francis Brown, Nov. 15, 1817, Dartmouth MSS., 817615.3, Dartmouth College.

62. Webster to Jeremiah Mason, June 28, 1817, Webster Papers, I, N. H. Hist. Soc.

63. Plumer to Plumer, Jr., Jan. 14, Sept. 30, 1817, Plumer, Jr., to Plumer, Jan. 18, 1817, Plumer Papers, N. H. State Lib.

64. For example, Webster used Chancellor Kent to attempt to influence Story. Shir-ley, *Dartmouth College Causes,* 304.

65. *Farmer's Cabinet* (Amherst), Sept. 27, 1817; *N. H. Patriot* (Concord), Oct. 7, 1817. Hill said that Webster made a very pathetic plea to the judges "as *alumni* of the College."

had ... more language than *light*." Somewhat later, Plumer learned indirectly from the chief justice himself that the judges had decided unanimously against the trustees, and replied that he had "never had any doubts on the subject." Even Chief Justice Richardson's opponents admitted that his opinion in favor of Dartmouth University was "able, ingenious and plausible," [66] while the university adherents hailed it with joy. "This," wrote Elijah Parish to Plumer, "seems to be the propitious moment for the friends of the University to come forward in the dignity of their power. It is only for you, my dear Sir, to say 'The University shall rise,' & it will rise with new splendor. The historian will date its brilliant era from the *administration of Gov. Pr.*" [67]

The rising was not so easy, however, and the historian must withhold his guerdons. While the university cause was winning in the courts, it was making little headway in Hanover, where the majority of the Dartmouth student body followed its old faculty into exile. At the end of his first year with the university, President Allen complied with a provision of the 1816 law by sending his annual report to Governor Plumer. It was a discouraging document. The student body numbered only sixteen, while the university's debts amounted to $3,000 and its annual income to $1,000. The only remedy for this situation, he believed, was a generous grant-in-aid from the state legislature.[68] Governor Plumer ignored this suggestion, but William, Jr., worked diligently in committee and on the floor for the university cause in 1818 and succeeded in obtaining a state loan of $4,000.[69] This money kept the university alive for a few more months but hardly "routed" the "Octagon party," as one enthusiastic Republican mistakenly asserted.

In spite of these discouragements, Plumer persisted, at least outwardly, in "a sanguine hope ... that we shall, if we are prudent & persevering, eventually render the institution prosperous, & a blessing to the nation." He exhorted Woodward to maintain a firm but moderate stand, equally avoiding "half-way, trimming, temporizing measures, & ... rashness & precipitation." [70] Plumer felt, however, that he was

66. Levi Woodbury to Plumer, Sept. 19, 1817, Plumer, Jr., to Plumer, Oct. 4, 1817, Plumer to Plumer, Jr., Oct. 7, 1817, Plumer Papers, N. H. State Lib. Richardson's opinion is published in *New Hampshire Reports*, I (Exeter, 1819), 113-36. The admissions were made by the *Portsmouth Oracle*, Nov. 15, 1817.
67. Elijah Parish to Plumer, Nov. 14, 1817, Letter Book, IX, Lib. Cong.
68. Woodward to Plumer, Mar. 8, 13, 1817, Plumer Papers, N. H. State Lib.; Allen to Plumer, July 7, 1817, Letter Book, IX, Lib. Cong.
69. *House Journal, 1818,* 97, 152.
70. Plumer to Woodward, Jan. 1817, to Thomas Searle, Jan. 13, 1817, Letter Book, III, Lib. Cong.

unable to do much more than render advice, in spite of the curious fact that both friend and foe persisted in regarding him as the "fountain head" of authority and the principal moving force behind the university.[71] "You greatly overrate my means of promoting the cause," he assured Dr. Parish, but then added that "such as they are, and as far as my feeble health and leisure will permit, I will devote them to her prosperity." [72]

Plumer had frequently stated his opinion that the college trustees had no legal ground upon which to carry their case to the United States courts. However, once the case had been appealed, he expressed no regret, except for the delay and expense involved in arriving at a final judgment. "I am confident," he wrote, that "the decision will be in affirmance of the judgment of our own court, & settle the question for other States as well as this." [73] The Supreme Court's decision, pronounced more than a year later, accomplished exactly the opposite result. Plumer kept in close touch, during this interval, with events in Washington, especially through Salma Hale, who took a jaundiced view of Daniel Webster's sentimental speeches.[74] There was little, however, that the Governor in New Hampshire could do to help the cause of the university in Washington except to offer long-distance encouragement.[75] When this failed, Plumer was indignant and inclined to translate his disagreement with the court's opinions into criticism of the court's ability. "In point of talents & legal science," he declared, "they are inferior to some of our State courts. They have evinced a strong disposition to extend their jurisdiction beyond what I think either the constitution or law contemplated." Under the stress of his mortification,

71. As one example, Dr. Benjamin Waterhouse of Harvard asked Plumer to obtain a tutoring post at Dartmouth for his son. Plumer to Waterhouse, Apr. 29, 1817, *ibid.*

72. Plumer to Parish, Nov. 29, 1817, Letter Book, IX, Lib. Cong.

73. Plumer to Plumer, Jr., Mar. 4, 1817, to Salma Hale, Jan. 15, 1818, Plumer Papers, N. H. State Lib.; Plumer to Woodward, Oct. 11, 1817, Letter Book, VIII, Lib. Cong.

74. Hale's accounts of the argument are very interesting, especially when compared with the traditional Choate narrative. He admitted that "Mr. Webster was as usuall able—very able—but also very disingenuous." Hale to Plumer, Mar. 12, 1818, Letter Book, IX, *ibid.* Hale also believed, however, that "Mr. Wirt grasped the cause with the mind of a giant, and made Webster lower his crest and sit uneasy." Hale to Plumer, Jr., Mar. 24 (misdated Dec. 24), 1818, Plumer Papers, N. H. State Lib. "From this," Hale commented, "you will percieve how much the speakers in our highest courts of law are indulged in their flights."

75. Hale to Plumer, Jan. 20, 1818, Plumer to Clement Storer, Feb. 23, 1818, Letter Book, IX, Lib. Cong.; Plumer to Hale, Feb. 5, 1818, Plumer Papers, N. H. State Lib.

Plumer even lost some of his faith in an independent judiciary. "This power must be restrained," he wrote, "or the States will in process of time be reduced to corporations and be restricted to making by-laws, and the legality of those laws subject to the decision of that tribunal." [76]

Shortly after Marshall's decision was announced, Governor Plumer received an agitated letter from President Allen announcing that he had been deprived by force of most of the university buildings, and had found it necessary to suspend instruction, although he still retained the key to a library that he could no longer use. Plumer advised him to keep the keys until the question was finally settled by the court that had "assumed jurisdiction." Notwithstanding what had occurred in Washington, he was "still of the opinion that the laws of N. H. of 1816 are strictly and literally constitutional; and I am inclined to think the court will ultimately be obliged so to decide." [77] A month later, Amos Brewster wrote to announce "the funeral of the University," but Plumer still insisted that the Supreme Court's decision would be reversed in the following winter.[78] This expression of unfounded optimism, soon to be crushed forever by Story's action in the "cognate cases," was the firm and final conviction of Plumer on the Dartmouth question.[79]

Whether John Marshall or William Plumer was right about the constitutionality of the acts of 1816 is now a highly debatable but largely academic question.[80] The immediate consequences of Marshall's decision, however, were difficult for both sides. It was many years before Dartmouth College recovered the prestige it had lost or gave any indica-

76. Plumer to Hale, Feb. 13, Apr. 8, 1819, *ibid.*
77. Allen to Plumer, Mar. 13, 1819, Plumer to Allen, Mar. 17, 1819, Letter Book, IX, Lib. Cong.
78. Amos Brewster to Plumer, Apr. 18, 1819, *ibid.;* Plumer to Brewster, Apr. 21, 1819, Dartmouth MSS., 819271, Dartmouth College.
79. These "cognate cases," on the ground of diversity of citizenship, were federal cases, bypassing the state courts completely. They could therefore be argued on a much broader basis than upon the single question of a violation of the Federal Constitution which had brought *Trustees* v. *Woodward* to the Supreme Court on appeal. Webster was originally eager to have these suits come to Washington, for he had little faith in the obligation of contract clause as the salvation of the college. After he had won his case on the original suit, however, he was determined not to argue these cases, and received Story's full cooperation. See Webster to Jeremiah Smith, Dec. 8, 1817, McIntyre, ed., *Webster's Writings,* XVII, 267-68; and Charles Marsh to Francis Brown, May 18, 1818, quoted in Frederick Chase and J. K. Lord, *A History of Dartmouth College* (Hanover, 1913), I, 154. The author is indebted to Professor Maurice Baxter of Indiana University for much helpful information on these "cognate cases."
80. Shirley, *Dartmouth College Causes,* 304; Plumer to Woodward, Mar. 21, 1817, Letter Book, III, Lib. Cong.

tion of becoming the flourishing institution it is today.[81] On the other hand, such a blow had been dealt the principle of public support for higher education in New Hampshire that Plumer was in his grave for decades before it achieved substance again.[82]

The best evidence, perhaps, that the triumph of the college cause was in harmony with the times—that New Hampshire was not yet ready for so radical a departure as public control of higher education—lies in Plumer's own reaction to the experiment. He had entered the struggle with high hopes, not merely that the clique in control of the college might be ousted, but that a genuine educational reform might be set in motion. He had given energetic leadership to the new movement and had ultimately succeeded in seeing the university established as a going concern, with a campus, a faculty, and at least the nucleus of a student body. At each step, however, Plumer had been forced to sacrifice a part of his master plan to the schemes of other men. He had lost a major engagement when the new board of trustees was made self-perpetuating, and he had struggled against the commission, by his own appointed trustees, of the same errors that had rendered the college unsatisfactory. He had blocked efforts to staff the university entirely with the relatives and family connections of John Wheelock, to create professorships of theology and ethics rather than of history and government, to open the chapel again to public worship and to pay President Allen for preaching in it. Eventually, Plumer lost his enthusiasm for this continuous battle. "Should the university of which we are trustees," he wrote to Salma Hale, "succeed in her controversies at law I shall expect but little from her. She appears to be following the old tradition and seems more anxious to please the priesthood than to pursue a manly and expedient course to fit men for the business and duties of this world."[83]

---

81. See Richardson, *Dartmouth College,* I, 345-46, for an eloquent argument in praise of Marshall's decision and Webster's services. Only two years after the decision, however, the college trustees wanted to apply again to the state legislature for financial aid and were only prevented from doing so by Webster, who wrote that "if the College must die, it is better it should die a natural death." Shirley, *Dartmouth College Causes,* 11-13.

82. In 1821, the state legislature established a literary fund, raised by a tax on bank stock, which was to be applied toward endowing a state college. The Dartmouth College trustees eyed this money hungrily, but it was actually spent on elementary schools. See Samuel Bartlett, "History of Education in New Hampshire," in Davis, ed., *New England States,* III, 1610, 1614.

83. Plumer, Autobiography, 347; Plumer to Hale, Dec. 28, 1818, Letter Book, IX, Lib. Cong.

Two years after Dartmouth University had perished and Plumer had retired, he devoted four of his "Cincinnatus" essays to an elucidation of his ideas on higher education. They go far to explain why he was sincerely convinced that Dartmouth College was on the wrong road and what he would have done to re-direct it. All the colleges of the time (1821), he complained, were subject to the clergy and devoted to denominationalism. As seminaries for the "priests," who were certainly in need of enlightenment, he had no objection to such colleges, but he considered them totally unfit for the training of young gentlemen in civil life. In their rigidly prescribed courses, their emphasis on grammar rather than literature, and their indifference to contemporary developments in science, the colleges seemed more adapted to medieval than to nineteenth-century conditions. When the colleges apply to the people or the legislatures for aid, wrote Plumer bitterly, they are public institutions, but when the legislature enacts laws for their better regulation, they are private corporations, exempt from interference or control. They required extensive reform to make them what they ought to be— "civil, public institutions governed by men of literature and science, teaching living languages, modern philosophy & useful arts." [84]

Plumer's definition of an education was derived from Locke and Milton: it should fit a man to perform skillfully all the tasks of life. Where, asked Plumer, was there a college in America that taught agriculture, commerce, manufactures, or mechanics? "What school have we to form statesmen, where they can learn politics & principles of government?" The present colleges, he concluded, with their devotion to logic, ontology, pneumatology, and a debased system of moral philosophy, deserved no public support. Let the rich and idle, who desired them as they were, maintain them. In carrying out its constitutional duty to encourage education, Plumer observed that the legislature of New Hampshire had provided for public common schools but not for the higher branches of learning. It had scattered gifts among the academies and Dartmouth College, which the Supreme Court had now declared to be *private* institutions. It was incumbent upon the state government, therefore, to turn from these fruitless enterprises and establish a system of state education. This would involve the creation in each county of

---

84. "Cincinnatus," Nos. 34-35, Plumer, Essays, II, 251-57, Lib. Cong., publ. in *N. H. Patriot* (Concord), Apr. 16, 23, 1821. In a letter to Salma Hale, July 31, 1817, Plumer Papers, N. H. State Lib., Plumer made out a strong case for the study of German. "We have few German scholars, & yet perhaps within the last thirty years Germany has produced more literary characters, & made greater progress in literature than any other nation."

an academy, in which "nothing but what is useful to improve the mind be taught," and the ultimate endowment of a state college or university "on the same principles" with a curriculum of "useful arts, science, and the higher branches of literature." This was Plumer's ultimate answer to the Dartmouth College decision, but he was seventy years ahead of his time. Not until the University of New Hampshire was established at Durham in 1893 did such an institution as William Plumer had hoped to create come into being on New Hampshire soil.[85]

85. Donald C. Babcock *et al., History of the University of New Hampshire* (Durham, 1941), chap. 4.

CHAPTER XVI

Elder Statesman

> "It has been my lot on several subjects to act alone, & in others with a lean minority.... A respect to the public as well as to myself, has induced me to form my own opinion & act in conformity to it." [1]

ON the last day of May 1818, ten weeks after he had been elected to his fourth term as governor, and a week before he was to take the affirmation of office, William Plumer wrote in his diary that he would decline re-election to a fifth term. "The state of my health, my desire for books, study, & writing, & my love of retirement render it necessary," he wrote of this decision. "We are now in peace & our finances are flourishing or I should not feel at liberty to decline." [2] He added that for months his sons had been advising him to take this step.

William Plumer, Jr., an even more persistent diarist than his father, confirmed these facts in his own journal, but added one that the elder Plumer failed to mention—that although he had decided to decline the office of governor he would "accept that of Senator should it be offered him." William, Jr., declared that it was "in hopes that his health might be improved, as it was before, by a southern climate, that he was induced to think again of a seat in the Senate of the United States." [3]

Plumer announced to his council at its first session after the legislature assembled that he was serving his last term as governor. Although the councilors were inclined to doubt his sincerity, he gave convincing evidence of it ten days later when he declined the renomination offered by the unanimous vote of the Republican caucus. There were undoubtedly ambitious politicians within the Republican party who heard the news of Plumer's decision with great satisfaction, having regarded

1. Plumer, Autobiography, 382.
2. *Ibid.*, 362; cf. Plumer, Jr., *Life of Plumer*, 476.
3. Entries for May 30, June 30, 1818, William Plumer, Jr., Journal, III (1816-21), N. H. State Lib.

him for some time as a serious obstacle to their advancement. Other party leaders, however, saw his retirement as the signal for a disastrous internecine feud, while Dartmouth University partisans felt "an obstinate reluctance to the change." They begged him, as he had once begged Langdon, to retain leadership for at least another year. When he remained adamant, they asked him to accept nomination again to the United States Senate, and since he did not categorically refuse to run, a second caucus meeting made him the official Republican candidate for that office.[4]

There are three available explanations for Plumer's acceptance of the Republican nomination to the Senate. The Federalists were certain that it was the result of a bargain between Plumer and aspirants to the governorship for an exchange of influence and that the Governor was eager to return to Washington. This explained his peculiar behavior in offering the chief justiceship to a Federalist; it had been a means of vacating Mason's seat in the Senate so Plumer could occupy it. William Plumer, Jr., also testified that his father wished to return to Washington, although he subsequently changed this story to a statement that the elder Plumer had been "willing to take the office, but not desirous of it."[5] William, Jr.'s narrative could have been colored by the fact that he had been elected to the House of Representatives and would greatly have enjoyed serving in the same Congress with his father.

Plumer's own account of this affair, written ten years later, tells a very different story. He had permitted himself to be named a candidate for senator, he wrote, not because he wanted to be elected, or would even have accepted the office, but in order to prevent the possible choice of Josiah Butler, who was an eager candidate for the post and who was supported by the Claggetts. His strategy had worked perfectly. The Republican malcontents who had supported Butler's nomination in caucus switched to John Parrott, a moderate Republican, as the man most likely to defeat Plumer, and the Federalists, unable to elect their own man, Jeremiah Smith, got behind Parrott for the same reason.[6] Thus, Plumer's subsequent defeat was a highly successful political tactic.

4. Plumer, Autobiography, 362, 364-66; Elijah Parish to Plumer, July 24, 1818, Dartmouth MSS., 818424, Dartmouth College; Levi Woodbury to Plumer, Jr., Aug. 2, 1818, Plumer Papers, N. H. State Lib.; Salma Hale to Plumer, Feb. 2, 1819, Letter Book, IX, Lib. Cong.

5. *Portsmouth Oracle,* June 20, 1818, Feb. 13, Mar. 13, 1819; entry for June 30, 1818, William Plumer, Jr., Journal, III, N. H. State Lib.

6. Plumer, Autobiography, 365-66.

This is a plausible explanation that fits most of the facts and is not inconsistent with the characters of the principal figures involved. It is the answer that Plumer gave to those of his friends who expressed regret that he had not been chosen senator, and it was finally accepted by William, Jr., and published in his biography of his father.[7] But there are overtones of rationalization and wounded pride in this explanation. Plumer would undoubtedly have accepted a draft to serve his party as a senator, but he obviously did not want the job seriously enough to work for it. One can hardly avoid sharing in the regret expressed by his son that the former Senator thus lost the opportunity, almost by default, of adding another period of useful service in the nation's capital to an already distinguished public career.

Although Plumer had wisely refrained from any premature disclosure of his plan to retire, he had been giving serious consideration since 1817 to the matter of his successor in the gubernatorial chair. Mature reflection had led to the conviction that Judge Samuel Bell would be the proper man to succeed him and hold the party together. He discussed the matter at length with the judge, and, in spite of demurrers based upon Republican divisiveness and the Hillsborough bank scandal, convinced Bell of his duty to submit to the will of the party, if it were clearly expressed in his favor. Plumer had either already expressed the will of the party or proceeded to create it. The same caucus that named him as a senatorial candidate endorsed his personal choice for his successor.[8] The Epping statesman had every reason to be pleased with the turn of events, even with his own failure to be elected to the Senate. His health was obviously unequal to the continued strain of official responsibilities; he was indulging not in fabrication but only in hyperbole when he so frequently said that he "daily felt the pangs of approaching dissolution." Two days after Bell's nomination, a weary ten-hour day spent in the council chamber confirmed Plumer in the wisdom of his decision to retire. "I have only time to add," he jotted in his journal before falling into bed, "I am this day fifty nine years of age."[9]

By the time he approached the end of his last year in the governorship of New Hampshire, the sixty-year-old Plumer had slipped easily

7. Plumer to Salma Hale, Aug. 24, 1818, Plumer Papers, N. H. State Lib.; Plumer, Jr., *Life of Plumer,* 478-80.

8. Plumer, Autobiography, 360-63. Plumer's son was a member of the caucus nominating committee, and boasted of having helped to secure the nomination for Bell. Entries for May and June, 1818, Plumer, Jr., Memoirs, I, N. H. State Lib.

9. Plumer, Autobiography, 366.

into the role of elder statesman. Younger men, such as Levi Woodbury, Salma Hale, and Ichabod Bartlett expressed filial admiration, while contemporaries, regardless of political affiliations, could now afford to recognize Plumer's merits.[10] Jeremiah Mason complimented the Governor on his appointments and expressed astonishment at his abandoning public life at the very apex of a distinguished career. Isaac Hill also pointed out editorially that Plumer's retirement was voluntary, following the example of Washington, Jefferson, and Madison, although his administration had been sanctioned by the votes of more of his fellow citizens than had ever supported any other man in New Hampshire for any office. Plumer had labored assiduously for the interests of the people, Hill continued, and had sought to remedy defects in the laws with "penetrating eye & a sound discretion." [11]

In this pleasant atmosphere, Plumer began the preparation of his last state document—his farewell address to be delivered to the legislature in June 1819. "In doing it I may be charged with egotism," he declared, "but I thot it might be the mean of preserving facts, & have a salutary influence upon the people, as well as on future administrations." On May 30, Plumer rode to Concord for the last time as governor and spent the following several days in performing the final official acts of his regime: visiting the state prison; administering the oath of office to legislators and councilmen; and parting regretfully with long-time friends and associates. By the fifth of June, the transition to the new administration had been completed and Plumer rode quietly out of Concord toward the life of study that he had so long anticipated. His son, who accompanied him on the homeward journey from Concord, noted as they rode through the June sunshine that he had never seen his father "more buoyant in thought, or happier in his anticipations of the future." [12] The retiring Governor certainly did not expect that future to be prolonged for thirty-one years, but neither did he anticipate sinking immediately into the grave. He planned a retirement of intense activity.

For the first few months, Plumer devoted himself principally to business affairs, organizing his estate in such a way as to provide a steady

10. An interesting example is a letter from a nephew of Bradbury Cilley in Fredericksburg, Virginia, who regretted that New Hampshire had lost a governor who had "raised it in a political point of view higher than it ever was before." John Williams to Plumer, Jr., Jan. 5, 1820, Plumer Papers, N. H. State Lib.

11. Plumer, Autobiography, 368; *N. H. Patriot* (Concord), June 1, 1819.

12. *Speech of His Excellency, William Plumer, to the Legislature, June 2, 1819* (Concord, 1819); Plumer, Autobiography, 372-73; Plumer, Jr., *Life of Plumer*, 492.

and moderate income without requiring much attention. His carefully maintained account book shows that on July 1, 1819, he had assets of $71,623.17. With this capital, Plumer was able to purchase property for his children, help set up his sons in business, consolidate his own land speculations, and make additional purchases of government bonds. As a director of the New Hampshire Bank and clerk of the proprietary for the towns of Millsfield and Errol he had to make occasional business trips, not unmixed with social calls and politics, to Portsmouth. These activities were essentially for conservation rather than acquisition. "I am now busily engaged in reviewing & counting my receipts & expenditures of the last year," he informed his son, in January 1830. "The latter have too nearly approached the former. I will devise ways & means to correct the procedure." [13]

As the weeks passed, Plumer gave increasingly more attention to the largest item in his inventory of personal property—his library, valued at $2,936.27.[14] "My devotion to reading and study not only continued but encreased with time, untill I felt an aversion to business & to writing," he explained to John Quincy Adams in a belated note of thanks for books which Adams had purchased for him in London.[15] Making his way daily through half a dozen newspapers, all the publications of the federal government that he could persuade his friends in Congress to send him, and books from dealers as far away as Philadelphia, Plumer did not find time hanging heavily on his hands.

Plumer's reaction to the "American System" that Henry Clay was gradually putting together during the postwar years changed considerably after his retirement. He had at first been favorably inclined toward a protective tariff, the Second United States Bank, and a program of internal improvements,[16] but the depression that overtook the burgeon-

13. Entry for July 1, 1819, Plumer, Property Book, N. H. State Lib.; Plumer to Plumer, Jr., Jan. 10, Feb. 7, 1820, Plumer Papers, *ibid.;* Plumer to Plumer, Jr., Jan. 3, 1830, Letter Book, VIII, Lib. Cong.

14. Plumer, Autobiography, 382. Plumer's library contained 1722 volumes and 912 contemporary pamphlets bound into 82 volumes. Plumer to Plumer, Jr., Jan. 10, 1820, Plumer Papers, N. H. State Lib.

15. Plumer to John Quincy Adams, Dec. 30, 1819, Letter Book, VIII, Lib. Cong. Plumer had purchased through Adams the only set available in London of Almon's *Remembrancer and Prior Documents;* John Q. Adams to Plumer, Oct. 27, 1817, Adams Papers, Mass. Hist. Soc. Plumer had also received from London a complete set of Hansard's *Debates* (to 1803), which he refused to sell to the Library of Congress; Plumer to Plumer, Jr., Jan. 3, 1820, Letter Book, VIII, Lib. Cong.

16. Plumer's message to the legislature in 1817 linked agriculture and manufactures together in the way that Clay and Calhoun had already coupled them. *House Journal, 1817,* 3-5. See also *Journal of the Senate, June Session, 1819* (Concord, 1819), 36.

ing economy during the last year of his administration diminished his enthusiasm for the program of the economic nationalists. The former Governor became highly critical of his protégé, Governor Bell, when the latter devoted almost his entire speech at the fall session of the legislature in 1820 to a eulogy of manufactures and the need for a tariff, "a subject it is evident he did not understand." At the same time, Plumer had incurred so many losses from depreciating bank notes that he memorialized the state legislature against rechartering "the Portsmouth Banck," of which he was a disgruntled stockholder. "It is not the interest of our country to have money plenty," he insisted; "it generates extravagance, idleness, negligence & a train of vices fatal to their opposite virtues." [17]

The inevitable result of this growing uneasiness was dissatisfaction with the Monroe administration, which seemed to Plumer to be plunging ever more recklessly along the road to ruin. "The expense of legislation is greater in the U. S. than it ever was in any other nation," he wrote to one congressman. What made this extravagance seem even worse in Plumer's eyes was the slashing of revenues while expenditures increased. The Governor had strongly opposed President Monroe's recommended repeal of the internal taxes in 1818. He proposed, instead, an application of surplus revenue to a program of paying off the war debt—cries of the creditors to the contrary notwithstanding. As did all Republican economists in that day, he pointed to the "wretched fate" of Great Britain where the permanent debt had become a burden almost too grievous to be borne. He charged Congress with similar prodigality, like "a young rich heir, who not having experienced the difficulty of acquiring wealth, dissipates the estate rather than improves it." [18]

Although Congress continued to spend money regardless of Plumer's sentiments, John Quincy Adams professed much respect for Plumer's opinions. "When the measures of [the] President have met your approbation, it has given me as much pleasure as if they had been my own," he assured his New Hampshire friend. "When you have censured, I have always perceived with new regret that it was not without reason." [19] Local statesmen often expressed a similar regard for Plumer's

17. Plumer to Plumer, Jr., Jan. 24, Nov. 24, 1820, Letter Book, VIII, Lib. Cong.; "Memorial of William Plumer," Repository, IX, 235, N. H. State Lib.

18. Plumer to Salma Hale, Dec. 8, 1817, to Clement Storer, Dec. 27, 1817, Letter Book, IX, *ibid.*

19. John Quincy Adams to Plumer, July 6, 1818, Adams Papers, Mass. Hist. Soc.

advice; in any case they were given it. But if Plumer still betrayed an interest in politics, it was purely in an advisory capacity. With unmistakable firmness, he rejected overtures to run again for governor or to re-enter the state senate in order to heal a party division. "I am resolved never to return to public life again . . . unless the state of public affairs should render it absolutely necessary," he declared.[20]

Despite Plumer's grumbling at the federal administration, there was nothing in the state of public affairs in November 1820 that required the sacrifice of his retirement. The moribund Federalist party in New Hampshire did not even bother to nominate electors, and the Republican leaders anticipated no opposition to Monroe. They decided, as a gesture of respect, to put the former Governor at the head of their electoral ticket. Plumer was at first inclined to refuse the nomination but could find no satisfactory reasons for rejecting so simple a service to his party. On October 31, accordingly, the *New Hampshire Patriot* announced an electoral ticket with "the venerable William Plumer" at its head. "The universal sentiment of the people of this state," it continued complacently, "is in favor of the re-election of MONROE and TOMPKINS, and the Electors of course will represent that sentiment. . . . New Hampshire has not within her bosom a son so degenerate as to forget our national benefactors." [21]

Plumer's lukewarm attitude toward Monroe was no secret in New Hampshire, but it did not generate any movement to prevent his choice as an elector, which was virtually uncontested. Plumer, in fact, was not alone in his distrust of Monroe. He represented a widespread feeling which, as John Randolph said, indicated that the political unanimity behind Monroe proceeded from indifference rather than approbation.[22] However, it was conceded long before 1820 that no candidate, Federalist or Republican, would contest the President's re-election. Those who wished to express their disapproval of the regime tended to concentrate their criticism upon the Vice-President, Daniel D. Tompkins. The New York Bucktail was far more vulnerable than Monroe, having been notoriously lackadaisical in his attendance in the Senate, frequently

20. Plumer, Autobiography, 373, 378; Plumer to Plumer, Jr., Feb. 21, 1820, Letter Book, VIII, Lib. Cong.; Plumer to Plumer, Jr., Feb. 7, 1820, Plumer Papers, N. H. State Lib.

21. Plumer, Autobiography, 378; *N. H. Patriot* (Concord), Oct. 31, 1820.

22. As reported by Plumer, Jr., to Plumer, Jan. 27, 1821, Plumer Papers, N. H. State Lib. For a good analysis of the opposition to Monroe's administration, see Glover Moore, *The Missouri Controversy, 1819-1821* (Lexington, Ky., 1953).

too intoxicated to preside when he did attend, and demonstrably more interested in New York politics than in national issues.[23] He became the victim of an interesting plot which may have been, indirectly, the catalyst that brought the uncertain elements in William Plumer's mind into a fixed determination.

The maneuver against Tompkins was initiated by no less a personage than Daniel Webster, who had only recently moved from New Hampshire to Boston. The people of Massachusetts, where electors were then chosen by districts, selected eight Federalist and seven Republican electors in November. Heading the list were the octogenarian former President, John Adams, and Congressman Daniel Webster. Webster harbored no intention of voting against Monroe, but Tompkins was another matter. "There will be a number of us, of course, in this state," he declared, "who will not vote for Mr. Tompkins, & we must therefore look up somebody to vote for."

The "somebody" who first occurred to Mr. Webster and his friends was the only son of New England in the President's cabinet, John Quincy Adams. It was important to know whether the Secretary of State would approve this use of his name, but Webster was not in a position to seek direct information. Accordingly, he wrote to his close friend, Jeremiah Mason, who was now one of Portsmouth's representatives in the New Hampshire legislature, and who would soon be traveling to Concord for the fall session. "If you can, without inconvenience," suggested Webster, "I hope you will see the Ex Governor [Plumer], as you go to Concord." Mason was asked to outline Webster's plan for giving vice-presidential votes to Adams, and to "ascertain what he thinks of it. Indeed," Webster added, "I know no one more likely to be able to learn from the Gentleman himself, how it would suit." [24]

This was an ingenious scheme, for Plumer placed great confidence in Mason and could readily communicate with Adams either directly by letter or indirectly through his son, who was now in Congress. Mason's visit was apparently successful, for on November 15, William Plumer sent the following letter to his son in Washington:

23. "You voted against the Vice President Tompkins for not coming here to preside in the Senate," wrote Plumer, Jr., to his father on Feb. 1, 1822, "but it would have been a much better reason, that, when here, his friends all wished him at home again. . . . he has now become so grossly intemperate as to be totally unfit for business." Plumer Papers, N. H. State Lib. See Julius W. Pratt in *DAB* s.v. "Tompkins, Daniel D."

24. Edward Stanwood, *A History of the Presidency* (Boston, 1898), I, 118; Webster to Jeremiah Mason, Nov. 12, 1820, Webster Papers, I, 55, N. H. Hist. Soc., printed in McIntyre, ed., *Webster's Writings*, XVI, 59-60.

A portion of New England is looking forward to the presidential election of 1824 with that view, as I learn from a communication I have this day received, some of the Electors will give John Q. Adams their votes to be Vice President. Their object in this is not to defeat the re-election of Tompkins, but to evince their confidence in Adams & prepare the public mind for his election as President four years hence. My object in writing you now is to request that you would without delay visit Mr. Adams, & in confidence ask him if he has no objection to this procedure. Write me, as soon as may be, the result of your visit. Delay will be injurious. I need not add that this is confidential.[25]

In this process of "communication" a subtle change had taken place. Webster had proposed to vote for Adams simply because there had to be "somebody to vote for." Plumer, however, gave this aimless plot a genuine purpose—"to prepare the public mind" for a campaign in behalf of his friend, which, as it proved, was actually to develop four years later.

On the afternoon of November 23, which could not have been very long after William, Jr., had received his father's letter, he sought an interview with the Secretary of State. According to his report of this meeting, he handed his father's letter to Mr. Adams, who read it very carefully and expressed his sense of obligation to the New Hampshire elector for his favorable sentiments. This was "the first intimation that he had received of a design to vote for him in New England," he assured the younger Plumer, but he "earnestly & sincerely desired" that no person would give him a single vote for the vice-presidency. Adams reported himself as replying even more emphatically to the young congressman, "my wish was that both [Tompkins and Monroe] should be re-elected unanimously; but, however that might be, that there should not be a single vote given for me, and I requested him to write so immediately." [26]

25. Plumer to Plumer, Jr., Nov. 15, 1820, Plumer Papers, N. H. Hist. Soc., printed in Everett Brown, *The Missouri Compromises and Presidential Politics, 1820-1825* (St. Louis, 1926), 53.

26. Plumer, Jr., to Plumer, Nov. 24, 1820, Plumer Papers, N. H. State Lib.; Brown, *Missouri Compromises,* 54. Adams recalled the details of this interview somewhat differently. He was merely informed that the elder Plumer had "intimated" to the younger a plan of several electors in New Hampshire and Massachusetts to vote for him. How Adams could have obtained this geographical precision from Plumer, Jr., who presumably had no information except that contained in the letter from his father, is something of a mystery. At any rate, Adams seemed to have sensed exactly what Plumer meant by "a portion of New England"—he even made the point that a vote for him from Massachusetts would be peculiarly embarrassing since his own father headed the College of Electors there. *Adams's Memoirs,* V, 205-6.

William Plumer, Jr., promptly reported the substance of this response to his father in two letters; the first a hastily scribbled note that he dashed off to catch the departing mail, the second a long letter reporting the conversation in far more detail than Adams devotes to it in his diary. Had the elder Plumer received either of these letters from his son, with their news that Adams so strongly disapproved of his scheme, he might have been robbed of his anonymous immortality among the footnotes of history. He departed for the state capital, however, before the letters from Washington reached his home.[27]

Sometime between November 15 and December 5, Plumer determined upon a bold change of plan. Rather than cast a protest vote against Tompkins, he would carry Webster's project to its ultimate conclusion and give a presidential ballot to his favorite, John Quincy Adams. Plumer himself does not reveal when or why he decided upon this course of action.[28] In the light of his character and previous behavior, however, it is logical to assume that he made up his mind to vote for Adams as president after he had failed to hear from his son, that the decision was entirely his own and was not discussed with any other person prior to election day, that he neither sought nor cared to learn how Webster or any other elector would vote, and that he would probably not have changed his mind, once it had been resolved, even had he subsequently learned of Adams's disapproval.[29]

The former Governor first met with his fellow electors, seven undistinguished Republican politicians, on the morning of December 5, for a short business session in which he was elected chairman. In the afternoon they met again and were favored by a lecture from their chairman.

27. From Concord, Plumer wrote to his son, George, in Epping, instructing him to "open William's letters to me but suffer no one but the family to read them. I received those you sent," he continued, "but not the information I wanted from William." Plumer to George W. Plumer, Dec. 4, 1820, Letter Book, IX, Lib. Cong.

28. Neither his autobiography, nor the *Life* written by William, Jr., in fact, mentions the original communication from Mason at all. It is apparent that both father and son regarded this scheme as unimportant or slightly discreditable, although the final act of casting the Presidential vote was proudly acknowledged.

29. This last assumption has some documentary support. On the day following the dispatch of his first two letters on the subject of his interview with the Secretary of State, Plumer, Jr., had anxiously written still a third note from Washington and sent it directly to Concord. Plumer, Jr., to Plumer, Nov. 25, 1820, Plumer Papers, N. H. State Lib. Plumer acknowledged its receipt on December 6, the very day on which he registered his vote for Adams, but failed to say whether the letter reached him before or after he had voted. Plumer to Plumer, Jr., Dec. 6, 1820, *ibid.* It hardly makes any difference, for by that time Plumer was thoroughly committed to the course which he had mapped out for himself. Brown, *Missouri Compromises,* 60-62.

This was an unusually solemn occasion, he declared. A heavy responsibility rested upon each of them, and he wished that they might have a "free and confidential conversation" on the subject of the persons for whom they should vote. The suggestion that any doubt existed on this subject must have struck the seven party stalwarts with astonishment, but their chairman had a reputation for eccentricity, and they, perforce, indulged his whims. Plumer dropped his bombshell at the outset by announcing that he intended, on the morrow, to vote for Adams and Richard Rush rather than for Monroe and Tompkins. He then explained that Monroe, in his opinion, had "conducted, as president, very improperly." The President's indifference to a proper balance between income and expenditures had led to the necessity, "in a season of profound peace," of augmenting the public debt by a three million dollar loan. Tompkins was simply intemperate and negligent; he had "not that weight of character which his office requires." Adams and Rush, in contrast to the incumbents, were able and well-qualified men.[30]

The reaction of New Hampshire's electors to this homily can only be conjectured, but they heard Plumer out and offered no objections to his proposed course of action. He, on his part, denied any intention of trying to influence their votes. He simply thought it due them in all candor to give notice of something that might otherwise come as a painful shock to them on the morrow. When they reassembled on the following day, Plumer voted as he had promised, and his fellows voted as the party expected. They then dispersed, apparently without recriminations or regrets.

Plumer's individualism attracted surprisingly little attention in 1820. The newspapers of the day were singularly indifferent not only to Plumer's precedent-shattering vote but to the election itself. As the returns from the various electoral colleges began to seep slowly into the columns of those few newspapers that bothered to print them, it appeared at first that the *Essex Register's* anticipation of "an unanimous vote" was being fulfilled.[31] "It is believed that Mr. Monroe has received nearly (or perhaps quite) the whole of the votes for President in the 22 States composing the Union," declared the strongly Federalist *Portsmouth Oracle* on December 9.[32] Ironically, the news from its own state

30. Plumer, Autobiography, 378-79.
31. *Essex Register* (Salem), Dec. 6, 1820. This statement was copied in the *National Intelligencer* (Washington), Dec. 16, 1820, and the *Scioto Gazette* (Chillicothe), Jan. 4, 1821.
32. *Portsmouth Oracle,* Dec. 9, 1820. The editor had neglected to include Maine and Missouri in his tally.

capital had not yet reached Portsmouth. When it did, however, it was an accurate report. Somehow, the *Oracle* obtained the substance of Plumer's remarks to his fellow electors, and other papers were soon copying the story that Plumer had voted against Monroe because he had "mismanaged the finances of the country" and against Tompkins because he "had neglected his official duties." [33]

In Plumer's own state the only newspapers that criticized his act were Federalist. The *Oracle* declared that Plumer would not have received a hundred votes in the entire state had his opposition to Monroe been anticipated. "But this vote is to be regretted," declared the *New Hampshire Sentinel,* "because it will probably be the only one throughout the United States in opposition to the reelection of the present incumbent, and thus to prevent a *unanimous* election will be pronounced *sheer folly.*" [34]

Federalists may have been eager so to pronounce it, but the great majority of Republican editors, embarrassed by this unexpected rebellion within their ranks, followed the example of Isaac Hill in refraining from public comment.[35] In New York, however, Plumer's vote against Tompkins added fuel to the fierce rivalry raging between two factions of the Republican party. The Vice-President's own organ, the *National Advocate,* rushed to his defense and accused Plumer of base disloyalty. It was inevitable, then, that this attack upon Plumer would elicit a defense from the opposition paper, the *New-York Statesman,* particularly since its editor, Nathaniel Carter, was a former New Hampshire resident. He praised Plumer lavishly as one who probably studied political subjects more than any man in the country. "He possesses a powerful and discriminating mind, a fearless independence, and an unbending integrity. . . . He had therefore no motive for voting as he did, but a sacred regard for the interest and welfare of his country." [36]

---

33. *National Advocate* (New York), Dec. 21, 1820. Also copied in *Farmer's Cabinet* (Amherst), Dec. 23, 1820; *Columbian* (New York), Dec. 21, 1820; *American* (New York), Dec. 22, 1820; *Boston Intelligencer & Evening Gazette,* Dec. 23, 1820; *New-York Statesman* (Albany), Dec. 26, 1820; *Richmond Enquirer,* Dec. 28, 1820.

34. *Portsmouth Oracle,* Dec. 30, 1820; *N. H. Sentinel* (Keene), Dec. 16, 1820.

35. Though completely discomfited by Plumer's unexpected vote, Hill exercised remarkable self-restraint. "For my part at the time," he later wrote to Plumer, Jr., "I regretted that the vote should have been given; and I regret still more that the subject should be handled to the disadvantage of any one. As it respects yourself, I pray it make no difference at Washington, as I think it will not in this State." Isaac Hill to Plumer, Jr., Jan. 3, 1821, N. H. State Lib.

36. *National Advocate* (New York), Dec. 21, 1820; *N.-Y. Statesman* (Albany), Dec. 26, 1820. The *Columbian* (New York) also defended Plumer's action.

William Plumer, Jr., read this article in Washington and found that many of his colleagues agreed with its sentiments. "I have been asked by several members to thank you for the independence which you have displayed," he assured his father, "& to say that they wish there had been more such votes in every part of the Union." [37] It seemed evident to him that his father had given unconscious expression to a considerable, though inarticulate, element of opposition to Monroe. In view of the generally undemocratic character of the electoral machinery in 1820 it was possible, and even probable, that a large and disgruntled minority existed without finding any way to reflect its existence in the electoral vote.[38] The situation gave rise to a demand that has been echoed down to our own day for a constitutional amendment which would make the electoral system more "analogous to the general usage of our country." [39]

The presumptive beneficiary of Plumer's defection accepted the tribute of his vote with that agonized masochism peculiar to the Adamses. The Secretary of State must have assumed that his objections to being considered a candidate for the vice-presidency had reached Plumer, and it was therefore with "surprise and mortification" that he learned of the defiance of his wishes by his New Hampshire friend in a manner that would embarrass his relations with the very head of the government. Being an Adams, however, he could not conceal a small degree of satisfaction in thus being singled out as a man worthy of the presidency itself. His mixed emotions are painfully evident in his diary: "If there was an electoral vote in the Union which I thought sure for Mr Monroe, it was that of Mr Plumer—I deeply regretted the loss of Plumers vote, because it implied his disapprobation of the principles of Administration, and although by giving the vote for me, he obviously exempted my share in the administration from any essential portion of the censure, I could take no pleasure in that approbation which though bestowed on me, was denied to the whole Administration." [40] When the

37. Plumer, Jr., to Plumer, Jan. 16, 1821, Jan. 15, 1822, Plumer Papers, N. H. State Lib. The younger Plumer mentioned Senator Macon specifically as one who admired his father's independence. He was himself inclined to join the opposition, although he had no personal feelings against Monroe. He confessed in his Memoirs, I, 509-12, *ibid.*, that he sometimes sympathized with the self-styled *Radical* malcontents who thought the administration "had departed . . . from the genuine Republican doctrine."

38. In the New York legislature, for example, the Clintonian minority voted for an anti-administration electoral ticket. Opposition tickets appeared also in Pennsylvania and Connecticut. See Charles Sydnor, "One-Party Period of American History," *Amer. Hist. Rev.*, 51 (1945-46), 439.

39. *National Intelligencer* (Washington), Dec. 12, 1820.

40. Entry for Feb. 14, 1821, John Quincy Adams, Diary, VI, Mass. Hist. Soc.

impeccable Adams composition became as awkward as this, it was a clear betrayal of extreme agitation. His feeling that Plumer's vote hurt his chances for the presidency in 1824 is manifest in every hastily-written line.

If the friend whom Plumer had attempted to honor feared him *donum ferentem,* the man who had earned his "disapprobation" might have been expected to show downright resentment. After all, Plumer *had* denied to James Monroe the intoxicating honor of unanimous re-election to the presidency. There was no way in which Monroe could have punished Plumer himself for his temerity, but the former Governor's son was within easy reach in Washington and might well have felt the weight of Monroe's displeasure. Plumer, in fact, confessed that the only apprehension he had felt over his decision to vote against Monroe arose from the possible consequences it might have had upon his son's career, and William, Jr., himself was not altogether free from this concern.[41] If Monroe was disappointed by Plumer's defection, however, he betrayed no sign of it. He even showed the younger Plumer a mark of favor by reappointing, at his request, the Portsmouth district attorney whom every other New Hampshire congressman had asked to have replaced.[42] It is also a tribute to the President's equanimity that Plumer's vote created no coldness between him and his brilliant Secretary of State.

The fact is that William Plumer's unexpected exercise of his prerogative as an elector in 1820 caused less excitement at the time than it has created since.[43] One reason for this lack of interest, perhaps, was the

41. Plumer, Jr., to Plumer, Jan. 16, 1821, Plumer to Plumer, Jr., Jan. 29, 1821, Plumer Papers, N. H. State Lib.

42. This affair added another fagot to the smoldering Plumer-Claggett feud. William Claggett wanted to succeed Daniel Humphreys, the seventy-six-year-old district attorney, and with unblushing effrontery, expected his former brother-in-law to work in his behalf. Clifton Claggett and four remaining New Hampshire congressmen petitioned against the reappointment of Humphreys, and Claggett pursued the matter with the same persistence he had employed for himself with Governor Plumer. Plumer, Jr., was careful not to speak against Claggett, but in effect he did everything possible to prevent his appointment. Plumer, Jr., to Plumer, Jan. 16, 1821, Plumer Papers, N. H. State Lib. See also entry for Jan. 8, 1821, John Quincy Adams, Diary, VI, Mass. Hist. Soc. After a visit from the elder Claggett, the Secretary wrote, "I am not much edified with the delicacy of [his] procedure."

43. The author has found nothing in the papers of Daniel Webster to describe his reaction to Plumer's vote, or to explain why he changed his own original plan and cast his vice-presidential ballot for Richard Stockton of New Jersey rather than for Adams. A Massachusetts Republican did attempt an explanation of this phenomenon to Monroe, but his letter is an incomprehensible jumble of dark hints about a proto-Abolitionist party. George Sullivan to Monroe, Jan. 11, 1821, Monroe Papers, N. Y. Pub. Lib.

fact that there was no reason to speculate about the motive for Plumer's abnormal behavior; it was well known. Except for a few vindictive Federalists who attributed his vote to ingrained eccentricity or to personal spite, contemporaries seem to have accepted the simple and logical explanation that Plumer thought Adams a better man than Monroe for the presidency.[44] Plumer himself certainly left no room for doubt as to his motives. He explained them carefully, first to his fellow electors, then to his son in Washington. "I was compelled, not only from a sense of duty, but respect to my own character, to withhold my vote from Monroe & Tompkins," he wrote to William, Jr., "from the first because he had discovered a want of foresight & economy; & from the second, because he grossly neglected his duty." There is nothing ambiguous in this statement. Nor was there ever the slightest hint of regret or misgivings about the singular deed he had done. "There is no one act of my official life which I reflect on with more satisfaction," he wrote in December 1821.[45] He felt that he, and not the 231 other electors, had been right, and that the people, in 1824, simply vindicated the good judgment that he had shown in 1820. Plumer would have been only a little less astonished and mortified than George Washington himself, if it could have been revealed to him that sober historians in the future would attribute his nonconformity to a wish to preserve for the first President the sole distinction of having been elected without a dissenting vote.[46]

William Plumer's vote in the electoral college of 1820—a typical gesture of independence—was his last public act. Although he lived another thirty years, he never again held a public office except that of

44. The *N. H. Sentinel* (Keene), Dec. 16, 1820, spoke sarcastically of "the odd old gentleman's ... propensity to be singular and overwise." The *Boston Intelligencer,* Dec. 23, 1820, pretended to have heard rumors "that Mr. P's vote is not entirely disconnected with the singular treatment Mr. Monroe received from him during his visit to New-Hampshire in 1817."

45. Plumer to Plumer, Jr., Jan. 8, 1821, Letter Book, VIII, Lib. Cong.; Plumer to Plumer, Jr., Dec. 14, 1821, William Plumer Letters, X (1821-25), Plumer Papers, Lib. Cong. (hereafter cited as Letter Book, X).

46. The connection of Washington's name with Plumer's vote in 1820 is one of the least credible, but most persistent myths in American history. There is not a shred of evidence for it in the papers of Plumer or any of his contemporaries. It apparently did not come into existence until thirty years after Plumer's death and sixty years after the event itself. It has been disproved by modern scholars, yet it appears in the works of some of the nation's foremost historians and still crops up regularly in college textbooks. For an attempt to trace the origin and development of this legend, see Lynn Turner, "The Electoral Vote Against Monroe in 1820," *Miss. Valley Hist. Rev.,* 42 (1955), 250-73.

justice of the peace.[47] During the decade of the twenties, however, he remained a familiar figure in New Hampshire through occasional public appearances and a constant stream of contributions to the newspapers. Then, at the end of the decade, he became again, as he so often had in earlier life, the center of a whirling controversy.

During the earlier years of his retirement, friends waited expectantly for those solid contributions to the field of history that Plumer had so long promised. But his scholarly pretensions had been too confidently inflated by Isaac Hill and therefore correspondingly derided by his opponents.[48] He was still toying with the idea of finishing his "History of North America" as late as August 1821, although he had actually come to realize that he commanded neither the talent nor the resources for such a task. Twice, responsible publishers asked him to add a volume to Jeremy Belknap's *History of New Hampshire,* bringing it to date, but he refused. Perhaps, with all his devotion to the muse, Plumer was also conscious that he would make a poor showing at the side of "the Tacitus of New Hampshire." [49]

Although Plumer was understandably reluctant to test his untried literary skill in the field of history, he made good use of his administrative talents in helping launch the New Hampshire Historical Society, the fifth organization of its kind to be chartered in the United States.[50] At a series of public meetings held in the spring of 1823, the preliminary organization of the society was effected by such younger men as Ichabod Bartlett, William Plumer, Jr., and John Farmer, an apothecary and

47. Plumer to Plumer, Jr., Dec. 27, 1824, Letter Book, X, Lib. Cong. Plumer said in this letter that in all his life there were only two offices he had ever sought, neither of which he had obtained—an evidence either of failing memory or deliberate rationalization.

48. "Don't count your chickens before they are hatched," scoffed the *N. H. Sentinel* (Keene), Mar. 2, 1816. "Wait until Plumer's history is published before planting him by the side of Marshall, Ramsay & Trumbull."

49. Plumer, Autobiography, 384; Plumer to John Mann, July 26, 1825, Plumer Papers, N. H. Hist. Soc.; Plumer to Jacob Moore, Apr. 9, 1825, to John Mann, Mar. 28, 1828, Letter Book, VIII, Lib. Cong.

50. Besides the Historical Society of his own state, William Plumer was elected to membership in the following organizations: Massachusetts Historical Society (1807); American Antiquarian Society (1815) and Councilor of the Society (1819); Historical Society of New York (1817); American Academy of Language and Belles Lettres (1821); Danish Royal Society of Northern Antiquaries (1837); American Statistical Association (1840); and Northern Academy of Arts and Sciences (1841). For the correspondence regarding these affiliations, see: Lyman Spaulding to Plumer, Nov. 20, 1817, Plumer Papers, N.-Y. Hist. Soc., John Francis to Plumer, Sept. 10, 1817, Charles Rafn, Copenhagen, to Plumer, Oct. 9, 1838, Josiah Fell, Boston, to Plumer, Mar. 12, 1840, W. Cogswell, Hanover, to Plumer, June 24, 1841, Plumer Papers, N. H. State Lib.; W. S. Cardell, New York, to Plumer, Nov. 3, 1821, Letter Book, VIII, Lib. Cong.

amateur antiquarian in Concord. The elder Plumer had been unable to attend these meetings, but he had been elected to membership and had assured the founders that they had his "best wishes for success." During the session of the legislature in June, Plumer found enough strength to travel to Concord, the first time for two years that he had ventured so far away from his rural retreat.[51] Meeting there with the other charter members of the society, lobbying among his old friends in the legislature, and conferring with his protégé, Levi Woodbury, the newly-elected governor, the Epping recluse played an active role in helping to launch the new organization. As chairman of the committee to draw up a constitution, Plumer himself drafted the document, "comprising but few articles... founded upon general principles, simple & plain, without descending into details." [52] This constitution was accepted without amendment by the newly chartered society at its first legal meeting on June 13, and Plumer was then unanimously elected its first president.[53]

Although William Plumer's duties during the next two years were largely honorary, he took them seriously and carried on a voluminous official correspondence. Illness, however, prevented his attendance at the society's meetings and finally led to the relinquishing of his office. His chief interest had been in the society's publication program, which he pursued with genuine zeal. In its first volume of *Collections,* he began reprinting in chronological order the principal documents upon which the early history of New Hampshire was based.[54] A disagreement be-

51. Nathaniel Bouton, "An Account of the New Hampshire Historical Society," N. H. Hist. Soc., *Collections,* 6 (1850), 9-32; Jacob Moore, "Memoir of John Farmer, M. A.," *ibid.,* 33-51; Plumer to Ichabod Bartlett, May 5, 1823, archives of N. H. Hist. Soc.; Bartlett to Plumer, May 1, 1823, letter in possession of Mrs. Bessie Plumer Norris of Epping, N. H., in 1938; John Kelley to Plumer, May 23, 1823, Letter Book, X, Lib. Cong.

52. Plumer, Autobiography, 388. A draft copy of the constitution with some interlineations and changes may be found in Plumer, Repository, IX, 255, N. H. State Lib. For the constitution and act of incorporation, see N. H. Hist. Soc., *Manual* (Concord, 1918).

53. For other accounts of the founding of the society, in addition to that by Bouton already cited, see one, probably by John Farmer, in N. H. Hist. Soc., *Collections,* 1 (1824), v-vi, and two by Elmer Hunt, "When New Hampshire was 200 Years Old," *Historical New Hampshire* (Apr. 1945), 1-6; "Historical Sketch of the New Hampshire Historical Society from its Beginning in 1823," *ibid.* (Apr. 1947).

54. Plumer to Jacob Moore, Aug. 2, 1823, to John Farmer, Aug. 8, Dec. 6, 26, 1823, to John Kelley, May 28, 1825, Letter Book, VIII, Lib. Cong.; Plumer to John Kelley, Apr. 29, 1824, Plumer Papers, N. H. State Lib. For Plumer's correspondence with the publishing committee, see Plumer to Farmer, Dec. 6, 1823, to Plumer, Jr., Jan. 26, 1824, Letter Books, VIII, X, Lib. Cong.; Plumer to Farmer, Feb. 7, 1824, Gratz Coll., Pa. Hist. Soc.

tween Plumer and the editors in regard to the scope of his plan "deranged" it so much that he refused to contribute to the second volume,[55] but he maintained a life-long membership in the society, paid his dues assiduously, and donated trunks full of books to the society's library.[56] After 1824, however, he ceased to play a personal role of any importance in the society's affairs. One has the feeling that he was disappointed in the society's limited view of its own mission, and that he turned from its primarily antiquarian outlook to projects that gave greater scope to his appreciation of genuine history.

One of these intellectual adventures in which Plumer became inextricably involved was a long series of newspaper essays that became, almost by chance, his literary testament to posterity.[57] In a conspicuous place on the front page of the *New Hampshire Patriot* for the 23rd of May 1820, appeared the first essay addressed "To the People" by "Cincinnatus." In a republic based upon public opinion, said the author, it was necessary to excite a spirit of inquiry—to furnish public men with information of their errors. This, the retired statesman inferred, was virtually the duty of a man in his position, and he proposed to fulfill his obligation to the public and to the rulers in succeeding essays. "To those who wish to know," he declared, "my politics are republican, my religion liberal—my name can neither add nor detract from my writings. My motive in writing is the *public good.*" [58] It is doubtful that anyone who read the first essay failed to penetrate the thin disguise of "Cincinnatus."

One week later, Plumer plunged into the substantive part of his series with "Cincinnatus" No. 2, on a subject of immediate and painful interest, "Hard Times." This led, by the inexorable logic of an elderly mind, through denunciations of idleness, speculation, extravagance, and gambling (including lotteries), to the trite conclusion that happiness was the reward of virtue, and that the essence of virtue was hard work. Nothing particularly distinguished these first public homilies; they were

55. Plumer to Richard Bartlett, Feb. 2, 1826, N. H. Hist. Soc. According to a note, signed "R. B." attached to this letter, the editors felt that Plumer's scheme would be "an unnecessary tax on the scanty funds of the Society."

56. Plumer to William Pickering, June 27, 1826, *ibid.;* John Farmer to Plumer, Apr. 1, 23, 1835, John Kelley to Plumer, Feb. 1836, Moore to Plumer, July 12, 1837, Nathaniel Bouton to Plumer, Nov. 22, 1841, Plumer Papers, N. H. State Lib.

57. Plumer, Autobiography, 375.

58. "Cincinnatus," No. 1, Plumer, Essays, II, 141-43, Lib. Cong., publ. in *N. H. Patriot* (Concord), May 23, 1820.

the usual blend of common sense, economic platitudes, and condescension. Nevertheless, Plumer was puzzled by the lack of public response to his moralizing. "I fear they will do less good than the labor they cost," he lamented.[59]

With the eleventh "Cincinnatus" article, however, Plumer began a series on the more controversial subject of education, to which his own thought and research could make a genuine contribution. Immediately his writing began to take on its accustomed verve, and reactions from his readers were not long in coming. His son wrote home from Washington enthusiastically about Plumer's penetrating discussion of the public school system and mentioned that it had been noticed in the *Aurora*. Even the Federalist press acknowledged that these were "useful essays," and a friendly printer seriously proposed to publish them in book form. But there was also vigorous criticism, particularly when Plumer tilted at his favorite windmill—the study of the "dead languages." Among others, "Cadmus," whom Plumer readily identified as a Portsmouth clergyman, stung him with one personal allusion— that those who knew nothing of the classical languages were in a poor position to criticize them. "Cadmus is uncharitable," protested Plumer, but he consoled himself with the reflection that the attack would draw attention to "Cincinnatus" and increase his following.[60]

After having devoted twenty-five articles and approximately 40,000 words to his thoughts on education, Plumer spent eighteen months in churning out thirty-four essays on agriculture. That the retired lawyer took his role as an agricultural expert seriously is indicated by the very pseudonym that he adopted for his essays—that of the good citizen who had voluntarily relinquished political power for the plow.[61] Then, in November of 1822, Plumer began a series of sixty-four numbers on

59. Plumer, Essays, II, 143-45, Lib. Cong., publ. in *N. H. Patriot* (Concord), May 30, 1820; Plumer, Autobiography, 375.

60. Plumer, Jr., to Plumer, Jan. 25, 1821, Plumer Papers, N. H. Hist. Soc.; *N. H. Sentinel* (Keene), Dec. 9, 1820; Jacob Moore to Plumer, Nov. 14, 1821, Letter Book, X, Lib. Cong.; *Portsmouth Oracle*, Mar. 3, 1821; Plumer, Autobiography, 383.

61. "Cincinnatus," Nos. 37-70, Essays, II, 260-388, Lib. Cong., publ. in *N. H. Patriot* (Concord), July 2, 1821 to July 29, 1822. Plumer did not share the contemporary enthusiasm for the gentleman farmer agricultural societies which were springing up everywhere. He was made a director of the Rockingham County Agricultural Society and placed on a committee for collecting a library, but after attending one meeting decided that there was "too much finesse & management" among the politician members. Dirt farmers, he thought, would profit more by education than from trying to emulate the agricultural aristocracy. Plumer to Plumer, Jr., May 8, 1820, N. H. State Lib.; Plumer, Autobiography, 377.

government, which occupied his attention for the next four years.[62] In these, he ranged over a wide field—political theory, the role of parties, nominations and elections, qualifications for public office, the operation of every branch of the federal, state, and local government. This series, perhaps the best of Plumer's writings, was followed by a miscellany of essays on the political implications of commerce and industry, on banks and currency, on slavery, taxation, war, the militia, military pensions, lawyers, medicine, and religion, which brought the long effort to a close.

When Plumer began his "Cincinnatus" series, he intended to write some twenty essays; before he finished, he had actually composed 186. His last article, on religion, was published in August 1829. Thus for nearly a decade, he wrote regularly upon subjects of his own choice for the newspapers. Such a scribbler today would be called a columnist and paid a handsome salary; Plumer wrote for charity and remained unclassifiable. Some of his articles merely reflected life-long prejudices— there were too many banks, the South was over-represented in Congress, the pension laws were fraudulent, the doctors were worse than the diseases they were hired to cure, the majority of clergymen were blind leaders of the blind. But these outbursts of petulance were interspersed with evidences of foresight and intelligent analysis. Plumer advocated income taxes, for example, nearly a century before their serious adoption and predicted that "if we are ever involved in a civil war, it will arise either from attempts to dismember & dissolve the Union of the States, or the election of a president, or perhaps from a combination of both those causes." [63]

After overcoming his initial discouragement, Plumer seldom had reason to feel that his literary labors were wasted. By the end of 1821, when he had finished fifty-seven essays, he felt they had "excited a spirit of enquiry, & of course have been useful." [64] One reader whose

62. "Cincinnatus," Nos. 76-138. Nos. 76-93 are in Plumer, Essays, II, 415-88, Lib. Cong.; Nos. 94-138 are in Plumer, Essays, III, 5-184, N. H. State Lib. They were published in *N. H. Patriot* (Concord), Nov. 25, 1822 to Jan. 20, 1823 (Nos. 76-79); *Portsmouth Journal,* Mar. 1 to Sept. 13, 1823 (Nos. 80-93); *Literary Journal* (Concord), Oct. 1823 to Dec. 1824 (Nos. 94-106); *Grafton Journal* (Haverhill), Jan. 8 to Apr. 2, 1825 (Nos. 107-13); *Portsmouth Journal,* Apr. 23, 1825 to Sept. 16, 1826 (Nos. 114-38).
63. "Cincinnatus," Nos. 159, 166, Plumer, Essays, III, 261-65, 289-92, N. H. State Lib., publ. in *Portsmouth Journal,* Dec. 1, 1827, June 7, 1828.
64. Plumer, Autobiography, 385.

spirit of inquiry found more political innuendo in the essays than pleased him was the owner of the paper in which they began publication, Isaac Hill. The Plumer-Hill alliance had never been entirely comfortable, although Hill had loyally supported Plumer's administration, even in policies which went against his instincts. The rewards that Hill had asked for his important services had certainly not been excessive, and Plumer had found few occasions to differ with him, except in the matter of patronage. Here, however, they had differed sharply, and the Governor had sometimes resented the printer's "uncourtly language" in terms that themselves were "severe and pointed." [65] Nevertheless, the men remained friends, and it was natural for Plumer to have offered his first "Cincinnatus" essays to Hill, who printed them in the *New Hampshire Patriot* with genuine enthusiasm.

Politics, however, brewed discord that ultimately made enemies of Plumer and Hill. The journalist was an undeviating party regular while the former Governor gave his allegiance to other principles. Hill was a Crawford man and he opened the columns of his paper to attacks upon the presidential pretensions of John Quincy Adams. His sniping at Adams struck the Plumers not only as treason to New England but as a case of flagrant ingratitude, since the Secretary of State had resisted attempts to deprive Hill of the federal printing contract for New Hampshire.[66]

In 1823, the old Claggett-Butler-Livermore faction in the Republican party rejected the caucus candidate for governor, Samuel Dinsmoor, and nominated Levi Woodbury as an independent. Hill denounced this insurrection, but it quickly gained momentum. In the ensuing campaign, both factions of the party were eager for Plumer's support and made exaggerated claims to being the sole possessors of his blessing. Strangely enough, considering the character of Woodbury's backing, Plumer decided to vote for him and announced his decision to the young candidate himself. The elements entering into this decision were largely personal.

65. Plumer to Plumer, Jr., Dec. 22, 1823, Plumer Papers, N. H. Hist. Soc.

66. *N. H. Patriot* (Concord), Jan. 20, 1823. The attempts had been made by the Butler-Claggett-Livermore phalanx in Congress and thwarted by the intervention of William Plumer, Jr., on Hill's behalf. Plumer, Jr., to Isaac Hill, Nov. 26, 1820, Dec. 14, 1822, Mar. 29, 1824, William Plumer, Jr., Letter Book, IV (1820-32), N. H. State Lib. (hereafter cited as Plumer, Jr., Letter Book, IV); Isaac Hill to Plumer, Jr., Apr. 11, 1822, Dec. 11, 1823, Plumer Papers, *ibid.;* John Quincy Adams to Plumer, Jr., Feb. 23, 1824, John Quincy Adams, Letter Book (1817-24), Adams Papers, Mass. Hist. Soc.

Plumer had no respect for the caucus candidate,[67] while he regarded Woodbury, who was free of the caucus taint, with almost parental affection. In his own mind it was simply a matter of principle.

The possibility that William Plumer might use the columns of the *Patriot* against its own candidate had obviously occurred to Hill. "As the author of these numbers is extensively known," he wrote to William, Jr., at Washington, "I hope nothing may be written and published, that will have the effect to second the views of a desperate little faction in this State, which has no better object in view than the command of the 'loaves and fishes.'" [68] On January 27, just after Woodbury had been nominated, Hill received from Plumer his eightieth "Cincinnatus" essay, a slashing attack on political parties and all of their operations. The article was couched in general terms and its criticism was leveled at "all parties," but the Concord editor, unduly sensitive, chose to interpret it as an attack on the sacred principle of party regularity. After a fortnight had elapsed, he wrote to Plumer, declining to publish No. 80 until after the March elections on the ground that it tended to give encouragement to the rebels who were attempting to destroy the Republican party.[69]

This was a serious error for so shrewd a politician as Isaac Hill. Plumer immediately demanded the return of his manuscript and on the next day offered the future numbers of "Cincinnatus" to Nathaniel Haven, publisher of the *Portsmouth Journal*, "a federal paper, & respectable," with the second largest circulation in the state. Consequently, the article that Hill had tried to suppress appeared during the week before election in the Portsmouth newspaper, together with a full account of why "Cincinnatus" had transferred his patronage. "We feel happy," declared Haven, "in presenting to our readers such sound political opinions—so well expressed—and so pertinent to the present condition

67. Cyrus Bradley, *Biography of Isaac Hill* (Concord, 1835), 57; Hill to Plumer, Jr., Dec. 2, 1822, Plumer Papers, N. H. State Lib.; *N. H. Patriot* (Concord), Feb. 3, 17, 24, Mar. 10, 1823; Plumer to Levi Woodbury, Jan. 28, 1823, to Plumer, Jr., Feb. 3, 1823, Letter Books, VIII, X, Lib. Cong.; Plumer to Plumer, Jr., Feb. 10, 1823, Plumer Papers, N.-Y. Hist. Soc.

68. Hill to Plumer, Jr., Dec. 2, 1822, Plumer, Jr., to Plumer, Dec. 6, 1822, Plumer to Plumer, Jr., Jan. 20, 1823, Plumer Papers, N. H. State Lib.

69. "Cincinnatus," No. 80, Plumer, Essays, II, 432-36, Lib. Cong., publ. in *Portsmouth Journal*, Mar. 1, 1823; Plumer, Autobiography, 387. Plumer had a strong presentiment of Hill's reaction to his essay, but said he would regret it "for I wished to make his paper a vehicle to convey an antidote for his errors to his numerous readers." Plumer to Plumer, Jr., Jan. 13, 1823, Letter Book, X, Lib. Cong.

of the State." [70] Hill had only succeeded in advertising the breach between himself and an honored Republican statesman.

Woodbury won an upset victory against the caucus candidate, and Plumer pointed to this as evidence that the people would always "resist the mandates of dictators" when a better alternative was offered. Hill was bitter about his defeat by a faction that counted "among its most powerful adherents some of the very persons who were before the subjects of its own reproaches." The Concord publisher maintained a desultory correspondence with William Plumer, Jr., until April 1824, when Hill announced what the Plumers had long suspected—that he would support the "regular" candidate, Crawford, rather than Adams. From that moment, the Plumers and Hill were on opposite sides in a war that permitted no quarter. [71]

After Adams was elected to the presidency, partly by the help of William Plumer, Jr., [72] Isaac Hill transferred his allegiance from Crawford to Andrew Jackson and entered enthusiastically into the four-year campaign to break down the Adams administration. Plumer was shocked and puzzled by Hill's unprincipled attacks and by the instinctive groping toward a new two-party system that was going on around him. In April he wrote to the President himself: "of all the oppositions I have lived to witness, & I have seen a number I do not recollect one so *malignant & unprincipled* as that which is organized against you. The deformity of its character, appears to me too gross to succeed; & if public spirit & public virtue is not at a very low ebb in our country, it must

70. Plumer to Hill, Feb. 12, 1823, to Haven, Feb. 13, 1823, Letter Book, VIII, *ibid.;* Haven to Plumer, Feb. 19, 1823, Letter Book, X, *ibid.; Portsmouth Journal,* Mar. 1, 1823.

71. "Cincinnatus," No. 83, Plumer, Essays, II, 446, Lib. Cong., publ. in *Portsmouth Journal,* Apr. 5, 1823; *N. H. Patriot* (Concord), Mar. 17, 1823. In the autumn of 1823, Plumer transferred "Cincinnatus" to the *Literary Journal* (Concord), a monthly magazine published by Jacob Moore and John Farmer. Plumer to Haven, Sept. 18, 1823, to Moore, Sept. 27, 1823, to Farmer, Oct. 11, 1823, Letter Book, VIII, Lib. Cong.; Plumer to Moore, Nov. 3, 1823, Etting Papers, Pa. Hist. Soc. Farmer welcomed "Cincinnatus," No. 94, to his pages with flattering words. John Farmer and Jacob Moore, the *Literary Journal, or Collections, Topographical, Historical and Biographical Relating principally to New Hampshire* (Concord, 1822-24), II, 311 (hereafter cited as *Literary Journal*). This arrangement lasted until Dec. 1824, when the *Literary Journal* suspended publication, and "Cincinnatus" went to the *Grafton Journal* (Haverhill). In Apr. 1825, it returned to the *Portsmouth Journal.* Plumer to Moore, Dec. 18, 30, 1824, to Messrs. Miller and Brewster, publishers of the *Portsmouth Journal,* Apr. 22, 1825, Letter Book, VIII, Lib. Cong.

72. Plumer, Jr., to Margaret Plumer, Feb. 13, 1825, N.-Y. Hist. Soc. Most of the younger Plumer's letters to his wife seem to be in this collection.

produce a re-action which will eventually prostrate & disappoint the prime movers of these conspirators. Of one thing, however, I have no doubt, that the manly, independent, & decisive course you pursue will *deserve,* if it should not *command success."* John Quincy Adams acknowledged gratefully that Plumer's approval was "among the most cheering incidents" that sustained him in the midst of his difficulties, but he gloomily admitted that the opposition had been "too successful in defeating measures of no small importance to the welfare of the nation." [73]

As the crucial elections of 1828 approached, Plumer lent the resources of his political wisdom to his son and a group of ill-assorted colleagues in their efforts to combine former Republican and Federalist elements into a new administration party. In February, he returned actively to the political wars with two sizzling contributions to the press. One article was a vicious attack on the Methodist preacher who was running against William, Jr., for the state senate, accusing him of falsifying his property record in order to qualify for the office and of defrauding his creditors. This recurrence of Plumer's occupational disease created considerable embarrassment for his son, who was himself suspected of having made this unprincipled attack against his rival for office.[74] Plumer's other article was a more moderate criticism of his former councilor, now Governor Pierce, for his desertion of President Adams.

At least four members of the extensive Plumer clan in New Hampshire became deeply involved in the memorable presidential campaign of 1828. So zealously did the former Governor enter into the spirit of the occasion that, for the first time in five years, he accepted an invitation to a public function, presiding at the traditional Fourth of July dinner in Epping and making a brief address on behalf of Adams and Rush.[75] Meanwhile, the *Patriot* had laid down a barrage of blistering editorials on the theme of "bargain and corruption," and introduced two Plumers as witnesses against Adams and Clay. These Jacksonian relatives of the ex-Governor, a brother and a nephew, claimed to have seen letters written in the spring of 1825 from William Plumer, Jr., to his father, describing at length a visit of Clay to Adams at which

73. Plumer to President Adams, Apr. 16, 1827, Letter Book, VIII, Lib. Cong.; President Adams to Plumer, Apr. 24, 1827, Plumer Papers, N. H. State Lib.

74. Plumer to Plumer, Jr., June 10, 1827, Plumer Papers, N. H. Hist. Soc.; Samuel Bell to Plumer, Jr., May 2, 1827, Plumer Papers, N. H. State Lib.; Plumer, Essays, III, 274-77, *ibid.;* entries for March, 1828, William Plumer, Jr., Journals and Memoirs (1828-38), N. H. State Lib. (hereafter cited as Plumer, Jr., Journals and Memoirs, IV).

75. Plumer, Autobiography, 392; Plumer, Essays, III, 292-93, N. H. State Lib.

the corrupt bargain had been sealed. The elder Plumer immediately published a denial that he had ever received any such letters,[76] but William, Jr., had to admit publicly that Hill's insinuation, though false, could not be proved so.[77] The literary garrulity of the Plumers had drawn them inescapably into Hill's trap.

In spite of these slanders, the state coalition ticket prevailed in 1828 and New Hampshire delivered its eight electoral votes to President Adams. It was the last political victory that Plumer ever had opportunity to celebrate, but even this one was nullified by the results in other parts of the country. "The nation, not you, will suffer by that event," he assured Adams, after learning of Jackson's election. "I have the consolation of knowing that I have done my duty, my whole duty. . . . But the prospect for my country is gloomy. I fear our free government, like the republics who have preceded us, is hastening with rapid strides to monarchy." [78]

The defeated President, in the midst of all his other troubles, was goaded at this moment into driving the old Hartford Convention wing of Federalist veterans away from his standard by reopening the bitter controversies of 1804 and 1814. In an attempt to refute certain other charges made against him during the campaign, Adams had published an account of earlier conversations with ex-President Jefferson in which the two men had freely discussed the Federalist secession movements of those years. A group of Federalists in New England, led by Harrison Gray Otis, felt their reputations, or those of their fathers, to be so damaged by the President's generalized statements that they sent him a letter of outraged innocence demanding proofs of his charges. At this point, Plumer, in spite of his declarations in favor of cementing union with the Federalists, leaped unbidden to the support of Adams by offering to furnish firsthand evidence of the 1804 design. The President was astonished to learn that his friend had even been involved in the conspiracy, but he did signify a wish to receive further information, and on December 20, Plumer wrote him a full account of what he knew of the project, omitting only the names of individuals. Before this letter

76. William Plumer, "To the Editor of the New Hampshire Journal" (publ. on Apr. 21, 1828), *ibid.*, 284-85. The younger Plumer actually had written his father on Jan. 4, 1825, saying that Clay intended to call on Adams, and again a week later, that the meeting had been held and that Clay would support Adams, whose success now seemed assured. This, of course, was all that Hill needed. Plumer, Jr., to Plumer, Jan. 4, 13, 1825, Plumer Papers, *ibid.*

77. Entries for 1825 and 1828, Plumer, Jr., Memoirs, II, N. H. State Lib.

78. Plumer to President Adams, Nov. 20, 1828, Letter Book, VIII, Lib. Cong.

could reach him, President Adams had answered the associated Federalists, declining to enter a controversy with them. Their answer was to publish the correspondence, together with an ill-tempered address, explicitly and emphatically denying the existence of any plan for a Northern Confederacy in 1804, except in President Adam's imagination.[79]

Stung by this outrageous denial, Plumer wrote again to Adams, giving the names of all the agitators in 1804 and freely admitting his own complicity. This bill of particulars so strengthened the President's case against his persecutors that he republished their pamphlet in Washington, together with a copy of Plumer's generalized letter of December 20. The circulation of this letter—the first published testimony to the project of 1804 by a participant and eyewitness—exploded a bombshell among the stiff-necked Federalist families in New England. Since Plumer had used no names in the letter that Adams had chosen to publish, it raised a variety of emotions in the breasts of surviving members of the Eighth Congress or their children—guilty apprehension, righteous indignation, and filial protectiveness. Tracy was dead, but a son-in-law sought to vindicate him by collecting letters from men who had been his associates from Connecticut in the Eighth Congress. These six old men unanimously denied ever having heard the slightest hint of the project which Adams and Plumer had pretended to reveal, and some of them added gratuitous reflections upon the veracity of the two "apostates to Federalism." [80] Of the six, only two, Hillhouse and Goddard, were remembered by Plumer as having been involved in the conspiracy. Plumer may have confused Goddard's membership in the Hartford Convention with his attitude in 1804, although Goddard betrayed a guilty conscience by writing two anxious letters to Plumer, endeavoring to ascertain what evidence he possessed. The denials of Hillhouse, however, shocked and surprised Plumer, for he remembered vividly the Connecticut senator's conversation at Aaron Burr's dinner, and the account of this affair in his Memorandum, written only two years later, constituted a nearly contemporary record of the incident.[81]

Plumer, however, did not remember either Hillhouse or Goddard

79. *National Intelligencer* (Washington), Oct. 21, 1828, quoted in Adams, *New England Federalism,* 23; *ibid.,* 43-92; Plumer to John Quincy Adams, Dec. 20, 1828, Letter Book, VIII, Lib. Cong.

80. Plumer to John Quincy Adams, Jan. 16, 1829, *ibid.;* Adams, *New England Federalism,* 93-106.

81. Plumer to Calvin Goddard, Mar. 20, Apr. 18, 1829, Letter Book, VIII, Lib. Cong.; Plumer, Autobiography, 396-97.

as the primary instigators of the plot. Hunt, Griswold, Tracy, and Pickering had been the ringleaders. They were all dead in 1828 except Pickering, who remained discreetly silent until he too died on January 29, 1829. Proof of the conspiracy, therefore, rested entirely upon Plumer and Adams. Motives of friendship, a sense of duty, and probably the peculiar satisfaction of the confessional had prompted Plumer to reveal his long-hidden secret, although he was quite certain of retaliatory abuse. But he refused to publish a reply to his critics. "I do not repent my writing," he confided to his journal. "The slanders of the press do not disturb my repose, & I think will never provoke me to reply to them." [82] Adams had reached the same conclusion. He prepared a long reply to the *Appeal* of the Boston Federalists, submitting parts of it to Plumer for criticism, but he did not publish it, and it remained in manuscript until 1877 when his famous grandson placed it in print.[83]

A peculiar result of the 1828 exposé was that it subjected both Adams and Plumer to obloquy from every political faction then trying to find its way into a party. On the one hand, the Jacksonian Democrats seized upon the quarrel to proclaim the two men as unworthy of the party they had entered in 1807.[84] Isaac Hill quoted Plumer's letter with editorial perversions in his *New Hampshire Patriot,* insinuating that the man who wanted to take New Hampshire out of the Union in 1804, opposed Jacksonian democracy with the same intent in 1829.[85] Hill's article appeared in March, just before the election that bound New Hampshire for thirty years to the Democratic party. At the other extreme were the remaining unreconstructed Federalists, who were even more enraged

82. *Ibid.,* 395. The *Portsmouth Journal,* Mar. 7, 1829, noted that "volunteers in other people's quarrels generally receive worse treatment than *the principals."* The *N. H. Sentinel* (Keene), Mar. 13, 1829, wanted to know who Plumer's confederates in the 1804 conspiracy had been, and "whether they did not all get into the *ark of safety together."* See also the *Columbian Centinel* (Boston), Mar. 4, 1829. Hill's *N. H. Patriot* (Concord) was, of course, the most vitriolic; the Mar. 9, 1829, issue spoke of a man showing "strong symptoms of a mind in ruins," and returning to his treason "like a dog to his vomit or the sow to her wallowing in the mire." The *Patriot* immediately concluded that Webster, Mason, Bell, Olcott, Wolcott, and even President Adams himself had been among Plumer's unnamed associates in the disunion movement.

83. Adams, *New England Federalism,* 107-330.

84. Plumer, Autobiography, 396. James Alexander Hamilton, son of the great founder of the Federalist party, but a Jacksonian Democrat, took offense at Plumer's mention of his father in connection with the Boston meeting proposed in 1804, and published a vindication in which he accused Plumer of being entirely selfish, seeking to advance his consequence with the Republicans and gratify his revenge on the Federalists for neglecting and discarding him.

85. *N. H. Patriot,* Mar. 9, 1829.

by Plumer's betrayal. Harrison Gray Otis, much more willing to believe the Connecticut perjurers than men who had abandoned Federalism, called Plumer a liar and added spicier remarks in a letter to Joseph Hopkinson:

A pretty figure is made by Govr. Plumer. Did ever a seasick Codfisher on the Banks of Newfoundland, disgorge so much flattery upon so unworthy an object as J. Q. A. has upon him. There is a case of one states evidence, supporting the character of another. It so happens that among us *Appelants,* there is not a man who has any acquaintance with Plumer, and but one that would know him by sight from the Devil. . . . This fellow Plumer used to take notes at dinner with the Federalists; while he dipped his hand in the sop [*sic*]. And I dare say has g[ot down some] of their convivial anathemas, as well as jocularities in his black book. It is amusing to think how Apostates smell each other out. This Adams & Plumer are antipodes in talent character, learning, and experience of public affairs, yet though born with their feet opposite, they come cheek by jowl by the attraction of Apostasy.[86]

So virulent was the hatred of the old Federalists for their former associates that for a time both Adams and Plumer thought a combination of "the nullificators from both ends of the union" likely. This fear was also expressed by the younger conservatives, whose political futures were at stake, and who were therefore disgusted with the mess dragged up unnecessarily, as they thought, by Adams, Otis, and Plumer. Daniel Webster was typical of this school of thought. The Democrats tried to connect him with the Federalists whom Adams had denounced; the accusation stung him into a libel suit.[87] Plumer's story that the section which Webster was soon to champion as the rampart of nationalism had plotted disunion in 1804 would not add to the consistency of Webster's position. Calling upon President Adams in March 1829, Webster grumbled sorely at both Plumer and Otis. As a law student in Thompson's office during the winter of 1803-4, he said, he had read letters from Senator Plumer to his instructor. They were "very violent against Mr. Jefferson, and full of all sorts of wild projects. . . . Plumer was a very weak man, without any steadiness of principle or solidity of judgment." [88] This testimony, of course, only verified the existence of the 1804 project, and Adams realized that Webster's own irritation was

86. Morison, *Otis,* II, 255.

87. John Quincy Adams to William Plumer, Jr., Jan. 9, 1830, Plumer Papers, N. H. State Lib.; Sydney Fisher, *The True Daniel Webster* (Phila., 1911), 227-28.

88. *Adams's Memoirs,* VIII, 118.

being vented on Plumer. "His character of Plumer is altogether incorrect," wrote Adams, who was willing to base his public reputation on his friend's good faith.

Plumer and Adams were vindicated as the whole story of 1804 emerged from the manuscripts. It was unfortunate that the revelation of a Yankee secessionist plot had been made in 1828 at the moment when the same feeling was growing so strong in South Carolina. Nevertheless, the frank contrition for what he called the greatest mistake of his life, and the impassioned plea for union that Plumer made in his letter to Adams, December 20, 1828, may have strengthened the hands of Webster and Jackson when they dealt with nullification so soon afterward. It is even more significant that Plumer's words were printed again in his biography in 1856, at a time when New England, and particularly New Hampshire, needed unity as never before in the final struggle for nationalism.

CHAPTER XVII

The Last Years

"Death is a debt we owe to Nature—we must all
pay—for there is no discharge in that war." [1]

PLUMER's diary conveys the impression that, except for poor health, his prolonged old age was spent in serenity and comfort in his Epping farmhouse.[2] At seventy-nine years of age, he was bald only in a small spot, though his thick, black hair had turned gray. Not quite so erect as formerly, he stood five feet, ten inches tall, and probably suffered from lack of exercise. His placid existence derived from having few wants rather than from uncounted abundance. "How much time is spent, and fatigue endured, for that which is unprofitable?" he moralized. It was a great comfort to him that he could dispense with servants and wait on himself. He arose at sunrise, regardless of the season, and washed his feet in a basin of water placed the night before at his bedside, sometimes breaking the ice in winter. After dressing, he made his way immediately to his office and in cold weather built his own fire from wood that he had himself carried from the woodshed. His breakfast would be bread, cheese, and a single cup of weak coffee. Once a week he shaved himself with a razor he had used for thirty-five years. His shoes, which he wore extra large because of an accident to one of his toes, lasted a year without mending. His hats were worn at least four years and his suits two. His clothing was always of superior quality, but he paid little attention "to the *tyrant fashion*," believing that "usefulness, convenience and propriety" were more important than "whim and caprice." [3]

Most of his day was spent in his library, which he had long since

1. Plumer to John Allen, June 4, 1784, Letter Book, I. Lib. Cong.
2. "The world has not left me, but I have retired from it," he confessed. Plumer to Justice Story, May 8, 1831, Plumer Papers, N. H. State Lib.
3. Plumer, Autobiography, 408, 409.

changed from a show place into a workshop. Although his book collection remained a source of infinite pride, over the years he began giving away many of his books and concentrated more on reading than admiring his volumes. Here, with a quill which he managed to use four months before discarding, sharpened with the only pen knife he had owned in thirty-two years, Plumer happily scratched away at his endless writing. At noon, he dined on meat or fish, vegetables, and two cups of strong tea. During each day, he consumed a glass of Madeira and half a glass of Jamaica rum. After dinner there was a half-hour nap in warm weather, and, in winter, an expedition to the wood lot, without an overcoat. Then followed an afternoon in the study, a light evening meal, conversation with the family, and so to bed between nine and ten.[4]

Existence on such a modest scale did not require much expenditure of money, and Plumer had so well husbanded his resources that his estate continued to grow throughout his last years of retirement. On January 1, 1845, when, in a faltering hand, he made a last, incomplete entry in his account book, he still had property worth nearly $54,000, although he had made substantial donations to his children. Interesting changes, however, had taken place in the character of this estate, reflecting in many ways the economic evolution of the nation. By 1834, undoubtedly because of his profound distaste for Jacksonian fiscal policy, he had converted the last of his federal securities into New England bank stock. He was also shrewd enough to liquidate his fifty-nine shares in the Bank of the United States after Jackson vetoed the re-charter bill.[5] Less perceptive, perhaps, was the abandonment of his speculation in Coös County lands. Most of this acreage he donated to his sons, but they found it increasingly difficult to protect against timber thieves and squatters. At the height of the land boom, therefore, the brothers unloaded their holdings in the wild northland at roughly three times the price their father had paid in the 1790's.[6] When the panic of 1837 struck, this looked like good business, and the Plumers did succeed in riding out the storm of depression without serious losses. Within another two decades, however, the lumber and paper mill center of Berlin,

---

4. *Ibid.*, 407-10.
5. Plumer Property Book, N. H. State Lib.; Statement of William Plumer's property, taxes, etc., Repository, IV, *ibid.*; Plumer to Nicholas Biddle, Jan. 23, 1835, Letters, XIII (1833-43), *ibid.*
6. Plumer, Autobiography, 401; George Plumer to Plumer, Jr., Jan. 29, 1820, Plumer, Jr., to Plumer, Dec. 2, 1822, to Mary Plumer, May 1, 1835, Plumer Papers, N. H. State Lib.; entries for 1835-36, Plumer, Jr., Journals and Memoirs, IV, *ibid.*; Plumer, Jr., Land Book, N.-Y. Hist. Soc.

now New Hampshire's second largest city, was to spring up on soil which the Plumers had abandoned.[7]

As Plumer came to the end of his adventures with "Cincinnatus," and as the excitement over his exposures in 1828 died down, he turned his literary activity exclusively to his "Sketches of American Biography," the first of which he had written as early as 1808.[8] Plumer's design in this epic project was to portray the "facts & traits of character" of every distinguished American who had lived since the time of Columbus. Much of his material was salvaged from the wreck of his "History of North America," but as he reached the eighteenth and nineteenth centuries, he discovered that a tremendous volume of fresh research was required. Crumbs of biographical information were solicited through extensive correspondence [9] and from official sources. As late as 1832, Plumer was receiving documents and biographical data from Secretary of the Navy Levi Woodbury, who expressed the hope that his old patron's sketches would soon appear. If they were to be published posthumously, however, Woodbury added gracefully, "I should rather adopt the sentiment of the Spaniard and pray they may not appear for a thousand years." [10]

As the years passed, Plumer's work became literally an obsession. "In a word, my time and thots are devoted to a single subject—biography," he declared in his seventy-eighth year. By that time, however, it had become abundantly evident that he would not live to complete his project, or to see any part of it through the press. Accordingly, he enjoined his sons, in the will that he drew up in 1838, to publish "as soon as may be after my decease . . . a handsome edition of my American biographical work." Complimentary copies were to be given to

7. Merrill, *History of Coös County*, 812.
8. Plumer, Diary, May 7, 1808, Lib. Cong. The collection of brief biographical sketches was a popular literary genre of the period, already successfully exploited by Jeremy Belknap, *American Biography* (Boston, 1794, 1798), and by William Allen, who later became president of Dartmouth University, in his *Biographical Dictionary* (Boston, 1809). In 1830, supposing that Plumer had abandoned any intention of publishing his sketches, Allen asked if he might use them in preparation for a new edition of his work. Plumer to Allen, Aug. 20, 1830, Letter Book, VIII, Lib. Cong.
9. For example, James A. Bayard to Plumer, Mar. 1, 1811, Miscellaneous Letters, N.-Y. Hist. Soc.; Samuel Phillips, Andover, Mass., to Plumer, Jan. 10, 1829, N. H. Hist. Soc.; Curtis Coe, Newmarket, to Plumer, June 10, 1822, Arthur Livermore to Plumer, Jan. 22, 1824, Letter Books, VIII, X, Lib. Cong.; Plumer to Cyrus Bradley, Aug. 1, 1833, Letter Book, XIII, N. H. State Lib.; Salma Hale to Plumer, Apr. 24, 1825, *Granite Monthly*, 5 (1882), 88; John Farmer to Plumer, July 25, 1825, Jan. 13, May 12, 1830, *ibid.*, 57, 167, 126-27.
10. Woodbury to Plumer, Jan. 6, 1832, N.-Y. Hist. Soc.

Harvard College and to each of the historical societies that had honored him with membership, and the profits or losses from the publication were to be shared equally by his four sons.[11]

Plumer's will was ignored, however, and the manuscript biographies remain to this day in the library of the New Hampshire Historical Society.[12] William, Jr.'s excuse for such unprecedented disobedience was that the sketches were not finished in the way that Plumer would have perfected them had he lived long enough to do so.[13] The variation in their quality—some were based entirely on secondary printed authorities and others concerned with nonentities—has discouraged the state historical society or any other editor from attempting their publication.[14] Plumer performed a valuable service for future historians by recording the lives of his own contemporaries—men whom he had known intimately in the legislature, the courts, and the executive councils of New Hampshire,[15] but the very qualities which give his sketches useful local color render them factually unreliable.[16] As his great-granddaughter declared, "Plumer said what he thought." [17] Perhaps that is why the man who hoped first to become the Tacitus and later the Plutarch of his times was finally remembered by those of his neighbors who read the newspapers only as a synthetic Cincinnatus.

Plumer's absorption in historical biography during the last two decades of his life may have been due in part to the hopelessness, from his viewpoint, of contemporary politics in New Hampshire. The Jacksonians, under Isaac Hill, had taken control of the state in March 1829 and did not relinquish their grip until 1846. William Plumer wrote an

11. Plumer, Autobiography, 407; William Plumer, Last Will and Testament, on file in Rockingham County Court House, Exeter, New Hampshire.

12. The finished sketches were donated in 1886 by Plumer's grandchildren. See vote of thanks to William L. Plumer *et al.*, by the society at its annual meeting on June 9, printed in N. H. Hist. Soc., *Proceedings,* 1 (1888), 376. They are indexed in *ibid.,* 435-57.

13. Plumer, Jr., *Life of Plumer,* 506-7.

14. For Washington, he used the biographies by Jared Sparks and Aaron Bancroft, and the histories of the Revolution by Gordon and Ramsay. See Plumer, Biographies, IV, 60-118, N. H. Hist. Soc.

15. Plumer's sketches of New Hampshire's most eminent sons in the Revolutionary period were published in vols. XXI and XXII of the *N. H. State Papers.*

16. In 1894, the New Hampshire Historical Society decided to print the Plumer biographies, but the resolution was soon countermanded.

17. Mrs. Bessie Plumer Norris, granddaughter of George Washington Plumer, and a lively lady with much of her great-grandfather's salty powers of observation, made this statement to the author in 1938, adding that this was the family's understanding of the reason Plumer's sketches had never been published.

occasional article against Hill and voted the Whig ticket, but with no appreciable effect.[18] In 1840, the spurious enthusiasm for "Tippecanoe and Tyler too" generated so much warmth in his eighty-two-year-old bones that he braved the November chill in order to attend town meeting and cast his vote for the Whig electors.[19] This was apparently the last time that Plumer left his house to attend a gathering of any kind in the village. The old man who as a youth had voted in this same town meeting for a vigorous national government and against democratic excesses had come full circle in his political evolution, ending as he had begun in a minority.

William Plumer, Sr., was never an abolitionist, but during the protracted debate over slavery he had for fifty years consistently taken a stand which coincided with the Republican party platform of 1856. In 1820 he had prophesied, as the consequence of the admission of new slave states, a "series of measures . . . that may prove fatal to the integrity of the Union," anticipating by forty years the defeats and vetoes of tariff, homestead, and railroad bills which drove thousands of Northerners into Lincoln's party.[20] When the abolitionist crusade began to gain momentum in the 1830's, Plumer pointed out its fundamental lack of realism in letters to John Greenleaf Whittier and other emancipation enthusiasts. He declared emphatically that he hated slavery and believed that slaveholders were "criminal violators of the Supreme Law." But who was to enforce the supreme law? Neither the free state legislatures nor Congress could emancipate the slaves or even mitigate their sufferings; that lay wholly within the province of the slave-state governments. These had shown some disposition to abolish slavery, and might show more if some method could be devised to "guard against the indigence and misconduct of the freemen." Transportation of liberated slaves had proven impractical; racial amalgamation was "too disgusting." Emancipation would come eventually, but the social problems must be solved first. The only thing that the abolitionists accomplished was disaffection between the North and the South, "and that without emancipating a single slave." [21] Much as he reprobated the ineffectual fanaticism of

18. "Cincinnatus," "To the Freemen of New Hampshire," Plumer, Essays, I, 207-8, Lib. Cong., publ. in *Portsmouth Journal*, Jan. 30, 1838.

19. Plumer, Autobiography, 414; entries for Oct. 1840, Plumer, Jr., Journals and Memoirs (1838-47), N. H. State Lib. (hereafter cited as Plumer, Jr., Memoirs, V).

20. Plumer to Plumer, Jr., Feb. 28, 1820, Plumer Papers, N. H. State Lib.

21. Plumer to John Farmer, Jan. 29, 1835, *ibid.;* Plumer to John Greenleaf Whittier, Aug. 20, 1833, Letter Book, XIII, *ibid.*

the abolitionists, however, Plumer never for a moment suggested that they should be suppressed, even under the warrant of safeguarding the Union.[22]

Plumer's reconversion to political conservatism was not matched by a return to the consolations of religion in his old age—not, at any rate, to any refuge in the bosom of orthodoxy. As early as December 1819, he recorded in his diary that he improved his Sundays in "reading, writing, & obtaining useful knowledge, & not in hearing sermons which outrage reason & common sense." [23] His long absence from church was noted in 1843 by the editors of a religious periodical then being published in Epping. They regretted "that so much occasion is furnished for the belief, that the gospel he preached in his youth has so little of his affection & confidence in the serious period at which he has arrived." [24] At the moment that the church paper was bemoaning his indifference to religion, however, he was reading "with attention and great pleasure" the entire six-volume edition of William Ellery Channing's works. The worthiest characteristic of Channing, in Plumer's opinion, was that he "freely, fully & uniformly avowed his opinions on all subjects & on all occasions with ... inviolable integrity." [25]

William Plumer was indeed a strange Yankee, rearing his children by Epictetus and Rousseau rather than the Old Testament, and being generally successful at it. By 1824, all but the youngest of his sons had married, and in due time Plumer was blessed with ten grandchildren. Jay remained a bachelor in his parents' house, managing the farm and

22. A pamphlet written by "Cincinnatus" and entitled *Freedom's Defense* ([Worcester, 1836], 24 pp.), has been attributed to Plumer. (Lib. Cong. catalogue card has the call number Z657.P73.) The evidence against Plumer's authorship, however, is all but conclusive. He does not himself mention having written such a pamphlet; no manuscript copy of it is retained among his papers; his son does not mention it in the standard biography; nothing else that he ever wrote was published outside New Hampshire; and finally, he says in his Autobiography, 406, for the year 1836, "Upon political subjects I have not, in the course of the last year, taken any part ... I neither read or examine political principles—I do not scarse ever read the whole of any one debate in congress which meets my eyes." At the end of the year he also noted that his reading and writing had been "almost exclusively confined to the subject of biography."

23. Plumer, Autobiography, 374.

24. *Congregational Journal* (Epping), Jan. 5, 1843. William Plumer, Jr., who was a religious man, conveys the impression that his father looked forward to immortality after the death of his youngest son in 1849; Plumer, Jr., *Life of Plumer,* 530-31. Since this event took place several years after Plumer had stopped writing, his change of opinion may have occurred. Prior to 1845, however, he had given no evidence of it.

25. Plumer, Autobiography, 418.

a nearby store. William, Jr.'s family lived in a house built in a corner of the family estate, while Samuel and George, after a short adventure into the west as far as Cincinnati, returned to build homes near their father. There seems to have been a warm, close family relationship, dominated by the patriarch in the old farmhouse at Epping. Some of the most charming letters Plumer wrote were those to his granddaughters when they went off to attend academies at Derry and Cambridge. "As the twig is bent, the tree's inclined," was his favorite admonition, and his grandfatherly advice covered every subject from better spelling to warmer underwear.[26] The third generation of Plumers was a lively lot. There was at least one black sheep among them,[27] but the majority seem to have inherited a considerable portion of their grandfather's intellectual powers with little of his stodginess. Old William Plumer was proud of his progeny, but did not permit them to upset the even tenor of his existence. In 1828, the second daughter of his son William died at the age of two. She had been his favorite granddaughter, and he paid an eloquent tribute to "the kindness of her temper, the strength, sprightliness, & activity of her mind." Yet he refused to wear the elaborate mourning dress of that sentimental age, and declared firmly that a black crepe on the arm was all the tribute he would pay to any relative's memory.[28]

It was natural that a man whose life had been prolonged for decades beyond his expectation should become obsessed with the subject of longevity.[29] Plumer outlived all the men with whom he had begun public life and acquired an almost morbid fascination with his own survival.[30] The deaths of his sisters in 1834 and 1841, however, affected him con-

26. Entry for Aug. 1820, Plumer, Jr., Memoirs, II, N. H. State Lib.; Plumer to Samuel and George, Oct. 31, 1837, to Sarah Plumer, Nov. 3, 1838, to Mary Plumer, July 23, 1839, Letter Book, XIII, *ibid.;* Plumer to Mary Plumer, May 27, 1835, to Sarah Plumer, June 24, 1843, Plumer Papers, *ibid.*

27. Entry for Feb. 1847, Plumer, Jr., Journal and Autobiography (1841-53), N. H. State Lib. (hereafter cited as Plumer, Jr., Memoirs, VI). During the previous year, the conduct of George's son had caused an estrangement between George's family and the rest of the Plumers.

28. Plumer, Autobiography, 392-93.

29. Plumer contributed an essay on longevity to the *Literary Journal,* II, 244. The MS. is in Plumer, Essays, II, 474-77, Lib. Cong. He also preserved tables of longevity in his Repository, IX, 273-74, 279-80, 325-26, N. H. State Lib.

30. President Francis Brown died in 1820, John Taylor Gilman in 1828, Clifton Claggett in 1829, John Samuel Sherburne in 1830, William Richardson and Josiah Bartlett in 1838, Jeremiah Smith in 1842, and Jeremiah Mason in 1848.

siderably and a fatal stroke suffered by his youngest son, John Jay Plumer, on May 1, 1849, completely unnerved him. This, and the sudden demise of his great friend, John Quincy Adams, in the previous year, were twin blows from which he never fully recovered.[31]

Plumer's other, and equally natural obsession, was with his own health, or lack of it. In spite of his tenacious hold upon life, Plumer was frequently a sick man, and, having little else to record in his uneventful later years, he indulged his taste for descriptive writing by a minute examination of his own symptoms. He boasted, however, in 1831, that he had not consulted a physician for fourteen years, and that no one except a member of the family had ever spent a night nursing in his home. Illness did not frighten him, but he did become concerned with the weakening of his powers of perception. In his seventy-third year he confessed that he feared a complete loss of vision and could hardly contemplate the calamity with equanimity. His observation of senility in other men made him realize that he would probably not be conscious of his own decline—an idea that appalled him more than the actual loss of memory itself.[32] But a weakened memory was almost the only "mental faculty" that gave him much concern. His imagination, his ability to reason, and his creative impulses remained strong to the very end.

When death finally visited William Plumer in the ninety-second year of his age, it came with a fine sense of dramatic propriety. On November 6, 1850, a convention of distinguished delegates met in Concord to revise the state constitution to which Plumer and his colleagues had given its existing form in 1792. The president of the convention, Franklin Pierce, son of Plumer's old associate and councilor, alluded in his opening remarks to the fact that "of all the great men who were engaged in forming the instrument under which we have so long lived a secure, prosperous and free people . . . but a single, venerated patriarch survives." [33] Word came on December 20 to William Plumer, Jr., who was himself one "of the most influential members" of this convention, that his father had taken a turn for the worse. Leaving immediately by train, William, Jr., was isolated by a severe snowstorm at Manchester, and

31. Plumer, Autobiography, 405, 415-16; Plumer, Jr., to William Stevens, Aug. 7, 1849, Plumer Papers, N. H. State Lib.; Plumer, Jr., *Life of Plumer*, 529, 531; Plumer, Jr., Memoirs, VI, Mar. 4, 1848, N. H. State Lib.; Plumer, Jr., to Mrs. Charles Francis Adams, May 5, 1848, Plumer Papers, N. H. Hist. Soc.
32. Plumer, Autobiography, 384, 400-4, 406, 412-13, 415.
33. *N. H. Patriot* (Concord), Nov. 14, 1850.

finally reached Epping two days after his father had died.[34] The end had come in the evening of December 22, 1850.

William, Jr.'s daughter, Mary—a true kindred spirit with her grandfather—had been alone at his bedside when he died. "He was quiet, and seldom spoke," she wrote in her diary, "but his breathing was faint and irregular. At length, as I sat listening anxiously to every breath, I heard him suddenly breathe a little harder and quicker than before. I sprang to the bedside in time to see his last gasp. He died without a struggle or a groan, or the slightest movement, except of his lips. As I stood over him, he looked so calm—it was so much like sleep—that I could not believe he was gone." [35] Thus it was, in the midst of a New England blizzard, that the indomitable spirit of William Plumer departed to whatever destiny it had prepared for itself through nearly a century of participation in American history.

The sons and grandsons of Plumer's contemporaries, still debating at Concord the merits and defects of "Plumer's Constitution" at the moment of its author's death, were strongly impressed by this historic association. Ichabod Bartlett, who owed much of his success to Plumer's patronage, rose in the convention to pay tribute to the man who "in all his various public offices [had] watched with such vigilance, and labored with such perseverance, for the interests and welfare of his constituents, as to secure their high esteem and lasting gratitude." Bartlett then moved and the convention unanimously passed the following resolution:

That in the death of the Hon. William Plumer, the State has lost an eminent statesman, a patriotic citizen and an honest man.

That for his long and faithful public services and exemplary virtues as a citizen, the whole people should cherish his memory with affectionate regard.[36]

As a mark of public respect, the convention then adjourned for the day, on the motion of Charles Atherton, distinguished grandson of the man under whom Plumer had begun his apprenticeship in the law.

Plumer's death, coming so long after he had dropped from public sight, was hardly more than a surprising curiosity to a generation ab-

34. Clippings from *Granite State Whig* (Lebanon), Jan. 14, 1851, in Plumer, Jr., Scrapbook, Plumer Papers, N. H. State Lib.; Plumer, Jr., *Life of Plumer*, 534.

35. Quoted in Plumer, Jr., *Life of Plumer*, 533-34; Mary Plumer to Plumer, Jr., Dec. 23, 1850, Plumer Papers, N. H. State Lib.

36. *Proceedings of the State Convention for Revising the Constitution of New Hampshire* (Dec. 27, 1850), printed copy in Plumer Papers, N. H. State Lib. Also printed in the *Daily Patriot* (Concord), Dec. 28, 1850.

sorbed in American expansion to the Pacific and already caught in the quickening current of an irrepressible conflict. The political struggles in which he had engaged were almost forgotten. The parties that he led had long since disappeared. Reforms for which he had fought were accepted as commonplace. In 1850, Plumer was an anachronism, and he remains to this day something of an enigma. His most ardent admirer would not suggest that he belongs to anything higher than the fourth or fifth rank of American statesmen. The only monument erected to his memory is one provided by his own sons in the family burial grounds, and his only existing biography is likewise a work of "filial piety." His birthplace has not become a public shrine, and his Epping homestead has slipped from the fingers of indifferent descendants.[37]

Yet America would not be what she is today, had not Plumer and hundreds of men like him believed profoundly in her destiny. His monument is not a statue on the State House lawn, but the State House itself, which he located and helped to build amidst sharp controversy. He left his indelible mark upon the constitution of his state, and even more, perhaps, on the intangible values which that state still places upon religious toleration and freedom of the press. He was a man of eccentricities and inconsistencies, but he was also a man of conviction, of stubborn courage, and of devotion to principles wider than his own horizons and nobler than his own character.

37. After Bessie Plumer Norris, the last of Plumer's descendants to occupy "Plumer-crest," died, the estate was sold outside the family.

APPENDIX A

THE SECESSIONIST MOVEMENT IN NEW ENGLAND: 1804

The account of the 1804 conspiracy in Chapter VIII has been written primarily from Plumer's point of view and from the evidence furnished by Plumer. It must be admitted that this evidence is uneven and less than overwhelming. None of it is precisely contemporary; neither Plumer's preserved correspondence nor his lengthy Memorandum reveal anything more than the fact that he himself favored a Northern Confederacy. The complete absence of contemporary revelation is disappointing but understandable—men engaged in a conspiracy do not ordinarily spread their activities upon paper. Plumer was careful later to destroy the incriminating evidence which did exist, such as his correspondence with Samuel Hunt.

Plumer's narrative of the 1804 plot therefore exists entirely in the realm of reminiscence, which is certainly not infallible proof. When his story was first published in 1829, it was vigorously challenged, even by some of the surviving participants in the conspiracy, and William Plumer, Jr., still felt it necessary in 1856 to enter into a long and detailed argument in support of his father's evidence. Such a defense is no longer necessary. The publication of letters by Timothy Pickering, Uriah Tracy, Roger Griswold, and the Federalist leaders with whom they had corresponded, in such works as John Church Hamilton's *History of the Republic* ... (New York, 1857-64), Henry Cabot Lodge's *Life of George Cabot* (Boston, 1877), and Henry Adams's *Documents Relating to New England Federalism* (Boston, 1877) laid bare the details of the recurring plans for a Northern Confederacy beyond any shadow of doubt. These letters confirm Plumer's memory in nearly every respect. He may have erred in a few slight matters, but such errors would implicate no one not already condemned by other evidence, nor alter the essential reliability of Plumer's story. His evidence, therefore, has been accepted at face value.

One strange fact, of which Plumer was very conscious, is that he suffered no contemporary attacks because of his secessionism. Writing long afterward (Autobiography, 134), he said: "But it is surprizing that during all the political contests, & they have been many & violent, in which I have been involved, & against some of the very men to whom twenty three years since I freely communicated that opinion, not an intimation has been made, either in the public papers or private circles, on this subject against me. This proceeded either from their sense of honor, forgetfulness, or the fear of being accused of the same error—perhaps all those causes contributed to their silence."

APPENDIX B

The exact statistics of the election of 1816, as described in Chapter XII, are:

Total vote in the
state 38,407   Necessary for majority 19,204
Total vote in 1815 . . 36,194   Necessary for majority 18,098

Increase in total vote,
1815 to 1816   2,123
Increase in necessary
majority   1,106

Plumer's total in
1816 20,338   Surplus over majority . . 1,134
Plumer's total in
1815 17,779   Deficit from majority . .   319
Sheafe's total in
1816 17,994   Deficit from majority . . 1,210
Gilman's total in
1815 18,357   Surplus over majority . .   259

Plumer's plurality
over Sheafe in 1816   2,344
Gilman's plurality
over Plumer in 1815   578
Plumer's increase
from 1815 to 1816   2,599
Sheafe's loss from
1815 to 1816   363
Scattering votes account for the slight
discrepancies.

Note on the Sources

William Plumer and his son, William, Jr., wrote voluminously on many subjects and carefully preserved nearly everything they wrote. Although Plumer himself carefully collected, bound, and catalogued his extensive papers, the collection did not remain intact after his death, but was divided, apparently by his grandsons, and disposed of variously. The bulk of these papers are presently located in three depositories: the New Hampshire State Library at Concord, the Library of Congress, and the New Hampshire Historical Society Library at Concord. There are scattered letters, however, in several other collections, the most significant of which are to be found in the Baker Memorial Library at Dartmouth College, the New-York Historical Society, and the Historical Society of Pennsylvania.

The major Plumer collection is held by the New Hampshire State Library, which contains more than half of William Plumer's papers. There are hundreds of letters, extending from 1782 to 1856, including those from and to several members of the Plumer family. Many of the letters from Plumer are drafts or copies, although hundreds are originals, collected by William Plumer, Jr., from such friends as Salma Hale, William Harper, and Bradbury Cilley. This collection was obviously gathered at one time into letter books, probably numbered from I to XIII. Volumes II, V, VII, and XI-XIII are in the State Library, but except for volume XIII, they have been dismantled. The other volumes are in the Library of Congress.

In addition to the letters, the New Hampshire State Library has many of the original manuscripts of Plumer's literary efforts as well as many miscellaneous Plumer books and papers, such as his property and account books, references to legal cases, precedents, and briefs, extracts from state and national documents, scrapbooks, and his commissions. The literary manuscripts include his Essays, Volume III, containing the "Cincinnatus" articles, written between 1823 and 1829; four of his Repository volumes—I, containing writings, 1801 to 1807; IV, notes and extracts, 1741-1805; VI, miscellaneous notes, 1776-1815; IX, Plumer's gubernatorial speeches and papers; and twelve large note-books in which Plumer inscribed the notes for his biographical sketches and made rough drafts of the biographies themselves.

Nearly the entire manuscript collection of William Plumer, Jr., and his children is also in the New Hampshire State Library. Besides miscellaneous property records and scrapbooks, there are four volumes of Letter Books (1803-32), eight volumes of Memoirs and Journals, running concurrently to 1828 and merged thereafter, and the notes for his father's biography, containing some interesting information which he did not use. There is also a manuscript Life of William Plumer, Jr., by his own son and daughter (William and Mary).

The most important Plumer manuscript in the Library of Congress is his Autobiography, a folio volume of 419 handwritten pages, written between 1826 and 1845, and purchased from Mrs. Bessie Plumer Norris in 1923. The Library also has seven volumes of letters to and from Plumer, mostly originals. These are stitched together into volumes numbered I, III, IV, VI, VIII, IX, and X, and are complementary to those in the New Hampshire State Library. Volumes I and II of Plumer's Essays, and volumes II and III of his Repository are also in the Library of Congress. A very important set of three manuscripts comprise Plumer's journal of events during his five and one-half years in the United States Senate. The first two of these, Plumer called his Memorandum of the Proceedings of Congress, but the third he called a Register of Opinions and Events, I, 1805-1807. (These three volumes have been edited and published by Everett Somerville Brown as *William Plumer's Memorandum of Proceedings in the United States Senate, 1803-1807* [New York, 1923].) The Library also has Plumer's Register, II, a diary which extends from 1807 to 1836, and his History of North America, as well as a volume of notes which he used for this work.

The principal Plumer holdings of the New Hampshire Historical Society are the five manuscript volumes of Plumer's Biographical Sketches, which contain more than 2,000 short biographies. (Thirty-four of these were published in Volumes XXI [1892] and XXII [1893] of the *New Hampshire State Papers*.) An index to the Sketches is printed in the New Hampshire Historical Society, *Proceedings*, 1 (1888), 435-57. The Society also has a few Plumer letters, a book of legal notes, a rough draft of the History of North America, and the manuscripts of a few other essays Plumer wrote for the early volumes of *Collections*.

During his lifetime, William Plumer published some forty-four essays in the newspapers in addition to the 186 "Cincinnatus" articles. Most of these are mentioned in the text, and the journals in which they appeared are listed in the footnotes. The original manuscripts are all preserved in his papers. He also published two works in pamphlet form: *An Address to the Electors of New Hampshire* (Portsmouth, 1804), by "Impartialis," and *An Address to the Clergy of New England on Their Opposition to the Government* (Concord, 1814), by "A Layman." His gubernatorial speeches and proclamations, some sixteen in number, were published by public authority. During his latter years, Plumer also published about half a dozen articles of historical interest in the *Literary Journal, or Collections, ...* (Concord, 1822-24) of John Farmer and Jacob Moore and in the *Collections* of the state historical society.

Six years after Plumer's death, a biography prepared by his oldest son, William Plumer, Jr., was published. This *Life of William Plumer* (Boston, 1856), actually appeared after its author's death and was edited and finished by a friend, A. P. Peabody. Its 543 pages are crowded with excerpts from Plumer's papers, but these were often so completely rewritten as to destroy much of their original character. The younger Plumer was an able craftsman and an essentially honest author, but the attitude with which he approached his task precluded an impartial account. Unfortunately, the half dozen or so biographical sketches of Plumer to be found in other sources are entirely derived from his son's biography. However, Sidney Perley, "The Plumer Genealogy," in the Essex Institute, *Historical Collections,* volumes 50-53 (Salem, Mass., 1914-17), is an example of genealogical research at its best.

The printed documents of the state of New Hampshire were indispensable for this study. Except for minor instances, they corroborate the statements of fact made in Plumer's letters and journals with remarkable consistency. They also, of course, add much information not to be found elsewhere. The state has been diligent in collecting and publishing its early records. The *Provincial, Town,* and *State Papers of New Hampshire,* 30 volumes, edited successively by Nathaniel Bouton, Isaac Hammond, and Albert Batchellor between 1867 and 1897 and published by the state legislature, contain the provincial charters and state constitutions, the legislative journals to 1792, town records, war records, official correspondence, and a wealth of miscellaneous material. After 1792, the journals of each house of the legislature were published sessionally in pamphlet form, and complete sets of these documents have been preserved in several depositories. Important acts, committee reports, speeches, and proclamations were also printed by the legislature; several of these directly concerned Plumer. It will be noted, however, that my study makes no references to the minutes of the governor's Executive Council. These minutes have never been published, and I was unable to locate them in manuscript.

From a period before the Revolution, the laws of New Hampshire were printed in the newspapers at the end of each legislative session, and were occasionally collected and codified by a special committee. Meshech Weare headed such a commission which published the provincial laws in 1761, and a committee composed of Jeremiah Smith, Nathaniel Peabody, and John Samuel Sherburne made a thoroughgoing revision in 1792. After another compilation in 1805, the statutes created by each legislature were published sessionally and periodically recodified until 1904, when the legislature authorized the standard *Laws of New Hampshire,* a chronological arrangement of all legislation to date in 10 volumes issued by the secretary of state. Most of the references to legal enactments in this study are to this work. See A. H. Hoyt, *Historical and Bibliographical Notes on the Laws of New Hampshire* (Worcester, Mass., 1876) for further discussion of this subject.

Court records in New Hampshire were not published officially prior to 1816 and have not been printed in any other form, except for the cases determined in the Superior and Supreme Courts of New Hampshire from 1803 to 1816. This was the period, except for the years 1809-12, when Jeremiah Smith presided over the state's highest court and kept a careful record of the cases which came before him. His manuscript was finally published in Boston in 1879. By that time, the official *New Hampshire Reports* had been published by the clerks of the Superior Court for sixty-three years. Unfortunately, all this activity came after Plumer had virtually retired from the bar.

Plumer first appeared in public print in 1782 through the columns of the *New Hampshire Gazette* (Portsmouth), the state's oldest newspaper and the only one existing in the colony before the Revolution. The *Gazette* managed to survive the vicissitudes of revolutionary times by maintaining a middle-of-the-road attitude, at least until 1801 when it was taken over by the Jeffersonians. Nearly all of the other early newspapers were Federalist. Chief of these was the *Portsmouth Oracle* which began publication in 1793, but almost equally important after Concord became the state capital were the *Courier of New Hampshire*

(Concord, 1794-1805), and the *Concord Gazette* (1806-19). A milder
Federalist organ in the west was the *New Hampshire Sentinel* (Keene,
1799———), while one of the most brilliantly edited papers in America
was the *Newhampshire and Vermont Journal,* later the *Farmer's
Museum,* at Walpole (1793-1810).

Although the Republicans gained control of the *New Hampshire Gazette* in 1801, and established short-lived papers in Concord, Walpole,
and Amherst at about the same time, they offered little competition to
the Federalist press until 1808 when Isaac Hill took over the *New
Hampshire Patriot* (Concord) and soon outdistanced all his rivals.
When Plumer finished his active political career in 1820, Hill was viru-
ally the dictator of the press in New Hampshire.

Newspapers in the early nineteenth century did not even pretend to
be objective reporters of passing events. Their principal purpose was to
pour scorn and contumely upon the heads of political opponents. This
should be remembered in estimating their historical value.

The hortatory or denunciatory pamphlet was a favorite form of propaganda in the early nineteenth century, but with few exceptions these
publications only amplified or repeated the material appearing in the
newspapers. Plumer himself, it will be recalled, published two rather
influential pamphlets and was the object of criticism in many others.
The Dartmouth College controversy gave birth to a multitude of tedious
and tendentious pamphlets, only one of which is listed in the footnotes
of Chapter XII. Election Sermons—the homilies officially pronounced
by invited ministers at the opening of each legislative session—form
another category of large dimensions. Most of the pamphlets used in
this work, however, were political, and were consulted in the remarkable Moore Collection of pamphlets in the Library of Congress.

The published memoirs and letters of John Quincy Adams, Thomas
Jefferson, James Monroe, and Daniel Webster, to which frequent reference is made in this work, are the standard editions, all of which are
incomplete in one way or another. There are two collections of published letters, however, which deserve particular mention. *Documents
Relating to New England Federalism, 1800-1815* (Boston, 1877),
edited and published by Henry Adams, corroborates to a remarkable
degree the evidence which Plumer gave in 1828 and 1829 of the constant flirting with secession carried on by leading Federalists after they
lost control of the national government. Equally revealing of the opposite trend during the decade of the 1780's, when unionists were trying
to hold the republic together, is the "Correspondence between Jeremy

Belknap and Ebenezer Hazard," published in the Massachusetts Historical Society, *Collections,* 5th series, volumes 2 and 3 (Boston, 1877). Belknap, New Hampshire's great historian, lived through these years in Dover and gives a firsthand revelation of their trials and tribulations.

No one writes a history or a biography independent of the works of other historians and biographers. My indebtedness to these is amply demonstrated in my footnotes and will be obvious to the informed reader. There seems little point in listing these secondary works again in this Note on the Sources, but this should in no wise be considered as an underestimate of their importance. Biographies, local histories, state histories, and studies of the national scene, in article and book form, were used extensively and added immeasurably to the scope and depth of this biography.

INDEX

Index

A

Abbot, Benjamin, 159
Abolitionist movement, 338
Adams, Henry, 125
Adams, John, 6, 67, 80, 81, 152, 312; foreign policy of, 64, 65
Adams, John Quincy, 101, 116, 172, 293, 309, 310; and Louisiana Purchase, 113, 114, 115; and John Pickering trial, 128, 132, 155; and Northern Confederacy, 136, 329-33; and Plumer, 175, 179, 199-200; opposes Essex Junto, 181; and embargo, 187; as Secretary of State, 283; and election of 1820, 312-15, 317-18, 319; elected President, 327, 328-29; death, 341
Agriculture in New England, 13, 323
Albany Gazette, 285
Alien and Sedition Acts, 65-66
Allen claim, 17-18
Allen, William, 248, 251, 296, 299, 301-2, 336n
American (Hanover), 266
American Antiquarian Society, 225
American Patriot (Concord), 187. See also *New Hampshire Patriot*
American Revolution, 4-6, 14, 22, 24, 28, 229
"American System," 309-10
Ames, Fisher, 134
Amherst, N. H., 15, 25, 74
Annals of Congress, 101
Antifederalists, 26, 145
Articles of Confederation, 45

Association Test in New Hampshire, 5
Assumption Act, 39
Atherton, Charles Humphrey, 29, 342
Atherton, Joshua, 15, 20, 28, 29, 45-46
Atkinson, N. H., 37
Atkinson Academy, 178
Aurora, 323

B

Bank of the United States, 309, 335
Bankruptcy Act, 102
Banks, New Hampshire, 275. *See also* New Hampshire, Bank of; Cheshire Bank; Hillsborough Bank; Union Bank; Walpole Bank
Baptists, 6-7, 12-14, 73, 75, 107, 160
Bartlett, Ichabod, 297-98, 308, 321, 342
Bartlett, Josiah, 203, 216, 280
Bartlett, Levi, 191, 203, 279
Bastrop grant, 169
Bayard, James A., 170-71
Beckley, John, 100
Belknap, Jeremy, 18, 320, 353-54
Bell, Samuel, 195, 217, 259, 261, 267, 307, 310
Bentham, Jeremy, 245, 293-94
Bentley, William, 233
Berlin, N. H., 335-36
Bill of Rights, 33, 47
Blennerhassett, Harman, 170
Bollman, Erick, 170
Bond, Nathan, 60, 61
Boston, 5, 42, 94, 141, 143, 283, 291; visited by Plumer, 60, 167, 214
Bradbury, Theophilus, 15, 30

Bradley, Stephen, 128, 169
Breckenridge Bill, 101, 114-15
Brewster, Amos, 235, 248, 251, 301
Brown, Francis, 234, 263, 264
Burr, Aaron, 82, 97, 115, 121, 134, 150;
Plumer's opinion of, 96n, 154; and
John Pickering trial, 127; and Northern Confederacy, 141-42, 143, 330;
conspiracy of, 169-71; and James
Sheafe, 237
Butler, Henry, 190-92
Butler, Josiah, 274, 278, 279, 306, 325

C

Cabot, George, 136
"Cadmus," 323
Canaan, N. H., 7
Carrigain, Philip, 140, 196
Carter, Nathaniel, 316
Caucus, Federalist, 75, 78, 88; Republican, 196, 198, 218, 279, 325-27
Centinel (Boston), 67
Channing, William Ellery, 339
Chase, Samuel, 154-57, 161
Chesapeake, 180
Cheshire Bank, 278
Cheshire Co., N. H., 7, 50-51, 166
Chester, N. H., 22
Cilley, Bradbury, 137-38
Claggett, Clifton, 29, 217, 241, 318n;
opposes Judiciary Act of 1813, 226,
256; clashes with Plumer, 261, 262-63, 267, 268, 269, 270
Claggett, William, marries Sarah
Plumer, 241; works for father's appointment, 262, 268-69; establishes
People's Advocate, 268; opposes
Plumer, 272-73, 274, 279, 318n, 325
Claggett, Wyseman, 29, 241, 262
"Claggetting," 262
Clark, Jonathan, 58, 59
Clay, Henry, 309
Clinton, DeWitt, 115-16, 216
Clinton, George, 121, 185
Cogswell, Thomas, 49-50, 138
Coleman, William, 16, 25, 94
Committee of Ten, 46-49

Concord, N. H., 19, 20-21, 28, 46; and
New Hampshire constitution, 51n;
and Republicans, 144, 205, 258;
Plumer leaves, 222-23, 260. *See also*
New Hampshire State House
Concord Gazette, 229-30, 239, 242, 261,
277
Confederation, 25
Congregationalists, 6, 10-11, 14, 34,
107, 290; clergy, 72, 187, 227-30,
234-35
Connecticut, 77, 139, 142, 149, 219, 231,
289
Connor, Benjamin, 80, 88, 89, 136; in
fiscal junto, 58, 59, 60, 69
Constitution, New Hampshire. *See*
New Hampshire, constitution of
Constitution, United States, 25, 36,
43, 45, 82, 112, 115, 117, 123-24
Coös County, 212-214, 335-36
Courier of New Hampshire (Concord), 71, 82, 352-53
Court of Common Pleas, 20, 167
Crawford, William H., 327
Crowninshield, Benjamin, 233, 296

D

Dartmouth College, controversy, 233-36, 238-39, 246-47, 301-2; Acts, 245-54, 270-71; Case, 297-301
Dartmouth University, 263-67, 295-302
Dayton, Jonathan, 109
Dearborn, Henry, 2, 14, 83, 209, 212,
214
"Decagon," 265
Delaware, 119, 149
Democratic party. *See* Jacksonian
Democrats; Republican party
Detached militia. *See* Militia, detached
Dexter, Samuel, 30
Dinsmoor, Samuel, 325, 326
Dover, N. H., 54, 84
Durham, N. H., 304
Du Pont de Nemours, 245
Dyer, Mary, 292-93
d'Yrujo, Marquis, 110, 169

E

Education in New England, 2-4. *See also* Dartmouth College; Plumer, educational theories
Edwards, Jonathan, 7
Eighth Congress, 115, 153-54
Election of 1816, 235-38, 347
Electoral college of 1820, 311-19
Embargo, 182, 186, 187
Enfield, N. H., 291, 292
Epping, N. H., 30, 72, 137, 214; and Plumer family, 2, 3; religious revival in, 6; elects Antifederalist, 26; "democracy" in, 80, 87; post office of, 183-84
Errol, N. H., 56, 309
Essex Junto, 136, 139, 153, 181, 193
Essex Register (Salem, Mass.), 315
Evans, Richard, 197, 262*n*; and "Veritas" article, 185; in Superior Court, 189, 217; praises Plumer, 193; and Judiciary Act of 1813, 226, 256
Exeter, N. H., 20, 22, 26, 58, 68, 74, 80
Exeter Junto, 43, 64, 136, 144, 195; fiscal policy of, 41, 58-62, 68-69, 75-76; controls New Hampshire, 74-75; Plumer against, 84-85, 86, 160, 185
Exeter riot, 23-24
Exeter Watchman, 277

F

Farmer, John, 321
Farrar, Timothy, 236, 261
Federalist party, 34, 71, 81-83, 160; in Epping, N. H., 26; Plumer joins, 57; and fiscal junto in New Hampshire, 61; and New Hampshire judiciary, 62; and New Hampshire election of 1796, 63; divided in New Hampshire, 64, 69; Plumer follows, 65; and political hysteria, 66; and spoils system, 67; indifference to public opinion, 68; strength in 1799, 72-73, 74; mistakes in New Hampshire, 75-78, 80; decline nationally, 97, 282; New Hampshire machine of, 143-44, 146; Plumer breaks with, 181; and New Hampshire election of 1813, 221; and Dartmouth College controversy, 236; and Plumer's appointees, 260-61. *See also* Caucus, Federalist; Judiciary Act of 1813; Pickering, John, trial of; War of 1812
Fletcher, Robert, 162
Fletcher v. *Peck*, 162
Florida, 173
Fort Plumer, 212, 214
Francophiles, 57
Francophobes, 57, 65
Freeman, Russell, 63, 69, 289*n*
Freeman's Oracle (Exeter), 22
French, Joseph, 22, 23, 24
French Revolution, 72
Frontier, 17, 68, 212, 213

G

Gallatin, Albert, 175, 204
Georgia, 6
Gilbert, Benjamin, 86
Giles, William, 155, 164
Gilman, John Taylor, 64, 120, 142, 223, 232, 251; heads Exeter Junto, 41; opposes state securities tax, 42; and fiscal junto, 58-62, 68-69; popular majority shrinks, 63; disputes with Plumer, 67-68, 79-80, 84-85; and Superior Court, 70; attacks France, 72; and Union Bank, 75-76; speeches of, 78; Plumer supports, 85-86, 108, 136; and Plumer's election to Senate, 87-89; defeated, 158; and election of 1812, 203-4; and militia, 220; defeats Plumer, 221, 233; Plumer, Jr., against, 230; fiscal advice to Plumer, 275; and state prison, 287. *See also* Judiciary Act of 1813
Gilman, Nathaniel, 88, 190-91, 196, 197
Gilman, Nicholas, 24, 25, 88, 89, 182, 196, 203
Gilmanton, N. H., 49
Goddard, Calvin, 135, 142, 160, 330

Goddard, John, 77, 196, 197, 216, 217
Gordon, William, 29, 63
Gov. Plumer, 222n
Grafton Co., N. H., 71, 205, 264
Greenleaf, James, 59, 60
Granger, Gideon, 83, 146, 183
Gray, Henry, 177-78, 296
Gray, William, 167, 177, 187
Griswold, Roger, 135, 141-42, 152, 331, 345

H

Haiti, 173
Hale, John, 29
Hale, Salma, 296-97, 300, 302, 308
Hall, Elijah, 259, 273
Hamilton, Alexander, 39, 141-42, 143, 149, 154
Hampstead, N. H., 22
Harper, John, 206, 208, 216
Harper, Robert Goodloe, 125, 127, 128
Harris, John, 268, 269
Hartford Convention, 143, 231, 233, 329, 330
Harvard College, 90, 158, 168, 178-79, 246
Hathorne, Benjamin, 138
Haven, Nathaniel, 326
Herald of Gospel Liberty, 187
Hill, Isaac, 242, 272, 308, 316; praises Plumer, 193; on Plumer's retirement, 223-24; warns of religious conspiracy, 234-35; and Dartmouth College, 245; and printing contract, 256; attacks John Quincy Adams, 325; breaks with Plumer, 326-27; controls New Hampshire, 337-38. See also *New Hampshire Patriot* (Concord)
Hillhouse, James, 135, 141-42, 330
Hillsborough Bank, 195, 217, 261, 307
Hillsborough Co., N. H., 20, 198, 259; convention, 20-21
Holderness, N. H., 7, 94
Holt, Peter, 72-73, 104, 107, 187, 227
Hopkinson, Joseph, 332
Hunt, Samuel, 134, 135, 142, 331, 345

I

Impeachment, of Woodbury Langdon, 40-41; Plumer's attitude toward, 123, 156; of John Pickering, 125-30; of Samuel Chase, 154-57
Impressment of seamen, 171, 182, 207
Imprisonment for debt, 18, 190, 288, 289n
Indiana Territory, 240

J

Jackson, Andrew, 327, 333, 335
Jackson, James, 164
Jacksonian Democrats, 331, 335, 337
Jacobin clubs, 57-58
Jacobs, Stephen, 264, 266
Jaffrey, George, 59-60
Jay Treaty, 57, 58, 61, 63, 172
Jefferson, Thomas, 87, 172, 230, 245, 308; Plumer supports, 39; and spoils system, 67; and election of 1801, 81, 82; Plumer visits, 94-95; and Supreme Court, 97; and Thomas Paine, 103; and Louisiana, 104-6, 111; and judiciary, 122; and John Pickering, 124; Plumer against, 147; character of, 164-65; and Burr, 171; and Napoleon, 173-74; and Plumer's historical writing, 175; and Plumer, 179-80, 183, 243; and Federalist secession movements, 329
Judicial reform, in New Hampshire, and Plumer, 32-33, 34-35, 48-50; by Federalists, 69-70; in 1816, 254-56. *See also* Pickering, John, trial of; Judiciary Act of 1813
Judiciary Act of 1813, New Hampshire, 225-26, 244-45, 255-56, 262

K

Kent, William, 144n, 191
Kentucky and Virginia Resolutions, 65-66

L

Ladd, Nathaniel, 26
Lake Umbagog, 212
Langdon, John, 78, 281, 306; and Federal Constitution, 25; elected U. S. senator, 37; Plumer against, 39, 40, 58; and John Taylor Gilman, 41; as Francophile, 57; and Union Bank, 75, 77; as candidate for governor, 86, 87; endorsed by Jefferson, 108; as speaker of the House, 142; as governor, 158, 160-61; Plumer asks for office, 167, 183, 184; and office-jobbing, 189, 217; Plumer joins, 193-95; and state charters, 195-96; and retirement, 196-98, 205; and militia, 210-11
Langdon, Woodbury, 40-41
Legislature, New Hampshire. *See* New Hampshire, Legislature
Leopard, 180, 181
Library of Congress, 99
Lincoln, Abraham, 338
Lincoln, Levi, 296
Livermore, Arthur, 163, 325; and Plumer, 7; character of, 29; and religious freedom, 34*n*; and Superior Court, 70, 71, 217; attempt to remove, 161
Livermore, Edward St. Loe, 83, 107, 127, 134, 137, 139, 163; character of, 29; and New Hampshire constitution, 45, 46, 49, 52
Livermore, Samuel, 23, 28, 29, 71, 81
Londonderry, N. H., 19, 22, 23, 24, 27, 57
Louisiana, 169-72
Louisiana Purchase, 109, 110-13, 114, 124, 133

M

McClary, Michael, 209
McClary v. *Gilman*, 33
McFarland, Asa, as "W," 229-30
Madison, James, 39, 131, 185, 221, 232, 293, 308

Mahurin, Ephraim, 212, 213-14
Marbury, William, 83
Marshall, John, 171, 301
Mason, George, 105
Mason, Jeremiah, 126, 136-37, 202, 218, 231, 269; as lawyer, 30-31; and Plumer's withdrawal from Federalists, 174-75; Plumer wants to appoint, 202, 259, 261; and judicial reform, 254; and Plumer's fiscal policy, 277; and Dartmouth College controversy, 298; praises Plumer, 308; and election of 1820, 312
Masonian Proprietors, 17, 59
Massachusetts, 1, 52, 77, 135, 149, 165, 167, 219, 312; General Court of, 6
Massachusetts Historical Society, 100, 180, 320*n*
Medical science, 13
Melemelli, Soliman, 163
"Merrimack Boating Company," 196
Merrimack Valley, 74, 87, 138
Militia, 5, 210-11, 242, 283-85; detached, 211-12, 219, 220, 232
Millsfield, N. H., 309
Miranda, Francisco, 170
Monroe, James, 105, 112, 172, 209, 282-85, 310-19
Montgomery, John, 213, 214
Morrill, David L., 198, 252, 256, 276-79
Morris, Gouverneur, 97, 102, 106
Morse, Jedediah, 132, 134, 139
Muzzy v. *Wilkins*, 34

N

Napoleon, 78-79, 97, 105, 112, 149, 171, 173
National Advocate (New York), 316
National Intelligencer (Washington, D.C.), 175
Naturalization Act, 65
Neal, Moses, 27
Newburyport, Mass., 2, 3, 6, 15, 115, 137
New Hamsphire, revolutionary constitution of, 10-11; constitution of 1784, 10-11, 44-45, 47-48, 52, 226, 255, 284-

85; religious establishment, 11; fiscal policy of, 16-18, 21, 23, 41-42, 58-61, 68-69, 275-78; constitutional convention of 1791-92, 45-52; trade of, 77; U. S. President from, 121; and War of 1812, 214-15; prisons of, 222, 287-89; constitutional convention of 1850, 341, 342

New Hampshire, Executive Council, revised in 1792, 47; Republicans control, 189, 190, 205, 231; Republican minority in, 217; of 1816, 259-60, 267, 272-73

New Hampshire, General Court, 23, 46, 47, 48, 50, 61. *See also* New Hampshire, Legislature

New Hampshire, House of Representatives, 47-48, 81-83, 117-18. *See also* New Hampshire, Legislature

New Hampshire, Legislature, Session of 1785, 18-19; of 1786, 20; of 1788, 36; of 1790-92, 39-43; of 1794, 58-62; of 1797-98, 64-71; of 1799, 72-73; of 1800-1801, 75-82; of 1810-11, 195-96; of 1812, 206-9, 214-15, 222; of 1813, 223, 225-26; of 1816, 242-57, 270-79; of 1817-18, 287-94

New Hampshire, Senate, 47, 80, 82, 195, 238

New Hampshire, Superior Court, 29, 57, 222; and Plumer, 30-33 *passim*, 54, 69-71, 84; and John Pickering, 62; and Dartmouth College controversy, 266-67, 297-99

New Hampshire, Supreme Court, 226, 255

New Hampshire Bar Association, 28

New Hampshire, Bank of, 42-43, 59, 61, 69, 76, 98, 309-10

New Hampshire Gazette (Portsmouth), 4, 10-11, 89, 185; bought by Republicans, 82; and Gallatin, 204; praises Plumer, 218

New Hampshire Historical Society, 320-22

New Hampshire Patriot (Concord), 219, 331; publishes Plumer's articles, 192, 193, 219, 228, 237, 322; praises Plumer, 218, 222, 280; attacks Federalist courts, 226-27; prints Plumer, Jr.'s articles, 230; and Jeremy Bentham, 294; favors Monroe, 311; and campaign of 1828, 328. *See also* Hill, Isaac

New Hampshire Sentinel (Keene), 244, 316, 331n

New Hampshire State House, 256, 260, 272-74, 343

New Haven, Conn., 177

"New Light," 6-7

Newmarket, N. H., 27

New Orleans, 104-6, 108, 110, 113, 170, 171

New York, 94, 116, 141

New-York Evening Post, 16, 94

New-York Statesman (Albany), 316

Norris, John, 101

Northern Confederacy, 133-50, 151, 186-87, 329-31, 345-46

O

"Octagon," 234, 251, 253, 254, 263-65, 295

Ohio country, 1

Olcott, Simeon, 81, 89, 129, 135, 295

Otis, Harrison Gray, 329, 332

Otis, Samuel Alleyne, 174

P

Page, William, 41, 45-46, 49, 50-51

Paine, Thomas, 147

Paper money, 16, 17, 20-21, 23, 26

Parish, Elijah, 248, 281, 299

Parker, Nahum, 166, 194

Parrott, John, 306

Parsons, Theophilus, 30, 31

Peabody, Nathaniel, 38, 178, 289n; Plumer defeats election of, 37; and New Hampshire constitutional convention, 45-46; investigates fiscal junto, 61; and Republican meeting, 190-91; and plot against Plumer, 203

Peabody, Oliver, becomes probate judge, 43; becomes state treasurer, 58; and fiscal junto, 58-61; and state tax, 68; as treasurer, 68-69; and Union Bank, 75-76; and Plumer, 88-89, 108, 138, 185, 195; and Noah Webster, 160

People's Advocate (Portsmouth), 268, 276, 279-80, 281

Perkins, Cyrus, 235, 248, 251

Peterborough, N. H., 20

Philadelphia, Pa., 65, 309

Phillips Exeter Academy, 93

Pickering, John, 15, 28; and New Hampshire constitution, 44, 45, 46; appointed to federal court, 62; impeachment and trial, 122-31, 136, 155

Pickering, Timothy, and Northern Confederacy, 135, 136, 139, 141-42, 149, 345; Plumer's opinion of, 165; and opposition to embargo, 186

Pierce, Benjamin, 259, 278, 279, 328

Pierce, Franklin, 121, 341

Pierce, John, 42-43

Pillsbury, Moses C., 288

Pinckney, Charles Cotesworth, 64, 172, 185

Plumer, Daniel, brother of William, 140-41, 157-58, 209

Plumer, Francis, ancestor of William, 1, 6

Plumer, George, son of William, 65, 93, 163, 178, 241, 286, 340

Plumer, John Jay, son of William, 65, 93, 287, 339-41

Plumer, Mary Dole, mother of William, 2

Plumer, Quintus, son of William, 158

Plumer, Samuel, father of William, 1-6, 14, 108

Plumer, Samuel, brother of William, 159

Plumer, Samuel, son of William, 56, 93, 163, 178, 204, 286-87; and treasury notes, 275

Plumer, Sarah Flower (Sally), wife of William, 27, 28, 56, 177

Plumer, Sarah (Sally), daughter of William, 56, 93, 177, 241, 262, 286

Plumer William, early life and education, 1-5, 9; toryism of, 5-6, 7, 238; religious beliefs, 6-7, 7-10; and religious freedom, 11, 14, 33-34, 47, 290-91; as lawyer, 15, 19, 20, 28, 30-34, 54, 159; as legislator, 16, 18-19, 36, 38-40, 42, 63, 68-69, 75, 80, 82, 195-96; family life, 26-28, 93, 339-40; political speeches, 26, 77, 82, 117-20, 182-83; as poet, 27; description of, 31, 92, 100, 134-35; as speaker of the House, 38, 40, 63-64; nominations, 43, 191, 198, 279, 305, 306; as constitution-maker, 45-52; retirements of, 52-53, 84, 176-80, 224-25, 308-11; wealth of, 55, 56, 168, 232, 309, 335; religious practices of, 72, 75, 290, 339; illnesses of, 84, 177, 284-85, 286, 296, 307, 341; as Jefferson's dinner guest, 95, 152, 164; in U. S. Senate, 98, 102, 110-13, 117-21, 129, 151-52, 156, 170; and official ceremonies, 98-99, 205, 260, 308; as secessionist, 134-50, 329-30, 345; and slavery, 146, 338-39; solicits offices, 167, 183-84, 190, 240-41; addresses to state legislature, 206-8, 220, 242-47, 272, 288, 290, 294, 308; as war governor, 210-16; gubernatorial appointments, 217, 258-63, 267-70, 288; educational theories, 245-46, 303, 323; as elector, 311, 314-15, 318-19;

political writings: on religious intolerance, 10-11; on paper money convention, 22; on constitutional revisions, 49; against James Sheafe, 237; during election of 1828, 328; Memorandum, 100-101, 114, 330; *Address to Electors of New Hampshire*, 144-46; *Address to Clergy of New England on their Opposition to the Government*, 228-30, 248; "Aristides" articles, 189-90, 192-93; "Cato" articles, 147-48, 175; "Cincinnatus" articles, 201, 303, 322-26; "Columbus" articles, 218-19; "Impartialis" articles, 144-47, 148, 175, 194, 238*n*; "Laymen" articles, 228-30; "Veritas" articles, 185, 277-78;

elected to offices: selectman and justice of the peace of Epping, N, H., 14; representative of state legislature, 1785, 16, 1788, 36, 1790, 1791, 38, 1797, 63, 1800, 76, 1801, 81; defeated by Antifederalist in 1788, 26; defeated by Exeter Junto in 1792, 43; to 1791 state constitutional convention, 45; to Epping, N. H., offices, 55; to U. S. Senate, 87-90; to state senate, 1810, 1811, 194-95; governor of New Hampshire, 1812, 205, 1816, 238, 1817, 281, 1818, 1819, 282; defeated for governor, 1813, 221, 1814, 231, 1815, 233;

political opinions of: and paper money agitation, 20-25; and Federal Constitution, 25-26; supports Federalist policies, 57-58, 64-67, 72-73, 104-5; opinions change, 160-61; opposes Federalists, 180-81; becomes Republican, 182-83;

as historian and scholar: 99-100, 168-69, 174-75, 225, 309, 320-21; historical writings: "History of North America," 179, 180, 199-201, 225, 320; "Sketches of American Biography," 336-37

Plumer, William, Jr., 163, 279, 305, 327, 341-42; birth, 56; at Phillips Exeter Academy, 93; as Federalist, 152; at Harvard, 158-59, 178-79; biography of father, 31, 95*n*, 345; as "Phocian," 230; against James Sheafe, 237; as federal loan officer, 240; and William Claggett, 262-63; and father's political techniques, 266-69; and treasury notes, 275-77; elected to Congress, 286; and election of 1820, 312-14, 317, 318, 319; and New Hampshire Historical Society, 320; and Isaac Hill, 328-29

Political Observatory (Walpole), 157*n*

Portsmouth, N. H., 3, 54, 74, 80, 214; politicians of, 15, 29, 78, 204, 267-68, 282; and Plumer, 19; and New Hampshire Bank, 42-43; defense of, 65, 209-11, 220; officers dismissed, 66-67; and Union Bank, 75, 77; fire in, 98; and Monroe's tour, 283-84

Portsmouth Journal, 326, 331

Portsmouth Oracle, and Federalists, 146; prints Plumer's articles, 147, 152, 175; against Richard Evans, 189; against Plumer, 194, 202, 238, 242; praises Plumer, 208; and Monroe's tour, 285; and election of 1820, 315-16

Prentice, John, 19, 28, 64, 70-71

Presbyterians, 34

Protestant test in New Hampshire, 47

Q

Quakers, 5, 107

Quarles, Samuel, 259, 273, 279

Quincy, Josiah, 180

R

Randolph, John, 162, 311

Religious freedom in New Hampshire, 10-12, 33-34, 47, 75, 160, 289-93

Repertory (Boston), 131

Republican party, 219; as Francophiles, 57; and fiscal junto, 62; in 1796, 63; and spoils system, 66-67, 83-84; grows in New Hampshire, 68; supports Samuel Livermore, 71; and religious liberty, 73; controls Epping, N. H., 74; and Union Bank, 75-77; and New Hampshire redistricting, 80; Plumer supports, 85; Plumer against, 86, 103, 140-41; changes principles, 97; and Portsmouth fire, 98; and Bankruptcy Act, 102; and Twelfth Amendment, 115-16; Daniel Plumer supports, 140-41; machine of, 143, 144, 148; Plumer turns toward, 157-58, 166, 183, 190-91; in Massachusetts, 167; Plumer joins, 198-99, 203-5; renominates Plumer, 218; defeated in 1813, 221;

controls Executive Council, 231; in Portsmouth, N. H., 267-68, 282; and dissension in New Hampshire, 271-72, 278-80. *See also* Caucus, Republican; Jefferson, Thomas; Pickering, John, trial of

Republican Address to the Electors of New Hampshire, 148, 149

Republican Gazette (Concord), 89

Rhode Island, 21, 119, 219

Richardson, William, 259, 261, 267, 269, 284, 298-99

Ripley, Eleazar, 248-49, 251

Rochester, N. Y., 291

Rockingham Convention, 22, 23

Rockingham Co., N. H., 30, 33, 43, 46, 85, 87, 167, 184, 259; courts, 30

Ross, James, 97

"Rotten Cabbage Rebellion," 178

Rousseau, Jean Jacques, 245, 339

Rush, Benjamin, 245

Rush, Richard, 315, 328

S

Saint-Memin, Charles Fevret de, frontispiece, 92

Salaries for public officials, 67, 70, 160-61, 243-44

Salem, Mass., 167, 233

San Ildefonso, treaty of, 110

Secession plot of 1804. *See* Northern Confederacy

Senate, U. S., election to, 36-37, 71, 77-78, 81, 87, 166, 217-18, 256, 305-7; Plumer in, 30, 94-176

Seventh Congress, 97, 115

Sewall, Stephen, 2-3

Shakers, 10, 291-93

Shays, Daniel, 22

Sheafe, James, 89, 124, 138; and New Hampshire Bank, 42-43; and John Pickering, 62; supported by Plumer, 71; elected to Senate, 77-78; resignation of, 87; and Northern Confederacy, 139; Plumer attacks, 236-37; Plumer defeats, 238, 281, 347

Shepard, Samuel, 6, 7

Sheppard, Joseph, 107

Sherburne, John, 57, 58, 282; character of, 29; Plumer opposes, 39-40, 124, and banks, 43, 77; as district attorney, 83; and trial of John Pickering, 128-29; accuses Plumer of toryism, 238

Smith, Elias, 187

Smith, Captain John, 200

Smith, Jeremiah, 144, 189, 224; refused bar examination, 20; friendship with Plumer, 29-30; as lawyer, 31; and judicial reform, 32-33, 226; and impeachment trials, 41, 155; correspondence with Plumer, 42, 57, 58, 60, 63, 66, 84, 130, 139; and constitutional convention of 1791-92, 45, 52; as congressman, 46; as judge, 81; becomes New Hampshire chief justice, 91; on Portsmouth fire, 98; on behavior of congressmen, 99; and Bankruptcy Act, 102; on Republican machine, 140, 143; quarrel with Plumer, 159; salary raised, 160-61; as governor, 188, 190; Plumer against, 195; and Henry Butler, 192; defeated, 203; and Dartmouth College controversy, 298; supports John Parrott, 306

Smith, Samuel Harrison, 175

Smith, William, 187

South Carolina, 64, 119, 185, 333

South Writing School, 2

Sparhawk, Samuel, 196

Spoils system, 67

Stearns, Josiah, 4, 6, 72, 184

Steele, Jonathan, 29, 128-29, 131, 217

Stewartstown, N. H., 56, 212-13

Storer, Clement, 198

Story, Joseph, 220, 233, 296, 301

Strafford Co., N. H., 30, 33, 205, 259, 279

Strong, Caleb, 135, 142

Sullivan, George, 29, 195, 297-98

Sullivan, James, 245

Sullivan, John, 23-24, 25, 38, 39, 62

Sullivan, John L., 196, 208

Supreme Court, U. S., 172, 300-301
Swartout, Samuel, 170

T

Tender Act, 18
Tenney, Samuel, 78, 89-90, 94, 160
Thompson, Thomas W., 87, 138, 139, 143-44 147, 252, 260
Thornton, N. H., 72
Toleration Act, 290-91
Tompkins, Daniel D., 121, 311-19
Tracy, Uriah, 152, 158; and Northern Confederacy, 135, 141-42, 149, 330-31, 345
Treaty of Ghent, 232
Treaty of Paris, 23
Tripolitan war, 138, 169
Turreau, General, 163
Twelfth Amendment, 115-20, 121, 133, 142

U

Union Bank, 75-77, 81-82, 84, 85
Universalists, 34, 160
University of New Hampshire, 304
Upham, George B., 259, 261

V

Varnum, Joseph, 94
Vermont, 119, 185, 289
Veto power, 257, 278-79, 293
Virginia, 39, 105, 119, 121, 133, 145-46, 157, 165
Vose, John, 178
Vose, Sen. John, 276, 277
Vose committee, 276

W

Walpole Bank, 257, 278
War of 1812, 207-8, 209, 213, 215, 228

Washington, D. C., 87, 88, 95-96, 162-63, 176; boarding houses, 94, 165
Washington, George, 62, 145, 148, 150, 152, 308, 319
Washington Benevolent Society, 216
Waterhouse, Benjamin, 90
Webster, Daniel, 87, 202, 204, 254, 257; as lawyer, 30-31; meets Plumer, 160; pamphlet by, 157n; opposes war of 1812, 216; opposes Plumer, 260; and Dartmouth College controversy, 253, 298, 300; and election of 1820, 312-14; disparages Plumer, 332-33
Webster, Ezekiel, 223
Webster, Noah, 245
West, Benjamin, 28
Wheeler, William Plumer, 222n
Wheelock, John, 55n, 234, 235, 236, 239, 245, 295, 302
White, Samuel, 129-30
Whitefield, George, 7
White Mountain, 56
Whittier, John Greenleaf, 338
Wilkinson, James, 169-71
Wingate, Paine, 34, 39, 70
Woodbury, Levi, 252, 269-70, 298-99, 308, 321, 325-27, 336
Woodward, William H., 144n, 248, 251, 260-61, 297, 299
Worcester, Noah, 72

X

XYZ affair, 64, 72

Y

Yale College, 246
Yazoo Bill, 162
Yrujo, Marquis d'. *See* d'Yrujo, Marquis

This Book

*was composed by Van Rees Book Composition Company
and printed by Van Rees Press, New York.
The text type is 11 point Old Style 1, leaded 1 point.
Binding was by Van Rees Book Binding Corporation.
The designer was Richard Stinely.*